# Polish Literature and National Identity

# Rochester Studies in East and Central Europe

Senior Editor: Timothy Snyder, Yale University

Additional Titles of Interest

*Coming of Age under Martial Law:*
*The Initiation Novels of Poland's Last Communist Generation*
Svetlana Vassileva-Karagyozova

*Revolution and Counterrevolution in Poland, 1980–1989:*
*Solidarity, Martial Law, and the End of Communism in Europe*
Andrzej Paczkowski
Translated by Christina Manetti

*The Utopia of Terror: Life and Death in Wartime Croatia*
Rory Yeomans

*Kyiv as Regime City: The Return of Soviet Power after Nazi Occupation*
Martin J. Blackwell

*Magnetic North: Conversations with Tomas Venclova*
Ellen Hinsey and Tomas Venclova

*Witnessing Romania's Century of Turmoil: Memoirs of a Political Prisoner*
Nicolae Margineanu
Edited by Dennis Deletant

*Plebeian Modernity: Social Practices, Illegality, and the Urban Poor in Russia, 1906–1916*
Ilya Gerasimov

*Making Martyrs: The Language of Sacrifice in Russian Culture from Stalin to Putin*
Yuliya Minkova

*The Balkans as Europe, 1821–1914*
Edited by Timothy Snyder and Katherine Younger

*An American in Warsaw:*
*Selected Writings of Hugh S. Gibson, US Minister to Poland, 1919-1924*
Edited and annotated by Vivian Hux Reed
With M. B. B. Biskupski, Jochen Böhler, and Jan-Roman Potocki

A complete list of titles in the Rochester Studies in Medical History series may be found on our website, www.urpress.com.

# Polish Literature and National Identity

## A Postcolonial Perspective

Dariusz Skórczewski
Translated by Agnieszka Polakowska

University of Rochester Press

The translation and publication of this book was supported by the National Programme for the Development of Humanities (NPRH), a program of the Ministry of Science and Higher Education of the Republic of Poland, in the years 2016–19.

NATIONAL PROGRAMME
FOR THE DEVELOPMENT OF HUMANITIES



First published 2020

Original Polish edition: *Teoria—literatura—dyskurs: Pejzaż postkolonialny* by Dariusz Skórczewski (Lublin: Wydawnictwo KUL, 2013)

University of Rochester Press
668 Mt. Hope Avenue, Rochester, NY 14620, USA
www.urpress.com
and Boydell & Brewer Limited
PO Box 9, Woodbridge, Suffolk IP12 3DF, UK
www.boydellandbrewer.com

ISBN-13: 978-1-58046-978-4
ISSN: 1528-4808

**Library of Congress Cataloging-in-Publication Data**

Names: Skórczewski, Dariusz, author.
Title: Polish literature and national identity : a postcolonial landscape / Dariusz Skórczewski.
Description: Rochester : University of Rochester Press, 2020. | Series: Rochester studies in east and central Europe, 15284808 ; 23 | Includes bibliographical references and index. | A translation of the original Polish edition.
Identifiers: LCCN 2019035341 | ISBN 9781580469784 (hardcover) | ISBN 9781787446687 (pdf)
Subjects: LCSH: Postcolonialism in literature. | Postcolonialism. | Group identity. | Polish literature—19th century—History and criticism. | Polish literature—20th century—History and criticism. | Poland—Civilization.
Classification: LCC PN56.P555 S5613 2020 | DDC 891.8/509353—dc23 LC record available at https://lccn.loc.gov/2019035341

This publication is printed on acid-free paper.

MIX
Paper from responsible sources
FSC® C013056

Printed and bound in Great Britain by TJ International Ltd, Padstow, Cornwall

To my wife, Magdalena

# Contents

# Contents

# Acknowledgments

Every book has its history and people who had a powerful impact on their final shape. This one is no different. And while the story behind the Polish original is partly recorded in the prologue, "How It All Began," people who made the English translation and its publication possible deserve special mention. Translating a scholarly book can present a challenge, and translation between two languages whose humanistic idioms are so different makes the task no easier.

Hence, I would first of all like to thank my translator, Agnieszka Polakowska, who spent countless hours carefully transferring the subtleties of the original and making my long Polish syntax accessible to an English-reading audience. I owe a debt of gratitude to Dr. Dorota Kołodziejczyk, who consulted on the translation and whose meticulous reading helped me revise the text, and Dr. Marcin Turski, who did the ultimate, thorough polishing of the manuscript and whose conscientious rereadings and friendly support made its completion possible. I am also immensely grateful to my friend and colleague from the Institute of English Studies at the John Paul II Catholic University of Lublin, Professor Magdalena Charzyńska-Wójcik, who was day and night ready to help with decisions concerning all sorts of language issues at the last stage of manuscript preparation, and Dr. Kinga Lis from the same institute, who revised the bibliography.

Separate thanks are due to Sonia Kane, editorial director at the University of Rochester Press, and Timothy Snyder, series editor, who provided me with advice and encouragement in the publication process. I also wish to thank the reviewers of the English manuscript, whose thoughtful comments helped me improve it. I feel profoundly grateful to Professor Stefan Sawicki; Professor Ewa M. Thompson; and His Excellency Professor Piotr Wilczek, Polish ambassador to the United States, for their support of and interest in my work.

Last but in no way least, I would like to thank my wife, Magdalena, for her unfailing belief in my capacity to complete the project, endless endurance, and angelic patience.

The translation and publication of this book would never have been accomplished without the financial support of the Polish Ministry of Science and Higher Education, from whose National Programme for the Development of Humanities (NPRH) I benefited.

# Prologue

## How It All Began

I first encountered postcolonial theory in the second half of the 1980s during my graduate studies at the Catholic University of Lublin, Poland, in a literary theory course taught by Józef Japola. The course was rightly considered crucial by Polish studies students, since it ended with perhaps the most difficult exam of our degree and the mention of postcolonial theory came during a lecture on the trends in literary theory. The term meant nothing to us at that time, because our theoretical and methodological horizons consisted, at best, of late structuralism, the Tartu-Moscow semiotic school, and Mikhail Bakhtin, including an open aversion to Marxist frameworks due to their purported responsibility for the Soviet totalitarianism. The current beneath the label was considered yet another oddity of Western culture rather than an ethically and socially valuable scientific pursuit, although we were aware to some extent that the Iron Curtain effectively separated us from not only material goods but also the free exchange of ideas and the grasp of power—knowledge relations in a "free world." Postcolonialism also tasted of something exotic that was absent from the other theoretical directions we encountered, such as feminism and gay and lesbian studies.

What could Polish studies graduates understand, however, from a handful of its most elementary ideas received without the support of primary texts (for they were not available at that time)? We were content to know that, at the only university that was not state run in the whole of the Eastern Bloc at that time, we got to taste freedom not only when hosting dissidents and Western politicians on our campus but also when talking about what was happening in the world within literary theory. We did not know at the time that this was possible as a result of the Catholic University of Lublin Polish Studies Department's efforts to provide its students with access to the avant-garde of theoretical and literary thought, and put into practice our university's laudable commitment to truth. Among other fields and forms of activity, our program participated in the circulation of ideas in this way, making the most of its limited means, despite the constant limitations of communism's repressive apparatus. We did so while clearly delineating our own methodological position and worldview in relation to other tendencies and directions in contemporary humanist discourse. No one among us could predict then that postcolonial theory would make its way to Poland and, what is more, in a domesticated form, free from the aura of exoticism. Could anyone guess that it would become part of the native theoretical landscape, inspiring and reinforcing studies of Polish literature while also stirring up a lively debate in local theoretical and literary discourse?

My first serious encounter with postcolonialism took place when I went to Rice University in Houston, Texas, in 2001 on a scholarship awarded by the Kosciuszko Foundation, an organization that has done, and continues to do, a great deal to raise awareness in the United States of the existence and value of Polish culture and academic thought. My three-year stay at Rice University granted me the pleasure and privilege of working with Professor Ewa Thompson. At that time, Thompson's book *Imperial Knowledge: Russian Literature and Colonialism* had just been published in Poland, and I credit our long discussions with stirring my interest in postcolonialism in Polish and East-Central European contexts and with shaping my conviction of the significance of this current of inquiry for contemporary humanities both in those regions and the rest of the world. It was also then that the initial outline of a future book, still hazy, emerged.

My intellectual adventure in postcolonial theory began conventionally enough, with the study of two classic works that were not yet well known in Poland: Edward Said's *Orientalism* and *Culture and Imperialism.* Reading Said while residing in a country that is the embodiment of the Western metropolis because of its political, economic, military, and scientific position in the world, I found myself observing what at that time baffled me as the underprivileged position of Polish culture and science. The confrontation of these two experiences emphatically confirmed the conclusion formulated in *Orientalism* about the acute consequences of epistemological domination over populations "erased" or "silenced" in the process of their othering by the stronger and more resounding discourse of the colonizer. My observations verified Said's perspective and inclined me to undertake this type of reflection in my native context.

It was not immediately clear to me, however, which direction to take in this approach to Polish literature and culture. I was equipped with two convictions. First, I understood that such an approach could not simply rename, or rebrand, existing categories of analysis, as suggested by research into communism and totalitarianism, for instance, or the history and culture of Poland after the period of its partitions by the Russian, Prussian, and Habsburg Empires (the end of eighteenth century to the beginning of twentieth century, for a total of 123 years). Second, I thought it necessary to take into account the particularity of the Polish experience of domination, subordination, and dependence, along with all of its historical realities. These convictions were reinforced by my study of the first articles that transposed the postcolonial questions onto the Polish ground, published by Clare Cavanagh and Aleksander Fiut, when my own perspective was beginning to crystallize.[1] I later presented both my doubts and an outline of my own proposal in "Postcolonial Poland: An (Im)possible Project," at a time when postcolonialism was still little known in Poland and the most common position toward it within academic circles, beside that of interest sprinkled with disbelief, was skepticism.[2] Given the reservations of some Polish literary and cultural critics, my research goals were from the outset accompanied by a desire to convince Polish readers of its value as a discourse. Some of the chapters in this volume carry the faint mark of this early position, chronicling the atmosphere that accompanied the birth of postcolonial studies in Poland.

This book probably should have been written sooner, yet it does not seem belated. To the contrary, the distance in time from my own initial considerations, together with an increasingly diversified and clear landscape of Polish postcolonialism, is responsible for the distinct tone it strikes. The varied ways in which the humanities and social sciences respond to the identity crisis faced by European (and not only European) societies in the era of globalization are also not without significance to the theses presented in the following chapters. This crisis takes on spectacular forms in Central and Eastern European societies that, having liberated themselves from the grip of Soviet domination, are now seeking self-identification and self-definition in the changing international system.

The essays collected in this volume center on postcolonial criticism and the Polish contexts it was to shed light on. Although they were written over a period of several years, they constitute a coherent whole focused on identity questions. Along with the postcolonial perspective that marks the main axis of argument in this book, the notion of identity binds the threads woven through individual chapters. Literature and the discourses adjacent to it are seen here as cultural practices that participate in the shaping of identity and at the same time as products of that identity. Cultural discourses, from the art of poetry to historiography and journalism, are considered here in the context of a broader and overriding identity discourse. Identity—especially collective, of a group or a community—is given particular emphasis in postcolonial studies. It also occupies a central place in my explorations. It brings together both theoretical considerations and individual analyses, providing their ultimate and most clearly drawn horizon even when it does not constitute their main theme.

Why postcolonialism? Colonialism usually connotes overseas conquests, the civilizing mission, and the exploitation of native peoples by whites. All this may seem irrelevant to the Polish historical and cultural context, as Polish lands were never an object of military invasion or economic exploitation by overseas powers. What, then, unites the global postcolonial experience with the part of the world in which Poles happen to live? Seemingly not much but in reality—almost everything. With the exception of geographic distance perhaps, since it just so happened that Russia, Prussia, and Austria—the three empires that partitioned Poland in the late eighteenth century—did not have to go far to obtain their desired colonies; it was enough for them to reach for neighboring territories. By an irony of history, Poland—formerly the Polish-Lithuanian Commonwealth that included large parts of the present-day Ukraine, Lithuania, and Belarus—lost its imperial position. The proximity of its territory to those of its occupiers (first the three partitioning powers, and later the Nazi Germany and Soviet Russia) occluded the fact that the nature of these conquests was similarly, and overtly, colonial. At a time when postcolonial studies was being established at American and British universities, Poles were still behind the Iron Curtain, unaware of the analogies between their situation and the condition of conquered people on other continents. As citizens of the Communist People's Republic of Poland, the satellite state of the Soviet Union, they lived in expectation of the restoration of national sovereignty and the fulfillment of the dream of returning to the Western community of free nations, which was to end the misfortune of long-term and destructive Soviet domination. The humanities in Poland surely had entirely different worries at that time. Separated, to a larger or smaller degree, from the intellectual currents in other parts of the world because of a screen of politics, ideology, and policing, Polish theorists and culture scholars were not so much unaware of them (in fact, the contrary was true: they were better informed than their colleagues in other countries of the Soviet Bloc) as prevented from entering into a global dialogue and exchange of ideas, for decades doomed to a spectator's position. This situation made the Polish humanities after the removal of the Iron Curtain significantly prone to passive rather than critical reception of theories produced within Western academic institutions.

All of this meant that Poles were not accustomed to thinking about themselves in the categories of postcolonial theory, since until recently these categories had seemed to be "exotic" and thus unrelated to Polish history and culture. These categories were not assimilated into, or integrated with, Polish humanistic thought and scholarly literature, so Poles did not consider the possibility that postcolonialism could offer theoretical models for the description of their contemporary situation. It is even possible that some among them were aggrieved by the thought of a comparison between their nation, for centuries located within the orbit of Western culture, and nations in Asia, Africa, and Latin America. Reaching for the instruments of postcolonialism, however, is necessary if reflection on East-Central Europe is to expand beyond the limits of totalitarian studies or communism and postcommunism studies. The postcolonial framework can help explain processes that have not been sufficiently interpreted. It "can help a number of eastern European cultures, located at the intersection of three empires (Ottoman, Habsburg and Tsarist/Soviet), to understand the postcommunist phase as a 'decolonization,' an attempt at liberating them not only from Soviet domination, but also from older colonial vestiges."[3] Knowledge of the nature, sources, and consequences of these processes, in turn, opens up perspectives for overcoming the cultural and mental effects of enslavement on the side of the formerly colonized and the residues of imperial thinking on the side of the former colonizer. Postcolonialism, interested in understanding the challenges faced by populations implicated in the history of colonial relations, also models these populations' self-perception, wherein rests its therapeutic potential. Postcolonial categories make us sensitive to the traces and remnants that linger in our discourses despite changes on the geopolitical map.

The first part of this book concerns some theoretical problems of postcolonialism that are of particular relevance to Polish studies. It focuses on the philosophical and ethical premises of postcolonial reflection and those issues that are unique for the Polish and Central European historical and cultural contexts, which must be considered in attempts to theorize these regions from a postcolonial perspective. I look into the conditions and the validity of applying postcolonial theory to Polish literature and culture, as well as the perspectives that open as a result of this approach, and suggest the directions in which postcolonial studies in Poland can develop. I also take a look at the different aspects of postcolonialism that have been delineated within Polish literary criticism thus far, seeking to answer questions about their role in the global and local knowledge production and about the scope of humanistic intervention in social life. Finally, I propose a blueprint of postcolonial studies that accounts for issues of identity of East-Central European nations such as Poland, which have experienced colonial domination and are striving—not without effort and frustration—to create their own modus vivendi within the realities of a globalizing, cosmopolitan, and transnational world. Within this project, identity constitutes a fundamental thematic category in Polish literature, starting with the time of partitions, through the period of foreign domination (including Polish domination over the former Polish-Lithuanian Commonwealth's other nations and ethnicities between 1918 and 1939), right up to the present. It is also a convenient analytical category that allows us to grasp and define some of the most important problems of Polish society after the fall of Communism in 1989, as well as to think through their previous diagnoses, formulated in alternative analytical idioms. The theory laid out in the first part of this book constitutes its general framework, while also providing support for the discussions of literary texts, and of historiographic and literary discourses, that follow in subsequent parts.

The book's second part gathers studies of literary representations of national and ethnic identities and their inseparable reverse—"foreignness" and "otherness"—in selected texts from Romanticism until the present day. Its conceptual framework borrows extensively, though not exclusively, from literary imagology—methodology informed by philosophy, anthropology, sociology, psychology, and literary studies, forged to explore perceptions of self and others, gaining popularity in various streams of contemporary humanities, including postcolonial studies.[4] These perceptions are recorded in, conveyed through, and either endorsed or challenged by literary works of various types: lyric and epic poems, novels, plays, essays, and others. Exploration of the awareness of national or ethnic difference through the analysis of literary representations of Self and Other that emerge from confrontations between nationalities and ethnicities and inform Polish literature—leads to conclusions about both Polish collective self-perception and self-definition, and the cultural dynamics of the kinds of colonial encounters that took place on the lands of the former Polish-Lithuanian Commonwealth and its current territories (which include Poland, Lithuania, Belarus, and Ukraine) starting at the end of the eighteenth century up to the second half of the twentieth century. Such reflection simultaneously prompts critical contemplation of the ways in which earlier texts can be read today with a view to identifying the processes of the ongoing reconstruction of Polish identity.

The third part of the book, in turn, searches for an answer to the question of how the contemporary humanistic discourse, both Polish and foreign (mainly Anglo-American), deals with the postcolonial identity of Poles. The issues taken up in this part prompt a reflection on the diagnoses offered by this discourse, the degree to which they are effective in describing the actual condition of the Polish society, and the ways in which they reproduce the theses of colonial discourse, thus orientalizing Poland.

This book grasps only some elements of the expansive and diverse landscape that emerges from viewing Polish literature and its accompanying discourses of the past two hundred years through a postcolonial optics. In choosing some elements of this constructed "landscape" over others, I was motivated by their representativeness of the local, namely, Polish, issues, their significance for understanding the Polish writing and culture, and the role that they can play in theory as areas that promote the reconstruction and reconfiguration of postcolonial studies within Central and Eastern European contexts.

I submit this volume to the reader with the hope that it will not be received as an homage to an academic trend; that trends in scholarship exist does not need to be proven, and postcolonialism has become admittedly trendy in Poland. Rather, I hope that it will stand as evidence of a thorough rumination on the role that literature and the humanities play, or are yet to play, within one society's search for a foundation of its identity at the beginning of the twenty-first century.

Chapter One

# Through the Lens of Humanism, with a View to Transcendence

This opening chapter presents postcolonialism in a series of snapshots, with a central role reserved for two scenes. The first emerges when we try to grasp the object in one glance in order to glean its most basic features. The resulting image of postcolonial studies viewed through the lens of humanism suggests the possibility, if not the necessity, of transitioning to a second perspective that considers the transcendental aspect of contemporaneity, of which postcolonial studies is an integral part. Accounting for the cultural circumstances of scholarly discourse and its implications allows for the formulation of a theoretical position, proposed in the final part of the chapter, for postcolonial criticism in the era of the exhaustion of postmodernism. Since this position also underpins this book, this chapter is a methodological statement, formulated from a spatially and temporally determined perspective—from the perspective of an East-Central European country after the Western "boom" of postcolonialism.

Looking at postcolonialism from a distance that helps to locate it in a *longue durée* perspective, I propose viewing it simply as a history of the human being. What cannot be stressed enough is that this chapter, along with the book it opens, presents my own perspective on postcolonialism, which is grounded in Christian humanistic thought with its vital component of personalism. I consider personalism a fitting philosophical framework for reflecting on the historical experience of populations that sought emancipation from the colonial grip (such as Polish society under Soviet rule).[1] The role of the person as acting agent is crucial for liberating processes, but it can be described in diverse ways that also depend on philosophical premises. Personalism offers an alternative to the secular philosophies, such as Marxism, that underlie the main currents of postcolonial studies, which have furnished individuals with nearly unlimited agency and offered prospects of absolute freedom. It accentuates personhood as the supreme value of human beings, treating both individualism and collectivism as contrary to human dignity. To be true subjects of history, human beings must act as persons, not merely as individuals. This means that their actions must reflect their self-governance: they act "assuming the awareness of who one is and the disposition of the will to choose the value which is proportional to that awareness. In this way freedom . . . reveals the spirituality of man which, thus conceived, does not have to be defined merely as the opposite to materiality."[2] This perspective on subjectivity is applicable to all life situations, including both colonial and postcolonial settings.

It must be stressed that the concept of "person," foundational for personalism,

> results from a philosophical reflection on human being and not only from a religious tradition, though, undoubtedly, the concept was discovered within Christianity. . . . [T]his concept stems from fundamental human experience and this is why it is essential for discovering the basic characteristics of human being. Also, the concept of person allows one to grasp the specificity of man, placing him in the privileged position not only in the world of nature but also in society. In this light it will result that personalism is not just one of many "isms," but it is a proposal of objectivistic interpretation of human fact.[3]

Christian personalism perceives human beings—persons rather than individuals—as social agents (acting persons) who are characterized by possessing dignity that results from their personhood. Persons realize their dignity through consciously performed actions, developing the full potential of their personality and thereby forming themselves as persons.

As I understand and apply it in this book, postcolonialism is not—or not only—a political, social, or economic history, although postcolonial criticism takes all of these aspects into account. It is also not a history of an idea, even though the attitude toward the ideas of Western civilization serves as one of the main indicators of a postcolonial position. Postcolonialism as I frame it can be described as a critical reflection on the history of human attitudes toward either domination over other populations or dependence on them. For it is not "hard" historical facts that are the subject of postcolonial research but rather the state of consciousness expressed in the discourse produced during the colonial encounter by human communities. The optics founded on this assumption create a space within the field of postcolonial studies for approaches that do not depersonalize the human being as the subject of experience or reduce this being to the function of the correlative of abstract social forces and discursive practices.[4]

Postcolonial theory, which provides the theoretical support for this study and supplies it with the self-reflection necessary to all fields of knowledge, is an interdisciplinary sociopolitical theory that seeks to explain broadly understood cultural processes resulting from the colonial encounter. Within its framework, literature is less an independent and final subject of analysis than a field that provides examples and allows for the exploration of sociocultural phenomena engendered by colonialism. Postcolonial theory is therefore characterized by an openness to the concepts and terminological stock of various scholarly disciplines and fields of knowledge, and by pluralism in using the results of their methodologies.[5] "New" humanism is perhaps one of the most clearly delineated positions within this multiplicity of approaches. It is based in the view that the consequences of the confrontation of traditional, broadly understood European humanism with Europe's increasingly multicultural reality were ambiguous and troubling because of their incompatibility with the humanistic project.[6] European humanism was revealed to be lofty in its universalist slogans yet destructive in its Eurocentrism, becoming a medium for totalizing discourses (for instance, orientalism) that were deployed against non-European peoples and bringing with it its antithesis—the barbarity of colonial conquests. In scholarship, the position of "new" humanism requires that the fundaments of humanism be reexamined to prevent epistemological—and in consequence also real—violence against people, nations, and cultures, a violence that begins when the object of cognition is forced into a foreign framework imposed by the "more powerful" discourse of the metropolis.[7]

It is hard to deny that this "new" humanism is, in fact, humanism par excellence—authentic and free of aberrations and deformations. It is a humanism that shows respect for the human being and his or her milieu, meaning community and its culture, the paramount product of a population regardless of its latitude, religion, skin color, and history. Through the lens of "new" humanism, postcolonialism—as I view it—would thus be a type of "corrective" discourse, restoring humanism's actual global and humane dimension, an aspect that was lost when the idea was used in the service of European colonial domination along with its inseparable legacy of ethnic and nationalistic conflicts, physical and mental enslavement, and economic and cultural deprivation.

Discourse, as both the product and the determining force of colonial division, is seen within the field of postcolonial studies from the perspective of conflict between social organisms, wherein one side is subjected to the repressive domination of the other participant in a specific political and sociocultural interaction that occurs as a result of conquest. This perspective serves as compensation for the shortfall of earlier humanistic approaches that either bypassed or insufficiently addressed the relationship between culture and politics. Postcolonialism distances itself from all traditions that emphasize universalism, autonomy, and political *désintéressement* of art and those that transcend external conditions and limitations. From the beginning, one of the tasks of postcolonial theory was to point out culture's entanglement in the network of relations of colonial power and subordination, as well as to formulate analytical methods of grasping and describing these dependencies. It is not by accident that literature has served, and continues to serve, as a field of strategic significance for postcolonial studies, even with the influx of culturally oriented analysis and the diminishing status of literature and the literary in contemporary postcolonial studies.[8] There are at least two reasons for this.

First of all, at its foundation postcolonialism is an emancipatory discourse that reclaims a community's right to a voice when, as a result of colonial oppression, it had been either previously deprived of it ("muted" or "silenced") or limited in its use of it. The interaction between subjects—the repressed and the repressor—constitutes the method of postcolonial studies, the "speculum" that allows it to look at the layers of cultural sediments of imperial domination.[9] This speculum allows the postcolonial critic to access and penetrate not only the world depicted in the literary work but also its depths—the deposits of discourse itself, which gives certain meanings and assigns specific values to the elements of this world. For the literary text always functions within a particular social circulation; it is embedded in a broad, institutionalized system of signs that consists not only of language and literary tradition but also of a dense network of unarticulated relations of power wielded by the metropolis over the peripheries.

Postcolonial studies aims to establish—within the realm of discourse—the desired symmetry between the former hegemon and the formerly subaltern population, which was lost as a result of political domination, as well as to problematize their encounter by pointing to its equivocal and ambivalent character—for both sides of the colonial divide. It thus cannot be reduced to revenge taken within the field of discourse.[10] It is hard to deny, however, the political potential of postcolonial criticism as a means of providing rhetorical support for the disenfranchised groups or entire populations from the former colonies seeking to regain their agency.

For the reasons stated above, the literature of a colonized or decolonized society constitutes the most important field of articulation of identity discourses for postcolonial critics. The texts of a population subjected to foreign domination are part of its efforts at self-definition and self-expression and part of its search for forms that can help resist and, potentially, overcome the conditions of oppression. In turn, the work of authors representative of the metropolis and in particular the canon of imperial literature(s) makes apparent the reality of discursive violence against the conquered, as well as indirectly provide information about the complex cultural processes activated by a conquest of a given territory. Postcolonial studies call attention to the particular density of problems caused by colonial oppression within the area of identity issues, at both the individual and community levels.

Like the most sensitive seismograph, literature registers all phenomena that transpire as a result of the interaction between a hegemon and the population of the peripheries, expressing them in the equivocal language of art. To clarify: this literary "register" means not simple mimesis here but rather a system of mutually intertwined cultural codes that allow for the "translation" of external reality into an artistic, textual representation. Postcolonial critics have not always paid sufficient attention to literature's polysemic potential, and many have overlooked the fact that a literary work extends beyond such phenomena. Literature can offer diagnoses that transcend the immediate context of both a work and its reception, and as such it requires careful and close study that is free from a priori prejudices and ideological distortions. The postcolonial critic, therefore, is taking a certain risk in adopting a stance toward a text that is perhaps greater than is the case for other interpretive methods. The task involves considering the double challenge presented by the work, which necessitates, on the one hand, constant reevaluation of the belief in literature's supposed pure aestheticism and political neutrality and, on the other, the careful avoidance of the temptation to view a literary text as an articulation of a solely political position. The ambiguity of this situation prevents reduction to theoretical dogmas and to the convenient, but schematic, explicatory constructions of a simplified, binary model of a world based on a colonizer—colonizer antithesis.

The second reason for literature's key place in postcolonial studies is partially connected to the first one. In a postcolonial context, the literary text is less the domain of aesthetics than a field where polarized and conflicted discourses—hegemonic and counterhegemonic—clash with one another. The scholar's task is to register, uncover, and interpret this historically anchored antagonism. As Said writes, in postcolonial studies "culture is a sort of theater where various political and ideological causes engage one another. Far from being a placid realm of Apollonian gentility, culture can even be a battleground on which causes expose themselves to the light of day and contend with one another."[11] As a domain of creative activity that constitutes an integral part of culture understood in this fashion, literature demands a particular kind of approach, one that can reveal, in Said's phrasing, the "worldliness" of texts, meaning their "material" existence in the past and the present. In other words, the approach should recreate the network of relations in which literary works are entangled by virtue of their contextualized existence, which situates them in relation to other writing, voices, and discourses. Their entanglement arises from the fact that the literary text, as a product of cultural activity, is a reaction to a certain reality and, indirectly, takes a position toward it. Postcolonialism wants to account for this fact, acknowledging its significance for the functioning of literature in the context of the colonial encounter.

Regardless of a given author's intention and awareness, a text's "being-in-the-world" depends on its participation in the Foucauldian "power/knowledge" system. This participation is veiled, however, by literature's alleged autonomous status: "Now the trouble with this idea of culture is that it entails not only venerating one's own culture, but also thinking of it as somehow divorced from, because transcending, the everyday world."[12] It is arguable, of course, whether art is not, at least sometimes and to some extent, a form of transcending reality that allows us to overcome the bleak, harsh, and earthly limitations of external conditions and contexts. Literature provides multiple examples of such transcending. It is nevertheless impossible to deny the sense of proposing a reading that would, on the one hand, illuminate a work's entanglement in "everydayness" and, on the other, reveal "the method colonized people use to assert their own identity and the existence of their own history."[13] There is no need to position these two ways of reading—situational and immanent—as mutually exclusive.

The ambivalence of literature is worth remembering when thinking about the perspectives of Central and Eastern European postcolonial studies. Literature inevitably belongs to the "structure of attitude and reference" that is anchored in historicity and exists outside of it, while simultaneously remaining the transhistorical domain of Kantian "disinterested pleasure," an object that brings satisfaction or aesthetic rapture.[14] Postcolonial criticism, both in its pronouncements and analytical practice, aims to uncover the previous layer of texts—their complex entanglement in the discourse of colonial power and anti-colonial resistance. It also frequently ends with this, satisfied, for example, with the unmasking of those places in the work where the hidden logic of power establishes its own laws not addressed by other interpretations. The most remarkable achievements of postcolonial criticism, however, among which the work of Said is still unrivaled, are also able to account for that most refined of human inventions—ars poetica. Postcolonial scholarship that reveals the tension between both tendencies (referred to as context centered and text centered in the methodology of literary studies) is currently of particular value as a formula for literary criticism that both respects that objective specificity of literature and remains sensitive to its sociopolitical and ethical functions, as well as its ties to other systems, institutions, and history.

The picture drawn here would be incomplete without mentioning one more factor that has impacted the ethical orientation of postcolonialism. In identifying this current's philosophical and intellectual background, textbooks and encyclopedia entries usually point to Marxism, for three main reasons: (1) Marxist critique of Western capitalism, which provides doctrinal support for the postcolonial point of view; (2) reference to revolutionary slogans, on the level of social praxis, by anti-colonial movements across continents; and (3) postcolonialism's methodological framing of social relations in dialectic categories, with special emphasis on the role of tensions and inequalities and on struggle as the means of eliminating them. This general kinship between postcolonialism and Marxism, however, should not lead to far-reaching conclusions, since "European theory and Western Marxism as cultural co-efficients of liberation haven't in the main proved themselves to be reliable allies in the resistance to imperialism—on the contrary, one may suspect that they are part of the same invidious 'universalism' that connected culture with imperialism for centuries."[15] It is telling that the motto of the book seen as the foundational work of postcolonialism, Said's *Orientalism*, features the meaningful quote from *The Eighteenth Brumaire of Louis Bonaparte*—"They cannot represent themselves; they must be represented"—which suggests Marx's complicity in Europe's discursive hegemony.[16] Even though Marxism endured as a radical critique of Western domination and imperial structures for many anti-colonial activists in Africa, Asia, and South America, its place in postcolonial thought is a much more complicated issue.[17] There is one aspect of this issue that is worth underlining here, since it usually escapes the attention of scholars who consider the issue of postcolonialism's ideological affiliation from leftist or poststructuralist positions. Within the Marxist vision of the world and of the human being, all significant phenomena and processes from the postcolonial perspective are dependent on materiality: dialectic materialism constitutes the justification as well as the ultimate horizon—and thus also a limit—for actions undertaken by both the individual and the collective. Within the postcolonial perspective, however, there is a place for the human being who is not determined by the logic of dialectical materialism. The consequences of colonial conquest—the loss of territorial sovereignty, the hegemon's merciless politics of exploitation of human and natural resources, the violence against and debasement of human dignity, the devastation of culture and of the psyche—are not the result of pressure from some abstract "conditions," independent of human beings and explained in terms of the historical imperative. They are the result of human actions with an unequivocal ethical standing, the recognition of which lies at the very foundation of postcolonialism's raison d'être, even if it is only rarely openly demanded.

The issue at hand leads to another significant issue, namely the ambivalent, and even internally contradictory, attitude of postcolonial thought toward postmodernism. On the one hand, in drawing on the works of such philosophers and theoreticians as Derrida, Foucault, and Lacan, among others, postcolonialism frequently falls into the self-referentiality typical of postmodernism. This self-referentiality stems from the sense that, first of all, social transformations have disturbed fundamental beliefs about the objectivity and truth of judgments about reality and, second, that culture is simply a domain of multiplied "empty signifiers" that cannot grasp reality. On the other hand, the ethical dimension of postcolonial studies, along with the respect of postcolonial scholars for truth, reality, and cognition, ensures that such approaches probe more deeply than postmodern ones, even when their horizon of humanistic consciousness and methods reference postmodernism, and indeed can oppose it in some of their forms. This is particularly true for the question of historicity and for the existential reality of both individual and collective experience. Postcolonialism, therefore, does not simply repeat or transpose the code words of the irreferentiality of language and the undecidability of textual meaning. Within its framework, the possibility of objective knowledge and truth as the aim of research is not undermined, even though all of these questions are subject to problematization within postcolonial theoretical discourse and despite the fact that doubts regarding the text suggested by, for example, deconstructionism or discourse analysis are the impetus of many postcolonial interpretations.[18] Does this mean that postcolonial studies, stretched between the intellectual tradition of Marxism on the one end and the impulses of postmodernism on the other, is inevitably condemned to the choice between these two variants or else to their medley?

The mentioned "ethical moment" of postcolonialism, so well emphasized by Said and the Indian scholars from the subaltern studies circle, among others, is a consequence of the belief in the factual existence of some objective measure of good and evil. This factuality, whether it is acknowledged or not, is rooted in universal natural law, with an ontological status independent of scholarly theorizations and ideological manipulations.[19] Among theoreticians who set in motion the postcolonial analytical machinery, it was the author of *Culture and Imperialism* who came closest to this conviction in his ethical stance, despite the fact that he never directly articulated it.[20] It is possible that Said's stance was influenced by his Christian upbringing and its specific religious, nationalistic, and cultural context: Middle Eastern and both Arabic and Judeo-Christian. Contact with this context shaped Said's worldview, bringing an aspect of engaged concern for the disadvantaged to his entire humanistic activity. Even without pinpointing its sources, however, it can be confidently asserted that the notion of harm in the life and work of this scholar had a very real and thus moral dimension. It was moreover irreducible to the relativizing verbal constructions deployed within the framework of this or that explicatory system. Put succinctly, Said's position is that harm is what painfully affects the human being, every human being, and not what is considered to be harm on the basis of this or that worldview-derived belief, ideological system, religious doctrine, and so forth. The proper reaction to harm, in turn, is a stance of outrage and protest—a stance that has real and measurable results, namely, those that find an extension in action and intervention in reality and that are thus (once again) irreducible to purely discursive constructions and not limited to textual and linguistic speculation over signification. Such defense of the disadvantaged, whose identity and existence are threatened by foreign domination, obviously assumes a certain quantum of objectivity and reality of social and cultural phenomena. As such, it implies a realistic, and to some extent essentialist, position; were it not so, it would amount to a mere juggling display of "words" detached from "things." Although historical forms of colonial oppression and anti-colonial resistance are changeable along with the forms of discourses that mediate in their realization and expression, there does exist a "hard nucleus" of these phenomena that calls for their examination, even if it is only substitutive and inscribed within a scholarly account. Why is this? Where does the general agreement about the evil of conquest and the evil of violence against representatives of other races, nationalities, religions, and languages stem from? What lies at the source of the imperative that directs people to condemn such behaviors and tells humanists to problematize their testimonies, pose questions to texts, and to attend to their answers?

In considering the legitimacy of the arguments that are the cornerstone of postcolonial discourse, we face a fundamental question about the original source, or else the decisive ethical sanction of the postcolonial complaint, which requires that scholars adopt a stance toward the facts, results, and victims of colonization. Postcolonial theory does not unequivocally resolve these issues within the scope of its propositions, probably concluding that the commonly held belief about the iniquity of violence serves as a sufficient argument. Answering this question requires leaving the theoretical ground of postcolonialism and looking beyond it, toward a system that can justify the thesis about the immanent evil of colonial conquest and the moral imperative to reject this evil. It is this *fundamental disagreement* that lies at the basis of postcolonial studies, investing it with meaning from both a purely epistemic perspective and from a social and ethical one. Without it, postcolonialism risks being reduced to a deconstructive play, however refined, with notions of justice, identity, dependence, harm, or responsibility. Is it only Marxist thought that fuels this fundamental disagreement?

The definition of postcolonialism as a political practice that is "morally committed to transforming the conditions of exploitation and poverty in which large sections of the world's population live out their daily lives" is certainly underpinned by Marxist thought in accenting the historical and class basis of social injustice, as well as the historical determinism of moral norms and the enslavement written into the human condition.[21] There is, however, also a different justification of the postcolonial ethic, which is non-Marxist or, more precisely, pre-Marxist. It comes via a fundamental text of Christianity that does not repeal the imperative of justice in social relations even as it defines the rules of an individual ethic. In the Sermon on the Mount, which played a significant role in shaping not only Christian world views, he who harms his brother—and the ontological equality of all people regardless of their race and skin color, and so on, is after all one of the axioms of postcolonial theory—is confronted with the perspective of the victim of his violence.[22] Moreover, the sermon strongly emphasizes the right of the oppressed to maintain their human dignity in relation to the aggressor, regardless of their (social, economic, civilizational) status.[23] When thinking about the ethic of postcolonialism, it is worth keeping in mind that the Sermon on the Mount and its message have circulated in European thought for many centuries.

Theoreticians usually silently bypass the question of the role that a Christian worldview and a Christian ethic play in the project of postcolonial studies, and they rarely take a Christian perspective into account in the context of their investigations.[24] The situation has at least two causes. The first is strictly ideological in character and tied to the fact that postcolonialism, especially in versions that highlight its postmodernist affinities, as is the case with most of postmodernism's currents, explicitly refers to philosophical traditions that are different from, even antithetical to, Christianity, starting with Nietzsche's "genealogical" reflections in *Beyond Good and Evil* and *On the Genealogy of Morals*. Through this optic, Christian thought is the self-expression of an unreflective subject that deforms and oppresses Others and conceals the "will to power" using religious discourse, dressing it in a cloak of resentment aimed at these Others. The second cause is linked to the fact that Christianity, when it is present in postcolonial studies, appears as an object of inquiry, a religion imposed by the West on the indigenous peoples of other continents by way of a civilizing mission. Not infrequently, postcolonial studies assigns responsibility for the aberrations of colonial rule to those who legitimized it, either directly or indirectly, by situating it and the Western civilization it represented within a sacred order, namely religious representatives (church dignitaries, missionaries) and the canonical texts they used for their purposes (the Bible).[25]

From this perspective, Christianity is a historical component of the contested colonial system; it is not given the chance to appear in its other roles, whether as the spiritual support of an oppressed population and an institution that preserves an endangered identity (as in the case of Ireland and Poland), or as a philosophical background, symmetrical and alternative to other systems and formations (such as Marxism and postmodernism), referenced in the process of thinking through the consequences of imperial domination. The impact of Christianity on the course and the outcome of intercultural contact is usually grasped in categories of destruction rather than of positive dynamics, and it is counterpointed by local cultures that are granted, somewhat a priori and routinely, the status of reservoirs of "native," precolonial virtues, which compete with values seen as part and parcel of European domination.

Is it possible to take a different approach to the question of Christianity's significance and place within the identity formation of the colonized and the colonizer and in the cultural experience resulting from the colonial encounter? The above outline of current postcolonial studies inclines toward skepticism. A postulate of referencing an alternative to commonly accepted intellectual tradition to justify postcolonialism's ethical project seems even more unrealistic. The issue appears predetermined given the configuration of positions within postcolonial studies up until now. The theoretical assumptions of postmodernism and the premises of the neo-Marxist critical theory of the Frankfurt school would likely demand that a prospective attempt to introduce Christianity to postcolonialism's field of inquiry be interpreted as an expression of either "cultural practice" or a historically determined "form of social consciousness," only this time of the inquiring scholar.

Even so, it is possible to reach a perspective on postcolonial studies without the patronage of either Nietzsche or of his successors (such as Foucault), but rather with recourse to the "late" Jürgen Habermas, presently one of the key representatives of the postsecular turn in the humanities.[26] From this perspective, postcolonialism would be a current of cultural studies that could no longer pass over, marginalize, or disavow the religious aspect of human experience to the extent that religious experience is implicated in the colonial encounter or in the process of dealing with its consequences. Its right of entry, so to speak, into postcolonial studies would be twofold: (1) as an objective component of academic accounts (*Homo religiosus* as part of the human condition that demands considerations along with other aspects of human existence), and (2) as a factor that shapes a researcher's stance, in relation to dominant positions with a (neo)Marxist or postmodernist provenance. The second point is particularly important, for it suggests the possibility of overcoming the monopoly of these frameworks at the same time as it unearths their indebtedness to the ethic of the Sermon on the Mount. It must be treated with a great degree of care, however, for there is no such thing as a "Christian stance" within the realm of academic methodology. It is possible to speak only about a horizon based on a Christian ethic and anthropology that makes visible those aspects of the object occluded by a different set of assumptions. Postcolonial studies in a postsecular variant, therefore, would be "forced" to formulate the problems and the perspective of Christianity differently than the traditional critique of its missionary expansionism has done. This would follow not from the possible claims made by opponents of liberal and leftist discourse in scholarship, however, but from the postulates announced by, among others, Habermas. Choosing this option, the option of compromise, which can reconcile the "sacred" and the "metaphysical" with the "secular" in contemporary humanities, makes it possible to avoid the potential charge of the ideologization of scholarship. Moreover, it opens up space for a discussion that leads beyond the framework of postcolonial studies and toward reflection about contemporary reasons and justifications for working in the realm of cultural studies. For it is not necessary to agree with the premises of postsecularism to notice the areas that it has created within the metadiscourse of contemporary scholarship that have not yet been cultivated. I am inclined to see this position as confirming a belief espoused in some academic circles—neither the first nor the last such confirmation within the history of human inquiry and thought—that the complete excision of metaphysics from the objective field and subjective horizon of the humanities is impossible in the long term.[27] As Barbara Skarga puts it, there exists "something that transcends us, and which opens new horizons before us."[28] This "something" is the sphere of transcendence understood in the most general terms, which eludes the language of both postcolonial and critical theory, a sphere that is likely to always return in some form to humanistic thought despite the variously motivated objections to such reflection.[29]

❧❧❧

The conclusions that follow from these reflections are not a summons to radically restructure postcolonial studies or—all the more so—a call for their vehement "Christianization," such as was attempted in the 1950s by some Polish Catholic writers and intellectuals in relation to Marxism.[30] Rather, the issue presented here should be treated as a cause for reflection on both the circulation of thought in the history of the humanities and the conditions and implications of the humanistic worldview. Marxism is likely to remain the main frame of reference within interpretations of sociocultural issues for postcolonialism. It is both possible and worthwhile, however, to broaden the horizons of postcolonial studies to include elements previously silenced in the name of either theoretical purism or the secularism implied by science. The double paradox of postcolonial discourse should be remembered here. To begin with, even though literature is its central area of exploration, postcolonialism rarely undertakes critical consideration of literature's aesthetic dimension, which in individual analyses sometimes comes off as a lack of respect for the specificity of the literary message. This deficit of Western postcolonial discourse—a claim that is not an excessive generalization but rather an indicator of a characteristic tendency—suggests that it be rethought and reworked. The rich text-centered tradition in Central and Eastern European literary studies can be helpful in this regard. Second, although postcolonial studies tends to eliminate this issue from its field of inquiry, indicating only its Marxist inspirations, the ethics derived from Christian thought are at the original philosophical source of the project from which postcolonial thought has sprung.

These factors create an opportunity to open postcolonial discourse to new stimuli, including those originating in Central and Eastern Europe, which will be the subject of chapters to follow. Having been sensitive primarily to what is historical, postcolonial studies can now confront questions about the role of the aesthetic that arise from a different, text-centered humanistic tradition. First and foremost, however—and to some extent in accord with the current Zeitgeist, which does not mean subservience to present-day intellectual trends—postcolonial studies is facing the imperative to search for meaning in a postmodern and postcolonial world. The various forms of this search are what binds the experiences of contemporary societies from different regions and continents in a globalizing world. In light of the post-secular questions posed today by philosophers who, until recently, did not hide their skepticism toward this direction of inquiry, the inclusion of the proposed ethical horizon of postcolonialism along with its metaphysical basis does not appear misguided, even if it were to be realized in the form of a compromise, as presented here, namely, through the translation of religious language into a "secular" one, distancing itself from religion without eliminating its perspective.[31] In a stronger version, in turn, it could open the realm of postcolonial studies to discourse that would make room for research into the religious and metaphysical motivations behind individual and collective actions (alongside, for instance, their social and psychological causes) and their cultural implications from the perspective of the colonial encounter. Even this version would not ask the recipient to identify with any faith or to affirm any ideology. By opening our eyes onto those dimensions of reality that, until now, have been either omitted altogether or interpreted one-sidedly because of the above ideological assumptions, this trajectory of postcolonial studies would recognize that the relation between transcendence and the sociocultural order has an immediate, analogous, and symbolic character and that the language of description of this relationship is not a perfect mirror image of reality but rather an element of social structure amenable to critique.[32]

Chapter Two

# Postcolonialism in Poland

The title of this chapter should not be read as announcing a systematized overview of the short history of Polish postcolonial studies; such surveys already exist.[1] Although the chapter does outline the reception history of postcolonial theory in Poland, its main task is to reflect on the particular conditions and perspectives of postcolonial discourse in a Polish context.[2] Since postcolonial theory was formulated outside of East-Central Europe, it is seen by some Polish scholars as a "foreign body," with its alien idiom and methodology viewed as inadequate for addressing local issues.[3] From this perspective, the foreignness of postcolonialism stems, in the first place, from the sociopolitical genesis of postcolonialism (the disintegration of Western colonial empires and decolonizing processes) and, second, from its ideological messages (Marxism that is burdened with objectionable, and easy to understand in Poland, connotations).[4]

It is thus not at all obvious that postcolonial studies have been assimilated into the realm of Polish literary scholarship. Their presence in Poland cannot be explained solely with reference to the enchantment of Polish humanities with imported ideas, despite a fairly widespread tradition of these kinds of borrowings.[5] When a translation of Edward Said's *Orientalism* first appeared in Poland (in 1991), it went almost entirely unnoticed; similarly ignored were Polish translations of anti-colonial classics, such as Frantz Fanon's *Les damnés de la terre* (which came out as *Wyklęty lud ziemi* in 1985).[6] No one could have suspected that these works would become important to Polish readers and for Polish studies after dozens of years—and not as criticism of scholarship about the exotic Near East, or as a diagnosis of the state of social consciousness in equally exotic Algeria, but as texts for Polish humanities scholars to reference in studying Polish culture.

Postcolonial studies arrived in Poland via neither *Orientalism* nor any other postcolonial classic, however. Its origins in Poland should be attributed instead to the reception of Ewa Thompson's book *Imperial Knowledge:*

*Russian Literature and Colonialism*, translated into Polish as *Trubadurzy imperium* (Troubadours of the empire) and published in 2000, a pioneering discussion that utilizes postcolonial ideas in interpreting Russian literature. The ground for its reception was presumably prepared by then. Since approximately the mid-1990s, Polish public discourse has included the opinion that "the honeymoon of restored freedom in our part of Europe has come to an end," and that liberation from the influence of the Soviet Empire did not help to resolve many problems facing the nations of East-Central Europe despite the passage of time.[7] The awareness of these problems served as a catalyst for change in Polish reflections on the conditions of Polish culture and research in the humanities. It may have been these transformations that fostered the reception of postcolonial theory in Poland.

Such speculations are not ungrounded, since the condition of decolonized societies is among the many questions that postcolonial theory considers. The postcolonial perspective includes problems that do not cease with decolonization but, to the contrary, start to intensify and make themselves known in certain forms of social behaviors and discursive practices in the postcolonial period. The explicatory potential of postcolonial theory gives attempts to apply it in the East-Central European context both an epistemic and pragmatic value.[8]

Is the use of postcolonialism as a model for explaining contemporary cultural and societal phenomena occurring outside of contexts of classic colonialism (as implemented by modern Western imperial powers), such as those of East-Central Europe, a misappropriation, however? Not being an overseas territory and without the history of organized racial exploitation—two criteria usually deployed by postcolonial theorists—the East-Central European geographical and historical frame of reference is foreign to postcolonial studies.[9] Postcolonial discourse was never interested in this part of the world, bypassing it for various reasons that stem from history, geopolitics, and the post-1945 distribution of power and knowledge about the world. On the one hand, this situation privileged the perspective of the Soviet hegemon, which nimbly concealed and disavowed the colonial nature of the imperial project, playing the role of spokesperson for the Third World's anti-colonial movements instead. On the other hand, it helped to entrench British imperialism as the paradigmatic model of colonial conquest, upon which postcolonial theory's subsequent conceptual constructs were founded. The dominance of English as the language of global postcolonial studies seals this state of affairs. In the realm of postcolonial theory that evolved within these coordinates, there was "no room" for reflection on the status of East-Central Europe. In its canonical form, the Eurocentric model of domination developed by postcolonial theory was not sufficiently sensitive to detect colonial signals coming from the continent's eastern regions. An additional hurdle that made such signals difficult for postcolonial studies to register was Europe's perceived status as the homogeneous "oppressor." Within such an ideological scheme, the possibility of assigning a different status—of victim—to territories dominated by the Soviet Union was, by way of extrapolation, fundamentally excluded. Consequently, as a subject of Soviet colonization, East-Central Europe was more foreign to postcolonial studies than the geographically distant territories of Asia, Africa, or Australia.[10]

Reversing this perspective, one could say that postcolonial theory can appear doubly foreign to the inhabitants of East-Central Europe. It is not only the postcolonial critics who are seen as belonging outside of the Old World, or even the Euro-Atlantic sphere. The very subject of their reflection was, until recently, quite exotic for Eastern Europeans, who were seldom exposed to representatives of non-East-Central European ethnicities because of decades spent behind the Iron Curtain. As a result, for a monolithic, single-race, and predominantly monoethnic East-Central European population such as Polish society after the Second World War, encounters with Third World countries were mediated entirely via available cultural discourses. This did not help such societies avoid adopting an "Othering" gaze upon the Third World. Consequently, instead of solidarity and identification with the postcolonial Third World, East-Central Europeans chose to dissociate themselves from it.[11] This sense of the "exotic otherness" of the postcolonial world within the context of the former Second World reaches deeper still: it derives as much from the sociopolitical genesis of postcolonial studies (the disintegration of Western colonial empires and the onset of decolonizing processes) as from their ideological messages (since 1945, Marxism has been associated in Poland primarily with an oppressive, and only recently disposed of, power system). Hence, attempts to embrace East-Central Europe within a postcolonial paradigm may be viewed by East-Central Europeans as counterintuitive and misplaced, since they "find being lumped together with the rest of the colonized humanity unflattering, if not humiliating, and want to be with the 'civilized' part of the world."[12]

From this perspective, some pertinent questions arise. Can reading Polish literature through a postcolonial lens lead to new and valuable discoveries? Is the application of postcolonial categories to texts by Polish writers an unproductive, not to mention risky, repetition of a methodological trend?

The authors of one of the first books of postcolonial theory open with an observation that became a foundational assumption of postcolonial studies, providing postcolonial research with historical justification and ethical resonance:

> More than three-quarters of the people living in the world today have had their lives shaped by the experience of colonialism. It is easy to see how important this has been in the political and economic spheres, but its general influence on the perceptual frameworks of contemporary peoples is often less evident. Literature offers one of the most important ways in which these new perceptions are expressed.[13]

If we accept the global reach of colonialism, then the fact that postcolonial theory from its conception passed over in silence the colonial struggles of East-Central European societies is one of the paradoxes of contemporary humanities.[14] The authors of the introduction to the Eastern European special issue of the *Journal of Postcolonial Writing* went as far as to assert that Western postcolonialism exhibited an astounding localism by this omission, which makes the present entry of Eastern Europe into postcolonial studies belated.[15] A familiar saying springs to mind: better late than never.

But to return to the question posed above: Can postcolonial theory serve as a point of reference for Polish historical experience and literature? After all, the situation, life conditions, and "fate" of people from the former Second World do not seem suited for writers from the so-called Third World. Indeed, for East-Central European readers, the challenges faced by Third World characters often seem part of a foreign space that is saturated with distant and unknown cares and needs that are satisfied by divergent means. On this basis, one could conclude that there does not exist a clear enough meeting point between these regions to justify their correlation. Indeed, doubts about the validity of extrapolating the categories of postcolonialism to East-Central Europe are being voiced from various directions.[16] Zdzisław Najder, an expert on the work of Joseph Conrad and a friend of Edward Said, unequivocally states that "in the cultural sense, Poland was never a colony."[17]

Was it really never a colony?

If consideration is given to factors such as "lack of sovereign power, restrictions on travel, military occupation, lack of convertible specie, a domestic economy ruled by the dominating state, and forced education in the colonizer's tongue," there is every reason to conclude that "Central Europe's nations were indeed under Russo-Soviet control from roughly 1948 to 1989 or 1991."[18] Here it must be added that the rule was strictly imperial in character, in line with the definition proposed by Michael W. Doyle: "Empire . . . is a relationship, formal or informal, in which one state controls the effective political sovereignty of another political society. It can be achieved by force, by political collaboration, by economic, social, or cultural dependence."[19] According to this definition, the powers that at the 1815 Congress of Vienna established their position in East-Central Europe, of interest here, meet this definition. Together with David Chioni Moore's sociopolitical and political arguments, as quoted above, this confirms the colonial status of this region from the second half of the 1940s (in Poland's case, from the end of the eighteenth century) until the end of the twentieth century (the 1990s).

Marko Pavlyshyn provides the following definition of the cultural aspect of colonialism:

> In culture, the colonial is that which tends to subject the cultural interests of the colonized entity to those of the colonizer. Strategies of cultural colonialism include the exploitation of the cultural resources of the colonized (people, institutions, cultural artifacts, historical memories); the control of cultural value so that prestige and the mystique of universalism attach to the metropolis, while the colony figures as marginal and parochial, graduating to significance only through the mediation of metropolis; and the regulation of cultural activity in the colony in such a way that competition for visibility and prestige with metropolitan cultural output is minimized.[20]

These, however, are only strategies, and thus external factors that condition the functioning of culture. There also exist impulses and motivations that are internal to culture and that are the consequence of those external conditions. Is Polish literature not a continuous "narrative of disasters," and is not our past made up of "mutinies and revolts, unsuccessful negotiations, prolonged military occupation, obdurate settlers, and a serious asymmetry in power" along with "a history of betrayal and disappointed (and disappointing) leaders"?[21] Were it not for the academic obligation of referencing citations, a reader could take this description for a superficial summary of the fate of the Polish people since at least the end of the eighteenth century. This citation comes, however, from Said's closing essay for a collection of studies under the telling title *Ireland and Postcolonial Theory*, focused on various aspects of the colonial legacy that the Irish culture struggles with. The Polish-Irish parallel in the context of postcolonial studies is a subject to which we will return.

Skepticism about attempts at postcolonial theorization of East-Central Europe has at its basis the belief in the incommensurability of the culture and history of East-Central European nations in relation to the newly established political organisms of Asia or Africa. According to Violeta Kelertas, the Balts are disinclined to see themselves as standing in line with the rest of colonized humanity, and this opinion can be extrapolated onto Poles and other inhabitants of the region as well.[22] From here stem the lively protests against these kinds of classifications, even if they are more often articulated behind the scenes rather than published in print, because of their perceptible political incorrectness.[23] A considerable number of inhabitants of East-Central Europe are more inclined to identify with the historical experience of Western Europeans than with the fate of the oppressed people in the Third World.[24] In the process, they overlook the fact that postcolonialism constitutes one of the fundamental ingredients of contemporary identity on a global scale. In this light, equating the postcolonial status with primitiveness and inferiority is decidedly out of place.

Despite this, attempts to utilize postcolonial theory in interpretations of texts from the Polish cultural sphere have frequently and for a long time met with charges of "foreignness," "artificiality," and "fashion."[25] To these charges one can add the already mentioned Marxist entanglements of postcolonial theory as well as the belief in the supposed specificity of East-Central European histories, which would make their description in other than traditional historiographic categories impossible. The list of incompatibilities is completed by a standard set of doubts that were raised also by scholars contemplating the sense of postcolonial studies in Ireland.[26] These doubts concern issues such as identification with Europe ("we have always belonged to Europe"), the interpretation of one's own historical experience ("we never saw ourselves as a colony or defined ourselves in those terms"), or the absence of racial difference ("colonization affects exclusively people of color, not whites"). Arguments offered by opponents of the "Polish brand" of postcolonialism undermine the very sense of using these theoretical tools to interpret Polish writing and sociocultural phenomena.

Yet despite this kind of idiosyncrasy, recent years have seen a growing number of precisely such attempts. The instruments of postcolonialism are increasingly being used to interpret the literatures and cultures of nations that are not "classically" postcolonial since they do not meet two criteria that are often, and erroneously, seen as prerequisite: geographical (they do not live in overseas territories) and racial (they do not represent a race other than white).[27] Such was the case with Ireland, for instance, which—despite its contiguity with British territory and lack of racial difference—was at one point under British governance and had a status no less colonial than Egypt or India. The works of scholars such as Declan Kiberd (*Inventing Ireland*, 1995) and Joseph Lennon (*Irish Orientalism*, 2004), together with the above-mentioned collection *Ireland and Postcolonial Theory* and a dozen of other titles by Irish scholars, now belong to the canon of European postcolonial studies, thus undermining the belief that only cultures of autochthonous populations of other continents can be the subject of this type of research. A separate place is occupied by Ewa Thompson's *The Imperial Knowledge:*

*Russian Literature and Colonialism*; the postcolonial spirit is also expressed by Ukrainian, Baltic, and Romanian scholars.[28]

Faced with the challenge of encountering a subject of a different character, contemporary global postcolonial theory has a chance to avoid stagnation and entrenchment within the comfortable paradigm of "Third-Worldness" and an opportunity to widen its set of interpretive schemata, founded until now on texts by Caribbean, Indian, and African writers. In many works about East-Central Europe that have been inspired by postcolonial studies, in turn, one notes the effort to legitimize methodology, as well as a willingness to creatively draw on the horizons that postcolonial studies opened for Polish and Slavic studies, rather than a mechanical transposition of Western postcolonialism's language and themes.[29]

In light of these remarks, it seems reasonable, even obvious, to conclude that postcolonial studies in a Polish context should (1) take into consideration the conditions stemming from Poland's political, economic, and discursive subjugation to the German, Austro-Hungarian, and Russian/Soviet metropolis, as well as the "surrogate" hegemony of the West; and (2) conduct a critical analysis of the cultural consequences of Polish domination in the eastern and southeastern territories of the former Polish-Lithuanian Commonwealth.[30] Adopting a postcolonial perspective on Polish writing of the past two centuries involves, therefore, an interpretation of Polish history as both a former colony (Russian, Prussian/German, and Austrian) and a former, premodern empire. Of course, a sense of proportion must be maintained in this process, since the expansion of the Polish-Lithuanian Republic is not parallel with the colonizing projects of the British and French metropoles.[31] Moreover, when discussing Russian colonialism, the specific characteristics that distinguish it from the Western model have to be addressed. For one, Russian/Soviet imperial domination of Central and Eastern Europe did not entail the alleged superiority of the "civilized" metropolis to the "barbarian" periphery. Numerous documentary and artistic testimonies of the nations subjugated by Soviet Russia speak to this point, presenting the Eastern hegemon through the prism of its primitive, uncivilized, ill-mannered, and corrupt officers who are held in disdain or hatred by those whom they invaded.[32] The debate about the concept and the identity of Central Europe that was launched by Czech dissidents and continued throughout the 1980s, mainly in Czechoslovak, Polish, and Hungarian intellectual circles, also concerned—to a significant extent—Central Europe's cultural distinctness from, and moral superiority over, the Eastern hegemon. Instrumental in setting the direction and tone of this debate during the 1980s was Milan Kundera's famous remark about the identity of Central Europe as a culturally "kidnapped" part of Western Europe that was taken by the East and forcefully incorporated into the Soviet sphere, resulting in the "tragedy of Central Europe."[33] According to Tomasz Zarycki, this concept,

> which peaked in popularity in the 1980s, can be seen as a result of the symbolic crisis of the Soviet Empire, which stimulated a search for new identities among intellectual elites in the region. All those who were able to argue about being located closer to the Western core rather than to Moscow, or any other of their significant symbolical others, started to look for new identities and ideological projects that could move them symbolically nearer to the triumphant West and further distance them from the weakening and eventually defeated Soviet Empire.[34]

Despite its difficulties with arriving at a commonly accepted definition of a unified Central European identity, the debate was critical for defining a common East-Central European stance toward the despised Soviet metropolis.[35] Its clearly anti-colonial context was markedly visible at the 1988 Lisbon Conference, where East-Central European, Southeast European, and Russian writers clashed over the notion of Central Europe. While the Russian participants rejected the notion along with Central Europeans' right to self-determination and solidified their imperialist, anti-Central-European discourse, the East-Central European writers saw the Red Army as a menace to East-Central European identity and pointed to the impossibility of divorcing literature's responsibility from (geo)politics.[36]

There is a long line of Polish literary works that raise the question of the Polish attitude toward the Russian Empire, starting with the "Digression" of Adam Mickiewicz's *Forefathers' Eve*, part 3. What may seem like a crowning argument against applying the postcolonial perspective to Polish discourse—that is, the lack of respect for the Russian hegemon among the subjugated Polish population stemming from the hegemon's alleged inferiority—speaks, in fact, to its adequacy. Military and political domination that, at the outset, was not supported by the civilizing mission argument (which constitutes the sine qua non of Western colonial projects) allowed the Russian/Soviet Empire to arrive at this argument with a confidence typical of empires and to present it to the world in a way that allows only for its undisputed acceptance. Versions of the "civilizing mission" were in fact implemented in the late eighteenth century by the three partitioning powers of Russia, Prussia, and Austria (as epitomized in Frederick the Great's slogan putting an equal sign between Poles and the Iroquois who similarly "can't be civilized, but by length of time and education") and in the twentieth century by the Soviet Union (through Marxist-Leninist ideology as the driving force of Moscow's imperial policy).[37] In both cases, these arguments found support in the discourse of modernity and served to rationalize the more or less explicit appropriation of lands, their natural resources, and the enslavement of local inhabitants, as is typical of colonialism. And, in both cases, these political, economic, and societal processes had powerful and long-lasting cultural implications for the subjugated population, some of which are explored in this book.

Letting our imagination run wild, it is possible to justify on the level of hypothesis a question that is otherwise tricky: Would the shape—that is, the ideas, representations, values, and ethos—as well as the present-day position of Russian literature and culture in the world be what it is were it not for Russia's role as an empire over the past two centuries? Ewa Thompson's *Imperial Knowledge* indirectly answers the first part of this question by pointing out how deeply the work of some Russian writers is grounded in an imperial "anthropology." As for the question's second part, regardless of the actual artistic value of particular literary works, their international visibility and accessibility is at least in part a factor of prestige attained by the represented population through a synthesis of power and culture. Prestige is a default characteristic of modern empires that translates into a growing circulation and recognition of their cultural output and the influx of confidence that further consolidates their global position. Even Adam Mickiewicz, a self-declared opponent of Russian Empire, succumbed to the suggestion of Russia's cultural superiority over the Polish periphery when, in a letter to his friend Edward Odyniec from 1827, he regretfully reported:

> I would like to publish in Moscow; Warsaw is distant, has difficult relationship, and a meager market. . . . Henceforth, therefore, Warsaw will be a secondary point in my literary endeavors. . . . Where, beside Warsaw, is Legouvé and Delil, or—worse still—Milvoie, etc.—now translated? The Russians shake their heads with pity and astonishment. We have kept ourselves back an entire century in literature! Here, Goethe's every new poem stirs up general enthusiasm, and is immediately translated and commented upon. Every romance by Walter Scott is immediately circulated, every new philosophical work is already in the bookstore; and what about us![38]

The quoted fragment clearly opts for distance from the provincialism of Polish culture and its calcified aesthetics in favor of the wind of Romanticism stirring the rest of Europe, including Russia. One should not overlook the possible colonial undertone of Mickiewicz's remarks—the resentment of a Polish poet whose perception of Russia, grounded in a sense of inferiority, reflects one of the most characteristic signs of a colonized population.

Russia does not fit fully the imperial paradigm as elaborated by theoreticians on the basis of the Western colonial projects: "Unlike Britain or France, which jumped thousands of miles beyond their own borders to other continents, Russia moved to swallow whatever land or peoples stood next to its borders, which in the process kept moving farther and farther east and south."[39] What Said fails to mention here, however, is that Russia was also moving west, with consequences that endure to the present day. A full analysis of the reasons why the Russian and Soviet Empires escaped the attention of postcolonial criticism for so long is impossible here. Among factors that must be mentioned are their skillful politics of self-representation and the lack of interest in the fates of Russian and Soviet colonies in Central and Eastern Europe typical of Western nations and twentieth-century humanities. Societies of countries such as Poland or Hungary, gripped by "reverse-cultural colonization," did not benefit from a phenomenon increasingly common among the emancipating elites of the British colonies, who—having received their education at British and American universities—could insist on speaking on their own behalf, on replying and writing back to the empire, thus creating the opportunity to be heard and to become liberated from an inferiority complex through an influx of confidence.[40] It is telling that, while the West is capable of critical analysis and reevaluation of its imperial activities, along with their social and cultural implications, it is difficult to conceive of a similar situation in the Russian context: "Permitting Gayatri Spivak or Homi Bhabha to shape Western academic responses to Western imperialism amounts to inviting, say, Poles or Lithuanians to instruct students at Russian universities about Russian imperialism. The inconceivability of such a project gauges the distance between the relative openness of Western discourse and the continuing self-imposed suppression of discourse in the 'Russian' Federation."[41] Besides other factors, the emergence of the postcolonial stance in the academic discourses of the United States and Western Europe was also a function of the "ideology of imperialist guilt."[42] Literary critics and scholars from former colonies who had received an education in metropolitan universities played a key role in the shaping of these discourses, clearing the way to the global "market of ideas" for groups that were until recently exploited by the West. The nations of East-Central Europe, in turn, have for a long time remained and, indeed, as current realities suggest, to some extent still remain subjugated, or "orientalized," in Saidian terms. The global public does not have access to their narrations and cannot thereby become interested in their experiences, since these narrations are usually silenced or shut out by the more resounding, and more visible, discourse of Russian literature, culture, and public relations. This both follows from and further solidifies the position of East-Central Europe as "a province of secondary status vis-à-vis Russia in Western academic studies."[43] Said's statements about the Western world's attitude toward "the children of decolonization" applies equally well to opinion about East-Central European societies that, starting at the end of the eighteenth century, has been forged in the humanities, in literature, and in culture: "They have no life, history, or culture to speak of, no independence or integrity worth representing without the West."[44] As the editors of *Over the Wall / After the Fall: Post-Communist Cultures through an East-West Gaze* note, "In public discourse, Eastern Europe has tended to appear through a veil of inherited clichés, reinforced by hazy journalism, unquestioned assumptions, and sometimes the nostalgia of diasporic communities."[45]

While postcolonialism treats colonialism as a discourse, historiography is more interested in "hard" facts—the expeditions, wars, and decisions of political centers and the insurrections of the peripheries—than the "soft" reality of texts and their mutual relations or the convoluted fates of its individual and collective interpretations. Yet, regardless of Polish historians' attitude toward the postcolonial paradigm, the issue of Russian conquests as a colonial phenomenon deserves conceptualization from a historiographic perspective. In fact, such attempts have been undertaken by Polish historians. In drawing parallels between the British, Spanish, and Russian/Soviet Empires, Jan Kieniewicz points to some methodological problems that arise from juxtaposing the varied forms of modern colonial enterprises.[46] Andrzej Nowak's studies in Russian imperialism bring insightful perspectives on the nature of Eastern Europe's colonial condition.[47] Both Kieniewicz's and Nowak's works provide support for, and inspire debate within, Polish postcolonial studies. Historiographic research cannot, however, replace the material that is of primary value to postcolonial critics, namely, literary texts and their contexts. Postcolonial studies treat colonialism less as a political and sociological phenomenon than as a cultural and textual one and understand it as a "project of representing, imagining, translating, containing and managing" a subjugated region that the metropolitan center undertakes "through textual codes and conventions."[48] The interaction and mutual impact of these processes results in the subordination of the population encompassed by colonial discourse regardless of the scale and intensity of the hegemon's violence. What is more, this subordination has more lasting and far-reaching consequences than this or that form of purely political or military domination: it takes away the self-worth of a population, leading to a proliferation of attitudes and behavior of victimhood, on the one hand, and to destructive resentment, for both individuals and collectives, on the other. In line with Gramsci's conceptualization of hegemony, the metropolitan center uses colonial discourse to convince itself, the subordinated population, and the global public that what is advantageous for itself is also good for the colonized. Colonial discourse thus reinforces the validity of the colonial subject/object relation, thereby consolidating the colonial divide.

❧❧❧

The number of works dedicated to Polish literature that reference postcolonial theory are still modest, although they increase from year to year. Interest in postcolonialism remains undiminished among some scholars in Poland and abroad, as evidenced, for example, by conferences, academic symposia, and thematic issues of journals.[49] This is due not only to the appearance of Polish translations of the classic works postcolonialism and the authority of their authors within global humanistic discourse. It is also the result of local theoretical initiatives that, prompted by different currents of Western postcolonialism, propose their own original and inventive frameworks to account for the specificity of local conditions: historical, geopolitical, and cultural. It is not an exaggeration that Polish postcolonialism does not so much believe in the magical power of imported doctrines as it tries to grasp the phenomena that are significant for the local Polish and East-Central European context. Among these phenomena are issues of the double status of colonizer and colonized, the specificity of Russian/Soviet as well as Prussian/German and Austrian imperialism, transformations of identity as a result of double colonization and the Western hegemon's ambivalent cultural role in it, and the orientalization of Poland and East-Central Europe in Western academic and cultural discourses.

Despite this, postcoloniality in Poland is not yet seen as a real and significant characteristic of an East-Central European mentality and of the cultural discourses in that part of the continent. Likewise, the idea that postcolonial theory can grasp the unnoticed, or poorly acknowledged, characteristics of literary and critical discourse from both the period of Poland's colonization and that of its imperial domination and colonial aspirations is not (yet) commonly accepted among Polish cultural critics.[50] Beside these biases, two external factors must be included among the causes of this state of affairs: the limitation of postcolonial theory to basically one model, based on conquest of overseas lands by Western imperial powers, and—stemming from this point—the monopolization of postcolonial studies (sometimes in the grotesque form of jealous appropriation) by scholars from Third World nations. It is not difficult to see that eliminating the second problem depends directly on whether literary and cultural scholars from East-Central European societies succeed in reconstructing postcolonial theory so as to encompass phenomena that have been omitted thus far despite their apparent colonial character, such as "white colonialism," colonization of neighboring territories, or the reverse-cultural colonization of Baltic and Central European nations by (first) Russia and (later) the USSR.

It is an unwritten rule of postcolonial studies that postcolonial research be initiated by academic representatives of a given group's diaspora because of their geographic, intellectual, psychological, and conceptual distance from their own community. Such distance allows for a perspective that can escape the native interpretive matrix, meaning the standard code system that serves to describe and interpret individual and social behaviors and creates a set of generally accepted axioms that tightly fill the conceptual and imaginative space of a given ethnicity. The case is similar for Ukrainian, Lithuanian, Bulgarian, and Romanian studies. The earliest postcolonial impulses arrived in these disciplines either from the outside, via contributions of members of their diasporas affiliated with university centers in Australia (Marko Pavlyshyn), the United States (Ewa M. Thompson, Violeta Kelertas), and Canada (Roumiana Deltcheva, Steven Tötösy de Zepetnek) or as a result of synchronization of research interests and materials arising from academic contacts.[51] The same holds for postcolonial studies of Polish literature.[52] At the end of the 1990s, interest in postcolonial studies surfaced also among Germanists, bringing forth studies of the cultural aspects and implications of the German imperial project in Central and Eastern Europe.[53]

What advantages does the postcolonial perspective offer for Polish literature and criticism? I want to indicate three main areas of benefit, all of which will be addressed in subsequent chapters.

First, postcolonialism supplies the methods and concepts that enable the description and reinterpretation of literary discourse along with other neighboring discourses, from a perspective of a specific and unique experience that links the aspect of being colonized with the aspect of colonizing others. Poland was not only conquered by several empires—Prussia, Austria, Russia, and then the USSR—but it was also once an empire itself, which encompassed the lands of present-day Lithuania, Belarus, and Ukraine. This opens up interesting horizons when it comes to questions of national self-representation, the representation of the Other, and the construction of self-identity in Polish cultural discourse. Grounding studies of these issues in postcolonial theory can help to rethink and reevaluate national, ethnic, and racial stereotypes and perceptions that have been preserved in Polish culture. They can help to plough through the collective consciousness and reexamine both how Poles perceive themselves and how others perceive the Polish people. The categories defined by postcolonial scholarship open insightful and productive avenues of thinking about the way(s) that political factors structured the double experience of Poles: as a former premodern quasi-colonial empire and as a formerly colonized and subsequently decolonized nation that still cherishes memories of its past splendor.

Recognizing these issues is necessary for all parties of colonial, or imperial, relations: both the colonizers and the colonized. It also remains within their individual reach, since the ethic of postcolonialism does not make reflection on one's own experience dependent on whether an analogous endeavor is made by Others—whether former oppressors or the formerly oppressed. This dimension of postcolonial research consists of two aspects, with the first being epistemological: postcolonialism allows a population to learn about itself, its mentality as well as its intellectual and moral condition as a collective that was subject to colonization or colonized others, or both. The second aspect is, in turn, interventional, since this recognition leads to another act of self-definition.

The second area of consideration is tied to the specific bidirectionality of influence that is written into postcolonial studies. Postcolonial criticism inevitably steps outside a single society and culture; it operates at the meeting point of *ethnoi*, cultures, and languages, impacting the interaction between discourses on both sides of the relation of subordination. It is impossible to overlook the fact that the role of postcolonialism is not exhausted in the "decolonization of minds" of conquered populations but also impacts the former oppressor's process of realization and acceptance of colonial culpability. Evidently, this aspect of the postcolonial project integrates in its purview two fields—politics and ethics—that left a powerful mark on the colonial era and that still imprint themselves on culture in the postcolonial era. The classic example of such bidirectional influence is the "writing back," to recall Salman Rushdie's now famous words, undertaken by writers, academics, and humanists from the former peripheries and addressed "to" the discursive field in which canonical texts, representative of the imperial center, functioned and continue to function even in a postcolonial world.[54]

How did Polish literature *write back*, and how does it *write back* now, to the imperial discourse of Germany or Russia? This is one of the questions that the subsequent chapters of this book address. Postcolonial studies plays a key role in a decolonized society's push for its own narrative and an independent existence as a subject in the global forum—for a confirmation of its presence that is symmetrical with existing power/knowledge structures. From another angle, narrative created by a self-conscious postcolonial society can also liberate the former hegemon's elite representatives—writers and journalists, thinkers, scientists, and politicians—from imperial modes of behavior and attitudes. Such was the case for many "exotic" nations of the British Commonwealth, who fought for their right to "fair representation" in English literature and in the British and American academic spheres. This phenomenon has yet to find its correlate in Polish-Russian and Polish-German relations. It is deferred not only because neither the Russian nor the German languages have ever been successfully imposed on the Polish population, a failure that blocked the possibility of Poles' postcolonial *writing back* to the former hegemons in their languages. While there are numerous works by Polish authors that can be read as instances of Polish literature's writing back to the postcolonial metropoles because of their availability in German or English (the lingua franca of today's world) and—less often—in Russian translations, it is still difficult to imagine a Polish university scholar lecturing on Russian imperialism to students in Moscow or St. Petersburg. To make matters seem worse, some German institutions of higher learning, for instance in Bremen, have closed their Polish departments in recent years, signaling the redundancy of cultural studies pertaining to former peripheries for the metropolis or, more bluntly put, the ignorance of the metropolis of its former periphery.[55]

The third area that makes apparent the advantages of postcolonial studies in the context of Polish literature and culture is strictly pragmatic and tied to opportunities for reconfiguring the situation of Polish studies programs in the United States today. Approaching Polish literature and culture through postcolonial thought opens the prospect of removing the restrictive and uncomfortable, as well as fairly anachronistic, corset of Slavic studies that such programs have functioned in so far. Admittedly, such reconfiguration does not rest in the hands of Polish studies scholars alone, depending as it does also on other, including administrative, factors. The advancement of postcolonial studies in Polish literature and culture may nevertheless invigorate, if not preserve, Polish studies abroad, as happened with Asian and African studies, which gained unprecedented momentum and scope through postcolonial criticism. The realization of this goal, however, depends primarily on postcolonial studies becoming a permanent and locally meaningful component of reflection on Polish literature and culture.

The areas outlined in this chapter point out the possible directions that postcolonial studies can take in a Polish and East-Central European context. These introductory remarks suggest that the categories proposed by postcolonialism, when applied to the literature of Poland (or another East-Central European society), allow one to grasp it in its specificity, which Aleksander Fiut aptly identifies with the central themes of unsanctioned peripherality, a sense of border mobility, and a problematic identity.[56] Using the three themes identified by Fiut, it is possible to propose the thesis that the first two are encompassed by the third at the same time that they constitute it. As such, the problem of identity appears as a key issue of nineteenth-, twentieth-, and twenty-first-century literature that requires repeated analysis. In this configuration, identity includes self-definition understood as self-knowledge, and self-definition in relation to others, meaning the orientation of one's "mental map" against the background of, and in relation to, other (foreign) cultural systems and styles of perception. Albeit not exclusively, the methods of postcolonial theory show the complex questions of identity in a light that reveals and accounts for those of its aspects that other perspectives fail to acknowledge or are unable to explain in a more coherent and incisive way.

Chapter Three

# National Identity in a Postcolonial Framework

## Necessary Clarifications and Opening Suggestions

> The lack of one's own identity means the transformation into an object for others, easy to manipulate, unresisting, and many a time given to being led by another, firm hand.
>
> —Skarga, *Tożsamość i różnica*

> Damnant quod non intelligent
>
> —Quintilian

Despite the postsecular and posthumanistic turns in the humanities, the classic issue of postcolonialism, namely the cultural and psychological implications of the colonial encounter, remains valid.[1] Its timeliness is especially resonant in East-Central Europe, where postcolonial studies has gained a considerable momentum over the past few years.[2] This level of activity is a response to the reconfiguration of political relations and to the dynamics of cross-cultural relations in the contemporary world, as well as to globalizing, neo-imperial, and neo-colonial tendencies and the nationalisms that they have revived. The postcolonial reflection in post-Communist European countries is developing in a specific sociopolitical context where disputes are waged over the economic, psychological, and symbolic residue of twentieth-century totalitarianisms (for example, the monuments and cemeteries of Soviet soldiers in countries of the former Eastern Bloc), the directions of post-Communist transformations and forms of democratic society, and, last but not least, the possibility and the limits of sovereignty—of the society and of the nation—in the era of globalization. Postcolonialism in its specific, East-Central European development thus provides the humanities with an entryway into the public debate that has been taking place across this region ever since the retreat of the last Soviet tanks, if not beforehand.

The postcolonial condition of the East-Central European space has a cultural and mental specificity that stems from its peoples' distinct long-term historical experience. In Poland's case, this experience can be charted as a sine wave, with phases of sovereignty and its loss coming one after another, starting in the seventeenth century up to the twentieth, at the hands of neighboring empires (Ottoman Turkey, Russia, Prussia/Germany, Austria). Despite these fluctuations, this sine wave is characterized by a constant parameter: a keen sense of the distinct nature of the East-Central Europeans nations and ethnic groups. To obtain a fuller picture, the sine wave representing phases of political dependence can be superimposed on a curve displaying national sense of self-worth wavering in proportion to the degree of the nation's political agency. When thinking about East-Central Europe from a postcolonial perspective, it is imperative to remember its strong internal differentiation, for the region includes not only relatively new nationalities that are considered to have been born or recovered as a result of nineteenth century national awakenings (Ukrainians, Belarussians), but also nations such as Poland or Hungary, whose identity developed significantly earlier and survived multiple external oppressions.[3]

These factors are historical in nature and have twofold implications. In the first place, they highlight the need for a differentiating rather than a standardizing approach in studies of the region. Such an approach would address the individual characteristics of specific national cultures and counter the tendency of squeezing them into the more or less monolithic paradigm of Slavic studies. The recognition of this diversity rings loud and clear in Milan Kundera's famous 1983 essay, which is anti-colonial in tone and serves as a milestone in the debate of Czech, Polish, and Hungarian dissidents about the region's identity during the Eastern Bloc's final stage of existence.[4] Second, these historical factors indicate the need for a specific focus on the question of identity as a means of broadening perspectives for this region's postcolonial studies. The issue of identity, particularly in its collective aspect, is thus the main theoretical problem to be addressed in establishing a postcolonial perspective on the sociocultural space of post-Communist East-Central Europe.

In this, as well as in the other chapters of the book, I refrain from simply equating communism and colonialism. The two should not be conflated, as each possesses unique characteristics. While the long history of Polish-Russian relations, particularly in the nineteenth century, could not but condition Poland's post–World War II relationship with the USSR and the efforts of Poles to rid themselves of what they perceived as a foreign hegemon, this relationship contained an ideological component typical of communism and absent from classical colonialism. Hence, in the subordination of the Polish Republic (renamed in 1952 the Polish People's Republic) to the Soviet Union in the wake of World War II, as well as of the other states of East-Central and Eastern Europe, some concepts involved were not specific to a colonial enterprise as we know it from the traditional nineteenth-century sense of the word but rather specific to a Communist regime. Among them were such concepts as "class enemy," "class struggle," "worker-peasant alliance," "internationalism," and, above all, "communism." This last concept comprised the ideology for a new humankind, and all of them were endlessly repeated and enforced throughout the Soviet-occupied Communist societies. However, there are "numerous grounds for treating the communist imposition in East-Central Europe as a particular historical embodiment of a persistent and widespread imperial drive which has characterized the behaviour of stronger states towards territories perceived as providing opportunities for economic, political or ideological expansion."[5] Hence, in the perspective applied in this book, communism is viewed as a historically, culturally, and geographically embedded version, or incarnation, of imperialism, its effects on Polish society tied up with Russian nationalism parallel to those that British or French domination had on the Irish or the Algerians. Communist imperialism of the Soviet Union threatened the identity of the subjugated Poles as much as Russian imperialism did during the Romanov Empire, and the continuity between the two is too strong to outweigh the other, apparently not colonial, or extra-colonial, aspects of the Soviet Communist enterprise.

An awareness of literature's role as a key channel of national identity formation was expressed by Polish writers as early as the first decades of the nineteenth century. Maurycy Mochnacki, a theoretician of Polish Romanticism, put forth a concept of the nation as involving the "recognition of self in its being-ness."[6] This conceptualization asked of the national collective to recognize and (re)define its own identity by means of art, primarily poetry, and reserved a leading place for literature in the process of discovering, understanding, and shaping the collective "I" of a given population. A question arises here about the language that should be used to speak about this identity, however. How is it to be articulated without erasing or deforming the traces left behind by the historical context on the one hand, and—on the other—while maintaining a suitable sensitivity to the relations in which this identity currently functions, both in a sociopolitical context and as the subject of contemporary humanistic studies? This problem is the subject of the first part of this chapter, "Identity in the Discourse of the Humanities"; part 2, "The Subjective Perspective," adds a philosophical context, while the third and final part, "Two Voices from the Peripheries," offers a comparative study of two cases of colonial identity discourse (Polish and Algerian).

## Identity in the Discourse of the Humanities

The notion of identity has become one of the central categories of philosophy and the social sciences.[7] Because of its broad range of meanings, it demands clarification and greater definition. The questions addressed in subsequent chapters pertain to one type of identity, seen as its most essential variant, cultural identity.[8] This approach depends on grasping identity in categories that, on the one hand, bind the individual to a given collective, accenting the longevity of his or her identity and the stability of remaining "oneself" (same-self) and, on the other hand, differentiate the individual from members of other groups, underlining his or her identity's distinctiveness and difference. The identity at stake in this discussion is not individually personal; it is not formed in the process of events and experiences lived through by an individual in the Braudelian perspective of "short duration," in other words, within the dimension of personal biography. Of interest here is rather collective identity, a social version of identity, which is co-experienced, co-mediated, and co-defined through intersubjective experiences. Along with other discourses, literature displays and provides evidence of the feelings, reflections, and experiences that are tied to the individual experience of the collective dimension of one's identity, taking up the question of identity in more or less systematized ways. The term "identity discourse" as used in this discussion connotes this entire and varied field of activity around the subject of identity.

Identity discourse concerns one of the core ideas of our time: the idea of individual versus collective identity. In the case of social groups—for example, nations—identity discourse addresses the fundamental question of "Who are we?" along with its more or less self-critical derivatives, such as, "What does it mean to be a . . . ?" "How are we different from others?" "How can we maintain and preserve our distinctness?" Diverse answers to these questions can be offered within a particular identity discourse, depending on the premises derived from an interpretation of, for instance, national history. An identity discourse of a nation is thus a complex entity. It is composed of a set of narratives that reflect and inform the processes that formed and continue to shape a given nationhood and that are transmitted by means of various channels, from mass and popular culture through literature, arts, journalism, and education to academic and nonacademic critical discourses. These narratives refer to and mobilize a variety of arguments for the existence of a given nationhood, such as "national liberation," "memory of a splendid past," "blood sacrifice," "national resistance," and "the civilizing mission," and they can be countered by other narratives within the same identity discourse that aim at interrogating the dominant, or traditional, narratives. Whichever narratives constitute it, and whichever direction it takes—whether antagonistic and exclusive or critical, dialogical, and inclusive—identity discourse of a given social group by definition aims at the solidification of identity and the consolidation of that group.[9]

Postcolonial theorists underline that colonial and postcolonial identity is the product of specific discourses that construct racial and cultural difference. Construed in this way, the study of identity concentrates mainly on problems of race and class, gender and sexuality, and hybridity.[10] Works on this subject generally draw on the Marxist model of social analysis.[11] This bears on the language of description and the direction taken in interpreting given sociocultural processes, which in turn is considered to be hampering the transfer of postcolonial theory to the countries of the former Soviet Bloc where the dominant ideology was that of Marxism-Leninism. Some East-Central European cultural critics can find it difficult to embrace postcolonial studies because of their "aversion to Marxism which historically has come to be regarded [in Eastern Europe] as an ideology of oppression."[12] A Marxist vocabulary awakes in them "bad memories" of past scholarly flirtations with Marxism, specifically the reductionist abuses of the Marxist method of literary and cultural analysis and interpretation that was implemented in the Soviet Bloc by means of administrative force, through indoctrination practices that condemned allegedly ideologically "incorrect" works and their authors en masse.[13] They point to the erroneous diagnoses proffered by some leftist Western intellectuals about the supposed effectiveness of the communist system.[14] This chapter aims to fill in an existing gap in the scholarship by proposing a conceptualization of identity that departs from Marxist language. The work of Charles Taylor provides some rudimentary explanations to aid this process:

> My identity is defined by the commitments and identifications which provide the frame or horizon within which I can try to determine from case to case what is good, or valuable, or what ought to be done, or what I endorse or oppose. In other words, it is the horizon within which I am capable of taking a stand.
>
> People may see their identity as defined partly by some moral or spiritual commitment. . . . Or they may define it in part by the nation or

> tradition they belong to. . . . What they are saying by this is not just that they are strongly attached to this spiritual view or background; rather it is that this provides the frame within which they can determine where they stand on questions of what is good, or worthwhile, or admirable, or of value. . . . [W]ere they to lose this commitment or identification, they would be at sea, as it were.[15]

The lack of frames (horizons) constitutive of individual identity leads to a crisis of self-identification, which Taylor further defines as

> an acute form of disorientation, which people often express in terms of not knowing who they are, but which can also be seen as a radical uncertainty of where they stand. They lack a frame or horizon within which things can take on a stable significance, within which some life possibilities can be seen as good or meaningful, others as bad or trivial. The meaning of all these possibilities is unfixed, labile, or undetermined. This is a painful and frightening experience.[16]

Two conclusions emerge. First of all, identity is a kind of semiosis: it is the result of "self-reading"—one's reading of one's self—which always takes place in relation to an external, objectified system of axiologically marked signs. Second, discovering this semiotic system and taking an evaluative (positive or negative) stance toward its vectors is a condition of having—meaning becoming conscious of having—an identity. This constitutes, or else determines, one's position within this system—a "place" that can be defined in terms of inclusion and exclusion. Moreover, as Taylor suggests, identity is a value for a human being: it is better to have it than not to have it. Identity constitutes an ontological support for the subject vis-à-vis others (both individuals and collectives). Its antithesis can be found not only in the lack of identity but also in the possibility of its loss when confronted with the "firm hand" of another, to recall the epigraph to this chapter. This possibility means that

> there exists within us fear of the loss of identity, a fear that is natural and present not only in individuals, but also in social groups. It is here that the great issue of identity—of the individual, as well as nations and cultures—is born. The category of identity thus becomes something more than a logical rule of thought, becoming a principle of world order, of our own existence, of the continuity of existence of our culture. It is not surprising that we are beginning to treat it as a value.[17]

In considerations of the postcolonial identity of East-Central European societies, meaning identity forged through the encounter with Soviet oppression, a particularly important role is attributed to their identity's national aspect, or dimension, viewed in the context of national discourse and national ideology. I use these terms at the risk of being charged with ideologization of scholarly discourse. I believe, however, that foregoing the terms of "nation," "nationalism," "national identity," and "national ideology" is no more ideologically neutral than their use, in contrast to critics who argue against the latter, such as Roger Brubaker and Frederick Cooper.[18] As Polish sociologist Michał Łuczewski points out:

> The most important objection to Brubaker's claim, inspired by humanistic sociology, underscores the indispensability of the category "nation" as giving justice to the self-understanding of human agents. Almost one hundred years ago, Florian Znaniecki faced something similar to Brubaker's dilemma. Though his point of departure made an identical distinction between *categories* of *practical reality* and *categories* of *thought* about *practical reality*, he drew reverse conclusions. He held that in social sciences we should use exactly such *categories* that are simultaneously *categories of practice* as well as *analysis*. Only such concepts can tie theoretical and practical reality. Only such categories are appropriate in understanding and explaining human actions. Using solely scientific equivalents bears the risk that we will create an artificial language without any bearing on social reality.[19]

I share Łuczewski's preference for language that adheres to social reality over one that creates its own reality. I endorse the use of nation-oriented categories as both relevant for and instrumental in the scrutiny of processes that began to transpire among Eastern and East-Central European societies in the eighteenth and nineteenth centuries. It was then that the modern identities of these societies were formed, and the processes that further shaped them have continued therein both during Soviet rule and after the collapse of the Soviet Empire. Postcolonial analysis of these processes that eschews nation-related categories for the sake of an imagined ideological neutrality and methodological purity runs the risk of throwing the baby out with the bathwater and removing from critical discourse on East-Central Europe concepts inherent to understanding this region's specificity. For both imperialism and colonialism, the variants born on the territories of East-Central Europe from the late Enlightenment through the end of twentieth century impacted not only individual existence but also entire communities: the identity of ethnicities and nationalities was thus jeopardized and had to be defended in order to be secured and maintained. This problem, however, is no way restricted to East-Central Europe. Frantz Fanon was aware of it when he wrote, in the context of the Algerian struggle for national liberation, "Colonialism has not simply depersonalized the individual it has colonized; this depersonalization is equally felt in the collective sphere, on the level of social structures. The colonized people find that they are reduced to a body of Individuals who only find cohesion when in the presence of the colonizing nation."[20] Nowadays, in the age of cosmopolitanism and globalization, nationality is often viewed as a factor of group self-identification that is exhausting itself. The very category of "nation" is disputed as no longer sufficient to describe the social realities of the apparently post-national late modernity, and national identity is substituted with other, post-national, supranational, or subnational, formulas of identity that accentuate—or dismiss—cultural, civilizational, religious, or ethnic facets.[21] As Nadine Holdsworth observes, "Current preoccupations with questions of globalization, internationalism, transnationalism and cosmopolitanism can give the impression that the nation is receding in significance and that to draw attention to it is somehow politically naïve or evidence of a retrograde parochialism."[22] In pursuing postcolonial literary and cultural studies, are we thus condemned to either giving up this analytical tool or else allowing this skeptical charge, critical of notions of nation and nationality, to bear on our interpretation of texts? To escape the supposed parochialism of the term "nation," should we simply replace the concept of "national identity" with that of, say, "cultural identity"?

Leela Gandhi underlines that, alongside the multiplicity of theoretical frameworks that subject the notion of identity to the processes of radical discursiveness, "we still need to listen carefully to . . . Fanon's categorical delineation of a situated, monolithic and combative national identity."[23] In the process, Gandhi does justice to scholars such as Said, who "concede the positive role of anti-colonial nationalisms in mobilising and organising the aspirations of oppressed and colonized people the world over."[24] It is telling that Gandhi, who as a proponent of the deconstructive method believes that "post-colonialism pursues a post-national reading of the colonial encounter by focusing on the global amalgam of cultures and identities consolidated by imperialism,"[25] also pays attention to the reality, not to say tangibility, of the national dimension of the colonial encounter. This shows that the question of nationalism, which frames the notions of nation and nationality in postcolonial theory, is significant regardless of one's epistemological position.

Nationalism has become one of the pivotal forces in mobilizing anti-imperial movements in Western European colonies, as attested by numerous critics of colonialism, including Fanon, Mahatma Gandhi, Chinua Achebe, Jomo Kenyatta, Patrice Lumumba, and Nelson Mandela. According to Siniša Malešević, "The steady erosion of colonial rule from the 1950s and the establishment of new independent states worldwide further extended nationalism, from a largely European or Northern phenomenon into a truly global and dominant ideology of modernity."[26] The militant potential of the term "nationalism," in light of the decolonizing processes that took place throughout the world during the second half of the twentieth century, seems obvious today. After all, colonialism "had to provoke resistance of the conquered people, which under favorable circumstances transformed into organized forms."[27] Among Western Europe's colonies in Asia, Africa, and the Caribbean, however, the nationalist bent of anti-colonial movements was not obvious and at times even absent (as exemplified by the activity of Aimé Césaire and Léopold Senghor), in contrast to the situation in Poland or Hungary, where the concept of national identity stabilized long before the experience of colonial oppression and was instrumental to their independence movements. In such cases, full emancipation from the grip of Soviet political, military, and economic hegemony does not mean a transition from an ethnic to a national phase of collective existence; in other words, it does not constitute a different, qualitatively new type of identity. Rather, it is an act or a process of rebuilding, reconstructing, recovering, or strengthening a weakened identity. It is both understandable and verifiable from a historical perspective, and surely not difficult to prove theoretically, that the nationalistic strivings of East-Central European societies subjected to the hegemony of the Soviet Empire until 1989 were anti-colonial at their basis. Their main premise was the real and objectively existent national community of interests and aims, regardless the problems with defining the nation. In the case of such societies, we are dealing with organisms that have constituted nations and ruled their own countries in precolonial times. For them, foreign domination marked a period when the national discourse was stifled, or intercepted, by the discourse of the hegemon. This could not occur without consequence to collective self-expression, both in the form of social activities and practices and on the level of reflection on identity. It is thus difficult to argue with the prognoses formulated on these grounds by some sociologists: "For the past fifty-five years, Poles were not allowed to freely express their national identity, outside of state-sanctioned means and narrations. Having this opportunity now, they will surely take advantage of the freedom they have. Undoubtedly, the first task of this 'work of memory' will be the redefinition of identity, but this redefinition will take place, with all certainty, within national categories."[28] The directions presently pursued in attempts to redefine Polish identity will be addressed in subsequent chapters. To undertake this type of reflection, however, it is necessary to recognize the position from which it can be sensibly conducted, without falling into a nationalistic rhetoric on the one hand, or—on the other—uncritically accepting post-national theses.[29] Some sociologists, such as Sławomir Kapralski, predicted that Eastern European societies will begin to "appreciate the charms of post-national life" after the relatively quick completion of the "work of memory."[30] Recent years, however, have revised this prognosis. Jan Kieniewicz's position on the topic is worth quoting: "It seems to me that the prophesied demise of the nation state's role was greatly exaggerated—especially as regards confrontation with the present global threats and the glaring crisis of the European Union."[31] The recent refugee crisis has proven that the majority of Poles, not unlike other East-Central European societies, are far from subscribing to the post-national rhetoric, opting instead for what they consider to be serving the cohesion of a nation state.[32]

The dual-faceted collective identity mentioned above, which rests on a similarity-dissimilarity model, obviously does not exhaust these complex identity issues. The field of inquiry is further complicated by the question of the objectivity or subjectivity of the criteria of a given group's distinctiveness. What serves as the basis of identification for a national collective? Is it a group of shared (not necessarily consciously) cultural values that exists objectively, or is it self-awareness arrived at by a collective—a concept of its own self that is prone to restructuring and formation, and thus rendered in discourse? In other words, is national identity a result of objective cultural characteristics, transcendent in relation to the linguistic image of the world, or rather the product of the beliefs held by members of a collective about their own distinctiveness?

Attempts to answer these questions produce new ones regarding definition (What is a nation?), genealogy (What is the source of a nation?), morphology (What are the elements of a nation?), and function (Why do nations exist?). These problems have been central to nation historians, anthropologists, and theorists for many years, and a review of opinions on them would require a separate book. One thing is certain: national and ethnic identity and the phenomenon of nations and nationalism tied to it constitute one of the central and most timely questions of the humanities, irrespective of the crisis that the nation-state faces today in the view of some scholars.[33]

Given the challenges of a scholarly explication of these issues, it is necessary to choose from among the research perspectives on offer. This choice should be based on the suitability of a given perspective for the identity model (along with its historical conditions) at stake here. Social constructivism enjoys particular popularity within the literary and other scholarly communities.[34] In this context, the comments of Andrzej Walicki, a Polish philosopher and historian of ideas, are particularly useful. They are a response to the voluntaristic model of the nation adopted by American theorists for historical reasons: "I do not consider my identity as a Pole to be imagined, fluid, or accidental; I like the feeling of there being something non-contingent inside me that defines me, and that this something is essential, inherent to my self, that it makes me myself and is thus mine to the core, even though it was not and cannot be a matter of choice."[35] While these ideas cannot be developed further here, Walicki's remarks signal a problem that must be acknowledged when deliberating the value of national identity frameworks proposed by social sciences. Contemporary, globally dominant, primarily modernist theories of the nation, based in the specific Western European (mainly British, French, and German) experience, are ill fitting in many regards when applied to the people of small and medium-sized nations of East-Central Europe, such as the Czechs, the Hungarians, the Poles, or the Slovaks. Moreover, when applied to citizens of such nations, their categories can perform "epistemological violence" on their subjects, having been established on a different ground. One example is the career of the term "nationalism" in studies of the development of East-Central European national ideologies, where it is used in a specific and stigmatizing sense developed by American scholarship under the sway of Hans Kohn's dichotomous division of nationalism into Western ("good," political, and civic) and Eastern, meaning Eastern European ("bad," cultural, and ethnic).[36] Kohn's dichotomy boils down to the opposition between civic and ethnic nations and continues to be used despite its inadequacy, the ambiguity of its terms, and its excessive generalizations derived from accepted ideological assumptions. Since its conception, it has generated qualitative judgments and quasi-scientific stereotypes, especially in reference to Central and Eastern Europe. Pointing to the need to challenge "the hegemonic (Kohnian) canon of nation-building," Monika Baár comments on the implications of its application to this region:

> According to . . . Hans Kohn, Western nationalism can be interpreted as a product of the Enlightenment, a rationalist ideology, centred around the notions of political legitimacy, active citizenship and the *Staatsnation*, while its Eastern counterpart was based on a romantic collectivism organized around the irrational, pre-civilized folk concept and the *Kulturnation*. The former is deemed individualist and universalist, and compatible with liberal ideals, whereas the latter is regarded as collectivist, exclusivist and therefore dangerous. Kohn's distinction and latent criticism, which was originally directed against Germany, soon became transferred into the context of Central and Eastern Europe. The shortcomings of this theory, especially its sweeping generalizations, have themselves been frequent targets of criticism.[37]

Nevertheless, this line of argument continues to occupy a strong position in scholarly literature. Especially visible among its supporters are theorists who associate the development of nationalism with modernity and modernization and hence subscribe to a vanguard version of national development, which was later imitated by latecomers in a distorted form, resulting in dependence and underdevelopment.[38]

Thus understood, "nationalism" connotes a dislike of ethnicity, national ideas, and the drive to attain a "strong" identity tied to them, which—in the context of Polish national endeavors—devastated the subject of study rather than increased the understanding of it. Said accurately grasped the essence of this problem as the paternalistic gesture of the West toward populations outside of its narrow, "elitist" circle, although he did not list post-Communist East-Central European populations among them: "In all these views, I believe, there is a marked (and, in my opinion, ahistorical) discomfort with non-Western societies acquiring national independence, which is believed to be 'foreign' to their ethos. Hence the repeated insistence on the *Western* provenance of nationalist philosophies that are therefore ill-suited to, and likely to be abused by Arabs, Zulus, Indonesians, Irish; or Jamaicans."[39] Conflicts and discussions around the nation's genealogy and ontology remain largely unfinished and inconclusive. A theoretical frame of reference for postcolonial studies in which questions of nation, nationalism, and national identity are posed in the context of East-Central Europe—outlined here in the example of Poland—is thus both a timely and useful proposal.

Contemporary theories of the nation and nationalism have been strongly influenced by modernist paradigm. Various models and conceptualizations of them were created within its framework, aligned primarily in two regards: they reflect a fundamentally constructivist point of view and define nationalism (seen as a source and cause of the nation) in categories of political, group interests. In light of these theories, nations are not only creations with a relatively short history but also "discursive facts," meaning beings that are "invented" and "constructed" (under the auspices of nationalistic ideology, brought to life through social engineering methods), and that have a non-objective, "imagined" status.[40] This understanding has developed under the influence of far-reaching theses (for social theory of the second half of the twentieth-century) that configure the nation as a communicative community created through interaction between many microparts of culture, as well as the product of both industrialization and the political maneuvers of elites inclined toward nationalistic ideology.[41] The proponents of these theses question the existence of a steady structure of identity. They consider it to be a component of the grand narrative of the nation and see identity as the intentional construct of this narrative aimed at realizing the interests of specific social groups.

The arguments put forth on the basis of such claims accent the processual (rather than substantive) character of the object of reference that they seek to explain. The theoretical constructions erected on top of such arguments are supported by the conviction that the nation is an abstract "contingency," which is invented, created, or "imagined"; stems from modernizing transformations; and is dependent in its ontology on the consciousness of its members.[42] Setting aside the significant differences among scholars such as Karl Deutsch, Eric Hobsbawm, Anthony Giddens, and Ernest Gellner, their views on this matter led them, along with their continuators and proponents, toward anti-naturalistic, anti-universal, and nominalistic positions. Understanding the nation as, for instance, a cultural artifact, the effect of "invented tradition," or the recent invention of "social engineering," dilutes the category of a nation as existing actually and substantively within a time and a space of a community.[43] That a nation can be viewed as such a community has been recently demonstrated by Michał Łuczewski's comprehensive and fascinating case study of the transformation of social relationships into national ones in a small village on the southern fringe of Poland.[44] The modernist approaches, such as Gellner's, in turn demand that the source of the nation be located in a nationalism born of an unidentified source.[45] Referencing this or that theoretical model is tied to a choice between two main philosophical traditions: nominalistic, which demystifies the world of ideas by separating it from the world of things, and realistic, which acknowledges the ontological rootedness of ideas.[46] This choice also has far-reaching consequences for interpreting literature and other discourses. Describing and explaining the process of nation building in the village of Żmiąca, which transpired over seven hundred years, Łuczewski offers a different outlook on nationhood than does Gellner, one that "leaves room for both freedom and determinism"; as Łuczewski claims, "Social reality does not fall to the whims of individuals, or the power of the structures."[47] I mention Łuczewski's approach (which he terms "integral" for combining the conflicting concepts of primordialism, modernism, ethnosymbolism, and constructivism) as an example of a very recent theoretical proposal that accentuates the nation as an objective, empirical reality that calls for being treated in terms of a community. Significantly, this proposal has been formulated in postcolonial East-Central Europe.

This is not meant to undermine the explicative value of modernist or constructivist theories of nation and nationalism. Answers to the scholarly questions that they pose deserve close attention and critical reflection. The work of authors such as Ernest Gellner, Benedict Anderson, and Stuart Hall brings valuable insight into postcolonial studies about the role of cultural discourses in the creation of both representations of collective identity and the cultural mechanisms of identification with a national community. Hall's take on the issues reveals the dynamics of the discursive processes that take place within the national community and at the juncture points between nations and ethnicities, including those in conflict with one another as a result of a colonial encounter. This list of merits could be expanded further still.

Drawing on concepts of theoreticians such as Gellner, Anderson, Hall, and others, however, does not require the full acceptance of their founding assumptions. Making use of methodological options that run against the grain of their conceptualizations can be epistemically useful. Such is the case with essentialism, which to some extent counters the intellectual tradition from which the work of these theorists derives. A polemic with this nominalistic tradition represented by constructivist theorists, however, is a separate undertaking. Here I can only address a question of prime importance from the perspective of these reflections. In this I am aided by Gayatri Spivak, who—despite the influence of Derrida's thought on her own writing—admits that "the moment of essentialism or essentialization is irreducible. In deconstructive critical practice, you have to be aware that you are going to essentialize anyway. So then strategically you can look at essentialisms, not as descriptions of the way things are, but as something that one must adopt to produce a critique of anything."[48] In my opinion, the East-Central European historical and social conditions are most effectively grasped with the use of Anthony Smith's ethnosymbolic position, as laid out in *The Ethnic Origins of Nations*.[49] In creating his theoretical model of *ethnie*, Smith shows that constructivism is not the only possible counterposition to primordialism—the paradigm that upholds the primal, "eternal" and "natural" origin of nations and that is opposed by Gellner's and Anderson's models.

Smith's own framework for the issue of nations, which he called ethnosymbolism, opposes primordialism while also countering constructivist conceptualizations. He based it on the analysis of materials from premodern times that are often overlooked by sociologists of nations. The fact that Smith's theory does not bypass issues taken up by constructivists, such as the significance of cultural and political discourse in the construction of identity, deserves emphasis; instead, these issues are differently conceptualized and explained. From the constructivist perspective, discourse precedes identity within the ontological order. Identity thus has the status of a purely discursive construct, a perspectivist entity, and as such is unstable and prone to the influences of nationalist ideology (the precise definition of which, as is the case with nationalism itself, comes with a separate set of problems). Taken to its ultimate limit, the concept can be expressed within a self-referential formula: "A national culture is a *discourse*—a way of constructing meanings which influences and organizes both our actions and our conception of ourselves. . . . National cultures construct identities by producing meanings about 'the nation' with which we can *identify*."[50] Seen from this perspective, identity appears devoid of an essential character and ties to individual or collective subjectivity, becoming a category that serves the power structure and is subject to the Foucauldian order of *savoir/pouvoir*.

For ethnosymbolists, in turn, nations exist because of the grounding of a real community within a symbolic world composed of such elements as language, myth, art, and religion—the "varied threads which weave the symbolic net, the tangled web of human experience."[51] This view accents the role of myths, historical memories, values, and symbols in the process of creating a nation. These elements add up to the foundation of ethnic identity, while this identity's development into a modern national identity is the effect of continuation of the premodern "myth-symbol complex"—in Smith's words, the *mythomoteur* of the nation.[52] The nationalism that was assigned an absolute causative power by scholars such as Gellner is submitted to strong limitations in Smith's model in the form of a shared culture that binds members of a population through common origin myths, historical memories, and cultural values. As a result, the history of a nation as "written" by nationalism does not constitute an arbitrary ideological construction, wielded and imposed on the population by the elites, but is rather its own kind of semiosis of the past—a process of investing myths, events, and figures with significance, of including them in reinterpretive narrations that possess the status and value of truth for a given collective at a specific historical moment. In this manner, the past and its contents are cultivated in the name of discovering the truth about oneself, meaning one's existence in a national collective.[53] It has little in common with a "construct," which suggests latitude, contingency, and arbitrariness, but is rather a discovery, reconstruction, and reinterpretation of past cultural models. Ethnosymbolism suggests a type of analysis of collective cultural identity that accounts for its *longue durée* perspective. It also takes into consideration the processual character of nation, although it understands this character differently than does constructivism: as a task for the members of a collective to be realized in part through mediating cultural discourses.

> "Nation-building" is not simply a matter of establishing the appropriate institutions or generating a complex class structure around a communications infrastructure. Nor is it a once-for-all affair. Creating nations is a recurrent activity, which has to be renewed periodically. It is one that involves ceaseless re-interpretations, rediscoveries and reconstructions. . . .

> At the same time, this "nation-building" activity operates within a definite tradition; it is not made over entirely anew by each generation, but inherits the mythologies and symbolisms of previous generations.[54]

Ethnosymbolism can be of significant operational value for Polish postcolonial studies. It lends theoretical support to the conviction that the nation is constituted in an invisible, yet nevertheless real way: "People *learn* their nation's history, they can *forget* and then, again, *remember* their national identity and they can *express* this national identity. Yet, in each of these instances we encounter the nation *sui generis*: it appears to exist above and beyond the agency of any of us as individuals."[55] At stake here is not just a general sense of the reality of the national substance that this conceptualization introduces to scholarly reflection on nations.[56] The category of nation derived from Smith's *ethnie* model is an important analytical instrument that gives a proper degree of consideration to the particularity of the Polish sociocultural formation, which in many ways differs from the national and ethnic entities of Asia, Africa, South and Central America, or Australia and Oceania that are the subject of Western postcolonial studies. The benefit of the ethnosymbolic perspective in a postcolonial analysis of identity discourse stems directly from some of the constitutive characteristics of Smith's model. Among other things, the ethnosymbolic framework warrants attention for the historicism that is inscribed in it and that underlines the identity forming and integrational role of cultural memory in nation-building processes.

From Smith's perspective, the nation and the realm of the national are characterized by a specific authenticity. These phenomena belong to the objective order—rather than an essential or an "imagined" one—which does not mean that they are unchanging, fixed within history, or separate from changeable cultural conditions.[57] Both of these categories are characterized by a dynamic of relations with other elements and with each other: "A nation . . . is a named human population sharing an historic territory, common myths and historical memories, a mass, public culture, a common economy and common legal rights and duties for all members."[58] Nationalism, in turn, signifies, on the one hand, the "awakening ['inventing' in Gellner] of the nation and its members to its true collective 'self,' so that it, and they, obey only the 'inner voice' of the purified community," while being, on the other hand, "a *form of culture*—an ideology, a language, mythology, symbolism and consciousness—that has achieved global resonance."[59] In this manner, Smith links the order of the nation's ontology with the order of intersubjective consciousness and cultural participation, and he avoids assigning an excessive role to the political factor of the state and the ideology that comes with it, as happens in Gellner's work.

By virtue of overcoming elite-centered modernist frameworks, including constructivism, the ethnosymbolic perspective reveals and problematizes in interesting ways phenomena from various regions and cultural strata that partake in the process of acquiring, or else of coming into awareness of, national identity. Among these phenomena is a tension, central also to Polish culture, between the leadership aspirations of the intelligentsia, who wish to claim "the rule of souls" for themselves, and the values engrained in folk traditions.[60] This tension determines the symbolic framework of Polish identity discourse. Reflection on Polish identity discourse needs to include the study of broadly understood "horizontal" structures of culture. Its study should be in part complementary and in part antagonistic with regard to the dominant, traditional, "vertical" frameworks that determined national values based on the degree to which ideas transmitted "downward" by the elites penetrated Polish culture.[61] Among such "horizontal" structures are Sarmatism (understood as an anti-elitist ideological current), republicanism, provinciality, and parochialism, as well as resistance to central power and dictatorship.[62]

Ethnosymbolism also attends to the stability and continuity of ethnic and national identity, which the modernist paradigm had put into question, without undermining the fact of its evolution or the impact of cultural and political discourses on its formation. In this way, it avoids the risky, if catchy, hypotheses that form the constructivists' main axis of argument. According to these hypotheses, nations owe their existence to "'invented traditions,' which are products of social engineering and are created to serve the interests of ruling elites by channeling the energies of the newly enfranchised masses."[63] From this perspective, the identity of a collective is not the cause but the result of emancipatory actions, which are usually discussed in terms of negative impulses of exclusion. Ethnosymbolism refers to a different, communitarian ethic: it accents the solidarity of the national community's members and stresses that their sense of group belonging is meaningful and positive. It also looks elsewhere for answers to questions about the sources and the nature of nation-building processes, focusing on the ethnic base, meaning "ethnic ties and sentiments."[64] The discovery of these bonds by the constituting collective assumes "continuity with the cultural past of the dominant ethnie."[65] Smith points out that "it is easy to dismiss these efforts and to treat them as inventions of nationalism, mythical fictions," but the effectiveness of national projects realized with the support of these historical and cultural factors of identity formation suggests, after all, the possibility of alternatives to constructivist interpretations—"the need for popular 'resonance' and 'appeal.'"[66] In other words, nations are not derived from purely discursive acts, and they are not only "ideas." To the contrary, they must be backed by a certain objective cultural tradition that is shared by a collective—both by its elites and its other representatives—and that is discovered and reconstructed by them. In this way, the ethnosymbolic explanation of nation and nationalism that valorizes the causative power of the collective (of the nation and, within its realm, of both groups and individuals) brings us to the issue of subjectivity, which is closely tied to identity and, from a postcolonial perspective, of particular importance to literary interpretation and other cultural discourses.

## The Subjective Perspective

The divergent notions of a subject and of subjectivity stem mainly from the varied philosophical traditions referenced by scholars of the issue, and not only in the field of postcolonial studies.[67] For explicatory reasons, contemporary theories, including cultural theory, readily make use of Althusser's concept of interpellation in their conceptualizations. From this perspective, the subject constitutes itself at the moment of subjecting itself to the institutionalized acts of language use that are addressed to it. Foucault's proposal to view the subject as articulated through previously existing discursive structures is also in constant circulation. According to Foucault, the subject is de facto the depersonalized discourse's object of power that is exerted over society's members by means of systems of knowledge. These frameworks are linked not only through a decentered subject but also through its specific "de-subjectification," depersonalization, and subjugation: they assign to the subject the status of an ideological (Althusser), discursive (Foucault), or linguistic (Lacan) construct, which is the effect of appropriation, control, oppression, and so on. The subject is reduced here to the role or the position reserved for it in the social structure. These types of frameworks are only a stone's throw away from the radical poststructuralist concepts of the subject that, as a result of putting the "metaphysics of presence" into question, deny it stability as well as an autonomous and sovereign existence. This understanding posits subjectivity as a category that is entirely dependent on culture and on its forms of articulation.

These frameworks have some analytical utility. They problematize the process of political empowerment of a national collective and call attention to its hidden agenda. It is difficult, however, to agree with the removal of causation from individuals and shifting it instead onto discourse, as Foucault's writings imply.[68] In particular, doubts arise around the lack of a human dimension in Foucault's framing of discourse—its purely depersonalized character—and its positioning as a dominant category and an instrument of the subject's subjugation. After all, can an impersonal and abstract "Discourse"—a constructed system of utterances that consists of signs and the rules of their use and is deployed by human collectives as a means of communication—really be responsible for all of the events that affect nations and societies? Is discourse understood in such a totalistic manner the only way of speaking, thinking, and creating knowledge about the world that exists? As Foucault asserts, along with later theoreticians of this issue (Ernesto Laclau and Chantal Mouffe), knowledge constructed through discourse constitutes the world that it supposedly only discovers: it categorizes it, orders and interprets it, and makes it comprehensible within the framework established by the limits of discourse. Admittedly, Foucault's proposition to view discourse "as a violence which we do to things, or in any case as a practice which we impose on them" undoubtedly suits the analysis of phenomena that occur at the intersections of politics and culture in situations of colonial oppression.[69] Reading *L'ordre du discours* in the context of relations between the empire (as the center—source and legislator—of discourse) and the subordinated population (as the object of discourse) makes tangible the reality of the Foucauldian "violence against things." It is a painful and dominant reality, yet it is neither an absolute one nor a final or permanent one. Yet limits to this violence do exist, and consequently so does the possibility of liberation from the web of discourse—if not on the systemic level and on a scale encompassing the entire population, then surely within an individual and personal domain. Said points to this in *Orientalism* when underscoring—in opposition to Foucault—the significance of the position of a text's author.[70]

Like much postcolonial criticism, the arguments presented here reference some ideas from the Foucauldian conceptualization of discourse.[71] While I do not accept all of its conceptual inventory, I recognize its potential usefulness on the level of microanalysis (meaning in descriptions of social dynamics) and especially in the context of colonial relations that shaped some part of contemporary Polish identity discourse. This book thus contains elements of discourse analysis aimed at exploring both surface and deep textual meanings, and toward a method of studying the social and institutional function of texts.

Discourse analysis accounts for the fact that each and every text stands in relation to and cocreates the sociocultural practices that gave rise to it. This helps to answer questions about the significance of a given utterance (whether literary, scientific, or political), which arises from its position within a broader field of discursive practices. The issues to be addressed concern who is speaking, to whom, and why. With what aim the message has been formulated? With the support of which resources of knowledge about the world, at which moment, and under which circumstances? From what position is this message spoken? This view of the text broadens the optics suggested by poetics and linguistics, adding to it the perspective of political science, anthropology, and cultural studies. It is erroneous to think "of the text as existing entirely within a hermetic, Alexandrian textual universe, which has no connection with actuality . . . not simply because texts are in the world, but also because as texts they place themselves—one of their functions as texts is to place themselves—and indeed are themselves, by soliciting the world's attention."[72] The reconstruction of this supratextual and paratextual frame, which every utterance is inscribed into and which Said called the "wordliness of texts," enriches research horizons with a dense net of meanings that appear only *after* a text is placed within an order beyond the limits of "the order of discourse." According to Said, a literary text permits the excavation of its semantic depths only if considered together with the history, anthropology, political theory, and life conditions in a particular time and place. To comprehend a text, one must recreate the extralinguistic rules that once played a part in its emergence and now participate in its social existence. At stake in this interpretation is the disclosure of these rules. The disclosure of these rules, the precondition for the reading I refer to here, facilitates access to meanings of a text seen as a product of specific discursive practices. Such disclosure also permits the grasping of the "ponderous, formidable materiality" of discourse with which every text struggles, as Foucault claims, while trying to carefully hide its dependence on it and unable to oppose its "materiality."[73] Yet the text is not simply an enticing game of signification that calls for innocent—meaning ethically unengaged—deconstruction. It is primarily a certain cultural reality that asks for an ethical stance to be taken toward the external, extratextual reality with its "hard" facts: oppression, injustice, subordination, and erasure (in both metaphorical and literal senses) of other nations and ethnicities. "If everything in a text is always open equally to suspicion and to affirmation, then the differences between one class interest and another, between oppressor and oppressed, one discourse and another, one ideology and another, are virtual in—but never crucial to making decisions about—the finally reconciling element of textuality."[74] Like every discourse, that concerning national identity is also contextualized: it develops within a specific situation and in a given language, and its semantic and rhetorical resources accent some things, omit others, and invent others still, so that all of its apparent descriptions are also acts of interpretation. This is always done from a specific (ideological, philosophical, social) position and thus in a certain relation to the object, to the other participants of the communication within the (national) community, to transcendental reality, and to the entire intellectual and discursive tradition that locates it.

Stuart Hall's opinion that ethnicity speaks from a specific place can also be used in the context of nationality. Identity depends on retelling the past. For this reason, narrations and stories constitute an important factor in the construction and the maintenance of national identity. At first glance, this perspective appears to agree with Smith's conceptualization, which highlights the role of *mythomoteurs* in national identity formation. Stuart Hall is not interested in approaching identity as something objectively given and possessing an established nature, however. Rather, he investigates the entanglement of identity with history, the always continuing process of changes that prevents the solidification of identity into a static, essential form: "We all write and speak from a particular place and time, from a history and a culture which is specific. What we say is always 'in context,' *positioned*."[75] Among other things, postcolonial analysis of identity discourse exposes these determining factors in order to problematize the seemingly evident formula of a homogenous, coherent, and continuous identity. It attains this aim by indicating the "cracks" within such a formula—the places of fissure or of *différance*, to recall Derrida's language, which echoes throughout Hall's essay on cultural identity:

> Cultural identity . . . is a matter of "becoming" as well as of "being." It belongs to the future as much as to the past. It is not something which already exists, transcending place, time, history and culture. Cultural identities come from somewhere, have histories. But, like everything which is historical, they undergo constant transformation. Far from being eternally fixed in some essentialized past, they are subject to the continuous "play" of history, culture and power. Far from being grounded in a mere "recovery" of the past, which is waiting to be found, and which, when found, will secure our sense of ourselves into eternity, identities are the names we give to the different ways we are positioned by, and position ourselves within, the narratives of the past.[76]

Since the determinations that Hall refers to constitute a permanent, inseparable component of human existence, they are "part of the equation" of human societies' conscious existence. On the one hand, we are indeed inevitably situated within rather than beyond discourse; we are thus circumscribed by its cognitive framework, its taxonomy, the axiology inscribed therein, the rules of creating and comprehending meanings, and so on. As a result, we can describe our identity only from a certain position; on the basis of some and not other "facts"; with the support of specific narrations, myths, symbols, and so forth. On the other hand, however, in constructing these identity narratives, we have some truth on the horizon—about ourselves, others, our community, our past—that we aim to discover (rather than construct) even when we do it in a faulty and partial manner. As human beings, we are subject to limitations: obstacles that are subjective in nature (rooted in the human being), as well as objective (stemming from reality) and linguistic (due to an imperfect medium).[77] It is a usurpation to assign the rank of dogma to conclusions drawn from partial premises. Claiming that we are thus simply "creating names," some arbitrary constructions, is likewise an abuse and leads to the relativization of the issue. I am instead inclined toward a belief in the "wisdom of language," that is, the possibility of formulating and communicating judgments that are cognitively valuable by means of language despite the mutability of the categories with which it operates, or else their relative longevity and thus historicity. Following the Polish philosopher Barbara Skarga, I too believe that "language is wise, . . . not accidental in character, . . . certainly not a conventional invention."[78] By way of only exemplification, I want to point out that the problem formulated by Hall can be considered from Smith's ethnosymbolic perspective and, because of different starting assumptions, lead to different conclusions: "Each generation . . . constructs its own social maps and chooses its special ethnic moralities, but it does so within a limited matrix formed by a strong social attachment to specific 'mythico-symbol complexes.'"[79]

Research approaches inspired by Foucault's and Hall's concepts are valuable indicators of the dangers, for instance, of risky generalizations, of eliminating or effacing differences in the name of an illusory coherence, and of omitting troubling facts that undercut the legitimacy of an adopted research method. Exposing social structures of knowledge does not need to end in relativism that shies away from essentialist aims. Nevertheless, for reasons presented above, linguistic or anti-logocentric concepts of the subject are insufficient in expounding national processes, since they cannot provide exhaustive explanations of the causes and mechanisms of the emergence and development of national formations; they therefore need to be complemented with other approaches. When these concepts are applied to Poles in a totalistic way, they occlude a basic and integral characteristic of the Polish subject and identity discourse: this subject understands itself as a continual "self" that admittedly participates in human history but that also believes in a transcendental order of things independent of human beings and their powers of cognition.[80] In the case of the Polish society, this belief is rooted in a culturally internalized and absorbed system of Christian worldviews transferred over generations through the channels of religion (primarily Catholic) and education, as well as of literature and arts. These worldviews—whether explicit or implicit, professed or debated—were present for centuries in Polish literature and arts as a reference point and a defining factor of Polishness. From the Middle Ages, Christianity was the main source of cultural values for the majority of Poles. Affiliation with the Catholic religion became central to Poles under the partitions, during which times "the [Roman Catholic] Church was often the only institution that had a Polish character. Thus Polish national consciousness came to be strongly tied to a Catholic religious identity."[81] Barbara Falk summarizes the historical position of the Roman Catholic Church among Poles as follows:

> Neither the Polish past nor present can be understood without grasping the complexity of the Church's presence and moral force in Poland, its notions of both the individual and the social order, its mixture of conservative ethics with progressive *and* nationalist politics, and the ongoing battle between Church and State—which both preceded and succeeded forty years of authoritarian Communism. The Church is deeply embedded in Polish society, culture, and history.[82]

Significantly, before Poland became an ethnically and religiously homogenous state dominated by Roman Catholic Poles as a result of the Second World War and the Holocaust, it enjoyed considerable religious and cultural diversity throughout its history—during its existence as the Polish-Lithuanian Commonwealth, the period of partitions, and as the Second Republic. In the Polish-Lithuanian Commonwealth, there were some places and regions where Catholicism was the religion of a minority. This diversity has undoubtedly remained an invaluable feature of Polish culture, with some of its aspects still awaiting discovery.[83] Thus, I am not advocating "a distinctly Catholic narrative of Polish history" here.[84] At the same time, I insist on paying adequate attention to the aforementioned broad and long-term transfer of ideas originating in Christianity to Polish culture. This transfer explains the consistent presence of Christian ethics, Catholic social teaching, and Catholic iconographic motifs in Polish literature and arts. It is also linked to the fundamental and still existing division of the European continent. Jadwiga Staniszkis has formulated a hypothesis about the undervalued significance of the so-called Western Schism in Christianity of the fourteenth and fifteenth centuries (meaning the breakdown of Western Christianity as a result of Protestant movements) for Europe's intellectual and political history from the Renaissance until the present. Her hypothesis explains on a macroscale certain historical processes, including the differentiation between the two parts of Europe, and presents the current challenges facing East-Central Europe's post-Communist societies in adopting the Western European style of political and judicial thought and state organization.[85]

In the realm of philosophy, a more essentialist concept of subjectivity can serve as a counterweight to the constructivist approaches. It is found in the personalist perspective that constitutes a critical avenue of Polish identity discourse.[86] Applying this perspective to the issue of cultural identity of East-Central Europe makes sense insofar as the "nominalistic intellectual revolution" bypassed this region.[87] According to Staniszkis, "The Catholic countries of Central Europe (Poland among them) did not go through the nominalistic revolution of thought, remaining in the realm of Aristotelian and Thomist realism. This fundamentally affected the distinctiveness of the concepts of state, law, and social order dominant in this part of Europe—a distinctiveness that lasts until this day."[88] This has left an imprint on the ways of understanding reality in this corner of the world, as well as in its sociopolitical, moral, and cultural dimensions. East-Central Europe is grounded in the classical ideas derived from Aristotle that have permeated the thought and lifestyle of Poles, aided also by Thomism, since the late Middle Ages.[89] Realism (as a position in the philosophical debate about universals), which in considerations of the social order, law, and state manifests itself in the belief in the ontological rootedness of ideas, also influenced Polish culture and social practice via Christian Aristotelianism. The latter can be found in Polish thought and public life from the fifteenth through seventeenth centuries in the form of a disciplined philosophical and political discourse developed by authors such as Paweł from Worczyn, Wawrzyniec from Racibórz, Paweł Włodkowic, Stanisław from Skarbimierz, Mateusz from Kraków, Stanisław Zaborowski, Andrzej Frycz Modrzewski, Jan Zamoyski, Krzysztof Warszewicki, Stanisław Orzechowski, Sebastian Petrycy from Pilzno, Łukasz Górnicki, Andrzej Maksymilian Fredro, and others.[90] It was also present and practiced by the citizens of the Polish-Lithuanian Commonwealth, as well as their successors—the conservative circles of nineteenth-century nobility that adopted the name "intelligentsia"—having become a widespread worldview passed down to successive generations of Poles via upbringing and education. Christian beliefs formed the core of this worldview and thus informed its values and ideals. In discussing the shared values of the Polish nobility, the Polish historian Tomasz Kizwalter mentions freedom and equality, and next to them respect for the law, love for the homeland, public concord, and respect for tradition.[91] The virtues listed by Kizwalter, constitutive of the republican ethos from which the Polish national ethos later emerged, did not appear like some deus ex machina. Rather, they were espoused by the authors mentioned earlier and constituted part of the Polish *Bildung*—the intergenerational transmission of values that resulted in a specifically Polish worldview. Another attempt to define this worldview points to its specific "sensitization"—"an inclination toward community, to other human beings, a sensitivity to all threats to truth and freedom, an understanding of the value of suffering and sacrifice, in a word—a humane ethos."[92] Leaning in great measure on immanent Catholicism, or, more broadly, Christianity, this worldview took for granted the clarity of categories such as "good" and "evil," the obviousness of the imperative to choose good, the sense of justice, the natural right to freedom, and the eschatological sense of history. All of these elements have impacted Polish subjectivity to a considerable degree, as attested by the ideas explicitly proclaimed in Polish writing since the Middle Ages.[93] Such is the case with Paweł Włodkowic's doctrine about the sovereignty of nations and countries, developed in the early fifteenth century, which voices the belief in the fundamental meaning of the human being as the subject of both individual and collective rights and responsibilities, and in the human dignity that flows therefrom. Further evidence can be found in the deep-seated intersubjective set of beliefs about the ontological and ethical order of the world that rests on these ideas and that is inscribed in the Polish way of thinking and the characteristic relationship of Poles toward reality. These beliefs have found and continue to find articulation in various situations and contexts: in the choices made by both individuals and social groups, in the interpretation and evaluation of foreign political entities and in reactions to them, as well as in public discourse.

Discussing Polish national "markers" is not the purpose of this chapter. I nevertheless want to highlight those components that consistently reappear in such endeavors. Zdzisław Najder, a distinguished scholar and critic of Joseph Conrad, the director of the Polish Section of Radio Free Europe (1982–87), and a dissident who spent ten years in exile, lists the following indicators of "Polishness" as observed from his émigré perspective: "the domination of non-utilitarian ideals, participation of ethical values in everyday decision-making processes, a sense of community that overrides all social, material, regional, or professional differences, rejection of violence as a means of enforcing change, the strong presence of tradition in culture, the increasing significance of religion, and finally the consciousness that our belonging to European and Christian culture is under threat."[94] At least from the early Renaissance, the Polish subject thus considers itself to constitute a specific version, or else a Polish variant, of the "Western" (rather than

"Eastern") subject, one formed in the realm of Western, Greek and Roman, Judeo-Christian and Catholic moral and cultural values.[95] This identification has not been left unscathed by geopolitics, however, which considerably complicates matters. The confrontation with multiethnic empires that surrounded the Polish-Lithuanian Commonwealth, itself a multiethnic empire, from the end of the early modern period onward, set in motion a parallel process, with the "Polish subject" distancing itself (in the areas of political ideas and identity discourse) from the emerging subjects of modern nation-states that transmit their own concepts of subjectivity by means of their identity discourses and politics, founded on different political, intellectual, and religious traditions.[96] On the one hand, therefore, it is possible to speak about its self-definition in relation to the "German subject," who has claimed the position of the center of Westernness for itself since the times of Frederick the Great, Fichte, and Hegel.[97] In its role of a civilizational model for the peripheral European "East," the "German subject" has gradually become a paradigmatic representative of the "West" for inhabitants of Polish lands. On the other hand, Polish identity discourse includes self-definition in relation to the "Russian subject," which defines itself within the dominant, Great Russian tradition by means of three key ideas: anti-Western, autocratic, and Pan-Slavic. The "Polish subject" can be seen, therefore, as a recognizable ontological category that became distinct and developed in opposition to and interaction with two concepts of subjectivity—Western European and Eastern, meaning Russian—both clearly demarcated since the time of Enlightenment and both evolving and at once stabilizing in specific, counterposed directions.[98] This dualism was accompanied by a sense of strong ties with Western European values, which served "to support the rejection of the 'Pan-Slavic temptation.'"[99] Moreover, the "Polish subject" maintains its own characteristic, East-Central European, anti-nominalist distinctiveness, which means that attempts to transplant Western European political ideas onto the Polish ground all too often resemble a façade: they have brought and still bring only surface-level results and they are seen as an artificial and foreign form rather than an authentic, integral component of Polishness.[100]

The works of philosophers Charles Taylor and Alasdair MacIntyre aptly account for subjectivity understood as a historically formed and continuous phenomenon.[101] Taylor emphasizes the moral foundations of subjectivity and their fundamental role in modern identity and subtly suggests that both categories be anchored in an objective, transcendent reality. Moreover, subjectivity for Taylor implies the possibility of a transformation of identity, one that allows for self-interpretation in light of the values brought to consciousness or else recovered in the course of such transformation. This is significant for the ethnosymbolic concept of the nation adopted here, especially in its historically and geographically embedded East-Central European variant. Taylor's considerations suggest that the terms "subjectivity" and "identity" are not interchangeable. Not every identity has a subjective character. Subjectivity constitutes a challenge for the individual, as well as for a collective, for instance, a nation: its status is not simply granted but is rather the object of aspiration. A collective ensures its subjective existence by undertaking the effort of grounding its identity and working to discover and redefine itself whether under conditions of foreign domination or after its cessation. As Taylor notes, "The horizons within which we live our lives and which make sense of them have to include . . . strong qualitative discriminations. . . . [L]iving within such strongly qualified horizons is constitutive of human agency."[102]

Notably, Taylor's "strong qualitative discriminations" are situated in opposition to the modernist concept of subjectivity that references Nietzsche. They do not translate into the imperative of individual rebellion against the collective or into the postulate of solipsistic self-improvement. Rather, they imply solidarity in mobilizing individuals and collectives to transform, in Taylor's terms, the shared "inescapable frameworks" of their lives by cultivating values that create goals and goods "independent of our own desires, inclinations, or choices, that . . . represent standards by which these desires and choices are judged. . . . The goods which command our awe must also function in some sense as standards for us."[103]

In this manner, we arrive at the issue of subjectivity's relationality: individual subjectivity is made complete in Taylor's conceptualization by a "higher" social subjectivity that possesses a "stronger" value—for instance, a national subjectivity. MacIntyre's neo-Thomist perspective offers the interesting prospect of widening the framework of the postcolonial exploration of identity to include the axiological horizon of subjectivity outlined by Taylor. Both philosophers share an anti-relativist stance on truth, stemming from their distance from postmodern epistemological skepticism as well as their awareness of the role of *narration* in the shaping (rather than construction) of identity.[104] According to Taylor and MacIntyre, both scholarship and practical life should strive for the most adequate of judgments, albeit without the pretense of arriving at a final and absolute truth, alongside their critical examination. Both philosophers are also of the opinion that the subject is not a product of discourse but retains a certain autonomy as well as substantiality and primordiality in relation to it, which counters constructivist conclusions.[105]

## Two Voices from the Peripheries

The understanding of identity and subjectivity outlined above delineates the general horizon against which the subject and the object of Polish identity discourse will be viewed here. This discourse developed in Polish literature and other forms of communication starting at the end of the eighteenth century: first, under the conditions of Russian/Soviet, Prussian/German, and Austrian domination (as well as after its end) and, second, within the context of Polish hegemony in the so-called Eastern Borderlands of the former Polish-Lithuanian Commonwealth. This view implies, of course, a subjective vision of literature and culture, which—following Smith—I see as components of a national, or a nation-building, discourse. The perspective on literature and its surrounding discourses presented in subsequent chapters is to a large extent an offshoot of this proposed horizon. This proposal can also serve as a departure point for research and discussions of the postcolonial identity of East-Central Europe's post-Communist societies. On the one hand, this approach avoids the dangers inherent in traditional, nationalistic methods of studying history, literature, and art, along with their buzzwords of "us" and "others," which are incapable of denoting the ambivalence of relations between the colonizer and the colonized. On the other hand, the proposed conceptual framework ensures that the baby is not thrown out with the bathwater by working against the total elimination of the issue of national identification from scholarly discourse.

By way of inviting reflection on the analytical possibilities of the perspective adopted, this final part of the chapter offers an experimental analysis of a fragment from an essay written by Leszek Kołakowski in 1973. Entitled "Sprawa Polska" (The Polish question), Kołakowski's essay points to a relationship between the subjugation of a population and its subjugated mentality, foreshadowing, as it were, present-day reflection on the implications that subordination by a foreign empire has for identity:

> If the nation is an active community of culture, if it thus lives insofar as it feels itself the subject of this life, meaning that it answers for itself, then the most effective means of destroying a nation is to strip it of this sense of responsibility, to make it believe that, as a result of its own powerlessness or immaturity, or due to external circumstances, it is forced to live as others command. The nation that would come to believe itself irreversibly deprived of moral freedom would lose all hope of regaining it ever again.[106]

Abstracting from Kołakowski's underlying argument about the contingency of human and national existence, with which I will not argue here, the above interpretation of colonial vicissitudes can be seen as a paradigmatic attempt to overcome the discourse of victimization, a trap that oppressed societies can easily fall into. Kołakowski does not bemoan the binding of nations with the chains of slavery, nor does he lament the losses, humiliations, and destruction experienced by Polish society. He also does not call upon traditional Romantic and Messianic rhetorics that support these kinds of approaches by hyperbolizing and simultaneously canonizing the role and status of innocent and passive victims of conquest during times of hardship. Faced with real force, manifested by the hegemon in all spheres (the "others" who "command"), Kołakowski pays attention to the conditions necessary for a nation to retain its subjectivity despite its political subordination and lack of sovereignty. Among these conditions are the rejection of fatalism and determinism, and reliance on models supplied by one's native culture. The latter demands a culture that is not solipsistic, however, but rather open to other cultures, with its cultural models serving to teach the nation to live in dignity, that is, in agreement with collective aspirations, regardless of external obstacles. It also requires an awareness that "the existence of the Polish nation is determined at this moment by Poles living in Poland, but without either their own foreign policy, or an army under sovereign command, or the freedom to transform institutional forms of social life, or any influence on international dealings and agreements between empires."[107] The description of the Polish nation's colonial condition and the possible route to overcoming subjugation that Kołakowski lays out strikes an interesting chord with the diagnosis formulated by Frantz Fanon in his classic essay "On National Culture." Although Fanon's analysis is grounded in a different geographical and political context, it concerns similar conditions of enslavement. As he observes, what is intriguing about the colonial period is that "the oppressor does not manage to convince himself of the objective non-existence of the oppressed nation and its culture. Every effort is made to bring the colonized person to admit the inferiority of his culture which has been transformed into instinctive patterns of behaviour, to recognize the un-reality of his 'nation.'"[108] This observation by the author of *The Wretched of the Earth* culminates in the following observation:

> The nation is not only the condition of culture, its fruitfulness, its continuous renewal, and its deepening. It is also a necessity. . . . The nation gathers together the various indispensable elements necessary for the creation of a culture, those elements which alone can give it credibility, validity, life, and creative power. In the same way it is its national character that will make such a culture open to other cultures and which will enable it to influence and permeate other cultures.[109]

It is remarkable that, with all the obvious differences between the Polish and the Algerian nations—historical, civilizational, cultural, and so forth—Kołakowski and Fanon arrive at such analogous conclusions. Indeed, it is impossible to interpret the essentially identical concern they express as anything other than an effort taken up on behalf of the nation. In both cases, this effort does not result in nationalistic distortions, since both authors are equally aware of such danger. Both also point to the strategic aim of hegemonic discourse, which is to set into motion and sustain the mechanism of self-deprecation among the conquered. They also offer similar diagnoses of the state of their respective communities and independently from each other indicate the same remedy: mobilization of national subjectivity by means of culture. Recognizing the defining, identity-building value of national culture, both Fanon and Kołakowski speak against its reduction to either the role of an anti-colonial arsenal or to a collection of clichés that erase the dynamic of nation-building processes and operate by means of simplified and stereotypical self-representations. Thus, Fanon underlines that

> we must not therefore be content with delving into the past of a people in order to find coherent elements which will counteract colonialism's attempts to falsify and harm. . . . A national culture is not a folklore, nor an abstract populism that believes it can discover the people's true nature. It is not made up of the inert dregs of gratuitous actions, that is to say actions which are less and less attached to the ever-present reality of the people. A national culture is the whole body of efforts made by a people in the sphere of thought to describe, justify, and praise the action through which that people has created itself and keeps itself in existence.[110]

Kołakowski, in turn, stresses with equal determination:

> We can believe in the unity of national tradition as long as we always remember that this unity appears only from our perspective, of people who came after, and as such is a projected unity rather than one contained within the experience of the historical actors of events. We are not allowed to believe, however, in national unity as an actual state of affairs, now or in the future—and this regardless of the measure to which the question of the nation in general engulfs other conflicts.[111]

From the perspective of the ontology of nations, the common point at which both authors arrive in their considerations of the "national question," despite starting from such different positions, is of particular importance. Specifically, they share the opinion that national culture is conducive to respecting and receiving other/foreign cultural models. They are also aware that the situation of colonization complicates this issue in a fundamental way: it opens the field to various deviations and anomalies of positions that shape the anti-colonial discourse with varying degrees of harm to the people's existence, including ethnocentrism, cultural exclusivism, isolationism, chauvinism, inverted racism, and xenophobia. Thus, both Kołakowski's essay and Fanon's work are a warning to those who wish to make national culture into an idol, a fetish, or else a weapon of rivalry with other groups. Kołakowski writes of the detrimental belief in "the self-sufficiency of national culture," which threatens to "dwarf" it; Fanon calls attention to the dangers of "painful cultural indecision which is found in certain countries which are newly independent" and underlines that, insofar as "it is the national consciousness which is the most elaborate form of culture," the self-consciousness that constitutes its final horizon is nevertheless "not the closing of a door to communication."[112] *Ubi Varsovia, ubi Algeria*—so far and yet so near . . .

Reading these texts in a context different from their formulation, after dozens of years and within a specific political, mental, and ideological climate and situation of reception, should not lead to hasty conclusions. However these texts are interpreted, it is impossible to prove that Kołakowski and Fanon are searching, each in his own way, for some hazy, nonnational or postnational antithesis for what is "national," or that the message espoused in their texts subverts the notion of national identity, or creates fissures within it. A deconstructive interpretation of this kind would be misguided and out of place. The warnings voiced by Kołakowski and Fanon have their place in the "order" of identity discourse that was developed among Polish and Algerian societies, respectively, during the period of their anti-colonial struggle. They reflect similar premises on which this discourse rested and offer similar solutions for prospective postcolonial states. The two case studies analyzed above can be treated as examples of theorizing the nation under colonial rule with a view to its liberation and reconstruction. Neither Kołakowski nor Fanon depreciates or disavows the nation as simultaneously the subject of culture and the object of self-reflection for the people, and neither subverts his respective field of national values, even if he does not necessarily subscribe to them in full. To the contrary, both recognize the facticity and significance of these values for the conscious, subjective existence of a national collective and point to the prospect of broadening the horizon attained thereby through contact with what is *other*, *foreign*, and *unknown*. Such contact can turn *distinctiveness* into an invaluable "value added" of national culture, since it widens the horizons of consciousness of a collective's members; it inclines them to affirm and accept otherness, to take responsibility for and demonstrate tolerance towards the "Other," and to create opportunities for the revision of stereotypes and the constitution of new bonds. Moreover, it reconfigures the existing axiological matrix of national discourse by adding new parameters to it and reshuffling its current elements. By these means, members of a collective have an opportunity to overcome their own epistemological limitations and to lean toward difference without giving up the support of their collective value system. The elimination of one's state organism, or even the drastic restriction of sovereignty as a result of an empire's interference, considerably weakens and even eradicates these types of experiences from the life of the collective; it leaves only its substitute forms in public discourse, which are accessible only to select elites or bluntly curtailed and deformed. Colonialism is a system that creates structural barriers that make it impossible, or at least very difficult, for a given nation to take an affirmative stance toward cultural forms differing from the dominant models of that nationality. It is perhaps here that one finds a key reason for why East-Central Europe, until recently within the sphere of Soviet influence and previously (primarily) of Russian, German, and Austrian ones, is still suffering from minor and major eruptions of radical, aggressive, and closed-off nationalisms of exclusion, as well as why it is perceived through the filter of these circumstances as regressive in terms of ethnic, national, and social coexistence, and as marked by atavism ("tribalism").[113]

It bears repeating here that both of the intellectuals under discussion, who come from two colonized societies separated by so much, then and now, and who function in such different traditions and contexts, nevertheless arrived at similar conclusions in their reflections about the nation. This telling and thought-provoking convergence supports the view that the nation as a category should not be seen as an aberration or relic of European origin (much less an Eastern European one), even during these times of supposed post-nationality.[114] To the contrary, the notion of nation is the central issue (object) as well as the dominant voice (subject) and the final destination (aim) of anti-colonial discourse along every geographic latitude and longitude. This can—and should—be seen as a substantive research problem of postcolonial studies that requires proper theorization. Postcolonial research still needs to account for the conditions of identity discourse indicated here, including the fundamental danger of colonialism and of neo-colonialism: the atrophy of a nation's awareness of itself in situations of its subordination or potential loss of sovereignty.

One must also be mindful, however, as Kołakowski and Fanon remind us in their own way, that the nation is not an ultimate value despite being the telos of anti-colonial discourse. The absolutization of what is national triggers an axiological chaos that impacts collective consciousness and public discourse as well as politics and results in extreme nationalisms. In fact, such absolutization harms the nation and its ethos, leading to national megalomania, cultural isolationism, and ethnocentrism in its "softer" version, and—in its more radical variant—to chauvinism and hostility toward other groups. This danger touches postcolonial societies in a particular way, an issue that has been presented avant la lettre by the Polish philosopher Władysław Stróżewski. His incisive diagnosis, applying the language of axiology, has such current relevance that it deserves to be quoted at length:

> I do not see the highest value in something because it is, for instance, Polish, but to the contrary: because it is an authentic value and I desire for it to be also Polish. When it becomes Polish, it does not gain in pure "valence," but gains one more specific realization, and thus that which all value is meant for. . . .
>
> Such is the normal situation. In abnormal situations things happen otherwise. And every situation of peril is abnormal. When the possibility of realizing values is threatened, it is necessary to accent the need for conditions of their realization. It is even necessary to fight for them. When they are recovered, everything should return to normal. The state of constant peril, however, or the state of loss of the appropriate conditions (among them freedom and independence), effects a transposition in the value hierarchy. A concrete form of execution that cannot become realized moves into the foreground. In consequence, an overemphasis can take place wherein the national completely overrides the universal. Their organic unity is severed. This consequence is one of the most serious effects of the loss of freedom and independence.[115]

Although formulated during the period of Soviet colonial domination, Stróżewski's diagnosis provides an adequate and still applicable recognition of the condition of the postcolonial nation. Its language accounts for both the ontology and ethics of the nation: it points to the subjective status of the nation as a tangible, historical reality and underlines the ethical dimension of the nation's existence. In postcolonial studies of literatures and cultures of East-Central European societies we should not lose sight of either the first or the second perspective. Both the devaluation of the nation while under the spell of theses about its supposed anachronism and its fetishization under the influence of chauvinist drives will lead to flawed conclusions and result in overstatements and overinterpretations in analyses of the processes undergone by these populations during the colonial and postcolonial periods of their existence. Some of the cultural stimulants and effects of these processes within the Polish setting will be addressed in the chapters to follow.

## Chapter Four

# Literature as Compensation

## Comprador Intelligentsia vis-à-vis the Hegemonic Discourse—Preliminary Theoretical Remarks

> The poverty of the people, national oppression, and the inhibition of culture are one and the same thing.
>
> —Frantz Fanon, *The Wretched of the Earth*

> Polish mentality is encircled, as if by a prison wall, by an enclosure that is invisible but also impregnable to the external light of knowledge.
>
> —Ignacy Radliński, *Nasza umysłowość* (Our mentality)

Until recently, the issue of attitudes adopted by nineteenth-century Polish elites toward the Russian Empire and its representative institutions was approached by Polish historiography from basically one angle. This "heroic" mode of describing the Polish experience of partitions and foreign domination accentuated the tradition of the struggle for independence.[1] The approach had the effect of downplaying other, nonheroic attitudes and acts of Polish collaboration with the enemy, which were viewed as occasional flaws on the otherwise nearly perfect image of noble and brave resistance. In other words, the narrative established by historiographical accounts for most of the twentieth century presented the uncompromising struggle against czarist despotism as the dominant position in Poland's partitioned society while marginalizing any evidence to the contrary. The literary and cultural output of Polish writers and artists of the nineteenth century can be read as derivative of this condition since it typically aligns the choices and decisions of the conquered population with Poland's national interests: the fight, whether active or passive, against the three hegemons, with czarist Russia viewed as the most ferocious and destructive.[2] From such a perspective, both ambiguous and openly contrary (for instance, collaborative or treasonous) positions were generally seen as incidental and of secondary importance to Polish scholarship. They were not, in any case, allowed to disturb the cohesive picture of the heroic whole.

The liberation of the Polish historiographic discourse from its earlier ideological restrictions, which came at the end of the 1980s, inevitably also impacted the situation outlined above. The question of treason, collaboration, renunciation, and national apostasy began to gain ground, aided by changes in historical research methodologies as well as an intellectual climate conducive to breaking earlier social and academic taboos—the contribution of postmodernist humanities in Poland. Shifting from the margins toward the center of study, these issues at times even acquired—whether rightly so is a matter of discussion—the status of the primary problem in the history of Polish society.[3] Regardless of the direction in which scholarship on these subjects has evolved and continues to evolve, however, open and veiled reflections on the character of Poland's subjugation and on its effect on individual and group behavior and stances were part of public discourse throughout the entire nineteenth century, the beginning of twentieth century, and after Poland's return on the political map of Europe in 1918. Presented in the form of more or less disciplined arguments, they were the product of writers, historians, philosophers, and journalists throughout all of the partitioned territories and in exile.

Polish elites played a dubious role in subordinating Polish society first to the Russian and later the Soviet hegemon (1772–1918 and 1939–89). According to Ryszard Legutko, this is why Poles have been reluctant to analyze this experience, choosing more often than not either to silence or to question the sense of such investigations.[4] This antipathy likewise explains the scarcity of publications on the subject. The question of the Polish intelligentsia's response to the colonial encounter between the Soviet center and the Polish periphery remains a touchy area of public discourse in Poland.[5] Works on the topic started to appear in particular after Czesław Miłosz's publication of *The Captive Mind* (orig. *Zniewolony umysł*, 1953), with its central metaphor of the "Hegelian sting" providing a needed context for the Polish intelligentsia's vulnerability to Marxism. Nevertheless, there is a shortage of critical works to aid exhaustive reflection on the colonial experience. Indeed, some of the existing accounts, including *The Captive Mind*, are in fact part of the subject of this reflection, for they too represent the postcolonial consequences of subjugating Polish intellectual elites to the politics of imperial Russia. After all, works on the issue include unreliable and even dishonest publications that met with the approval of the Communist regime.[6] In general, the relevant body of work is greatly varied in generic and thematic scope.[7] It ranges from interviews and conversations, through authorial treatises on the times, to detail-oriented sociocultural analyses, and includes texts classified as pamphlets and lampoons, among them Wiesław Paweł Szymański's *Uroki dworu* (The court's charm). The qualitative criteria applied to these various forms of writing were rooted in ideology and milieu but were sometimes arbitrary. The differences between the frameworks they employ is a topic for separate consideration; here, a single example should suffice.

Henryk Słabek's book *Intelektualistów obraz własny* (Intellectuals' self-portrait) represents one branch of the discourse of "rapprochement" aimed at explaining the Polish elites' cooperation with the Soviet occupier; it is particularly effective at revealing the aporias and crossroads of this discourse. To prevent "simplifications" and "harmful judgements" of the motivations behind the engagement of elites in the cultural politics of Communist Poland, Słabek's analysis proliferates in paradoxes. Thus, the author can point to the supposed "evangelical element" of communism as well as to the elevated status of the Catholic Church in subjugated Poland.[8] Słabek uncritically, sometimes even naïvely, buys into the rhetoric of specious testimonies rationalizing the decision to participate in the Sovietization of Polish sociocultural life (the case of Andrzej Walicki).[9] Słabek draws his conclusions from an analysis of statements and actions of key figures of Polish postwar intellectual life and contributes to the construction of a discursive model that presently dominates social and political writing in Poland and can be termed the discourse of empathy for, or of the diminished responsibility of, individuals who collaborated. Słabek's final thesis about the complete wrongheadedness of the belief that Polish society underwent Sovietization is the consequence of a stance that, because of a lack of methodological instruments, stops short of identifying the colonial aspect of the subordination of Polish society and its elites to the Soviet Union.[10]

The issues taken up in existing interpretations of the Polish intelligentsia's response to the Soviet hegemon undoubtedly need to be accounted for more fully.[11] There is still a need for studies of singular events and processes as well as for in-depth, comprehensive overviews of the entire Soviet domination period; there is certainly documentary value in such approaches. This chapter, however, offers a different perspective on the participation of members of the Polish artistic milieu in the Soviet project of subordinating Poland and Polish culture. I eschew explicit moral judgments of individual stances and choices, the judgments that are so well domesticated in Polish public discourse. The historian Jerzy Jedlicki warns against extending the conclusions drawn from an analysis of individual decisions to an entire group when he states that "[the] hottest topic was always the dilemma whether intelligentsia, when tested, is accustomed to reveal more submission than resilience, more opportunism than non-conformism—for it is known that plentiful evidence can be found for all of these tendencies."[12] This kind of reflection leads to either an accusatory or an apologetic stance toward specific individuals. It also inevitably multiplies existing frameworks of these phenomena and becomes inscribed within the matrix of actual conflicts, be they ideological or political. Reserving the readers' as well as my own right to personal judgment, this discussion shifts focus from concrete and individual choices and actions, including the biographical approach to the subject that kindles so much emotion with every new discovery of previously unknown facts and events from the lives of specific individuals. Instead, it looks at certain characteristic structural dependencies that are inscribed within the colonial situation and pertinent in this context, with a particular emphasis on colonialism's cultural implications. Exploring and naming the mechanisms at work in the colonial situation is a matter of primary importance for the humanities; it is a prerequisite to understanding the processes that affect a subordinated society's culture and a useful context for analysis of individual cases within this subject field.

The following discussion seeks to establish an analytical and explanatory position toward the cultural aspect of collaboration. Alasdair MacIntyre's truism that "all power tends to coopt" has serious ethical, social, and cultural repercussions.[13] Placing the problem of collaboration within the structure of colonial dependence reveals another significant aspect of collaboration. The fact of someone's collaboration only points at the deep entanglements between culture and (geo)politics, and, while dramatic in its forms, it is certainly not the only, nor even the most dangerous, among them.

❧❧❧

With this preface, it is time for considerations announced in the title. The starting assumptions of this discussion can be summed up in two, fairly obvious statements:

1. Every population produces only one culture that is not exchangeable with any other, but which given different conditions could have undergone different transformations and arrived at a form other than the one it actually assumed.
2. The culture of a colonized people has its specificity.

Pressure from a geopolitical context, such as the colonial situation, disables or impedes some of the directions in which the culture of a given population might have otherwise developed were this population not subject to these conditions. Hence, the culture of a colonized national or ethnic group faces a limited array of possibilities if compared to that of a free society. The awareness of lost chances and missed opportunities leaves an imprint on the colonized culture. This imprint is transformed by that culture into an immanent value and then reproduced. In becoming integrated into the culture, the new component is perceived as an element of a supposedly natural, and hence unavoidable, order of things. This semblance of naturalness makes it difficult for a society subject to foreign domination to recognize its own condition and its cultural consequences.

The triumphant perspective that presents the colonized people as conquered but unbroken, so at home in Polish public discourse, needs to be supplemented with another point of view, one that shows more than an image of a nation and its literature frozen in a proud gesture of resistance. Opposition to empire-imposed rules comes with "compelling seductions," to reference a category suggested by Leela Gandhi.[14] As Gandhi points out, "Power traverses the imponderable chasm between coercion and seduction through a variety of baffling self-representations."[15] These two instruments of imperial power only seemingly exclude each other. In reality, they constitute a coherent system of channels whose efficiency is guaranteed by their complementarity: the more coercive measures of colonial administration, the more tempting the rewards for concessions made by members of the oppressed elites. From the point of view of hegemonic discourse, the role of the "baffling self-representations" of imperial power is critical to the process of "colonizing the minds." Consequently, the colonizing power "offers itself both as a political limit and as a cultural possibility."[16]

As a result of colonial subordination, public discourse of the subjugated population is organized and modeled by factors previously absent from or unknown to it. These factors, foreign in origin and character, constitute the particular situation in which a culture develops. Moreover, they are conditioned by the penetration of the public space by the hegemonic discourse of the metropolitan center of power.[17] The empire realizes its objectives toward the conquered peripheries by means of this discourse and other, more material mechanisms. The effort to deal with the colonial situation is the common denominator of the processes that the colonized are subjected to as a result of these factors. While these strivings take various discursive directions and forms, they all derive from one of three possible attitudes toward the hegemon: resistance, collaboration, or accommodation.[18] The "cultural possibility" offered by colonialism leans toward the latter two positions. Literature, as the most refined form of cultural communication, is subject to the influence of other discourses and is simultaneously an active force in the formation of a (national, social) collective's symbolic universe. In the case of literature, each of these attitudes comes with a characteristic manner of organizing the matter of perceived "reality":

1. Each delineates the field of phenomena recognized as actually existing, eliminating from the discourse what does not fit. Elimination is done by means of labeling and stigmatizing (for example, in utterances stylized into public indictments, appeals, critiques, and self-critiques), exclusion, omissions, and silencing (e.g., through censorship and self-censorship).
2. Each establishes interpretive frameworks for what it takes as the real state of affairs (for instance, by suggesting specific macro- and micro-relations between the story motifs and its characters' decisions and actions).
3. Each incorporates this interpretation of reality into public discourse, converting it into an evident cultural feature of the subjugated population at the given period of its existence.

The transformations that take place in a society subjected to foreign domination reconfigure the matrix that supports the reproduction and development of culture. One of the signs of such a remodeled culture is its self-marginalization, expressed through an inferiority complex in cultural contacts with members of free societies—a bitter pill to swallow whether it is meticulously concealed or, to the contrary, ostentatiously demonstrated. This complex is also heard, perhaps even more clearly, during the postcolonial phase, meaning after the cessation of formal dependence on the metropolis. This process of cultural self-marginalization affected (post)colonial elites, especially intellectuals and artists, whose search for ways of dealing with the colonial situation left them particularly prone to absorbing the hegemonic discourse. The very existence of an "intelligentsia" in East-Central Europe and the significance attached to this group's existence and function point to the strictly colonial roots of its social role. The intelligentsia is a domain of "dependent countries, under authoritarian rule and without the effective motors of enterprise and a level of economic development."[19] Thus understood, it served as a substitute and a surrogate for the nonexistent state, or else its semblance; it also usurped for itself—or unwillingly played—the role of an admittedly substitutive but also autochthonous center of power, defining itself and its responsibilities in relation to the order imposed by the metropolis. This situation had far-reaching implications not only for the intelligentsia's ethos and status, but first and foremost for the culture produced by its creative spheres and assimilated and reproduced—or else contested, rejected, and even derided—by the rest of society. More than a century ago, the Polish writer Stefan Żeromski spoke of this unprecedented, and simultaneously abnormal, substitutive function of literature positioned as the domain of freedom and a means to survive foreign hegemony. The formula called for writing to not only be "at the service of an unhappy homeland" but also to act as an organizational, political, and educational replacement of "the Polish consulate, the Polish legal counsel, the Polish school and all offices."[20] Such an integrative, therapeutic, and homeostatic function of writing is noticeable among oppressed populations and commonly acknowledged. Thus understood, writing under colonial conditions has become not only an artistic but also a political act, mobilizing the colonized people for resistance and, in a long-term perspective, to rise and overthrow the foreign oppressive regime.

Besides the aspect discussed above, there exists yet another aspect of literature's compensatory character. At the very beginning of twentieth century, in a book about the work of a late nineteenth-century Polish painter, Aleksander Gierymski, the art critic Stanisław Witkiewicz thus described the climate in which Polish art developed after the bloody suppression of the anti-Russian insurrection of 1863, also addressing its implications for the spiritual and mental condition of his compatriots:

> The lost great political wager filled the spirit with a lack of faith in its own value and in the strength and the ability to act, creating a type of people with an obsequious humility toward "Europe," who were afraid to compromise themselves and dared not counter Europe with manifestations of their social life. It was a sort of plague of doubt and lack of faith in oneself that created peculiar doctrines and brought the negative critique of the past to historiosophy. . . . This anemia, this derisive self-irony . . . penetrated many minds, and the best ones to boot.[21]

Witkiewicz's language is free of the emancipatory jargon of contemporary humanities and his diagnosis of a "colonized mind" strikes one even now with its insightfulness and precision. Among issues raised by the author are a diminished sense of self-worth, a paralyzing fear of contact with the cultural metropolis and its evaluations, and lack of belief in oneself as well as a destructive distancing from one's own past and scorn for oneself. All of this adds up to an autobiographical narration of a colonized subject that sounds strikingly familiar in the now post-Communist Poland. Here, however, another issue noted by Witkiewicz needs to be underlined: the significant scale of passivity among the elites. As Witkiewicz intuited, the phenomenon could be catastrophic in its social effects; it also constitutes the second aspect of literature's compensatory character. The following diagnosis well captures this condition: "People born and educated in somewhat happier conditions in the country are dying out, and the young are looking toward a future without radiance, without perspective, in bitterness that grows daily, inactive and hopeless."[22]

Approximately eighty years after the publication of Witkiewicz's book on Gierymski, the literary critic Andrzej Kijowski asked a question that reveals its dramatic scale when viewed in light of its historical context's imposing continuity: "What are we still capable of as a nation, and what are we no longer capable of. What . . . long-term effects has our centuries-long dependence already had."[23] Kijowski's questions constitute a horizon that stretches beyond the boundaries of literature as the domain of art to include what Maurycy Mochnacki, a Romantic critic whom Kijowski carefully studied, understood according to the concept of national literature. Kijowski's observations stemmed from a concern similar to that expressed by Mochnacki for the social impact of culture in a colonial situation. They also led him toward analogous conclusions about the lack of originality and authenticity resulting from the complex of peripherality, and about the defensiveness and constant search for recognition. One of Kijowski's diagnoses integrates culture with the social processes taking place within a colonized population:

> The pain of failure. In a country . . . that . . . for two hundred years found itself in the custody of empires working harmoniously on its subjugation, degradation, and finally extermination, where the selection of unqualified management became the constant principle of power, conspiracy a form of life, and scheming a means of political action, in a country forcefully kept below its possibilities and aspirations, this "basic pain," the pain of not fulfilling its function in the world and not realizing its talents, is almost the stuff of folklore now; here, you sing, joke, and swear about it. Here, customs and language form around this pain, from it emerge national plagues (drunkenness, poor workmanship, emigration), the whole of culture is marked with it.[24]

These assertions suggest that the discourse of colonized elites in some part retains, even in the most unfavorable circumstances, the ability both to critically analyze the situation of its own people and to articulate it in a language free of resentment toward its community. This is a significant claim, since this "positive energy" makes it possible to discursively undercut the domination of the hegemon and, in the long term, to "disown the burdens of their colonial inheritance."[25] However, Kijowski's critical analysis of the consequences of foreign domination highlights their almost material realness, which manifests itself in the inevitable change of the subordinated people's cultural priorities.[26] Kijowski thesis about the results of the cultural absorption of foreign elements that are implanted by the hegemon's physical presence, and which also follow from the secondary, cultural implications of being suffocated by his omnipresent materiality, is also important to these considerations. As derivatives of colonial dependence, these elements enter into social circulation that, in turn, assigns a specific profile to cultural behaviors and artifacts ("marking"), which leads to the explosion of a metaphoric "pain of unfulfillment." The degenerated and deregulated forms of social life as well as the recalibrated and modified forms of culture are thus revealed to be as much the direct effect of imperial domination as the result of structural subordination to its discourse.

In the discussion about East-Central Europe that took place in the Paris-based literary quarterly *Zeszyty Literackie* (*Cahiers Littéraires*) during the 1980s, the poet Adam Zagajewski made note of a characteristic subservience to power politics that can be described, on the macrostructural level, as the demobilization of social capital.[27] Dynamic individuals, unable to orient their actions in a desired direction as a result of communism's oppressive socioeconomic system, are governed by the principle of rational choice, which includes the options to emigrate, to transfer their energy resources to other realms, or to serve within the administrative structures of the colonial state. While the criteria and results of this choice are rarely the subject of free discussion when it is made, they sometimes become the object of stern judgment by future generations, long after the fact. The foundations of each of these decisions can be located in one of the three types of stances mentioned earlier. In the context of this discussion, more pertinent are the specific consequences of these decisions not only for individual lives but also from a sociocultural perspective. Emigration depleted a particularly valuable segment of the national populace. The long-term effects of collaboration with the regime lasted far into the postcolonial period and were obviously moral as well as social, political, and economic in nature, resulting in the emergence of the so-called post-Communist cleavage.[28] *Homo sovieticus*, or the Communist man—a mentally enslaved individual, obedient and passive—is perhaps the best exemplification of this post-Communist legacy that has haunted Poles, as well as other Eastern Europeans, after the end of Soviet domination.[29] The demobilization of social capital during Soviet rule that necessitated the transfer of energy resources to other realms, psychological in nature, and its scope and reach are hard to measure. It often took the form of "the obsession with a wasted life," to use the writer Leopold Tyrmand's phrase.[30] The Polish "periphery" was not able to make use of the creative potential of talented, dynamic, and active individuals, which on the one hand drained it of strengths, possibilities, and talents and intensified universal frustration. On the other hand, in a society with a relatively high level of education and cultural development, it redirected such people toward, for instance, the artistic path. As Zagajewski ascertained, "A certain portion of active people, out of despair for having been deprived of history, politics, and economy, effected a somewhat forced sublimation and engaged with culture."[31] Culture that appears on the horizon of reflections about the results of political dependency is thus denuded of its aura of aristocratic dignity and transformed into the domain of compensation.

In speaking about compensation I have in mind one of the fundamental principles that organize the intellectual and cultural life of subordinated societies, which is part and parcel of the colonial condition. According to Zagajewski's diagnosis, however risky it may sound today, culture becomes a substitute field of action for individuals who are unable to release their creative potential in areas such as politics, industry, or science because of imposed restrictions. At issue here is their inability to participate in modernizing processes, or the difficulties of such participation, with the oppressive colonial power system blocking their access points—and their compensation for this loss. This phenomenon is not limited to the present time or to the Polish colonial experience, of course. Rather, we are dealing with a universal rule that stems from authoritarian domination. Looking at the past, the extravagant development of the aesthetic and spiritual sphere during Romanticism can be seen in part as the result of compensatory activities, undertaken within a realm where it was possible to succeed on the basis of native values, without relying on the distribution mechanisms of colonial power and under conditions that made realizing Enlightenment's myth of progress either impossible or significantly more difficult. Concurrently, the free nations of Europe were bringing to life the ideal of progressivism and thus overtaking by many decades colonized societies in civilizational development. These statements by an Irish cultural historian can also be applied to the Polish situation in the nineteenth century:

> Culture, in a sense, became a consolation for injustice, for all those areas of experience—nature, community, the past, even physical pleasure itself—excluded from the march of progress. It was left to Romanticism, then, to pick up where the Enlightenment left off, offering the imaginary realms of myth, nostalgia, and artistic creativity for those deprived of equality, liberty, and fraternity in the political and economic spheres.[32]

While this characterization of the phenomenon does not pertain to Soviet colonization, it does emerge with remarkable sharpness in its context because of the acute limitation of developmental perspectives for native managerial, industrial, and economic elites by the politics of the Eastern hegemon, which depleted the Polish economy and gravely impacted the process of shaping

Poland's leadership class. The compensation at stake here is somewhat reminiscent of the mechanism of defensive sublimation, and it leads to a specific kind of distribution of creative powers and energies that is not encountered in non-colonial societies. While grounded in a system of prohibitions and restrictions and harmful to civilizational development, these types of shifts are certainly often fruitful in their consequences for the peripheral culture. A familiar paradox arises here: what is detrimental to the *bios* of a people and harmful to their existence can be beneficial for their symbolic code, namely, art. Experiences difficult in extremis, as are all types of deprivation and forms of oppression, repression, or subjugation, help give birth to the masterpieces that subsequently determine the hierarchy of a national culture's accomplishments. This is a fortunate coincidence for literary critics, although I am proposing a different, reversed perspective on this issue here.

Performing the compensatory function understood in this way involves the following strategies of literature's social impact, all of which can be subordinated to one of the previously listed stances of resistance, accommodation, or collaboration:

1. neutralizing or eliminating motifs deemed undesirable or inconvenient for the empire;
2. working within ideas, themes, and artistic strategies that correspond to the metropolitan center's point of view;
3. avoiding subjects that are painful or difficult for the peripheries and that the colonized population does not have the energy to contend with (for being engaged in resistance against the metropolis or in the search of suitable means of adaptation) or is unable to do so;
4. constructing the discourse of modern Polish identity around the axiom (articulated, among others, in the theses of the counterhegemonic discourse) of Russia's civilizational inferiority as the Eastern hegemon and the civilizational superiority of the Western hegemons (Germany and Austria), as well as around the feeling of resentment that is characteristic of colonized people and stems from the fact and consequences of foreign domination; or
5. demonstrating the illusory nature of the transformative power of the imposed (official) culture in relation to the life of a society, which leads to a growing chasm between the sphere of internal consciousness and hidden convictions of individuals, and the realm of external, real actions in social micro- and macrosystems.

One more item can be added to this list: allusiveness understood as a communicative and aesthetic strategy. Literature, as is known, plays with the restrictions imposed by the hegemon's cultural politics, with institutionalized censorship being only one instrument of the latter's rule.[33] In so doing, it relies on various accessible means, such as satire, irony, parody, parable, allegory, allusion, and metaphor. In the hands of Polish authors, these artistic methods reached a pinnacle in a series of works that are seen as both outstanding and important items in public discourse even long after their publication.[34] These literary accomplishments must be given a positive evaluation since they constitute lasting symbols of literature's victory over human weakness and the oppressiveness of geopolitics. Indeed, they testify to art's advantage over history's limitations. These works are (and are likely to remain) the hallmarks of anti-colonial discourse. Emphasizing these texts' emancipatory, liberating resonance overshadowed their reverse side, however. It occluded the fact that this literature, given its specific social function, engaged in a specific appropriation of public discourse. This is troublesome from the perspective of Polish society's further development, since its public discourse was rendered vulnerable to limitation, deformation, and impairment, and constrained in other aspects necessary for the normal functioning of a society. The discursive direction taken by developing allusive and symbolic forms specific to itself, which were seen as proof of the uncompromised spiritual sovereignty by the nation and its elites and as an unquestionable cultural good in terms of protecting Polish identity, diverted Polish public discourse from paths pursued by societies untouched by colonial oppression.[35]

❧❧❧

The three theses presented below constitute the departure point for this theoretical description of the cultural situation of a colonized population that accounts for the role played by the intelligentsia, referred to here as "comprador intelligentsia," during the period of Soviet domination. To speak of comprador intelligentsia in these circumstances, a modification of the following definition by Kwame Anthony Appiah is needed. "Postcoloniality is the condition of what we might ungenerously call a comprador intelligentsia: of a relatively small, Western-style, Western-trained, group of writers and thinkers who mediate the trade in cultural commodities of world capitalism at the periphery."[36] The term "comprador intellectuals" refers to that part of the colonized elites (which includes artistic and academic circles) whose members are the "beneficiaries, more or less aware of their country's exploitation by colonial powers."[37] In the East-Central European context, the comprador intelligentsia was those intellectuals who used their nationality and talent, along with their public position and authority among their compatriots, in the service of the colonial power, becoming intellectual henchmen for the

Soviet regime and benefiting from it. As a result, "members of the intelligentsia loyal to the communist government, were seen as servants of the Kremlin."[38] The aim of this description, however, is not to judge individual stances and choices but rather to construct a model of Polish culture viewed through a postcolonial lens, as culture of a population subordinated to foreign imperial hegemony after a centuries-long history as a sovereign nation-state with a relatively high level of cultural development.

Thesis 1: From the beginning of the nineteenth century, with a short break between the two world wars, Polish culture developed in a state of permanent restrictions on the freedom of expression and on the right to guide its development. This led to the erosion and substitution of the themes undertaken by writers, as well as to an attitude of resentment and an inferiority complex in relation to the "West" (rather than the "East," which Ewa M. Thompson's category of "surrogate hegemon" grasps well in its relation to culture and other areas of social life).[39] The suffocated public discourse during the colonial period, in turn, severely limited authentic discussion of this situation. Not surprisingly, the thus-idealized West was not just turned into the object of cultural idolatry in Poland's postcolonial period but has been granted the status of a real hegemon by some politicians and cultural critics.[40]

Thesis 2: National culture is the result of processes of selection and accumulation. When it is built with the support of substitution and illusion, however, it becomes fraudulent to a significant extent with respect to various spheres of collective experience through absorption of the hegemon's discourse and its transmission to specific realms of sociocultural life.

This aspect of colonial dependency has already been noted by the Polish writer Józef Mackiewicz in 1962: "Under the Russian partition there existed . . . a Polish national literature, published by Polish publishers and only censored by the authorities. Today it is published by the authorities and opted for, inspired, and directed by them."[41] The literary critic Zdzisław Łapiński called this state of affairs "amputation," tying it to the period of socialist realism: "What is most striking in the evolution of Polish literature at the turn of the forties and fifties is the gradual elimination by its authors of various components of their own poetics, or putting it differently: successive phases of self-mutilation."[42] The "self-mutilation" that Łapiński refers to is by far the most conspicuous in the literature of the socialist realist period, but certainly not limited to it. This thesis indirectly addresses the questions that Łapiński's metaphor provokes. What replaced the amputated organs? What kind of prostheses were used for this purpose? And what were the cultural consequences of this operation undertaken on the living tissue of a national culture?

The novelist Maria Dąbrowska pointed out the implications of this situation in a diary entry from 1949, where she summed up the consequences of Polish culture becoming assimilated into the dominant (Russian) culture, in other words, of its undesirable hybridization (of unique, native characteristics), as follows: "Russia acts like a corrosive acid that eats through the soul of the nation and transforms its organic contents into an unrecognizable amalgam that stinks to boot."[43]

Thesis 3: The influence of anti-colonial discourse on a culture subjected to foreign domination is ambivalent. While it can provide protection, it can also make the colonized culture its hostage, tying it up in obligations agonistic to hegemonic discourse and creating a simplified, bipolar image of both sides of the colonial encounter. By virtue of its existence, the hegemon sets into motion the sociocultural discourse of the conquered, which from then on is implicated in the search for a justified choice among the three possible attitudes—of resistance, accommodation, or collaboration—toward the empire. The literary critic Jan Błoński puts is in no uncertain terms: "The slave exhausts himself entirely in the relationship of dependency, even if he wishes to sever this relationship; the shadow of power falls upon all of his actions."[44]

These theses lead to rather depressing and discouraging conclusions. The hegemonic discourse does not so much deprive the colonized of the chance to "speak in their own voice," to use Gayatri Spivak's famous phrasing, as it completely drowns out this voice, making it inaudible, that is, ungraspable in the epistemic structures imposed by the dominant discourse. At stake is the fundamental impossibility of obtaining the "permission to narrate," which is written into the system of imperial domination.[45] In summing up this part of the discussion, one can say that culture under conditions of subordination is not able to effectively articulate itself, in other words, it cannot speak the way the culture would have spoken under other conditions; its articulations are always burdened with the irremovable weight of the colonial experience articulated in the theses outlined above. All attempts to lift this weight from the shoulders of culture—any simulations of sovereignty made in the form of literary programs, for example, or individual textual undertakings—are subjected, within the closed system of a given culture, to critical evaluation based on criteria that correlate with colonial conditions.

❧ ❧ ❧

The comprador intellectuals are "indoctrinated into the culture of the colonial power," and, while formally belonging to the subordinated population, they mediate in the process of a multilevel exchange between the colonial metropolis and its periphery.[46] Using resources available to them and their native cultural code, albeit in a modified form as a result of its penetration by the hegemonic discourse, comprador intellectuals realize—whether consciously or not—the interests of the imperial center. They act on either mercenary impulses or the conviction, which comes with the internalization of the hegemon's logic, that what is desirable from the point of view of the metropolis is also beneficial for the populace in the provinces. In this manner, they "speak to" the members of the subjugated population, including their rival groups within the elites. Their discourse about their role and activities is legitimating and persuading in nature. Comprador elites also have a double role in relation to the metropolitan center's elites: they advocate on behalf of their population and its interests in relation to the metropolis as well as translate the directives of the hegemon's politics, including cultural politics, into a native cultural code. Collaboration par excellence is not the only attitude displayed by the group, for various types of complicit and accommodating attitudes are also at play. Postcolonial studies fosters understanding of the processes that secure the control of the metropolis—and in effect its dominance—over the peripheral society along with its mental and cultural existence.[47] Here, attention must be paid to the impact of accommodation attitudes on culture rather than the issue of advantages gained by "native" beneficiaries of colonialization (mainly artists-collaborators).[48] Accommodation involves a broad spectrum of stances characterized by external adaptation to performing roles that answer the demands of the colonial system, different degrees of internal acquiescence to this situation, and an evolving attitude toward the hegemon, from antipathy and distance to rationalization, satisfaction, and support.[49]

Applying the category of compensation, the impact of accommodating attitudes on culture can be linked to the construction of a substitute culture. Three complementary models of culture's functioning in Poland during the period of Soviet domination emerge as hypotheses here, involving both highbrow and lowbrow registers:

1. Culture as the effect of latching onto substituted themes that are either actively proposed or suggested by the hegemonic discourse or discovered by the creative elites on their own initiative, for instance, in order to overcome "boredom" or "cultural stagnation." (Literary works that were the effect of this exchange were often described in critical discourse and popular opinion as "mendacious.")
2. Culture as a realm of lethargy and of activities that are specious, inauthentic, or irrelevant from the point of view of social needs and defined outside of the metropolis's control. From the collective's

perspective, artistic doctrines diverge from what is important to it at a given moment, serving as a "survival niche" for artistic circles, rather than as a sphere for articulating opinions of significant weight to the subordinated public.

3. Culture as the hostage of anti-colonial discourse is the result of negotiation between the options of subordination and insubordination to the hegemonic discourse. The choices made by the creative elites are located between the two responses and often explained with recourse to the same argument: the defense of culture (understood as the preservation of its substance or the rescue of its sovereignty).

In his 1962 essay on the condition of Polish literature, under the meaningful title "Wyznania uduszonego" (Confessions of the suffocated), the literary critic Kazimierz Wyka put forth a thesis that was quite radical and that now strikes a chord with these theoretical suggestions: Polish literature "could have been different" and "should be different."[50] The critic sees the objective and obstructive conditions of Polish culture as devastating for its development, but he is more concerned with the elites' acquiescence to "the results of intellectual slavery, and the implications of philosophical and ideological minimalism as the supposedly necessary conditions of post-partition writing and a post-partition nation."[51] Wyka expressed this opinion under circumstances that did not differ much, in their essence, from the situation in place a century earlier. In questioning nineteenth-century literature's choice of substitute themes, that is, easy and safe issues, Wyka identified the existence of "internal censorship" that "was worse [than external censorship], since it did not come from force, but from approval, from consenting to harmless and non-aggravating functions of literature" that lead in a straight line to "wasted possibilities," "motifs taken no further," and "issues never taken up at all."[52] Attentive readers could have applied Wyka's diagnosis to their times by noticing traces of Aesopian speech in the critic's presentation of the argument.

As this example shows, the "enslavement" at stake here cannot be discussed only in categories of political oppression, as a formalized colonial dependency realized exclusively from "the outside," "foreign" in its nature, and thus relatively easy for the subordinated population to identify. The "enslavement" that Wyka writes about had those roots originally, but the activity of the imperial apparatus of repression, which also functions in culture (through censorship and cultural politics), was not its only source. An even more significant role was played by interiorized mechanisms of self-control and subservience that directed on the one hand the creative and communicative-mediating process (in media and academic discourses, among others), and—on the other—public reception. Significantly, for these mechanisms, a society under foreign domination has at its disposal—in an exemplary situation, desirable from the hegemon's point of view—a cultural "dictionary" limited to the categories and cognitive structures that fall in line with the hegemonic discourse. Writers among comprador elites, carrying out for various reasons the cultural politics of the metropolis, ensured that this "dictionary" filled out the linguistic universe of their society, as happens according to an often validated claim that "language has always been the companion of empire."[53]

This is one aspect of culture in relation to the hegemonic discourse. To balance this description, an opposite aspect of culture's peripheral status vis-à-vis the empire needs to be noted. The ramifications of cultural complicity in the colonial encounter on the part of the subjugated population include its organic, inevitable, and as such disastrous dependency on hegemonic discourse. This dependency is not limited to following the directives of this discourse, as happens when art respects the "dictionary" rules in echoing the ideology and interests of the empire. In another sense entirely, dependence on hegemonic discourse underpins discourse oriented against the empire, which seeks areas of philosophical, creative, and intellectual freedom. An awareness of the limitations imposed by the external situation of culture and of the dangers of culture's colonial entanglement also finds expression in this incisive diagnosis:

> As long as independent culture remains determined almost exclusively . . . by a worldview organized around the opposition of authority—anti-authority, it will be imprisoned within this temporary and narrow horizon, it will befit this opposition and this horizon, and it will be narrow, shallow, and barren. Authentically independent culture decides for itself the areas of its interest, horizons, aims, it chooses its partners and opponents on its own, and it does not allow its opponent to decide on its obsessions, aspirations, and tasks.[54]

This second instance of dependence through negation is of a radically different type, of course. Although they are two sides of the same phenomenon—two ways of relating to hegemonic discourse—it is impossible to equate them. They derive from extremely different attitudes on the part of the participants in the discourse: collaboration or accommodation on the one hand, resistance, disagreement, and rebellion, on the other. Differentiating among these positions, the elementary duty of a scholar, requires accounting for their axiological contrast. They also had a contrary impact on the shaping of identities among members of the subordinated population. Nevertheless, they converged on one point: they sealed the state of cultural submission.

One of the tasks of postcolonial studies is to describe this dynamic and its social implications, with consideration of its fundamental differences and subtle variations, in line with the observation that "the forgotten archive of the colonial encounter narrates multiple stories of contestation and its discomfiting other, complicity."[55]

❧ ❧ ❧

Undoubtedly, Polish literature of the past two hundred years, including the period of Soviet domination (1944–89), provides a record and evidence of courageous and uncompromising stances rather than mediocrity and submission. Their proportion and the moral aspect of everything that filled the spectrum in between these extremes are likely to be the subject of multiple analyses still. Assessments both of individual facts and efforts to synthesize the question of "writers against violence," however, cannot lose sight of the essential issue that this discussion highlights: the specific and systematic relation of literature and of its surrounding discourses to the hegemonic discourse, as dictated by colonial domination.

A colonized culture finds itself in a specific position owing to its situation of subordination. Colonialized nations are conditioned by colonialism even when they attempt to extricate themselves from it. Books, whether published officially or in samizdat editions, in Poland or by the diaspora, cannot avoid these circumstances; they must inevitably situate themselves in relation to these circumstances somehow, with a stated attitude toward external realities being transformed into an integral element of the literary code. As a result, cultural discourses, including literature, criticism, and journalism, are tainted by colonial domination: they soak up this domination even when they declare opposition to it and do oppose it through various contestatory actions.[56] The tasks of postcolonial studies should include bringing out this stigma from the texts, facilitating awareness of its existence, and revealing how this stigma impacted literature—a unique form of communication, inscribing it with a Foucauldian element of power, camouflaged and interiorized. It also seems necessary to agree with critics calling for a rereading of the whole of contemporary literature, given the restrictions during the Communist period on free scholarship and criticism and on free circulation of their opinions. A model of functioning based on free flow and self-propulsion is unknown to the culture of a colonized society:

> The issue here is that, for the most part, interpretations from the period of the Peoples' Republic, especially of literature pertaining to sociopolitical and historical matters, could be translated into the language of criticism

> only to a small degree. One must realize that the full decoding of the meanings and senses of circulating works was impossible not only due to the restrictions of censorship, but also because undertaking a genuine interpretation of a work would have been a type of political denunciation of the author.[57]

Taking all of this into consideration, the claim that a colonial situation causes the destruction of the subordinated population's culture seems more than valid. This destruction has taken place on two planes, individual (biographical) and collective (discursive). Studies in the biographies of members of the Polish creative elite during the Communist period, among them Czesław Miłosz, Tadeusz Różewicz, and Wisława Szymborska, to mention the most prominent names, contain records of these authors' more or less evident failings and weaknesses, at some stage of their lives, related to the *power-career* nexus under colonial conditions.[58] The body of such critical investigations has been growing, and even if the discoveries presented therein have not brought about a significant reinterpretation or a reevaluation of a given literary output, and not everything may have been exposed yet, the general conclusions of such approaches can be predicted without much difficulty, as they come close to the trite observation "X was not clean, either, and his life was not spick and span."[59] The challenge lies in exploring the latter plane, that is, how hegemonic discourse intervened in that of the subjugated elite, effecting its more or less subtle transformation and eventual creation of a self-regulating mechanism, which replicated the ideas and values benefiting or simply characterizing the hegemon. Here it must be remembered that culture was not just a victim, or the ultimate or main target of the hegemon's actions, but rather a means of achieving an aim that can be defined by paraphrasing Lord Macaulay's "Minute on Indian Education": "to form a class" of people who will be Polish "in blood" but Russian "in taste, in opinions, in morals, and in intellect."[60]

Taking this context into consideration reveals a different aspect of Polish anti-colonial discourse; its study should complete our understanding of the subject matter under discussion in a way that ensures that the image of a subordinated people's culture arrived at with the help of postcolonial instruments is not one sided. Given that the discourse of contemporary humanities continues to privilege analyses of the "methods of enslavement," their conclusions can start to look that way. This can be prevented by research into the defense mechanisms used in response to foreign hegemony, which the language of postcolonial theory is uniquely suited to grasp. The identity angle of Polish postcolonial studies stressed in this book makes this postulate all the more significant. Polish history, also recorded in literature, shows that the loss of independence has always impacted the status of its collective subject's identity. The complex interaction between enslavement and defense that took place at various phases of the colonial encounter has not yet been described in light of the dynamics of political and cultural relations between the metropolis and the periphery. These dynamics can be grasped and problematized in part with the help of postcolonial studies. Importantly, although despite a long history of destructive colonial oppression the Polish nation did not perish or vanish without a trace (or into oblivion), as a result of this interaction Poles' national identity was by no means in status quo ante (as it was before). To the contrary, Polish identity underwent transformations, internal shifts, and modifications, of which only a small part is presented here, in general terms and in the form of theoretical propositions. Awareness of this fact, supported by detailed research into literature and public discourse in the context of foreign domination, opens a new perspective onto questions of national continuity, on the historical changeability of factors of national identification, and on the problem of the self-awareness of elites and of their changing cultural role throughout history.

## Chapter Five

# Confronting the Romantic Legacy

Indeed, our literature should counter what has been written for us so far, we have to look for a new path that opposes Mickiewicz and all the Spirit-Kings.

—Witold Gombrowicz, *Diary 1953—1956*

## "Narrating the Nation"

Postcolonial studies provides ample evidence that, regardless of geographic location, the experience of foreign hegemony deforms the subjugated population's perception of reality. Literature offers numerous examples of this deformation. The modes of representation employed by authors from colonized nations and the image of the world inscribed in their work are tainted to varying degrees by the implications of their encounter with the colonial power. This contamination, moreover, results not so much from the servility of the collaborating authors as from the colonial situation itself. As the previous chapter's discussion of the comprador elites shows, it is structural in character for a colonized culture and also encompasses oppositional stances, thereby influencing anti-colonial discourse. Neither does the colonial experience exhaust itself on a thematic level; it impacts other aspects of the text, such as the means of signification, its style of expression, and even the choice of composition and genre. Among its other roles, literature functions as an instrument of individual and collective self-analysis, even self-therapy. As such, it is instrumental in the construction of collective identity and a natural space of narrating the nation.[1] Literary works that emerge under the condition of subjugation inherently participate in the transmission thereof and actively shape mental attitudes, stances, and behaviors acquired as its result, even when they undertake to critically dissect or outright reject them.

For postcolonial studies in Polish literature and culture to adequately address the issue of modern Polish identity, it must look at Romanticism. It was during this period that the various formulas of what Homi Bhabha terms "narrating the nation" were established in Polish literature, journalism, historiography, and philosophy. This "narrating" is understood in the broad, cultural sense as underpinning national culture and identity.[2] The process is neither simple, nor one dimensional, nor consistent, but it is rich in tensions between the nation's present, always experienced as fragmented, and the images of its past, built into its collective tradition by means of discourses to solidify collective self-identification. As Bhabha claims in his characteristic style, "The language of culture and community is poised on the fissures of the present becoming the rhetorical figures of a national past."[3] The implication in this formula seems worth reflecting on. In Bhabha's formulation, narrating the nation is a complex and dynamic process of assigning significance to figures of the past (myths and legends; historical events; and figures real, invented, or phantasmal) aimed at creating a coherent and meaningful image of the collective present. It is the result of two forces, which represent the "splitting" of the national subject: (1) the "social authority" accumulated (and simultaneously camouflaged) in the discourse dominant at a given historical moment; and (2) either the submission or the subversion of the remaining members of society, who are the subject of this discourse. Out of the mutual interaction of these two pursuits a "story" is created, which—by reinterpreting less and more distant heroic deeds, defeats, as well as images of the everyday—is tasked with assigning significance, in the here and now, to the ontology of a collective treated as a whole, a nation.

Narrating the nation takes on a particular form in the case of colonized peoples. While leaning on the institution of one's state under "normal" circumstances allows a nation to hide the contradictions that emerge between the above two tendencies behind the authority of "tradition," faced with foreign domination, these antinomies are exposed and become the governing principle of constructing the national discourse. The work of the Polish Romantics provides numerous instances of such themes and problems as myths of origin, the state's rise and fall, social and ethnic antagonisms, displacement and alienation, and, finally, the historical incarnations of the national idea viewed from the Romantics' perspective. A new type of consciousness emerges at that time, as visible in the Romantics' literary output—a type that, to use Bhabha's categories, breaches the purely "pedagogical" perspective in favor of a "performative" one, wherein the nation is seen as "a liminal signifying space that is *internally* marked by the discourse of minorities, the heterogeneous histories of contending peoples, antagonistic authorities and tense locations of cultural difference."[4]

All of this does not transpire, of course, outside of history and the local realities of collective practical knowledge embedded in a context of a concrete time and place. During a time when national aspirations were awakening and solidifying in a Europe of the Congress System, Polish poets, historians, and philosophers looked for ways to articulate the experiences of collective and individual existence under the rule of empires—an experience that was difficult, if not impossible, to come to terms with. With the recent grandeur of the Polish-Lithuanian Commonwealth still present in the memory of Polish society, a more topical issue emerges: of loyalty to the new state along with its complex implications, including the question of treason. These issues were taken up also in literature, which participates in the construction of identity discourse by constantly casting the past over the present. Finally, it is impossible to overlook the fact that both the horizon of the cultural authority of the "elites" and the perspective of the "people" are inscribed with the point of view of the "slave." This happens on various registers of sensitivity and rhetoric, which take the form of different matrices of perception and behavior, and the resulting point of view is inevitably subject to the pervasive hegemonic discourse along with its extensive means and institutional support. This perspective enacts a radical decomposition of the life and culture of the subordinated population, which has at least four implications:

1. It inclines toward stereotyping of one's self-image and the image of Others, including—in the first place—the hegemon.
2. It narrows the horizon of collective action to survival and rescue from annihilation, and it limits the horizon of collective reflection to debates about methods of achieving this aim and to interpretations of the steps taken (in other words, explanations addressed to one's own population).
3. It aids the cultivation of memory of one's distinctiveness and of sacrifices made, feeding into the discourse of victimization.
4. It instils in a society the belief in the inevitability of state-driven civilizational oppression, which comes with the imperative to either reject or undermine the authority of state structures.

These transformations, the list of which could be expanded, have other consequences, too: they solidify the peripheral status of the subordinated population's culture, strengthening at the same time the international position and prestige of the metropolis. In the European salons of the first decades of the nineteenth century, Poles still felt themselves to be, and to a certain extent actually were, partners among representatives of the cultural discourse of Western Europe. They were slowly losing this awareness, and, consolidated by the contemplation of incurred loss, they in fact participated less and less in the intellectual, scientific, and social development of which Western European countries partook throughout the nineteenth century. Only a few individuals even among the educated Polish, Lithuanian, and Ukrainian elites shared an interest in, and understanding of, the modernizing processes that encompassed the rest of the continent at this time. To a significant extent, this was the effect of colonialization, which forcefully regroups the vitality and possibilities of the functioning of both individuals and an entire collective deprived of sovereign state structures. Earlier participation gives way to marginalization, which in turn—along with an activated mechanism of self-marginalization—produces attitudes of withdrawal and defensiveness. These attitudes, which identity discourse reevaluates, are seen as qualities that preserve identity, defined in opposition to Others. Society remains oblivious and indifferent as a whole—not by choice, however, but because of the inertia of the colonial apparatus that steers social life, which effectively ensures that native residents do not harbor excessive aspirations that could strengthen the periphery's position in relation to the metropolis. While obtaining an education at universities in St. Petersburg and Vienna or participating in the administration of the Polish periphery (an option open to only a few) were sometimes welcomed as tempting propositions of advancement, a career thus realized most often came at the cost of emancipation from Polish circles and cessation of actions benefiting one's own nation. This met with disapproval and various forms of stigmatization among one's compatriots. This picture can be complemented with a list of such elements of imperial politics as the colonialist imposition of a foreign language (Russian and German in relevant partitions), or discrimination against the colonized, with their culture and religion, at various administrative levels, where activities were focused on forcibly obtaining approval for the empire's "civilizing mission," and so on.[5]

These phenomena, duly recorded in writing during that period, are part and parcel of the life of the colonized, irrespective of the geographical latitude and longitude. Still, few comparative studies of this issue have been carried out to date. Since the attention of people deprived of their own state is focused on the need to constantly define their stance relative to the metropolis and, based on this definition, to establish the limits of "loyalty," a spontaneous process of a gradual loss of shared "places" and of the separation of Polish discourse from those of Western societies takes place. Although Polish Romanticism was responsive "to modern aesthetic trends and modern European philosophy," and "in Polish literature of that period those strands were present," Polish Romantics were primarily involved with national issues.[6] These issues became "the subject matter and the main problem of Polish Romanticism," contributing to the growing particularism of Polish literature.[7] Alongside the absence of statehood, this particularism made Polish culture gradually less visible and recognizable as Polish to Western audiences over the latter part of the nineteenth century. This only confirms the belief, which was disseminated over time among the sovereign nations of the continent that "there was nothing between the Western European Germany and a new Russia, identified with Eastern Europe."[8]

## "Decolonization of the Mind" and the Haze of Romanticism

Romanticism impacted the shape and character of Polish symbolic culture during the periods of foreign domination (1772–1918, 1939–45, and 1945–89) to an unprecedented degree. The great nineteenth-century poets—Adam Mickiewicz, Juliusz Słowacki, Zygmunt Krasiński, and Cyprian Norwid—created a code used by Poles to communicate the experience of their loss of sovereignty and aspirations for liberty during both the period of partitions and the five decades of Soviet domination. For this reason, rethinking Romanticism is an indispensable challenge for Polish post-Communist society. Many of the questions posed by these authors to their contemporaries have retained their relevance. A central place among them is held by the issue of the sources of Polish identity, which some find in the "Westernism" and others in the "Easternism" of the Polish cultural profile and its individual components. Does Polish identity stem from a sense of ties to the "Occident" or the "Orient," or is it a combination of these two? Or is it perhaps rooted in neither?

The motifs characteristic of Polish Romantic literature, such as the loss of sovereignty; the struggle against the hegemon; the "reign over souls," or national Messianism, were preserved in nineteenth- and twentieth-century Polish culture in the form of universal symbolism, generally understood by Polish society. Romanticism is still considered the fundament of modern Polish subjectivity, and the study of Romantic poets has molded the imagination of young Polish readers for a long time and to an unrivaled degree; it has determined the framework of their later worldview, civic attitude, and hierarchy of (both aesthetic and existential) values. Its expression can be found in life preferences and ideological choices, or else simply the Polish "way of thinking" among both old and young generations. Even presently, in the twenty-first century, despite reforms of the educational system and the influence of pop culture and postmodernism, the works of the Romantics have not ceased to organize Polish collective consciousness. They are effective still, predominantly in the realm of ideas encompassing the obligatory code of the "Polish patriot." The same canonical texts—Adam Mickiewicz's *Forefathers' Eve* and *Pan Tadeusz* and Juliusz Słowacki's *Kordian*—constitute the main component of the humanistic education of successive generations; they play a part in shaping their worldview, value system, and life stance and to a degree act as a filter for interpreting current social, political, and philosophical impulses. All the absurdities that Witold Gombrowicz ridiculed in his *Diary* and *Trans-Atlantic* stem from Romanticism thus read, taught, and understood, and their superficiality, anachronism, and immaturity is all the clearer in today's world. Among these absurdities is the belief in Poland's unique status as the "bulwark of Christianity" and, later, as the innocent victim of collusion between empires, at the heart of the idea of Polish martyrdom. For many decades, two mutually reinforcing ways of reading the canonical works of Polish Romanticism have dominated Polish schools and public discourse: the first, psychological and biographical; the second, historical and national, with both contributing to the mythologization of the Romantic legacy. These models of reception fall short on criticism and lack the minimum necessary distance to deal with a subject that is still actively functioning within the collective consciousness.

Consequently, this Polonocentric deformation has long been part of the national reception of Romanticism. Its evidence is easily found when looking at the singular career of one Romantic idea—of national Messianism—in the common consciousness of Poles. The notion that the suffering of one's nation has a unique role in redeeming humanity does not have a Romantic genealogy, of course, nor is the idea Polish in its genesis or specific only to Polish culture. Nevertheless, the problem in the Polish context is that, from Romanticism onward, successive generations were instilled with the belief that the Messianism proclaimed by Mickiewicz in part 3 of *Forefathers' Eve*, for instance, is a great reason for national pride. The Messianic way of thinking made its way into general Polish consciousness during the nineteenth century, as attested by memoir entries from that time. It has settled in and impacted the Poles' understanding of history and their place in it until today.[9] Through works of high art, Messianic ideas "impacted the imagination and mentality of several generations of Poles: they shaped their way of thinking about history and Poland's place in the world."[10]

Significantly, Messianism was not exclusively a Polish property during Romanticism. Messianic ideologies were produced also by the French and the German nations. The aberration was thus not a specifically Polish characteristic, as Andrzej Walicki, an expert on this issue, underlines.[11] The image of Messianism drawn up in Walicki's interpretation, however, is missing an evident enough compensatory feature of a colonial nature. To begin with, given the religious and historiosophic depths that Walicki credits Messianism with, it is easy to overlook the fact that at the base of Polish Messianic thinking stands an inferiority complex.[12] This complex, in accordance with the rules governing colonial discourse, had to find an outlet in Polish thought and culture burdened by a struggle against the hegemon. It found it precisely in Messianism as a specific form of the discourse of victimization. Moreover, in contrast to Messianic currents in Western Europe, Polish Messianism did not run its course when the philosophical and sociopolitical climate changed in the second half of the nineteenth century. To the contrary, it persisted along with subordination of public space to the hegemon's discourse and politics. For a century and a half, successive generations of Poles were taught to think in Messianic categories, primarily through the work of the great Romantic poets and of their interpreters. Historical conditions meant, among other things, that this idea enjoyed considerable influence in Poland up until the 1980s. It found its late expression during martial law when the Solidarity movement was crushed by General Wojciech Jaruzelski's junta, an action that he justified as a means of forestalling a Soviet invasion but that can also be interpreted as a comprador's attempt to please the hegemon. The Messianic idea translated into the political and geopolitical thinking of parts of Polish elites and the way its society comes to terms with its collective fate. The concept of the "chosen nation" is one well-established relic of Messianism, with a "posthumous" existence that is still cultivated, if often by veiled means. At issue is thus not Messianism as such—a defined historical phenomenon—but rather its social existence:

> Messianism used to be the primary defendant in all trials of the Romantic legacy in Polish culture. At times, it provided foreigners with arguments in the creation or popularization of a negative stereotype of the Polish national character, wherein the lack of a sense of reality is supposedly tied to surges of collective megalomania. Neither is Messianism a historically anachronistic phenomenon in the consciousness of Poles today. It still provokes masochistic examinations of the national conscience, with attacks on society's Messianic moods by disciples of "level-headed politics" repeating at history's every turn.[13]

This observation, while accurate, demands a follow-up. It is telling that Czesław Miłosz in *The History of Polish Literature* offers only scant remarks on Romantic national Messianism—once considered "one of the most powerful

Polish historiosophic concepts during the nineteenth century."[14] Miłosz was aware that accentuating Messianism in line with the Polish tradition would have been not only inappropriate but also imprudent for readers from different linguistic and cultural contexts: "Polish Messianism cannot find understanding in the West, which is hardly surprising."[15] Indeed, Miłosz considered this phenomenon of "collective hypnosis" unwise, euphemistically speaking, and disastrous in consequence.[16] He saw in it the traces of a colonized mentality—"the compensatory kink of small nationalism"—in other words, an expression of the "necessary fictions" that feed all colonial societies until they come to terms with the psychological residues of foreign hegemony and their own subjugation.[17] According to Miłosz, Mickiewicz's Messianism "belongs to the order of compensatory ideas that oppressed human communities excel in when they make up various mythologies for themselves."[18] Miłosz considered this Messianism to be a tawdry phenomenon and—in assessing the consequences of Poles' reception of *Forefathers' Eve*, part 3—wrote that Mickiewicz "pickled them alive in Messianic nationalism."[19] As Elżbieta Kiślak observes, Miłosz "consistently stifles motifs that he suspects of nationalist background: patriotic martyrology and folklore. Both in the textbook and in his essays, the desire to pass over in silence, or neglect these Romantic myths is at war with the desire to unmask and disgrace them."[20] The arguments that swayed Miłosz in *The History of Polish Literature* are understandable, even if the phenomenon's elimination, depreciation, and even degradation is a poor choice of framing within a historical and literary synthesis.

It is worth noting that Miłosz's perspective on Messianism, situated at the end of the twentieth century and conditioned by his views on the issue of the nation and nationalism, has much earlier and no less incisive precursors, such as Kazimierz Chłędowski, who noted the following opinion in his diary:

> This "Messianism" of the Polish nation is one of the most harmful inventions of our Romantic school; the poets convinced the nation that God applies different standards to Poles than to the Germans, the French, or the Spanish, and commanded it to always count on having things handed to it on a silver platter. These ideas contributed to national laziness, turning Poles into a nation of dreamers uncertain of their own power, own work, but expecting that Providence will reward them.[21]

The heterodox idea of national Messianism presented in *Forefathers' Eve*, part 3, and *Books of the Polish Nation and Polish Pilgrimage* was also the subject of a smart polemical stance taken by Norwid, who considered Mickiewicz's Messianism "a mystical radicalism and a gnostic spiritual aristocracy of the called."[22] In this light, even given the historical arguments in support of Messianic ideology, it is difficult today to treat national Messianism as anything other than an intellectual and religious excess, a pseudo-Christian political religion that, as a remnant of anachronistic political idealism in the Polish mentality, requires critical commentary to settle accounts with the postcolonial past. Norman Davies suggests that Messianism be looked at as a link in a specifically Polish "tradition where the 'Word' has precedence over the 'Fact': where more attention is paid to what people would have liked to happen than to what actually occurred."[23] From this point of view, Messianism becomes a gesture—one of many in a series of gestures made throughout the history of Polish culture and politics—of a "refusal to accept the political situation as reality."[24] If it has any value, it is a historical one, arising from the circumstances in which it was originally preached. It is impossible to transfer it into the present and apply it to contemporary challenges. The problem is that the effects of Messianic thinking are still noticeable in the political thought and collective behavior of Poles: "patriotic devotion spun Poland's calamities into an apotheosis of martyrdom, which plunged minds into rapture over an extraordinary, to be sure, but also hopeless situation, paralyzing the will to act and transform."[25]

To conclude this part of the discussion, one might add that proponents of Pan-Slavism used the Messianic idea instrumentally in the past to delude Poles with the possibility of normalization of relations with Russia. In 1916, Russian philosopher and poet Vyacheslav Ivanov wrote, "I want to believe that there shines above Slavdom the morning star of love, and that the third day of its sojourn in the tomb dawns for Poland—the day of resurrection. . . . From the onset of Polish Messianism, characteristics of Slavophilia can be observed in it, understood as a faith in the special destiny of the entire Slavdom to fulfil a global mission."[26] Nurturing Messianic ideas thus introduced a double load of "necessary fictions" into social circulation: it explained the sense of collective suffering as "sacrifice" and provided a national collective without a state with a supranational mission, which was to end with the politically impossible "reconciliation" with the hegemon. History, of course, continuously tested both of these convictions, exposing the illusoriness of their underlying assumptions.

## The Question of *Pan Tadeusz*

Alongside *Forefathers' Eve*, Adam Mickiewicz's *Pan Tadeusz* is the second work that for a long time defined the Polish way of thinking and perceiving reality, setting up the ideological and moral horizons of the Polish *Weltanschauung* and instilling the criteria used by Poles to judge themselves and others. Its impact is partially due to this epic poem's artistic excellence. Successive generations of readers have been enchanted with the mastery of Mickiewicz's verse and rendered defenseless against the meanings implied by the masterpiece, as was noted by the few critics who dared to take a skeptical stance toward some of Mickiewicz's ideas.

Among voices critical of *Pan Tadeusz*, Cyprian Norwid's is worth pointing out. Norwid recognized and acknowledged the epic value of the work, which he called the last European epic. He also spoke of the poem's message with irony, however, stating that its heroes "eat, drink, go mushroom picking, and wait for the French to arrive and make a homeland for them" (jedzą, piją, grzyby zbierają i czekają, aż Francuzi przyjdą zrobić im Ojczyznę).[27] From that point in time, opinions that this work, whose beauty is so powerfully enchanted in the word, injects poison into Polish souls, are not uncommon. Some even speak about the "*Pan Tadeusz* syndrome."[28] Mickiewicz's apotheosis of Napoleon is seen here as a link in a series of political "comedy of errors" displayed by Polish Romanticism and its later followers. A link of such special rank, however, that literary scholars are still tempted to assign positive historical value to the myth, as if absolved by the equivocal assessments of figure of Napoleon in Polish historiographic discourse.[29] Those who view *Pan Tadeusz* as the source or else an emanation of the "Polish syndrome" see the axiology of the poem's represented world as proof of the author's political naivety.[30] They denigrate *Pan Tadeusz* for its alleged uncritical praising of traditional social forms and social order. They also perceive this axiology as an argument in favor of passivity, the conviction that "things will turn out somehow."[31] In their opinion, such axiology preserves less-than-praiseworthy models of conduct from the period of the decline of the Sarmatian Polish-Lithuanian Republic and fosters the rehearsal of some most naïve or obsolete political concepts of that period. The critic Andrzej Kijowski has this to say about the Polish sentiment for France and the Napoleonic myth, which is built in part on the uncritical reception of Mickiewicz's work:

> In Poland's case, the irrational nature of the cult of Napoleon is particularly obvious, drastic, even. . . . The consequences of the Napoleonic myth are huge, and appear in convictions that are most deeply rooted in the collective consciousness, in dogmas on which the collective life of Poles rests, and finally in literary motifs that determine the type of Polish literature, constitutive of its separate, strange, almost exotic beauty.[32]

Given that successive generations of Poles were nourished by works that could not recognize and describe the experience of Napoleon's humiliation of Poland and instead built on its basis a myth of a generous liberator, they found it difficult to rationally assess historical facts from the eighteenth and nineteenth centuries in Polish history in a broader European context. This is a symptom of a characteristic affliction in Polish society: a shortage of effort to critically and independently understand the events and processes taking place on the continent and to determine the country's position, which, as critics such as Kijowski suggest, has often translated into unfortunate political decisions or reckless, unconsidered actions. Freedom and independence frequently appear in the collective Polish mentality as something that justifies, without considering benefits and risks, the unsheathing of swords along any geographic latitude, under any command, and in anyone's interest. This is backed by a belief that this type of "nobleness" will be returned by foreign decision makers, which is grounded in wishful thinking rather than Realpolitik. Such was the case for both Polish legionnaires fighting in Napoleon's name on San Domingo and Polish soldiers fighting alongside Allied forces on the fronts of World War II. Was the case any different in Iraq and Afghanistan in the twenty-first century?

What is the part—meaning responsibility—of Polish Romantic literature and the ideas it expressed in this situation? Does it simply try to rationalize national defeats and find sense in suffering after the fact? Or does it aid in entrenching and nurturing the discourse of victimhood, on the one hand, and in propagating irrational heroism and proclaiming an easy and non-binding return to a past Arcadia, on the other? Not all of Polish literature is trapped between these contradictions, clearly, yet the field they demarcate has set to a large extent the intellectual horizons of several generations. Jan Prokop has identified a particular type of a sociocultural tie between authors and audience that emerged in nineteenth-century Polish society, with the Polish family as their target audience. Considering the peculiar implications of text circulation generated by this cultural model, Prokop listed the following as one of its results:

> Norwid gets defeated, while mediocrity emerges victorious; the latter does not task readers with difficult and ambitious intellectual effort, far from the belief that writing constitutes [*sic*] a challenge to generally held stereotypes and habits, that it is a dangerous and risky adventure. . . . Hence, unreflective literature flourishes, which aims to hearten the spirit, protecting hearts and minds from the acute experience of reality, offering a patriotic opium in the form of Towiański's version of moderately martyrdom-oriented Messianism . . . , or a little-binding nostalgia for the good old days of the [Polish-Lithuanian] Commonwealth. In this manner, the average of various stances emerges, which includes on the one hand passive

> martyrdom for the salvation of humanity, and on the other hand conformism, the acceptance in anticipation of a miracle that will come without effort on our part.[33]

The problem presented here does not pertain only to Napoleon, who as antihero was barely present in the works of some Romantics (Norwid, Teofil Lenartowicz) and could not compete with the almost omnipresent apotheosis of the emperor. Later critics of *Pan Tadeusz* point out other implications of the ideas Mickiewicz has presented there. For example, Jan Nepomucen Miller critiqued its anachronistic cult of "kindly homeliness" and charged the poem, in his specific style, with "infecting and cutting down souls with the poisonous breath of its satiety, sybaritic virtues of the Lithuanian provinces, and optimistic self-delusion" and "entrenching, conserving a certain type of parasitic life that oppresses us like a nightmare for centuries."[34] Attention was paid to the moral aspect of actions taken by the heroes from Soplicowo during their confrontation with the Russians.[35] While these opinions, voiced by various critics, share a lack of respect for the stereotypes espoused by literary scholars, these critics point to the cracks and ambivalences in the world of Mickiewicz's masterpiece, which conflict with a good-natured acceptance of *Pan Tadeusz* as a model universe of the national past and require maintaining a distance toward it and approaching with caution and skepticism many traditional commentaries of literary scholars. Marek Troszyński's study, in which he juxtaposes Mickiewicz to Juliusz Słowacki, is situated along this axis. It is devoted to the "significant conflict" between two opposing traditions in Polish literature that are rooted in a stance taken toward the idea of knighthood and chivalry.[36] According to Troszyński, Słowacki's lofty and tragic opus is the fullest Romantic embodiment of the first of these traditions; it cultivates the myth of a proud knight, a man of absolute honor and loyalty. The second tradition, in turn, ironic and trivializing, which caricatures and sacrilegiously negates the first, is to be found in Mickiewicz's work and culminates precisely in *Pan Tadeusz*, where—according to Słowacki's commentary—"a sword duel is laughed at while those who look to be offended with the help of a stick meet with total adoration."[37] Troszyński points to the continuation of this opposition, fundamental to Polish culture, in the work of Zbigniew Herbert and Czesław Miłosz, whom he aligns with Słowacki and Mickiewicz, respectively.

What place should Mickiewicz's national epic poem occupy in contemporary Polish culture given the issues raised by the history of its interpretation? It is impossible not to consider the idealizing code activated by the poem's invocation when interpreting *Pan Tadeusz*. "O Lithuania, my Homeland, thou art like good health . . ." has the function of an "axiologically charged sign."[38] As many critics have noted, *Pan Tadeusz*, written in 1834, recuperates the lost time and space of the gentry Commonwealth by mythologizing not only the events of 1811/12 (Napoleon's march on Moscow and the hopes for liberation it stirred up among the inhabitants of the Polish lands) but also the customs and traditions of the Polish and Lithuanian gentry before the partitions.[39] This lost reality is usually subject to idealization in literature, and Mickiewicz depicts it with a great deal of nostalgia. Instead of unconditional trust, however, this idealizing code should receive critical attention and be seen as a historically rooted instrument of the semiosis of the national reality's significant moments and motifs, which reveals much about Polish identity discourse. In other words, the fact that Mickiewicz could create an "unreal legend" does not have to be seen as the best or the only possible form of cutting the Gordian knot of what has been termed "the Polish fate" in Polish identity discourse.[40] Part of this fate was the vicissitudes of the territories of the former Polish-Lithuanian Republic and their inhabitants under the hegemony of the Russian Empire. The problem is that Mickiewicz's model of shaping reality is both identified with the imperative of complete affirmation of the world of *Pan Tadeusz* in the consciousness of Poles, and it overpowers other, competing points of view with its persuasiveness. Paradoxically, from this perspective *Pan Tadeusz* provokes and forces a discussion—but not with the "Polish center" created within it (which would not make much sense) but rather with Mickiewicz's proposed choice of an escape into myth in dealing with the situation of colonial subordination. Acknowledging the existence of the "idealizing code" is not equivalent to taking it for an infallible, authoritative model of Polish identity discourse under conditions of colonial domination. In reality, this code was merely one possibility of translating the experience into the symbolic language of literature: through the revivification of the past of the Polish-Lithuanian Commonwealth by "painting a provincial microcosm"—a world that seemed "gone forever" when Mickiewicz described it.[41] The suggestiveness and inertia of this code, however, meant that it acquired canonical status in the commonly held convictions of Poles and was seen as the only possible formula for rationalizing "the Polish fate."

The list of opinions on the subject of *Pan Tadeusz* and its presence, role, and consequences in Polish public discourse—in school textbooks, politics, journalism, and so on—certainly could be expanded. In terms of a hierarchy of arguments, the leading position on this list would surely belong to Witold Gombrowicz's novel *Trans-Atlantyk*, termed by Stefan Chwin as the "anti–*Pan Tadeusz*" because of its multilayered references to Mickiewicz's poem.[42] Indeed, seen as part of a discussion about Polish identity and a means of shaping its discourse, Gombrowicz's novel exceeds the framework of a polemic with a single text. It has the form of a debate with the entire cult of Romantic thought, along with its extensive stock of symbols and inflated rhetoric, as well as later incarnations of reinterpreted Romantic ideas, meaning everything that can be described, according to preference, as the haze or *longue durée* of Romanticism. According to Gombrowicz, Mickiewicz, as the creator of a collective therapy of "virtuous familiarity" that was fatal in its consequences, "accomplished what he was able to, namely supplied us with beauty that suited our national interests at a given moment. . . . [H]e accessorized our weakness with the headdress of Romanticism, made Poland into the Christ of nations, countered the iniquity of invaders with our Christian virtue, and trolled the beauty of our landscapes."[43] Gombrowicz's ironic commentary would probably be superfluous were it not for the deep disproportion in the public discourse and common understanding of Poles between the weight given to Mickiewicz's opus as opposed to the work of other great Romantic authors. Indeed, the Mickiewicz read by the majority of Polish audiences is usually interpreted unequivocally (in line with a national agenda) and uncritically (stamped with the mark of "inviolable authority").[44] The antidote to Mickiewicz's excessive presence could be sought in reflection on the ideas and opinions of other Romantics, such as Słowacki, Krasiński, and Norwid. Such an approach allows for serious consideration of their intellectual content and for its evaluation as an intellectual proposition with a value that a postcolonial society has a right to question, here and now.[45]

## The Need to Rethink Polish Romanticism

The epigraph of this chapter, sourced from Gombrowicz's *Diary*, illustrates well the belief in the necessity of a postcolonial revision of Polish Romanticism encompassing a critical rethinking of the diagnoses, stances, ideas, and opinions of the Romantic bards. Condemning Romanticism, along with it national mythology and rhetoric, is not the point here. The problem with Romanticism is that, for political reasons, it could not be broadly and freely discussed outside of an exclusive circle of specialists for many years. During the Communist period it was used by the Soviet-imposed authorities to legitimize their authority by placing Romanticism within the context of revolutionary and "progressive" traditions. "Marxist-oriented literature historians, culture activists, writers and poets readily lent a helping hand, reproducing officially approved concepts and images."[46] As Anna Artwińska notes in the book comparing Mickiewicz's reception in Communist Poland with that of Goethe's in East Germany, Romanticism in Polish People's Republic "was an object of suspicion as an ideologically inappropriate tradition—overly religious and overly anti-Russian."[47] Since its moral and political dilemmas were seen as a forecast/prophecy of the future Polish fate, first and foremost determined by Russian/Soviet hegemony, its language became the universal code for the experience of Soviet colonization. Hence, the imperatives proclaimed by Romantics and the imponderables of their poetry were still seen as compulsory in the popular, unofficial (clandestine) reception of Romanticism during the Communist period. As a result, any questioning of the Romantic legacy perceived this way meant an attack on the core of the Polish ethos and was classified as treason, defection, or at the very least controversy. All of this culminated in the creation and consolidation of a characteristic mode of approaching Romantic texts. It is not surprising, therefore, that the average Polish reader, brought up to read these works as if they contained religious dogmas, was unable and is still not ready to enter into discussion with the points of view presented therein. The Romantic legacy seems like a voice coming from holy books, and its single, orthodox interpretation loses its attractiveness and impact under different conditions of reception. Alina Witkowska wrote in the early 1990s, in a cautionary tone, "Ever more frequently, especially young readers are losing the mental connection with the Messianic, martyrological, patriotic message. It bores or irritates them. The stubborn insistence on former rules of interpretation will lead to the depopularization of Romanticism, and perhaps even to its enclosure within an archive of worthy relics where it will meet with a worthy death."[48] Yet the fact that the ideas and role models of Romantic literature are not authentically internalized by younger generations of "coerced" readers, primarily high-school students, does not mean that the problem does not exist. To the contrary, the schizophrenic approach to Romanticism continues, since students' exam essays about Romantic poetry simply regurgitate traditional formulas.[49] This is one of the reasons why Romanticism is not read "against the grain" with enough vigor and its sacrosanct ideas are not sufficiently discussed outside of a narrow circle of literary historians. The second reason stems from the fact that Poles—captured, surrounded, and in awe of the beauty of the poetic world of Romantic masterpieces and their untranslatable idiom—have become accustomed to receiving these texts' ideas on bended knee along with all of their inventory, to soaking up this world and transmitting its order and telos to successive generations as the most valuable of deposits.

The interrogation of Romantic masterpieces is not an easy task, nor is it risk-free. As Miłosz wrote about *Forefathers' Eve*, part 3, "The most beautiful poetry that has been written in Polish captures us and does not let us go, so how is reason to buck against it?"[50] The task, of course, is not to deny the artistic value of eminent Romantic masterpieces but rather to ensure that this value is not routinely extrapolated to the whole of their contents, to prevent readers from viewing the reasons and diagnoses contained therein as a priori irrefutable, as if they were revealed truths. Such an approach clearly had and still has serious consequences, which are by no means limited to a knowledge and understanding of literature as an art form but extend also into the sphere of philosophy, ratio, and praxis (as Bismarck has been claimed to have said, Poles are politicians in poetry and poets—meaning idealists and inappropriate dreamers—in politics). In this stance toward the legacy of remarkable individuals, Gombrowicz saw symptoms of Polish self-satisfaction, intellectual laziness, and evasion of life. For is this evasion not treated with overwhelming permissiveness in *Pan Tadeusz*, finding there its powerful articulation? Is it not heard in the helpless convulsions of Romantic and post-Romantic Messianism, whenever the intellectual energy to seriously confront reality was lacking or channeled into the long-unused avenues? Looking at the intellectual proposals articulated in works of Romanticism would help to move the Polish identity discourse beyond the Romantic paradigm, freeing the language of that discourse from "poetic and theatrical shamanism."[51]

Even the most critical of readings, of course, cannot do harm to Mickiewicz's masterpieces, both from the point of view of their rank in the history of Polish literature and on the level of individual reception. They will remain, most likely forever, eminent poetry not on account of their professed ideology or religious and political worldview—their "Polish metaphysics"—but despite these factors, which constitutes a significant difference.[52] Their unmatched artistry does not preclude the option of testing them on other than an aesthetic level—of examining them within an intellectual order. This concerns not only Mickiewicz's own convictions and beliefs, whether those articulated and implied in his poetry or those contained in his other work (for example the Paris lectures, recently explored as an autonomous and complete text).[53] It also pertains to everything that can be extracted from his works now, after years of experience and repeated interpretations within changing contexts and without the Romantic mind-set. This test of Romanticism's intellectual relevance derives from a different reception context—the situation of a contemporary reader, formed under the pressure of a present that forces the text out of its native, historical environment and includes it, as yet another voice, within its polyphony. At the same time, reflection on the means by which Mickiewicz and his contemporaries posed and solved problems, as well as the historical conditions and real consequences of their choices—given the present-day knowledge of nineteenth-century geopolitics and its implications—can reveal the mechanisms by which identity discourse functions in a developing, modern nation.[54] One of the issues that certainly appears on the horizon of this postcolonial reflection on Romanticism is the entire complex question of identity, which cannot be reduced to Mickiewicz's nationality.[55]

## The Case of Słowacki

In the polyphony of the contemporary world, the note of postcolonialism rings ever more clearly. Of particular interest from this perspective, beside Mickiewicz's Paris lectures and the work of Norwid, is Słowacki's Protean opus. As Alina Kowalczykowa, Słowacki's renowned monographist, writes, "there are especially many motifs that seem to harmonize with our intellectual anxieties" in his work.[56] The rest of this chapter presents in point form six issues of interest from the perspective of a postcolonial reclamation of agency.

1. Unlike most Romantics (with the exception of Norwid), Słowacki was aware of the ambivalence inscribed in Polish identity. The source of this ambivalence is the loss of a position that assures a strong subject position. In Słowacki's plays and epic poems, its result is the proliferation of opposing pairs of self-stereotypes, which are often embodied in a single literary character. Słowacki's conceptualizations of Polish identity in his work are rarely unequivocal. In their choices and actions, these textual Poles oscillate between loftiness and triviality, nobility and villainy, and loyalty and betrayal, especially in the plays *Kordian*, *Mazepa*, *Sen srebrny Salomei* (The silver dream of Salome), *Ksiądz Marek* (Father Marek), *Horsztyński*, and *Fantazy*, as well as in the digressive poem *Beniowski*. Their Polishness is both affirmed and criticized, in a word—difficult. These characters have psychologically complex forms and constitute themselves in the process of dynamic interactions. Słowacki appears to intentionally complicate his heroes' relations with Others, such as Russians, Ukrainians, or Jews. He thus escapes the trap of mythomania, of multiplying stereotypes, and of univocality. His writing does not contain the simplified opposition of *good* Poles and *bad* foreigners. Evil in Słowacki's oeuvre is not embodied in the oppressor or the Other, which means that Poles are not automatically purged of it.

In Słowacki one never finds a complete answer to the question of responsibility for the fall of the Polish-Lithuanian republic in any one of his works. Instead, this responsibility is presented as ambivalent. On the one hand, the author questions that type of Polish historical thinking that assigns blame for the national calamity exclusively to foreigners. On the other hand, in projecting responsibility for the status quo from the colonizers onto collaborating individuals in Polish society, Słowacki seems to overlook violent foreign imperial conquest as the major reason for the fall of the commonwealth. In fact, there is no contradiction between these two positions, as Słowacki's reflection on the reasons for Poland's decline is scattered across his entire oeuvre. In attempting to represent the horrific experience of defeat, which absorbed him close to half a century after its occurrence, the poet is unable to grasp and exhaust it in one take. He could not create a work encompassing and explaining the whole of Polish experience. Instead, this experience is parceled out and represented in its multiple aspects, in separate scenes and with variously placed accents. For instance, while *Father Marek* offers a portrait of an individual perpetrator from a group of those victimized by a foreign hegemony, the *Silver Dream of Salome* presents a view of Ukraine ablaze that makes Russia the invisible beneficiary of this fact. This very Russia appears in *Father Marek*, however, while in *The Silver Dream of Salome*, despite its absence, it plays a silent role of a complementary "requisite hypothesis."

The ambivalence that informs Słowacki's opinions on many things is also at play in issues of the historical significance of the Polish-Lithuanian Commonwealth in human and European history and the social roles and individual stances related to it. Słowacki sees in individual actions and social interactions both the residue of an imperial mentality (the sense of pride among military commanders and soldiers, the discourse of power evoked by their words and actions) and the symptoms of colonization (seen in the grotesque images of decomposition and degradation of Polish discourse that dominate in *The Silver Dream of Salome*, *Fantazy*, and *Kordian*). This ambivalence does not boil down to noticing this double experience, but rather it goes beyond the opposition grasped therein. It includes yet another equivocation, arising from the tension between the traumatic and destructive sense of being subordinated and the consciousness of a mission, which is dictated both by the ethos of unbreakable obligation and of the knightly act, and the imperative to bring civilization to the remote territories of the Russian Empire (Siberia). Słowacki encloses a psychologically attuned analysis of this condition in the epic poem *Anhelli*.

2. Słowacki's writing offers an interesting diagnosis of the colonized society's condition, which can be described in terms of interconnection with the hegemon. The idea refers to the assimilation of the colonizers' manner and appearance, the "milling" and "digesting" of their characteristics that is typical of subjugated populations, even to the exchange of traits between the

colonized and the colonizing.[57] This leads on both sides to a significant and problematic—from a cultural as well as moral point of view—reconfiguration of the identity profile. In terms of language, manner, and mentality, Hetman Kossakowki in *Horsztyński* is not distinguished by much from the Imperial Russian Army soldiers who run rampart around the castle; similarly, the crass, repressed, and debased Warsaw crowd ahead of the czar's coronation ceremony in *Kordian* blends in with the unchecked mob of Russian soldiers in *Father Marek*. One of the key differences that defines these characters and groups is the notion of honor and the attitude toward it—a constitutive and fundamental parameter of Polish knightly culture that distinguishes it in an elemental way from the hegemon's Eastern culture.[58] The Russian general Krechetnikov in *Father Marek*, as well as the major in *Fantazy*, in turn, are figures capable of a nobleness that is rarely heard of among representatives of Polish society. Conversely, Horsztyński, a character stylized as an unblemished, heroic patriot, appears unable to fully carry the burden of tragedy, the glory of which falls—how ironically—onto the bravely dying opportunist Kossakowski. The world of Słowacki's heroes is a realm in which "moral arguments are substituted by the rights of the stronger—the empire's national interest."[59] It is a world where the degradation of language, the relativization of its semantics, and the depreciation of the honor code necessarily lead to the splitting of identity and loss of subjectivity of the heroes. In the sociopsychological order, resentment and mimicry are adequate terms to describe the phenomena that Słowacki observes with particular acuity.

Readers also find a rich gallery of mediocre characters in Słowacki's plays—traitors, scoundrels, wicked individuals, and opportunists like Ślaz in *Lilla Weneda* or Hetman Kossakowski in *Horsztyński*. They can be characterized as model examples of the comprador elites. These are the antiheroes of history, people of a sort well known to Polish society during the Communist period—the prefigurations of those who by flattering the Soviet occupant unscrupulously found prominent positions in the colonized society. In Słowacki's works, these figures take a more or less active part in the hegemon's project—the multilayered transmission of power among the subordinated population by its vestment in local elites. Informers, traitors, collaborators, or simply people who gave in to harmless accommodation through subservience, are the various prototypes of the elites collaborating with the colonizer. Such behavior was known to Słowacki through personal experience to some extent, and it existed and grew in Polish society for almost the entire nineteenth and twentieth centuries. It is not so much Słowacki's fascination with this psychological profile that explains the multitude of such characters in his work but rather his awareness of the specific and unprecedented nature of this phenomenon, with its purely colonial foundations, in Polish social life. Słowacki was able to observe and precisely outline the inevitable and long-term result of foreign domination, which left its trace not only in the symbolic sphere but also on individual and social behaviors.

3. Polish Romanticism is a period of rapid reconfigurations and shifts across the mental map of Europe. Numerous testimonies to this fact are found in historiographic and political discourses, autobiographical writing, and literature. "At home" ceases to mean "in Europe" and begins to designate a realm opposite Europe. How does Słowacki respond to this tendency? It would be pointless to look for characters in his writing who imitate cosmopolitan opinions and behaviors so mercilessly derided in *Pan Tadeusz*: "His works do not contain a trace of tendencies toward national isolationism that were then frequent, no fears about the melting away of Polishness through bonding with foreigners. The only wall he erected was that separating us from Russia of that time, which had rapidly become hateful."[60] Słowacki's writing must be studied in the context of Romantic discourse, which can be termed the discourse of identity negotiation, of searching for a place between the East and the West. This discourse had many faces, even within a single author's body of work (as was the case with Mickiewicz), and it was not limited to the issue of attitude toward the "Slavic idea," or Slavophilia, nor was it exhausted in the search for, and reconstruction of, mythical ancient sources of national existence, which was characteristic for the epoch (and can be seen, for example, in Słowacki's play *Lilla Weneda*). Attempts to extract a Polish discourse from a mental geography in which Poland is irrevocably part of the East (or the North) are perceptible in his works. These efforts do not follow an anti-colonial model, however, with its paradigmatic form presented by Mickiewicz in the prologue to *Forefathers' Eve*, part 3, wherein the inherent anti-Easternness of Polish culture and ethos is highlighted. Słowacki does not take Mickiewicz's approach of using simple antitheses that counter Polish "virtue" with Western "corruption" and "materialism," and Polish "saintliness" with Eastern "despotism." The central opposition for Polish Romanticism of West-East is either eliminated in Słowacki's oeuvre or shifted elsewhere, which gives his works a different, surprisingly contemporary, postcolonial tone.

Two very different examples illustrate this point. In the poem "Paris," Słowacki enters into a polemic with the proud self-image of the Western metropolis carrying out its civilizational mission, an image that coheres with the main principle of European orientalism.[61] In the play *Mazepa*, in turn, he deconstructs European orientalizing discourse in the form of a spectacular turn: the title figure of a "tamed native." An arrival from the periphery, the

Ukrainian hetman Ivan Mazepa is initially shown as an exotic specimen of manliness used to fulfill the empty desires of women, in accordance with the myth created by Western Enlightenment, but he becomes a fully developed hero with a potentially tragic dimension, who is morally superior to the metropolitan center's representatives. Where the "Eastern pole" is concerned, Słowacki does succumb to Russophobia, and he does not create simplified images of a dehumanized Russia. In his work, the "East" is heterogeneous and internally deeply varied. It is cocreated by Poles, Ukrainians, Ruthenians, Russians, Catholics, Eastern Orthodox, Uniates, and Jews (*The Silver Dream of Salome*, *Father Marek*). It is worth recalling here that in the unfinished play *Książę Michał Twerski* (Prince Mikhail Tversky), Słowacki creates a phenomenal vision of the transformation of Ruthenia into Russia, taking up a significant issue from the point of view of future development of Polish anticolonial discourse, namely, that of the sources of the Russian imperial project and of Muscovite despotism.

Although Słowacki is original and independent in both his research and its artistic rendering in his own writing, he is not entirely free of the Western orientalizing discourse, traces of which can be found in his works. This can be seen, for instance, in *The Silver Dream of Salome*, where emphasis is placed on graphic scenes of the slaughter of Poles by Ukrainians, sourced from a classic and orientalizing (in Saidian sense) work, Claude Carloman Rulhière's *Histoire de l'anarchie de Pologne* (1807). This issue triggers further questions. To what extent did Polish Romantic discourse constitute a reaction to the orientalizing texts of both Western and Russian hegemonic discourses—literary, journalistic, and, first and foremost, historiographic? The opinions of Polish Romantics, poets as well as journalists and historians (Joachim Lelewel, Maurycy Mochnacki), can be interpreted as voices raised under the pressure of European discourse, which positioned Poland on the continent's geopolitical and cultural map for a long time. To what extent were these works an answer to statements made by such thinkers and writers as Voltaire, Herder, Fichte, Rousseau, or Rulhière? To what degree, if at all, were these answers given from a position of a "strong" identity, and—conversely—to what degree was this foreign voice accepted as authoritative and consequently interiorized and absorbed by the Polish discourse as its own?

Against a background of problems that appear as a result of the questions posed above, Słowacki's ideas seem to occupy a particular place in nineteenth-century discussions about Polish identity in relation to Russia and the West, which is worth more careful study. To what extent was Słowacki able to escape the trap of defining the identity of the national collective through reference to these two signposts traditionally evoked in attempts at Polish self-definition? Regardless of the answer to this question, one thing is certain: instead of participating in a discourse based on the antithesis *inferiority-superiority*, Słowacki turned toward the space of Sarmatism—a category that constitutes the main, autonomous defining point of Polishness in his writing.

4. In the course of reflecting on the roots of Polish identity contained in Słowacki's oeuvre, the reader encounters the aforementioned category of Sarmatism, or Sarmatianism, which occupies a special place in his value system. It constitutes an embodiment of the concept of "knighthood" and the realization of the knightly ethos, which counters the allegedly degenerate Sarmatism of *Pan Tadeusz*. It is worth underlining here that Słowacki's attitude to Sarmatism was not that of a colonized subject deprived of his own, original tradition.[62] To the contrary, he was able to extract from Sarmatism the beauty of custom and the magnificence of gesture, to grasp its notions of honor, pride, dignity and a sense of greatness without forgetting about its degraded forms—the cult of simplicity, rowdiness, arrogance, and megalomania—that he saw as its negation and proof that its pure prototype had been squandered. First and foremost, Słowacki situated Sarmatism as a timely task, a responsibility understood as the incarnation of the knightly ideal, without reducing it to the dimension of an obsolete myth of the past, celebrated collectively in an atmosphere of self-satisfaction.

One could say that Słowacki's work is a record of the search for an individual voice, a personal record of an identity discourse. This search takes place between two extremes, with one end constituted by the embodiment of an ideal and the other by its opposite: between knighthood and knightliness as a former, noble tradition and a current, degraded aristocracy and nobleness. In the words of Słowacki's poem "Agamemnon's Tomb," the two poles of Polishness are marked by an opposition between an "angelic soul" and a "boorish skull." To repeat: the identity discourse proposed by Słowacki is ruled by a fundamental principle of ambiguity, since identity in his writing is indicated by precisely these two coordinates. Słowacki's oeuvre thus agrees with Gombrowicz's much later postulate laid out in this memorable form: "would that a Pole could like himself in two opposites forms—as the person that he is in a given moment, and as the person who destroys who he is within himself."[63] In the place of the model offered up by *Pan Tadeusz*, which is based on the principle of harmonious coexistence and erasure of antinomies and conflicts, Słowacki constructs a model of "difficult" identity, defined through the coexistence—rather than the removal or leveling—of antagonisms.

5. Słowacki does not stop at defining Polish identity. Rather, he confronts it in a manner that is very close to contemporary sensibilities—with the identity of the Other, treated subjectively. As a result, his writing stands apart from the discourse of the Polish Borderlands, which orientalizes Ukraine as the former so-called Borderlands of the Commonwealth and is represented, for example, by writers of the Ukrainian school (such as Antoni Malczewski, Seweryn Goszczyński, and Michał Czajkowski, among others) and the political conceptualizations of Maurycy Mochnacki. Słowacki's works are characterized by a remarkable sensitivity toward otherness: ethnic, national, linguistic, as well as religious. They anticipate some of the current tendencies in literature and the humanities. Słowacki's ability to give voice to the experience of an Other, to recognize the subjectivity of an Other, offers some proof that Said's postulate from the closing remarks of *Orientalism* can be fulfilled, while also negating theses about the allegedly *exclusive* and *hateful* character of Polish nationalism, which was to surreptitiously take root in Polish writing already during Romanticism.[64] The manner in which Słowacki evokes Ukraine in *The Silver Dream of Salome*, for instance, appears to break with the orientalizing practice of his contemporaries—Polish, as well as English, German, or French authors—which Said assesses as follows: "I consider Orientalism's failure to have been a human as much as an intellectual one; for in having to take up a position of irreducible opposition to a region of the world it considered alien to its own, Orientalism failed to identify with human experience, failed also to see it as human experience."[65] Słowacki's Ukraine is not a native realm to which Polish lords have an exclusive right, nor is it the domain of Polishness in the sphere of language, culture, religion, or politics. To the contrary, he problematizes these and other determinants of Ukraine's "Polishness." As a result, they lose their obviousness and demand discussion, which the poet engages with using the full range of factors constitutive of subjectivity, both Polish and Ukrainian. In the place of axioms imposed by other Polish Romantic writers and critics, Słowacki presents tension and uncertainty. Neither is the Ukraine of Słowacki's oeuvre a foreign territory, however, in the sense of an exotic sphere where the refined, orientalizing longings of the civilized, Western subject can be fulfilled. Its function takes on a more complex and subtle form in the poet's rendition. Słowacki juxtaposes the antithetical images of "pastoral" and "horrid" Ukraine that are common in Polish culture to an image of Ukraine unmarked by its separatism, confronting his audience with the necessity of reflecting on and understanding its point of view. Both of the crimes committed in the play are equally felonious; both perspectives—Polish and Ukrainian—have equal standing. Słowacki proves

capable of recognizing—granting?—the subordinated Ukrainian population its subjectivity, agency, and a separate identity, which their Polish neighbors and kin must take into account. In his writing, Ukrainians are neither ornaments on the patterned rug of the mythological Eastern Borderlands of the Polish-Lithuanian Commonwealth, nor a thoughtless and formless mass stripped of consciousness and identity, but a subject and partner in discourse. A characteristic trait of their identity and that of figures representative of other ethnicities is their hybridity—the transgression of inflexible ethnic and cultural boundaries resulting from colonial violence. This issue, which Słowacki poses in an intriguing way, opens a broad question that is clearly, though not exclusively, exemplified by *The Silver Dream of Salome*—which, in terms of identity, presents an immensely varied gallery of characters.

6. The last and completely separate problem that broadens the horizon of research beyond Słowacki's oeuvre is the orientalization of his writing within Western European academic discourse. This especially concerns his plays. As Alina Kowalczykowa justifiably writes, "*We know* that he belongs to the most remarkable playwrights of European Romanticism, and that, were it not for linguistic and national barriers, he should occupy a place at least alongside of Victor Hugo."[66] Therein lies the rub: were it not for barriers of nationality and language. At stake here are not only "technical" issues, such as the lack or inaccessibility of translations. Kowalczykowa references a telling opinion of an English scholar: "While we cannot rate Słowacki highly as a playwright, his scenes display poetic power, and the later development of the Polish stage owes much to his inspiration."[67] The hierarchies utilized in many Western literary textbooks, which rely on this kind of elimination, or depreciation, of the subject, can be jarring for Polish readers; in appearing arbitrary, they raise questions about the validity of the accepted criteria. In fact, this is not a case of arbitrariness, nor of misunderstanding Polish literature, but rather of the merciless logic of orientalizing discourse that for years consolidated this, and not another vision of writing among the nations of East-Central Europe, including Poland, which were subjected to foreign hegemony. Of fundamental significance among its assumptions is the conviction that the cultural artifacts of the people residing in these territories do not possess their own inherent goodness as the products of the populations but rather acquire it exclusively via the epistemological initiative of the Western subject in the process of their exploration and evaluation. This is the source of the sometimes significant discrepancies in the historical and literary hierarchies presented by Polish and foreign literary syntheses and encyclopedic editions.

❧❧❧

To conclude, let us return to Gombrowicz's *Trans-Atlantyk*. When it comes to a discussion of Polish identity, this text stands half in agreement with and half in (seeming) opposition to the epigraph to this chapter, leaning, so to speak, more to the side of Słowacki than of Mickiewicz. Gustaw Herling-Grudziński forecast that *Trans-Atlantyk* will gain rather than lose in currency with time.[68] The reception of Gombrowicz's work, over fifty years now, has so far confirmed this prognosis. Some aspects of Polish mentality critiqued in *Trans-Atlantyk*, such as national pride verging on narcissism or patriotism that amounts to no more than a superficial celebration of its orthodox forms, are ongoing and thriving, or—to use Gombrowicz's words—"keep dying yet cannot die."[69] Only when the literary audience in Poland receives *Trans-Atlantyk* simply as a work of art, a fantastic satire on Romanticism and its haze, rather than a tool of national shock therapy, will one be able to say that the phase of collective life critiqued by Gombrowicz has come to an end. A conclusion of this phase, marked by the experience of colonial subjugation and an internalized inferiority complex, would be verified by the change in reception of not only Gombrowicz's *oeuvre* but many other texts key to the discourse on Polish identity in the nineteenth and twentieth centuries. One can assume that it would also overcome the colonization discourse that has persisted since the end of eighteenth century, along with its social and psychological attributes and symbolic depository.

Chapter Six

# The Natives' Exclusion by the Empire's Poet?

## (Adam Mickiewicz, *The Crimean Sonnets*)

Our departure point is a true story. In 1908, King Leopold II of Belgium, the self-appointed "liberator" of lands he had seized more than twenty years earlier and called the Congo Free State (now the Democratic Republic of Congo), finally gave up his claim on the African territories. As the author of some of the most extreme atrocities in the history of Africa, Leopold knew well the secrets held in his state archives. Aware of this inconvenient legacy, he ordered that the archives of the Congo Free State in Brussels be destroyed. It took eight days to burn the collected documents. The occasion prompted Leopold to remark to his military advisor, Gustave Stinglhamber, that "I will give them my Congo, but they have no right to know what I did there."[1] In this manner, he not only got rid of the evidence of the crimes committed by the hegemon but also erased the textual traces of the hegemon's presence.[2]

This anecdote demonstrates one of many strategies used in colonial discourse to solidify its position as the exclusive source and medium of authoritative knowledge about the world. As long as this discourse has institutional support and is the only voice heard within the realm of politics and culture, its status remains secure, and the image of the metropolis and the periphery it creates becomes validated and "true." In other words, it is taken to be factual, and it is respected as uncontestable.

This strategy depends on the rhetorical rule of detraction (removal). For empires, elision and silence are convenient camouflage for the violence they perpetrated. It can be effected in various ways and pertains not only to "hard" colonial discourse, for instance the actions of the empire's administrators (as was the case in the anecdote above), but also its "soft" forms, such as literary representations. For colonialism, understood as a system of a multichannel distribution of imperial power based on territorial annexation and human exploitation, creates and promotes a myth of the colonizer to convince the subjugated populace along with the rest of the world that the values and ideas held by the metropolis are superior to those of the colonized people, that they are universal and uncontestable and thus deserving respect and acceptance. This politics of self-representation, which typifies all authoritarian rule, is an especially prominent element of the civilizing mission of modern-day empires. To realize this politics, colonial discourse harnesses various rhetorical strategies, including depreciation (the degradation of the subordinated population's image) and hyperbolization (the amplification of the periphery's defects and of the metropolis's attributes). Against this background, the rhetoric of elimination we deal with here is distinguished by its radicalness and far-reaching implications, up to and including exclusion. Hence the postulate of postcolonial criticism for textual interpretations to look carefully at both what is included and what is excluded by the author.[3]

In 1825, following a trial for his membership in a secret student organization and his deportation to Russia, Adam Mickiewicz found himself in Odessa. From there, he took several trips to the Crimean Peninsula. His encounter with Crimea bore fruit in the form of a cycle of eighteen poems known as *The Crimean Sonnets*; they were first published in 1826 in Moscow along with the so-called Odessan sonnets, a cycle of twenty-two poems, and quickly translated into, as well as published, in the Russian language.

Critics have long ago noticed Mickiewicz's omission in the Crimean cycle of its exotic, oriental subject: "There is an absence of cities, Ukrainian villages, and Tatar auls in the *Sonnets*. . . . Crimea looks as if it were uninhabited."[4] They explained this omission by claiming that the Crimea as perceived and registered by the poet was a "poetic Crimea," and, as such, "it never existed on the earthly realm."[5] The cycle admittedly includes the indigenous figure of Mirza, but his status is quite problematic. Some see the figure as discursive in nature—neither a Tatar, nor a Turk, nor a Persian, but rather a kind of alter ego for the poet.[6] Speaking rarely, and in an "eclectic 'eastern' style," he is perhaps "something of an occidental ventriloquist's oriental dummy, wearing a 'turban' and mouthing a stylized, syncretic language inspired by, and on a few occasions directly borrowed from, such classics of the Western orientalist canon as Hammer's *Geschichte der schönen Redekünste Persiens*, de Sacy's *Chrestomathie arabe*, and Goethe's own poetic representation of the Orient, the *West-östlicher Divan*."[7] Others see Mirza as a teacher and master whose erudition towers over the Pilgrim's or else as the Pilgrim's dialogical partner, who provides him with authoritative answers to key questions asked in the poems' tercets.[8] This perspective would highlight the strong subject position of the figure and the humanism of the poetic account of an "encounter with the Other." Still others suggest that the figure be read in categories of hybridity, as a character who simultaneously belongs to local culture and is alienated from it through contact with a Western subject's perspective.[9]

Regardless of how the figure of Mirza is interpreted, he is exactly what the poetic subject of *The Crimean Sonnets* needs in an interlocutor to play the two roles that his European intellectual lineage grants him and that he embodies in line with the aesthetics of the age: of a traveler amazed by the lush environment of the East and of a human being suffering from Byronic spleen, who undertakes an inner journey aimed at self-discovery in parallel to his travels across the Orient.[10] Beside Mirza's ambivalent, hybrid figure and the anonymous Muslims exiting the mosques in "Bakhchysarai at Night" ("Bakczysaraj w nocy"), *The Crimean Sonnets* present no authentic natives who are treated as subjects and equipped with their own, either Tatar or Karaite, identity. They do not function within the cycle as independent individuals possessing their own historical and personal narration; indeed, they are actually absent from it, erased from the Crimean Peninsula's enchanting and at times threatening landscape. The substitution of human subjects with bewitching oriental landscapes, as realistic as they are fantastic—whether seen or imagined by the newcomer from the Occident—is a striking characteristic of the entire cycle. It is surprising for two other reasons. First, as the reception of *The Crimean Sonnets* proves, the substitution has not been the subject of critical, historical, or literary questions and doubts. Second, it is not entirely compatible with the cycle's motto—"Whoever wants to understand the poet, must go to the poet's country"—since the motto is an expression of European "geographical curiosity" but also a declaration of an empathetic attitude.[11] Readers and literary critics have usually taken the represented world of these sonnets as a product of poetic license, for this reason exempt from critical discussion. Studies of the representation of reality in the sonnet series' imagery have concentrated on the analysis of Mickiewicz's poetic language and intertextual references. At most, it was noted that the human world in *The Crimean Sonnets* appears "primarily in the deep background and most closely connected to the rest of nature."[12] No attention was paid to the troubling conclusion that emerged in the process of reading—that the imperative of *sympathy* and *understanding* expressed in the opening citation from Goethe does not seem to extend to Crimea's native inhabitants. Yet the Pilgrim, a figure of the author with a pivotal function in the cycle that is supplemented by that of Mirza, perpetuates with his presence the polarized division of the world represented in the sonnets. This division leads to the occidental-oriental clash that takes place in *The Crimean Sonnets* in a veiled, but after all indisputable, manner. In other words, the Pilgrim and Mirza are symbols of the mutual otherness and impenetrability of both realms, understood not so much in terms of geographical territory but as two incompatible and untranslatable discourses confronting each other. The symbolic apogee of this clash of discourses comes in sonnet 15, "The Road along the Chasm of Chufut-Caleh" ("Droga nad przepaścią w Czufut-Kale"), taking the form of disobedience that the Pilgrim, a newcomer from the West with a European soul, displays toward Mirza, his guide through the Orient. The Pilgrim's disobedience means that he can arrive at an understanding that is unattainable for the native, in this way reaching the dominant epistemological position that is owed to him in line with the rules of orientalist discourse and that is transcendent in relation to any prior knowledge of itself the East may have possessed:

> Murza, I peeped! I pierced this planet's cleft
> And saw a sight . . . I'll tell it from the grave,
> Men in the flesh lack tongue to tell such things.[13]

When the Pilgrim sees the ruins of a castle in Balaclava, the sight reminds him of a pestilence-infected medieval town—a kingdom of death (the castle, incidentally, went to rack and ruin owing to the Russian presence in Crimea during the rule of Catherine II). Alina Witkowska, the author of a monograph *Mickiewicz: Słowo i czyn* (Mickiewicz: The word and the act), thus describes the lyrical hero of *The Crimean Sonnets*:

> It might seem that nature is the alpha and the omega of being. Based on this less than optimistic lesson for the human being, the traveler across Crimea could even arrive at a more far-reaching conclusion about the impermanence of all historical forms. Since the traveler is a descendant of a conquered nation, he could take heart from the joy of destruction and the promise of the fragile instability of even the most powerful subjugating powers. He could, but he would have to be someone other than the Romantic Pilgrim, a very unequivocal figure that cannot be reduced in scope to the fanatical opponent of despots.[14]

This fragment explains why Mickiewicz gave up on striking a historiosophic, or simply independence-seeking, note in both this poem and the entire cycle. According to Witkowska, this would have countered the artistic concept of the work, which stresses the general and humanistic rather than only the particular and national dimension of existence. The reader of *The Crimean Sonnets* does not have any doubts as to the function of this kind of characterization of the cycle's actual two main heroes—the Pilgrim and the oriental scenery that serves as his background. Exotic nature meets in Mickiewicz's text with the relics of an Eastern civilization that has been turned to dust. The historicity and contemporaneity of Crimea and its inhabitants, in turn, are removed from view to highlight the figure of the unfortunate wanderer along with his spiritual biography and human fate. Indeed, literary critics have on multiple occasions shown that Mickiewicz was no different from his contemporaries when it came to fascination with the East; *The Crimean Sonnets* superbly realize the literary conventions utilized by their author and deploy them in such a way as to help develop a masterpiece.

Witkowska, an excellent scholar of Mickiewicz's work and biography, nevertheless overlooks an important issue in her critical text. To use Levinas's language, the lyrical hero of *The Crimean Sonnets* shrinks from assuming disinterested responsibility for the Other. More than that: he does not acknowledge the Other's sovereign existence, nor does he pay attention to the Other as an ontologically valuable and autonomous subject. In fact, the opposite is the case: when depicted, the Other is a depersonalized being, its subjective status eliminated from the discourse. To put the matter differently still, the universalization of the experience of exile and longing as well as the poet's growing sense of his worth as a poet come about in the context of local nature in the sonnets and via this nature's lofty and deeply metaphysical perception. In reality, however, universalization occurs at the cost of suppressing the human dimension of what is local and what—for reasons described in *Orientalism*—is viewed as not deserving of the honor of "universality."

The omission, or else the passing over in silence, of the existence of a social space of Crimean nature and architecture, whenever a newcomer from the Occident confronts an exotic (in his view) East, appears as a typical strategy of Western cultural discourses. The Western subject, in speaking about the Orient and its inhabitants, does so because of its own predicament, dilemmas, and needs, whether they are epistemological, spiritual, ethical, emotional, or of any other nature, rather than out of a desire for the subjects it is describing to exist autonomously. In line with this logic, the East remains an exotic and enchanting background for Mickiewicz's hero and his personal spiritual therapy. It has the function of a catalyst of experiences and reflections: "Psychological and philosophical themes play a primary role in the Crimean cycle. . . . The Pilgrim searches for solutions to his internal tensions and experiences within the exotic landscape."[15] Witkowska adds, "In participating in the spectacle of nature, delving into its wonders and marvels, the Pilgrim journeys into the depths of his self."[16] If an indigenous inhabitant appears among this scenery, it is either Mirza—a figure who is a correlate of the cycle's protagonist—or the anonymous (and challenging in terms of interpretation) "man lower than vermin" in "The Castle Ruins at Balaclava."[17] Beside these instances, local inhabitants basically do not appear in *The Crimean Sonnets*, and their existence, if it comes into play at all, is signaled metonymically, for example as the implicit cause of the rustling wheat fields in Alushta Valley in the sonnet "Alushta by Day": "Gold-eared grain croons the matinal namaz" (11, 2, 425).[18] In his representation of the East, Mickiewicz does not really depart from the multitudes of nineteenth-century orientalists recruited from among Western writers, scientists, and travelers whose accounts were subjected to analysis by Said. Mickiewicz's Orient—Crimea—is presented as a mysterious space of an enchanting realm that awaits being vested with meaning by the Western subject and has basically one function: to be the Western subject's source of illumination, wonderment, or else existential or philosophical insight.

This mode of representation is aided by the Romantic nature of the powerfully drawn subject, the "I" seen, for example, in the sonnet "Baidary": "Rock, forest, combe, in serial throng, stream by, / Cascade like waves and vanish at my feet" (10, 2–3, 424).[19] Within the framework established by Romantic individualism, the poetic subject thus confirms his dominant position in relation to the space perceived through personal experience. This experience is not direct in character, however, even though no evidence exists to deny its authenticity or undermine the legitimacy of the poetic statements formulated on its basis. Rather, it is mediated by systems of knowledge and of representation, which aid the Pilgrim's observation and interpretation of the places he encounters and which dictate that he see the "Orient" in Crimea—a construction of cultural discourses conceived as an antithesis of the Western world. The attitude of the lyrical persona in *The Crimean Sonnets* toward this place, formed under the influence of the author's knowledge of the orientalist works of Goethe, Byron, and Hammer-Purgstall, as well as Sergey Muravyov-Apostol, at least in some measure coincides with the perception of the Orient recorded by Western European travelers both before and after Mickiewicz wrote his sonnet cycle, as exemplified by Chateaubriand's *Itinéraire de Paris à Jérusalem* (1811), Lamartine's *Voyage en Orient* (1832–33), and Nerval's *Le voyage en Orient* (1851).[20]

In speaking of *The Crimean Sonnets*, it is necessary to remember that we are dealing with a highly polysemic work of uncommon subtlety written by a great poetic talent. Yet it is not an overstatement to say that the cycle's modeling of the East follows the rules of orientalizing discourse. According to these rules, the West encounters a "radically new form of life in the Orient."[21] The East evoked in individual sonnets is characterized by an amorphism typical of orientalist works. Its representation blurs the boundary between rational and disciplined perception of what is real and the subjective experience of the lyrical persona that takes place on the border between reality and dreams. As a result, to the newcomer from the Western world, Crimea appears as a realm with indistinct, hazy borders that exudes sensuality and is fused with illusion. Set within this framework, the territory is the epitome of otherness and an embodiment of metaphysical mystery.[22] It also constitutes, as was already mentioned, the background for the psychic and spiritual experiences of a foreign subject who is engaging with it while genealogically and spiritually alien to it and from an epistemologically and discursively dominant position. This subject is constituted by a Western style of thinking and inherently unable to give voice to local inhabitants. The point here is not to accuse Mickiewicz of insincerity in his fascination with the Orient either in its natural dimension or its cultural one (with the latter confirmed by his choice of the sonnet form, which was seen by the Romantics as having an Arab or Persian pedigree).[23] From the perspective of postcolonial theory, it is irrelevant whether the interest in the subject of orientalizing discourse is authentic. European orientalists were usually genuinely absorbed by the people and the cultures of the Near and the Far East. The problem of orientalism is located elsewhere, namely, in pinpointing the perspective from which the subject of its interest is viewed.

The cultural order of the East does not exist "in and of itself" but is defined (discovered) from the outside by a subject who defines and gets to know itself in relation to and against its background. In addition, the encounter between the two has a predetermined structure governed by a strict division of roles: the subject who views and relates its perceptions *needs* an object that is radically different from itself. This object is indispensable—the condition of the subject's existence, the means by which it is constituted. Those who are subject to observation and description, in turn, *must* at once dazzle with exoticism and silently agree to this description. The point of view of an orientalist is situated outside the studied culture and separable from its world, including its values and ideas. This world is from the outset considered to be different and foreign, and it is represented as such by means of an essentializing language, whether that of a scholarly description or of a literary travel account. The epistemology of orientalizing discourse is an epistemology founded on difference: within this discourse, knowledge is derived from a basic opposition of the Western subject's situation to the Eastern world, which is viewed as radically different. This knowledge, moreover, is less a knowledge of the Orient than a disguised form of the subject's self-knowledge, where the actual object of study—the East—is relegated to the role of a splendid decoration or of "an appendage to Europe."[24] All of this occurs on the authority of universalizing generalizations that the subject uses in its encounter with otherness and which either exclude local cultural codes or employ them to express the subject's own experience.

Is this not the situation in Mickiewicz's cycle? In reading *The Crimean Sonnets*, one has an impression that its author shares in a desire typical of an orientalist stance and wants to, in Said's words,

> formulate the Orient, to give it shape, identity, definition with full recognition of its place in memory . . . to divide, deploy, schematize, tabulate, index, and record everything in sight (and out of sight); to make out of every observable detail a generalization and out of every generalization an immutable law about the Oriental nature, temperament, mentality, custom, or type; and, above all, to transmute living reality into the stuff of texts, to possess (or think one possesses) actuality mainly because nothing in the Orient seems to resist one's powers.[25]

What is local in *The Crimean Sonnets* is called into service on behalf of the universal, with the cycle's lyrical "I" acting as its spokesperson. He arrives in Crimea with a conceptual apparatus and epistemological prejudices developed in the context of his own culture, and it is through their prism that he views and describes the world known to him from multiple readings and grounded in oriental stereotypes. The extent to which Mickiewicz utilized these models, or exceeded their findings, is a subject for a comparative study. Certainly, as an educated representative of his times, the author of *The Crimean Sonnets* could not help but be influenced by orientalism as a system of knowledge about Eastern countries and peoples. This system reproduced and suggested ready-made matrices for perceiving the Orient and its "typical" traits.

"Oriental sensuality," ascribed to the inhabitants of the East and extrapolated by poetic means onto their surrounding environment, is one typical determinant of the Orientalist stance. This is the perspective glimpsed in the sonnet "Alushta at Night," when the lyrical subject contemplates the supposedly specific "Eastern night," which is permeated with sensuality as intense as erotic experiences:

> Oriental night!—Oriental odalisque,
> Your fondling bears me to the brink of sleep;
> Your eyeball flares, arousing me afresh.[26] (12, 12–14, 426)

This example throws into sharp relief the central problem of orientalism, namely the treatment of the Orient as a jumping-off point for the Western subject's self-presentation, which is written into the structure of Western discourse and lies at the root of its rationality. The East is grasped and brought to a standstill in its most characteristic gesture or aspect, only this characteristic belongs not to the realm of ontology but to the realm of representation. It is an effect of essentializing discourse about the East, which is externally imposed instead of deriving from the East's process of self-identification. The Orient *is* what it is because it is *seen as such* by the Western subject. In "Alushta at Night," similarly to numerous works of nineteenth-century European poets and writers, the East is personified by a woman lavishing tenderness on her lover. The subject assumes the role of a manly conqueror who dominates his weaker and helpless lover. The graceful and sensual (white) feminine figure belongs to the East; she is its emblem and its embodiment, and her position within Muslim society only reinforces the stereotype of sexual laxity so subtly evoked by Mickiewicz in his sonnet. In this way, both sides of the orientalizing discourse are permanently consigned to roles that are defined by its rules. Thus configured, the represented world of *The Crimean Sonnets* is not equipped to either permit the existence of the values represented and upheld by the autochthonous population or to allow for a presentation of its point of view. Crimea functions as a peculiar "theatrical stage open only onto Europe" as if in a gesture of surrender to its epistemological possession.[27] The Orient, like the enchanting night in Alushta, exists simply to become the object of a lyrical story like the one told by Mickiewicz. The discourse about it encloses it within such a framework and does not leave space for the possibility of a different function, one that would take into account its autonomous goals. This mysterious and unpredictable imaginative space of the Orient is presented in accordance with, and as a result of, European values and existential explorations; it speaks in the language of European imagination.

The fundamental opposition between a European subject and the almost entirely absent native inhabitants of Crimea in these sonnets appears to coincide with the model described by Said on the basis of analyses of French and British orientalizing discourses: "The Oriental is irrational, depraved (fallen), childlike, 'different'; thus the European is rational, virtuous, mature, 'normal.'"[28] This dialectic explains the reason why the penultimate work in the cycle features "man lower than vermin."[29] Little is known about this figure other than that he lives in the Balaclavan fortress and plays a synecdochal function in Mickiewicz's work. This reading relies on a specific interpretation of the adjective used by Mickiewicz: *podły* in Polish, which can be variously rendered in English, including as "lower," "baser," and "odious." In *Słownik języka Adama Mickiewicza* (The Adam Mickiewicz dictionary), Konrad Górski suggests that it is indicative of "meanness" or "pettiness," rather than simply of a low social status, the sense in which this adjective had thrice functioned in Mickiewicz's other works (as also noted by Górski) and which was its basic meaning in the Polish language at the start of the nineteenth century.[30] If the latter sense is applied, the description would have quite the opposite meaning, suggestive of misery and the poverty of human existence among the Crimean ruins and thus calling for compassion. This would clearly reverse the interpretive direction of at least this sonnet.[31] Settling this issue, however, does not alter the fact that Mickiewicz's poetic representation of the Crimean people is dominated by a strategy of exclusion that is analogous to some extent to that employed by Tolstoy when he "excised" the Polish narration from the *War and Peace* storyline.[32]

❧❧❧

Considerations so far suggest that Mickiewicz's orientalism construes the Orient as an Other who stands in opposition to the West and is fundamentally different from it, as if the East was a territory that exists for the benefit of a European observer. The orientalism of *The Crimean Sonnets* has another specific characteristic, however, and cannot be unconditionally identified with a stance typical of a nineteenth-century Western European writer, historian, or ethnographer. Mickiewicz does not leave the reader in any doubt regarding the identity of the subject of *The Crimean Sonnets*, and the fact that he is an exile lies at the paradoxical core of the discursive practice exemplified by this masterpiece of the Polish Romantic lyric.

The lyrical subject of *The Crimean Sonnets* is endowed with the poet's biography and thus can be viewed as the poet's *porte-parole*.[33] Mickiewicz makes this connection clear to the reader by dedicating his cycle to his "Crimean traveling companions"—a reference to the journey through Crimea that he undertook in August and September 1825. The fact that the experiences and emotions of the lyrical subject are linked to the poet's biography is further supported by parallels between Crimea's and Poland's situation vis-à-vis Russia. The same empire that had conquered Mickiewicz's homeland (in a process sealed with Poland's third partition in 1794) had also annexed Crimea a decade earlier (1784). The ambivalence of the political situation implied in *The Crimean Sonnets* is amplified by the fact that the announcement of the Russian translation of these sonnets, made by Mickiewicz's friend Prince Petr Andreevich Viazemskii, coincided with the Imperial Russian Army's bloody hostilities in the Caucasus, led by General Alexei Petrovich Yermolov, against the populace of Chechnya and Dagestan.[34] Mickiewicz's cycle could have been used as a literary argument in Russian colonial discourse. The Polish poet supplied this argument by writing about Crimea, which had been recently conquered by Russia, and by agreeing to his work being published in the hegemon's language and to its reception in the capital of the metropolis that had also conquered his own homeland. As Roman Koropeckyj asserts in an intriguing (and radical in its conclusions) essay:

> For readers in Moscow and St. Petersburg, increasingly concerned by Muslim resistance to the empire's expansion in the Caucasus, Mickiewicz's sonnets furnished a reassuring reminder that Russia had in fact already notched a triumph over Islam—in a land whose khans, as Muraviev-Apostol had put it three years earlier in his *Journey through Tauris*, "not so long ago . . . demanded tribute from Russians" but which "is at last under the boot of Russia," the "silent dust" of its once terrible rulers resting "behind a [cemetery] fence." . . . And in a sense, the Polish poet's representation of the Crimea too serves to safely ensconce the world of the Islamic peninsula, but behind a fence, as it were, of form. Tightly contained within the unyielding confines of the sonnet, its Muslim inhabitants aesthetically packaged by someone *from* the Slavic Occident *for* the Slavic Occident, Mickiewicz's Orient, or rather, as he so tellingly calls it in an 1827 letter to Lelewel, his "Orient in miniature" . . . , could be viewed as a place whose Islamic otherness was exotic but not incomprehensible, alien but, unlike the "Tatar" auls of Chechnya and Daghestan, no longer threatening.[35]

Undoubtedly, there is some evidence to support this interpretation of the Polish poet's artistic representation of the Crimean Peninsula, which emerges less from the poetics of the sonnets than from the situation in which Mickiewicz's cycle found itself or, rather, into which it was drawn (or perhaps itself had entered). This situation placed its author in the role of a "Slavic poet," which, given Russian politics, was almost identical with "the poet of the empire."[36] As a result of this context, *The Crimean Sonnets*, a masterwork and Mickiewicz's debut in the Russian language, are not defenseless against contemporary attempts at locating them within the Russian imperial discourse of the first half of the nineteenth century. Significantly, even the greatest literary works are at risk of (not necessarily intentional) participation in the power order, since along with other texts they constitute the broader constellation of a given discourse. They *create* the objects that they only seemingly *represent* and determine the rules by which they are to be understood and evaluated, with the subject of their reflection included in systems of thought that the work's author was not even necessarily aware existed.

Koropeckyj's analysis of the discursive context of *The Crimean Sonnets* serves, among other aims, to identify precisely these implications. Koropeckyj's interpretive direction proposed is not uncontroversial, however. He charges Mickiewicz with legitimating Russia's actions, in effect appointing him the empire's agent. In what follows, I will present reasons that undermine the validity of this interpretation by querying *The Crimean Sonnets* and their interpretations in ways that require further consideration of these issues.

As shown thus far, *The Crimean Sonnets* inscribe themselves well onto the schematic of the rhetorical appropriation of the Orient by Western colonial discourse. Koropeckyj goes one step further in his interpretation to claim that they ratified and, in their silencing, accepted the Russian annexation of Crimea. This is quite a radical interpretation. Can Mickiewcz's sonnet cycle actually be equated with the texts analyzed in *Orientalism*, for instance? As Said demonstrated in *Orientalism* and *Culture and Imperialism*, in the writing of Victor Hugo, Charlotte Brontë, Jane Austen, Joseph Conrad, Rudyard Kipling, Albert Camus, Jules Michelet, François-René de Chateaubriand, Arthur Balfour, Lord Cromer, and many others, we encounter rationalizations of Western empires formulated on various rhetorical registers by writers, scientists, and travelers from the metropolis. Is this the case in *The Crimean Sonnets*?

There is a troublesome ambiguity in Mickiewicz's text. After all, the omission of Tatar, Turkish, and Karaite presence in the cycle and its replacement with an Orientalist spectacle is performed—let us assume in a way that coincides with interests of the metropolis—by a representative of a likewise colonized ethnic group from a different province of the same empire. As a poet, he is allowed the privilege to represent the subjugated Other. Yet this Other is not given the chance to speak in his or her real voice in *The Crimean Sonnets*. This is surprising in an author as sensitive as Mickiewicz was to the injury of the conquered and the despotism of the Eastern power. What the Russians did to Crimea and its inhabitants is neither directly nor indirectly implied to the readers in these poems. In a similar fashion, visitors to the Belgian archives will not discover what King Leopold II did in the Congo. Indeed, the cycle does not even suggest that Crimea was home to some Others whose culture, everyday life, and own country were destroyed in confrontation with the aggressive Muscovite metropolis. These Others have been erased from the sonnets, which remains the case even if their omission or silencing was grounded in artistic considerations (evoking a specific atmosphere, for instance, or maintaining thematic purity and consistency of construction). This style of representing Crimea might have suited not only the key players of Russian politics but also its "run-of-the-mill" supporters, even those as liberal as Prince Viazemskii. Does this make Mickiewicz a eulogist of the empire?

This lacuna in Mickiewicz's representation of Crimea could be explained, of course, with the necessity of relying on symbols as means of circumventing czarist censorship. Scholars of Polish Romanticism called this practice "deluding the despot."[37] It is also possible to argue that we are dealing not with any kind of lacuna here but simply with the lyrical transformation of individual experience and the record of subjective perception. Such a record would exclude the poetics of a realistic account of the intercultural encounter, leaving no room for a description of the Other. It is clearly difficult to deny that the artistic project underpinning Mickiewicz's sonnet cycle is governed by its own logic, which flows from, among other things, conventions of the sonnet form. *The Crimean Sonnets* evoke an imaginative rather than a realistic space. The author is entitled to create it by the freedom of expression inscribed in the art of writing and all representational art. This space, the domain of creativity, imagination, and fiction, is and has the right to be a space of strangeness that is distant, and indeed even distinct, from real space.[38] It can be entirely independent of this space, in line with the order of mythical geography, which is constructed from the lyrical transformations of impressions and emotions. Aesthetic arguments facilitate the thesis that the hyperbolization of nature's representation in *The Crimean Sonnets* is matched by the parallel exclusion of the human world from representation. Both of these correlated poetic methods seem to serve in equal measure the author's intent: to transgress the fate of an exile through liberation from domination by nature and surrender to "the captivity of memory."[39] Ultimately, however, from a position where ethical rights supersede even the most refined aesthetics, can these arguments justify the silencing of the Other's existence, its elimination and erasure from memory? Does this "poetic anthropology" not convey some meaning through not speaking about a Crimean local? Does this not lead to the discursive annihilation of the Other, regardless of the artistic aims that motivate it?

Scholars of Mickiewicz have noted that the symbolic language of *The Crimean Sonnets* provokes conflicting interpretations rather than conveying a clear message.[40] Two interpretive trajectories can be clearly discerned in their studies so far. The first positions the Romantic exoticization in Mickiewicz's text within the perspective of a Western subject confronted with "otherness." The second underscores the enigmatic character of *The Crimean Sonnets*, with the exoticism of the cycle viewed as camouflage for the political ideas about the situation of exile. While different, both of these interpretive trajectories lead to conclusions in which the Orient functions in an ancillary manner and not as a subject. Mickiewicz's Crimea is an argument in support of his own case: the personal one (in the dispute between a Romantic and the classicists) and the autobiographical as well as national one (as the allusive figure of a lost homeland). It is difficult to see its value as autonomous, however, which would call for an adequate research perspective, aimed at and open to encountering the Other. The reader does not encounter the Orient "in and of itself" in *The Crimean Sonnets* but rather—as Polish critics unanimously emphasize—"the tragic vision of the land of exile" dressed in the form of "pessimistic reflection on the fragility of power, love, and fortune" or "a religious experience" that "put on Muslim vestments."[41] It is paradoxical that, as the discussion so far suggests, in both this vision and the land that provided its metaphorical support, people turned out to be redundant from the point of view of poetic economy.

How is Mickiewicz's text to be understood then from a postcolonial point of view? It seems almost self-evident that a postcolonial interpretation of *The Crimean Sonnets* should first and foremost pay attention to their veiled, anti-imperial tone. Indeed, this tone has been frequently discussed by Polish literary critics. In this chapter I suggest an interpretation that avoids reproducing such theses and does not stop at showing the parallels between the fates of Poland and Crimea under Russian rule. This kind of reading leads directly to interpretations that canonize the cycle's patriotic aspect, as seen in the following: "By attempting to show the strong and the weak sides of the czarist system in *The Crimean Sonnets* through the suitable metaphorization of Crimea's natural environment and realities, Mickiewicz in a sense suggests not only the possibility of a struggle against the occupier, but also its means."[42] The postcolonial reading proposed here should tackle the dynamics of the relation between the lyrical subject and the exotic, oriental object. How to interpret, then, the exclusion noted in this chapter's title—a marginal issue within Mickiewicz's cycle that has become a central research problem here under the influence of interpretations offered by contemporary critics such as Roman Koropeckyj?

*The Crimean Sonnets*, the poetic account of Mickiewicz's travels across a land seized by the Russian Empire, seems devoid of feelings of solidarity with other non-Russian people of territories annexed by Russia. Mickiewicz made such declarations of solidarity toward the Russian Decembrists in his poem "To My Friends Muscovites" ("Do przyjaciół Moskali") (1831) in response to their political manifesto. However, he spared sympathy toward the Crimean Tatars who were not attributed the tiniest bit of political agency in Mickiewicz's cycle. This counters Kubacki's thesis, which he based on an overinterpretation of sonnet 9, "The Harem Tombs" ("Mogiły haremu"). Kubacki suggests that the sight of the crying Pilgrim builds a bond of community between him and Mirza—a community representing people subjugated by czardom.[43] It is not the ruins that prompt the Pilgrim's reaction (as Kubacki claims), however, but the titular harem tombs. As Megan Dixon rightly notes, Mirza seems to place an excessive value on the tears of the Pilgrim, whose isolation and disinterest diminish in the context of the preceding sonnet 8, "Potocka's Tomb" ("Grób Potockiej").[44] The orientalist perspective is thus strengthened rather than undermined here. The hero as well as lyrical subject of *The Crimean Sonnets*, while a tragic figure for being an exile, a wanderer, a foreigner, and so forth, remains primarily a newcomer from the West, a proponent of the anthropology and aesthetics of the Enlightenment, and a European in every sense of the word. In this he is like the protagonists of Pushkin's poems from the Southern period, such as "The Prisoner of the Caucasus" (1822) and "The Fountain of Bakhchisarai" (1823). He differs from them, however, in not becoming involved in interactions with the inhabitants of the Crimean Peninsula. As a result, in Mickiewicz's sonnets we are not faced with the issue that is so clearly marked in the poems by Pushkin: the open confrontation between two mentalities, civilizations, religions, and cultures.

In the first place, then, Mickiewicz became a part of the orientalizing current of European literature, albeit clearly in an ambivalent way, through a specific mode of representation, or more precisely underrepresentation, of the local population in *The Crimean Sonnets*. Second (and consequently), contemporary interpretations that view Mickiewicz as a participant in Russian colonial discourse do not take into account his role as a Polish national poet. It is possible to imagine a different literary scenario, such as that realized a century later by the Polish author Ksawery Pruszyński in the short story "The Trumpeter of Samarkand" ("Trębacz z Samarkandy"), where the Asian natives are given the opportunity to speak in their own voice and represent their own point of view.[45] Mickiewicz chose a different path in *The Crimean Sonnets*, despite the fact that he was capable of including a "foreign" voice in his narrations, as evidenced by the contrapuntal, internally dialogized structure of some of his earlier works, such as the ballad "Romanticism" ("Romantyczność") or the poetic tale *Grażyna*.[46] He left behind a work of unparalleled poetic artistry that diligently registers the oriental environs while depicting the Crimean Peninsula as devoid of an autochthonic population. Did this population not deserve to be represented in a manner reflecting its human dignity in the text of the Polish poet? Or should the problem be differently configured?

Despite the strong theses of Roman Koropeckyj and arguments that support an orientalist reading of *The Crimean Sonnets*, Mickiewicz's masterpiece contains elements that unsettle the homogenous "structure of attitude and reference" that absorbed our attention up until now.[47] Here and there, in a subtle and noninvasive manner, the lyrical subject's sympathy toward the native population does make itself felt in the cycle. It can be discerned in the mode chosen by the author to register the figures of the local people and interpret the traces of their presence. The attitude of the lyrical "I" toward the Crimean autochthons signaled by these means is entirely free of the paternalism that saturates the texts of many Western writers who traveled across the Orient. For instance, in one mention Mickiewicz calls the inhabitants of Bakhchiserai "pious" (*pobożni*; "Bakhchiserai at Night," 7, 1, 421). That the author captures precisely this aspect of their attitude in a fleeting report of their everyday life deserves a mention, since it counters Koropeckyj's thesis that we are facing an orientalist abstraction in the cycle.[48] The lyrical subject's stance of empathy, which is signaled by this epigraph, not only renders these "pious inhabitants" less abstract but also gives them very human characteristics. Next, the seat of Crimea's former rulers, which has fallen into disrepair, is not a nameless place. Mickiewicz presents it as the work of the people to whom the lyrical subject dedicates a compassionate comment, which allusively denotes the depopulation of the Crimean lands: "Still vast, now desolate Girai's demesne" ("Bakhchiserai," 6, 1, 420).[49] In turn, the fountain—that poignantly anthropomorphized witness of the disintegration of an architectural masterpiece and of the khans' state—is "seeping pearl-tears, it sobs across the waste" (6, 11, 420).[50] What or who is it crying over?

Clearly, in a form as condensed as a sonnet, every word carries weight, and attention should be paid to every nuance of its semantics. Each object of poetic description can carry weighty, symbolic, or allusive meaning. Such is the case with "Bakhchiserai." Its interpreters have usually underscored the passage of time and the evanescence suggested by the motif of the fountain's flowing water in the first tercet.[51] I propose shifting attention to its second tercet and the presence therein of personified concepts invoked by this oriental spring: "Love, glory, potentate! where are you now?" (6, 12, 420).[52] The significance of this rhetorical question extends beyond the evocation of the Latin topos of *ubi sunt*—"where are (they)?"—with its concomitant nostalgia. As if with three short strokes of a painter's brush, these notions sketch a portrait of the now-destroyed Crimean state along with its axiological and ideological profile. One would be hard pressed to find here a note of superiority toward the East, which orientalizing discourse views as separate from "advanced, civilizing powers."[53] Indeed, the opposite is more the case: Mickiewicz's Orient certainly does not represent the forefront of human culture, but it is representative of its greatness, even though culture proves fragile in confrontation with the natural world. In the above-quoted verse, the reader can hear the poet's affirmation of Crimea's grand past and its human dimension. It is thus difficult to see *The Crimean Sonnets*, as Koropeckyj does, as "the desiderata of the empire's 'civilizatory' mission for its Muslim colonials."[54] The history of this part of the world acquires an autonomous value in the quoted sonnet 6 ("Bakhchiserai") rather than a relative one (in other words, one measured with reference to the lyrical subject's native context). As a result, this history prefigures the experience of destruction that was likewise the fate of the poetic subject's homeland, as the reader learns from Mickiewicz's other works. The specific bond of shared experience thus forms between the Orient, which the Pilgrim makes an effort to understand, and the Occident, to which he belongs by virtue of genealogy. Both spheres—Crimea and the European homeland of the lyrical hero—are symmetrical at this moment, and both are equally important.

Such instances in Mickiewicz's cycle throw into question the charge of the poet's cohesive orientalizing stance suggested by the previous analysis. This leads to the conclusion that in the masterful artistic construction of *The Crimean Sonnets*, which creates "such a tightly fused whole that nothing can be added or subtracted from it anymore," nevertheless there exists some rupture—fundamental but difficult to grasp.[55] It has been the aim of this inquiry to point out this internal indecisiveness, which pertains to the lyrical subject's attitude toward the human dimension of the world that constitutes the object of his description. It transcends the two semantic planes that are key to the cycle: "the situation of tourism" and the wandering "in a country of one's own individuality"; situated in their deep background, it is a factor that arranges the meanings evoked on both planes.[56] Taking into consideration the dual signals given off by *The Crimean Sonnets*, the lyrical subject's stance can be characterized as oscillating between reluctance to engage with the actual realities of life in Crimea and admiration not only for the absolute perfection of Crimean nature but also for the devastated and forgotten Crimean culture. This culture still shows traces of its former glory but now inclines the lyrical subject (and reader) toward mournful empathy and philosophical reflection over the impermanence of human creations. It is possible that the mentioned reluctance to engage with both the Crimean world and its civilization stems from a sense of their foreignness.[57] Such speculations are left unresolved by Mickiewicz's cycle, which highlights the existence of equivocal and controversial places within this text. An ethical reading of the work requires that these places be respected for their heterogeneous and divided significance rather than be tied to a consistent, homogenous sense.

The ambiguity encountered in *The Crimean Sonnets* needs to be explored to find the reasons behind it and determine its general character. The following hypothesis can frame that effort: confronted with the exotic space of Crimea, its inhabitants and their actual status quo, the lyrical subject is torn between the felt imperative of empathy and a sense of this attitude's inappropriateness due to the order of discourse that frames and silently influences the development of his lyrical story. The strategy of exclusion ultimately chosen in *The Crimean Sonnets* constitutes the consequence of Mickiewicz's own situation as the work's author and as a poet with a complex and multifaceted identity. On the one hand, the lyrical subject, who functions as Mickiewicz's *porte-parole*, himself belongs to a nation conquered by an empire: he and his implied compatriots are in an analogous situation to the Crimean populace, which inspires a search for traces of a possible awareness of a similar historical fate and of empathy for the Other's experience. On the other hand, the subject of *The Crimean Sonnets* arrives in the Orient equipped with structures of perception and categories of understanding proper to the Western European orientalizing discourse. Since he moves mostly within its limits (transgressing it at times), he is predisposed and entitled to play the role of an orientalist writer. (In this context, a significant theoretical problem arises that cannot be fully developed here: To what extent can a writer overcome these conditions and predispositions and oppose the orientalizing discourse, and to what degree is he its prisoner, and perhaps even victim?). To top it all off, his utterances are the record of negotiating between the two positions indicated here—positions that define his own ambiguous identity in the context of an encounter with Crimea.

In asking about the reason, or reasons, for this exclusion, it is necessary to remember that the Pilgrim is a subject whose own status limits his freedom of artistic expression. He has already accepted the conditions of the discourse of the Russian hegemon, which obligate him to formally pass over in silence the nature of the Russian presence on the Crimean Peninsula along with its implications. This claim needs to be taken as a necessary hypothesis since it is prerequisite to further interpretive questions. If it is accepted, then it should also be acknowledged that in *The Crimean Sonnets* we are contending with a structural limitation of the possibility of subordinated discourse. Following this line of reasoning, the traces of the Other's textual existence noted above can be read as an attempt to articulate the aporia that permeates the entire sonnet cycle and that can be summed up in the paradoxical formula of "absent presence." From this angle, the rhetoric of omission and of concealment through silence that leads to exclusion in the end would be a compromise that serves the construction of an artistic representation, as well as the ultimate limit of the discourse of the colonized, who are represented by the poet exiled from his own homeland. This framing of the issue leads to the conclusion that Mickiewicz's text, which in principle bypasses the Others in silence, nevertheless points to them subtly and indirectly, as it finds itself unable or unwilling to fully express the trauma of the Russian occupation. From this perspective, Mickiewicz's text is more than a work of an orientalist's nimble quill. Despite all of the previously presented reservations and doubts, the artistic imagination behind *The Crimean Sonnets* does not belong to an obedient or diligent eulogist of the empire. Instead, Mickiewicz's cycle constitutes a poetic attempt at doing justice to what is "local" within the limits established by the orientalizing discourse. In a form of a compromise, the sonnets testify to letting otherness speak and to respecting the subjectivity of the Other within a framework permitted by worldviews of the time.[58]

In the end, Mickiewicz's Crimea as embodiment and metonymy of the Orient is as awe inspiring, indeed bewildering, in terms of its natural dimension as it is unclear and aporetic in terms of its position in relation to the lyrical subject, who represents an antithetical, Western world. This duality provides a mirror reflection of the position of the subject, which is likewise ambiguous, with the subject assuming a set of diversified roles in *The Crimean Sonnets* that prompt the process of its self-definition in relation to the Orient's otherness, both consciously recognized and intuitively sensed. This perception of Crimea as the oriental Other is a reaction to difference and likely the inevitable result of an intercultural encounter, not only in the nineteenth century, and it impacts the forms and rules of Crimea's literary representation: its space, environment, history, culture, and life at that time. It reduces Crimea's present almost exclusively to images of ruins—signs of the past. It sets into motion the mechanism of redefinition and modification, in consecutive parts of the cycle, of the subject's own stance toward the realities of the country he visits, which enter the represented world of *The Crimean Sonnets* not in their entirety or multifacetedness but in pieces, glimpses, and fragments. This specific kind of filter, which allows some semantic signals through while blocking others, is evidence of the choices made by the Romantic poet based on the repertoire of discursive practices available during his epoch. The principle that governs the effect of this semantic filter on textual representation is a challenge for interpreters. Its functioning is the reason why the world of Mickiewicz's Orient is characterized by ambiguity: on the one hand, it excludes almost entirely the human element; on the other, it cannot be entirely inscribed within a model orientalist discourse since it respects only some of its norms while transgressing others. The foreignness of reality as experienced by the lyrical subject of

*The Crimean Sonnets* is triumphantly transcended in relation to the natural environment (meaning it is tamed, "conquered," and possessed by him) with the help of suggestive poetic figures of speech. When it comes to the world of people, however, the cycle leaves the contemporary reader uncertain and divided, a state that seems to characterize the equivocal relation between the lyrical subject of the poems and the world that they reveal. For reasons presented herein, even after two centuries, Mickiewicz's masterpiece inspires various, often conflicting, readings while constantly raising new questions.

Chapter Seven

# Identity as an Object of Inquiry

## (Paweł Huelle's *Castorp*)

Hailing Paweł Huelle's novel *Castorp* in 2004, Polish critics often compared it to Thomas Mann's *The Magic Mountain* and looked in it for traces of Mann's characters and leitmotifs, including the narrator, philosophical discussions of the epoch, reflections on sickness and death, the experience of time, and, first and foremost, the "figure on loan."[1] The book itself seemed to invite these types of interpretations. Successive layers of the work's palimpsestic structure were thus peeled away to reveal its allusions and references to other source texts, literary genres, and musical forms.[2] Simultaneously, critics underlined the difficulty of the task undertaken by the Polish writer in using *The Magic Mountain* as an intertext.[3]

There exists in literature a fashion of writing either sequels or prequels to existing canonical narratives. It is the kind of apocryphal tradition that Huelle's novel certainly falls within. I do not intend here to follow the path already well trodden by critics, however, and compare the work of the Gdańsk-based author with that of his German predecessor in order to assess the prequel's success. I also will not pursue the trail already taken up in many reviews of *Castorp* and search for elements of a coming-of-age story, a philosophical novel, a "postcard" from mythical Gdańsk, and so on. This journey goes in a different direction. For the situation in Huelle's *Castorp* is to some extent reminiscent of that which moved Jean Rhys to write *Wide Sargasso Sea*, a novel that "answers back" to the narrative told by Jane Eyre in Charlotte Brontë's famous romance.

The reconstruction, or rather deconstruction, of Bertha Rochester's fate in Rhys's work is contrapuntal in relation to its prototype in Brontë's narration, where her character is repulsive and almost entirely stripped of human traits. Rhys's Antoinette Cosway (for such is Bertha's actual name in *Wide Sargasso Sea*) attains the status of a literary protagonist who offers a counterpoint to Brontë's version of her biography by narrating it from her own, non-British point of view. It hardly needs saying that, while both stories come to an identical end—the madness and suicidal death of Antoinette (a.k.a. Bertha) in the fire at Thornfield Hall—what occurs beforehand belongs to different orders. Rhys *writes back* to Brontë, with "writing back" understood not only as a reply but also as an independent act of speaking up, of becoming independent from a dominant discourse and its canonical version of the story, in accordance with Salman Rushdie's famous postcolonial formula.[4] "Writing back" describes the work of writers from former colonies who, by referencing the metropolitan literary canon, enter into a polemic with the image of the peripheries established therein; they unveil aspects that were left unarticulated by the dominant discourse and problematize them in ways that call for the critical reconsideration of both these works and their interpretations in term of power relations entrenched in the canon.[5]

The reader of *Castorp* is dealing with a phenomenon that is, in some respects, analogous. While Huelle's manner of narration is strikingly similar to Mann's, and therefore not as clearly contrapuntal as *Wide Sargasso Sea*, the Gdańsk episode of Castorp's life nevertheless explains the specific perspective from which the protagonist perceives his new surroundings and his own place within it.[6] This perspective has the marks of postcoloniality, and it is here that the similarity of relations between the novels of Rhys and Huelle and their respective intertexts is located. However, I position Huelle's novel as "writing back" not just to Mann's work but rather to the entire discursive field in which it is situated: an assembly of symbols and worldviews inscribed in numerous nineteenth- and early twentieth-century texts of the German literary canon, which will be discussed further in due course. Within this assembly, an important role is played by the "East," which is understood less as a purely geographic category than as an imagined object of German imperial aspirations compensating for the lack of overseas territories and the proximate goal of expansion realized by political, military, economic, and demographic means.[7] Theodor Fontane's novel *Effi Briest*, for instance, which Huelle's protagonist references, is located within this discursive field. Far from being a misappropriation, therefore, the use of postcolonial theory in the analysis of *Castorp* opens up intriguing perspectives on the novel.

When *Castorp* is viewed from this perspective, its meanings emerge from a series of transgressions that go beyond the typical colonial narrative.[8] In a typical narration, the specific distribution of characters' roles, goals, and actions is requisite and rests on established hierarchies of races and skin color, and social positions and roles. These hierarchies determine the logic and order of story elements, the means of representing what is "native" and what is "foreign," and the choice of what to include in as well as exclude from the work. These factors constitute the ideologically and axiologically marked rules that govern the represented world of colonial narratives. In Huelle's work, these rules are transgressed on four levels: space, language, identity, and literary genre.

## Space

Frantz Fanon has thus described the specificity of space appropriated by the empire:

> The zone where the natives live is not complementary to the zone inhabited by the settlers. The two zones are opposed, but not in the service of a higher unity. Obedient to the rules of pure Aristotelian logic, they both follow the principle of reciprocal exclusivity. No conciliation is possible, for of the two terms, one is superfluous. The town belonging to the colonized people is a place of ill fame, peopled by men of evil repute. The colonized man is an envious man. And this the settler knows very well; when their glances meet he ascertains bitterly, always on the defensive, "They want to take our place."[9]

Indeed, Gdańsk in *Castorp* is not just "a cultural melting pot, already provincial and living off the remnants of its Hanseatic glory, ever more undermined by increasingly apparent contradictions."[10] It is a city with a complex history in which Polish, Kashubian, and German cultural elements coexist, intersect, and blend or compete. Seen through the eyes of the novel's protagonist, the city aligns with the criteria of literary representation of a colonized space identified by Fanon. It is a realm saturated with and dominated by Germanness, which not only sets the key orientation points of urban and suburban scenery but also hermetically fills them in. Following in Castorp's footsteps, we move among Prussian barracks, a German academy, and a sanatorium for German patients, encountering German students and hearing the German language in every corner of the buildings and the city. The local population constitutes an enclave pushed to the margins of the novelistic universe—it occupies strictly defined regions and does not mix with the dominant population: "The Kashubians and Poles, whom he could not tell apart by language, were like a grey layer of earth: long since buried under the cobblestones, it only occasionally revealed its existence in places assigned to it for centuries.[11] Castorp's perspective has a typically colonial footing. Within it, the city constitutes a heterogeneous realm with fundamentally disjunctive spheres and impenetrable boundaries. Along with his compatriots, Castorp belongs to the territory of dominance, which also includes a select few educated representatives of the subjugated population (such as Dr. Ankewitz, a.k.a. Anke), while the Polish and Kashubian populace inhabits the peripheries of the represented world.

Huelle's Castorp does not stop at exploring the city; he derives his most powerful aesthetic stimulus from excursions beyond its limits. On those hikes, he blissfully contemplates the foreign landscape, with the narration referencing specific topoi that are recognizable to Polish readers. This staffage is constructed with the use of images that are deeply ingrained in Polish cultural discourse: weeping willows, a stork in a meadow, a birch copse. In Huelle's novel, however, they are part of a configuration that departs from their standard—identifying and emotive—functions. They are no longer the emblems of Polishness, since Castorp, whose perspective the narrator adopts, is unable to recognize the identity trope within them. They are simply the normal objects of a young man's rapture. As such, they underline his dominant position and their own defenselessness in relation to him, soliciting, so to speak, their discursive appropriation and subjugation. They seem to exist only to provide the metropolitan center's representative, who is cultured and sensitive to beauty, with aesthetic satisfaction. Gdańsk and its vicinity, which Huelle's novel recreates with subtlety, possess traits of otherness that allow the Germans to view them on a par with the exotic regions of German colonies in Africa.[12]

Castorp's admiring perspective on the Polish landscapes he discovers aligns with the orientalizing approach explored by Said. The relation of the subject to the object of observation is marked by fascination, but this fascination is of a conqueror who, through an epistemological act, carries out a symbolic appropriation of an exotic territory that stimulates his imagination. The areas explored by Castorp and his peers from the nationalist youth organization Wandervogel (from which the protagonist quickly distances himself) are presented as wild, deserted, and untouched.[13] This creates the impression of virgin territories waiting to be taken possession of.[14] Franz Schubert's song "Das Wandern," which the protagonist sings during one such excursion, symbolically seals this act of appropriation. The song is more than an artistic response of the sensitive young man to nature encountered in the Pomeranian province. The work of the brilliant Austrian composer from the Romantic period becomes the most appropriate textual instrument for expressing Castorp's experience of contact with the ethnically Polish and Kashubian natural environment. Interestingly, his friends resort to an analogous act when they sing, in a similar situation, the song of another Romantic poet—Joseph von Eichendorff's "Wer hat dich, du schöner Wald (aufgebaut so hoch da droben?)" (Who made you, you beautiful forest [built you so high up there?])—to the music of Felix Mendelssohn-Bartholdy. Both Castorp and the stalwart German boys from the Wandervogel patrol find themselves unable to contemplate the foreign landscape on its own terms. They do it by relying on the works of German Romanticism, enfolding the local space in the conceptual framework of the empire's cultural discourses. In appropriating the territory, this discourse simultaneously "appropriates the means by which such acts of appropriation are to be understood" and in doing so "effaces its own mark of appropriation by transforming it into the response to a putative appeal on the part of the colonized land."[15] This only underlines one of the central dichotomies of colonialism: nature is the domain of the periphery, while culture belongs to the metropolis. Art is thus presented as no longer innocent; instead, even the apparently insignificant act of singing in the bosom of nature engages it in a symbolic appropriation of an ethnically non-Germanic territory.[16]

The significance of space for the postcolonial interpretation of Huelle's novel is already revealed in its exposition, which establishes the epistemological perspective that provides the intellectual support of the represented world. This perspective is determined by the interaction of the Occident and the Orient, signaled in the novel's opening dialogue between Consul Tienappel and Castorp. Huelle is, of course, directly indebted to Thomas Mann here. The latter's work contains after all images and emblems of the East (suffice it to mention the enigmatic figure of Clavdia Chauchat from *The Magic Mountain* or the Polish boy Tadzio and his family from the poignant story *Death in Venice*, congenially translated into film language by Luchino Visconti) and subtly conveys the tension of encounters between Western subjects and representatives of the secretive Eastern world.

The archive that fills out the background of the representation of an intercultural encounter in *Castorp* is not limited, however, to Thomas Mann's opus. It encompasses a more extensive tradition of Western European orientalism:

> Along with all other peoples variously designated as backward, degenerate, uncivilized, and retarded, the Orientals were viewed in a framework constructed out of biological determinism and moral-political admonishment. The Oriental was linked thus to elements in Western society (delinquents, the insane, women, the poor) having in common an identity best

> described as lamentably alien. Orientals were rarely seen or looked at; they were seen through, analyzed not as citizens, or even people, but as problems to be solved or confined or—as the colonial powers openly coveted their territory—taken over.[17]

The Germans also had their orientalism. Its discourse encompassed, among other things, lands located beyond the empire's eastern border and neighboring territories already included in it, and it has identical or similar characteristics to those quoted above.[18] As early as at the onset of the novel, the reader enters the very core of this type of discourse. The opinions of Uncle Tienappel on Castorp's intended studies at the Gdańsk Polytechnic demonstrate convictions typical of the colonial point of view, where "the East as such" was not meant to obtain "top marks" (1). Equipped with the authority of the oldest family member and his expert knowledge on the subject of world relations, the consul gives his young relative instructions in advance of his trip to Gdańsk. Within the novel's reality, the city plays the function of a settlement colony in the conquered periphery; it is an imperial enclave protected, admittedly, by the garrison, but located in a place only partially tamed and civilized; a sojourn here carries a certain risk, akin to dangers that awaited the British who went to India or the Caribbean or Africa. Castorp's destination, according to his uncle's argument, is a dangerous and unpredictable space for a Western subject, a place where "manners forged so painstakingly might plunge into chaos" (2). Among the warnings given to the protagonist, elements characteristic of the *polnische Wirtschaft* rhetoric within German discourse are interwoven with universal myths of temptations and dangers that the unsuspecting newcomer encounters in the "near" Orient and that literatures of imperial powers abound in: "Consider, please, how easy it is to stray from one's chosen path. A meaningless word, a moment of weakness, an instant of forgetfulness can destroy many years of effort. In the East these things happen more often, although there is no rational justification for it" (5).[19] The prediction contained in this warning is completely fulfilled in Castorp's life. As the reader finds out in the course of the narration, the protagonist succumbs to the East in its most representative figure, which is so often exploited in imperial texts—that of a tempting woman perfumed with the sensual fragrance of musk, who after the first accidental meeting in a sanatorium appears in front of the hero as if in a dream, with her "gently protruding cheekbones, combined with a special, slightly capricious air about the mouth, gave her face exotic allure, a sort of ambiguous, appealing foreignness" (106–7).

Colonialism in *Castorp*, however, is not reducible to performing the orientalizing discourse, having at least two other aspects that must be considered to understand the postcolonial connotations of the novel. The first encompasses the realities of Huelle's represented world, which are enclosed in veiled structures of colonial dependence that govern the plot. This is accompanied by conceptualized thematizations of the colonial question realized in the form of characters' monologues or relevant subplots introduced by narrator's comments. The reader thus meets Pastor Gropius, who "after two decades among the blackest tribes of Bantustan" (10) received an offer to take over a congregation in the provinces closer to the metropolis, namely near Gdańsk, as well as the Dutch merchant Kiekiernix, who—while on a cruise sipping rice vodka imported from China, which was by then already probed by Western colonial powers—kindly informs his fellow passengers of Gdańsk's peripheral status ("a squalid, provincial hole, as proved by the fact that there was no decent theatre there" [11]). The same Kiekiernix who describes Europe mired in local conflicts and rivalry over colonial influence in territories abroad as a "cesspit" (21) also initiates Castorp into the secrets of the true, meaning *colonial*, source of the wealth of nations, namely the "millions of slaves" (19). A Protestant cleric, in turn, delivers a speech in defense of German imperialism, legitimating it with the civilizing mission—the universal argument of the proponents of the colonial project. The rhetoric of this mission replicates tropes present in assertions of British and French authors and politicians from nineteenth and early twentieth centuries: "We have been late in reaching Asia and Africa, indeed. But in the east of Europe? For hundreds of years we have brought law, order, the harmony of art and technology. If not for us, the Slavs would long since have fallen into anarchy. It is thanks to our benefaction that they have found their place in the family that bears the name of civilization and culture" (20).

Kiekiernix's answer is strikingly similar to arguments of anti-colonial activists. It is worth quoting at length, since on an ideological level it determines the direction taken by Huelle in the rest of his narration:

> Just imagine, one day an armada of foreign, Indian or Chinese ships docks at Amsterdam. They order us to worship their god, they kill our king, rape our women and force the men to work in their mines or on plantations. Syphilis, smallpox, pneumonia, cheap liquor and opium do the rest. Afterwards their preacher tells us to thank them for the care, thanks to which we are now in the family of civilization and culture. That is exactly how the Indians, Asians and Blacks feel nowadays. (20–21)

To this list one may add Kashubians and Poles. The opinion of the Dutch merchant can be treated as an argument, provided by the novel itself, for embedding its plot in the sociopolitical realities of the early twentieth century. This situates the plot in a broader context of artistic conventions and rules of representations that typified Western European writing of the colonial era. This is the extent of Huelle's respect for the rules of mapping the space that were set by the colonial discourse. In *Castorp*, the reader is simultaneously dealing with the transgression of orientalizing clichés of spatial construction. What are the signals of this transgression?

For the novel's protagonist, the Prussian presence in Gdańsk is an unpleasant burden embodied by Mrs. Wybe, the widow of a Prussian officer. Castorp's attempt to venture beyond the limits of urban space during the above-mentioned excursion is only partially successful, since it is interrupted by an accidental and unwelcome meeting with his countrymen. His outsider's attitude does not fully explain the mode in which other Germans operate within Gdańsk's unique setting. Castorp, who in the end becomes an understanding liaison between the two spheres—German and Kashubian—distances himself from his kinsmen, especially those who represent a chauvinistic Prussian mentality.

Castorp strolls the streets of Gdańsk and of the neighboring resort town of Sopot (Zoppot) in a spirit of discovery. Despite his youth and a certain philosophical naïveté (he has not yet met Naphta, who will trigger his desire to seek out answers to weighty questions), he is enriched through his contact with a conquered culture, thus differing from his prototype from *The Magic Mountain*. Huelle's Castorp gets to know the subjected culture of Poles and Kashubians through German eyes—those of a colonizer still unaware of his nation's historical and political role. His acquisition of insight into his own identity and growing awareness of belonging to a nation that imposes an imperial hegemony in East-Central Europe is a significant, albeit very subtly interwoven, thread of the narrative fabric that impacts the novel's interpretation.

The decolonization of space in *Castorp* is accomplished also by means of toponymy. Although the narrative develops from the viewpoint of a German protagonist, in the Polish original (unlike the English translation) German names are substituted with Polish equivalents, as exemplified by cities (Gdańsk instead of Danzig; Sopot rather than Zoppot, as was the case in Stefan Chwin's novel *Hanemann*), suburbs and neighborhoods (Oliwa, Orunia), and streets (Kasztanowa in lieu of Kastanienweg). The novel displays a space that, on the one hand, is and *wants* to be German (a claim supported by the German names of hotels and ships and terms such as *Kurhaus* rather than "sanatorium"), while on the other manifesting its inherent foreignness, unintelligibility, and mysteriousness, epitomized by the uncertain, impossible to identify localization of the building that hosts participants of the erotic and narcotic orgy. This space exceeds Castorp's reach; as a result of the intrigue that he becomes involved in by having Wanda followed (when she is still a mysterious, unknown woman), it expands and extends into other realms of the non-existing Polish state, such as Warsaw and Lublin, which Castorp has to look up on Russia's map in his atlas.

## Language

In light of the above remarks, the statement "We only speak German here!" (122) can be seen as emblematic of the position of language used by the novel's characters. In *Castorp*, the German language fulfills an analogous function to that of the English language in British colonial novels: it points to symbolic violence and domination.[20] It is the language of the administration and of communication between characters, regardless of regional differences that are scrupulously caught by the protagonist's ear. It is also the language of power and thus an instrument of oppression: its contamination is met with resistance motivated by the purist stance represented by imperial officials. For this reason, the Polish accent of the clerk, which is derided by his social circle, pushes his pity-inducing figure to suicide, while Dr. Ankewitz, a Polish exile from the Russian partition, can practice psychiatry not only because he is the protégé of Polish landowners "scattered about the three monarchies" (132), but primarily because of studies completed in the metropolis and his excellent knowledge of the German language.

The hegemony signaled by means of language is sometimes undermined in the novel, however. The normative status of the German tongue is first undercut during Castorp's encounter with a local boy who is, in fact, initially presented in line with the directives of colonial representation: the ragged child with "bare feet shod in flimsy sandals" (53) is a typical representative of a "native" part of the city, and he remains unnamed, stripped of individuality, his identity uncertain.[21] Despite his inherent inferiority, however, the boy bests the protagonist with his linguistic competence, as Castorp becomes painfully aware in the course of their conversation. In a colonial novel, such a confrontation would likely meet with a comment about the civilizational retardation, or primitiveness, of the incomprehensible rustling Polish speech or else with praise for the Prussian educational system fulfilling its phantasmagorical civilizing mission by imposing the colonizer's language of knowledge and science on the purportedly undereducated local people.[22] Huelle's hero does not succumb to triumphalism, however, nor does he adopt a superior tone. He does not view what he encounters in the peripheries in terms of a "distorting mirror of *modernization* or, otherwise put: a *treasury of modernizing deficits*."[23] To the contrary, he reflects on the odd sensation of not having "access to something that to others seems as plain as day" (54). This statement reverses one of colonial discourse's basic premises, namely, the epistemological competency of the subject, which affirms its authority and consequently gives it power over the object of cognition.

The supremacy of the German language in Huelle's novel is also undercut by the relations between Frau Wybe and her female Kashubian housekeeper. The character of the Kashubian (named Kaszibke in the Polish original) is interesting from an anthropological perspective and breaks with the colonial stereotype so often utilized in imperial narrations, where figures of servants and slaves sourced from the subjugated population, and thus located on the lowest rungs of the social and ethnic/racial hierarchy, are consigned to silence and obedience.[24] The Kashubian can be seen as a vivid illustration of the recovered voice of the "subaltern others," to paraphrase Gayatri Spivak's famous formulation.[25] The Kashubian, playing the role of a servant girl in a German house, reverses the traditional relation of dominance with her behavior, which reveals the diligently concealed "underside" of colonial relations—the colonizer's dependence on the colonized. Admittedly, Frau Hildegarde Wybe teaches the girl to play the piano using suitable rhetoric, which fulfills her cultural mission and simultaneously realizes one aim of the colonial project. At the same time, however, she gives in to the Kashubian in everyday household tasks, which the astounded Castorp does not fail to note. The housekeeper takes the liberty of raising her voice to her employer, and her simple but emphatic language and determined, self-assured gestures are indicative of the power that the servant wields over Frau Wybe. This reversal of the relation of subjugation at play here symbolically undermines the supremacy of the metropolis. The conclusion drawn by the widow when justifying herself to the protagonist, that "it was all different in Berlin" (62), acquires a particular significance from this perspective. The Kashubian's character reveals the ambivalent effect of colonization: the servant is a mirror reflection of the colonizer, but a reflection that is distorted and caricatured, adulterated and as a result ominous for the colonial order imposed on the periphery. As a representative of the colonized population, the Kashubian is a challenge to the colonial authority personified in Frau Wybe, acting to destabilize its dominance over the conquered. The resulting fissure in the relations between both parties of the colonial encounter points to the mimicry as defined by Homi Bhabha: the colonized copies the behavior of the colonizer, yet this reproduction is never total, carrying within it mockery as well as a threat.[26]

The third transgression of the linguistic parameters of colonial narratives, which operate on the basis of refusing to give the subordinated population the right to its own authentic voice, is tied to the figure of Wanda Pilecka. The mysterious Polish woman exists fully as a subject in the novel. She is presented as a partner in conversations held freely in various languages. She sits at a shared table vis-à-vis the protagonist, and her remarks at times perplex him. She speaks with her lover in French, with Castorp's sensitive ear also detecting a foreign note here, which initially makes his identification of Pilecka's nationality more challenging, leading him to the incorrect conclusion that she is Russian. When they connect directly over a meal, they converse in German; the protagonist detects a foreign accent as well in this case, "somewhere right at the bottom of the words," although as he himself admits "not necessarily a Polish one" (210). We thus arrive at another key issue in Huelle's novel—the sense and awareness of one's identity.

## Identity

In *Castorp*, identity and related issues of belonging and loyalty to one's own community are presented via a series of ruptures and transgressions of the order of colonial discourse. The hired detective's discovery that Wanda is Polish comes as a surprise to Hans Castorp. It is only more surprising to discover that her lover is a Russian officer, a revelation that disturbs Castorp's clear and unequivocal image of Polish-Russian relations built on knowledge of Polish history acquired in a German school. The protagonist thus begins to grow aware of the limitations of the discourse to which he had been unwittingly subject up until now, bound by Foucauldian structures of knowledge and power reproduced by metropolitan institutions. He discovers that his cognitive horizons do not extend beyond the frameworks of imperial education:[27]

> In history classes at school he had had one lesson about Poland: the anarchy and drunkenness of the nobility had led to the partitions, because the cancer in the middle of Europe had to be cut out as soon as possible for reasons of hygiene. (211)
>
> Herr Stelling, the geography teacher at his school, had lectured on many lands and exotic races, but had never once mentioned that on the eastern borders of the state there were such people as the Kashubians. (28)

Castorp is largely unaware that his cursory acquaintance with the now Prussian periphery of Poland and its ethnicities, limited to a handful of stereotypes sprinkled with disdain and perpetuated in part by the German educational system, is the outcome of imperial history and geography. Based on the information at his disposal, it is not difficult to guess which books were part of Castorp's German education. The opinions about Poles and Polish political history cited above are a part of Castorp's metropolitan résumé and include theses proclaimed by Leopold von Ranke and other German historians in the service of imperial ideology.[28] It is also conceivable that the protagonist's childhood and early adolescence involved family study of the *Conversations-Lexicons* by Brockhaus and Meyer, a custom in nineteenth-century middle-class German households.[29]

This knowledge, which was initially collected, systematized, and disseminated by imperial scientists and officials to justify the *Drang nach Osten* and subsequently passed onto the protagonist, is presented in the novel as an element in the discourse of power. With its help, this discourse categorizes reality and segregates it into two spheres, with one of them (German) representing civilization, culture, and progress, and the other (Polish-Kashubian) presented as the domain of primitivism, barbarism, and backwardness. The first claims the role of the sole vehicle of reason, goodness, and beauty, in this way perversely transforming the myth of a disinterested transmission of cultural values; the second, in turn, is placed in the position of an immature and passive recipient dependent on the benevolence of the first side in its actions. Castorp lives in a world structured according to this fundamental opposition without being aware of it at first. His mode of thinking is saturated with concepts formed under the influence of orientalism that "explained the behavior of Orientals supplied Orientals with a mentality, a genealogy, an atmosphere; most important, they allowed Europeans to deal with and even to see Orientals as a phenomenon possessing regular characteristics."[30] Only an encounter with the aforementioned cases of canceling the monopoly of colonial discourse makes a dent in Castorp's uncomplicated worldview, opening onto other axiological and cultural systems than the one instilled in him as the only proper and viable system.

In terms of its protectionist attitude toward objects of description, Castorp's inherited epistemological warehouse of concepts, ideals, and values is close to that gathered and perpetuated by British and French scholars, writers, and travelers relating to the conquered peoples. It consists of historiographic, anthropological, and ethnological information delivered in accordance with the code of orientalizing discourse. This code "shares with magic and with mythology the self-containing, self-reinforcing character of a closed system, in which objects are what they are *because* they are what they are, for once, for all time, for ontological reasons that no empirical material can either dislodge or alter."[31] Backed by the authority of science and viewed as professional and competent, this knowledge, as Said argues, never produced a neutral, disinterested description of the colonized people. What is more, it does not *need* their realness but eliminates, substitutes, and makes it redundant. The cognitive perspective, entangled in the situation of a colonial encounter, is harnessed to the mechanism of perpetuating the rule of the metropolis over the periphery and its inhabitants even when this is accomplished solely by the soft means of discourse, for example, with narrative techniques.

Castorp's cognitive situation on arrival in the *Ost*-colony places him amid a defined repertoire of discursive practices characteristic of the (not only) German colonial discourse at that time, derived from the myth of the "noble savage."[32] Among others, these practices include idealization, aestheticization, exoticization, and eroticization of the indigenous population.[33] Not infrequently, these practices coexist within a single text. This also seems to be the case in Huelle's novel, where they participate in ordering the elements of the plot as well as play a stylistic function, introducing indicators of a colonial narrative into the work. Is this where their role ends, however? Does *Castorp*, in terms of its discursive practices, simply copy the artistic models of European colonial writers? Answers to these questions can help define the eponymous character's point of view and in whose name he speaks, as well as determine what type of overarching formal structure is at work in the novel. There is also a reason to think they would be helpful in interpreting Huelle's novel as a contemporary work of a Polish author situated within a specific historical, cultural, and geopolitical order.

The idealization of "savages" has a long history in the European tradition that goes back at least to Michel de Montaigne's time and his essay *Of Cannibals* (1580). The practice, however, does not mean breaking with the Western point of view through the rejection of the European value system with its inherent racial differentiation and its more or less latent sense of superiority. On the contrary, it is realized by projecting what is Western onto "the savages." As such, it does not affirm them in themselves while preserving their inherent "wildness." Rather, by introducing "alien" elements to their identity, this practice disfigures them, rendering them idealized—a representation far from realistic. In the texts of writers and travelers, the Other becomes subsumed, so to speak, into the Western value system. The subject who narrates this otherness remains within the limits of its own culture throughout the intercultural encounter, without crossing the foreign culture's border and authentically entering its realm. In a colonial text that employs idealization, the Other serves to "expand the territory of Western imagination," as a result of which its representation becomes another form of "Western culture's dialogue with itself."[34]

The practice of aestheticization in colonial discourse, in turn, is the subject's textual means of coming to terms with a foreign reality perceived as culturally, and often also aesthetically and ethically, distant. The aesthetic stance helps to overcome the disgust that arises in the observer at the sight of local poverty, and it is accessible to the Western subject because of the latter's particular position of authority: "The power to perceive poverty as aesthetic value is a privilege not granted to the poor."[35] It is a luxury that the hegemon can afford in order to hide within the safe walls of a discourse, which separates him from the realities and concerns of the conquered peoples' life.

What is Huelle's attitude toward these techniques of discourse construction? The exoticization of images of the periphery and its inhabitants plays an important role in the novel, as has already been demonstrated. The case appears different for idealization. Rather than the author's approval, the reader encounters a polemic with this practice in the novel. The "Oriental" Other is consistently depicted as possessing its own sovereign mystery, a mystery to which the protagonist is denied access. If the strategy of idealization as defined above can be applied here, it is so only in a fragmentary form, in the context of the Other's aestheticization.

The strategy of aestheticization comes into play in episodes where the protagonist observes behaviors that are in some way characteristic of the local population. In this way, these behaviors are separated from and elevated above their original basis in "normal" native life. Such is the case, for instance, with the young Kashubian woman that Castorp meets during one of his walks. He becomes aware of her presence when he hears the song that she sings while working, which elevates the girl's simple existence to an aesthetic level in his eyes. The description of an intercultural encounter, given by a representative of "civilization," modifies the dry and detailed style of an "ethnographic description." As a result, the protagonist reinterprets the behavior of the "object" with empathy and in categories that exceed the standard framework of colonial discourse, opening a space for the construction of the Other's subjectivity:

> The girl had fetched a basket full of fish from over the side of a fisherman's boat, and was carrying it inland across the wide beach, propping the weight of the load on her right arm. Her bare feet squelched into the sand at every step, her linen skirt hampered her movements, and her headscarf, which seemed to be tied too tightly over her hair, was slipping onto her brow, obscuring her vision. Despite, or maybe because of this, the girl was singing with joyful abandon, as if the entire drudgery of existence did not concern her at all. (101–2)

Also worth mentioning is an incident in which the discursive practice of aestheticization is utilized and then reversed. On a train to Zoppot, Castorp surreptitiously reads a local paper held by another passenger, with his attention caught by the news of a brutal murder of a German employer perpetrated by two Poles. He finds out about the event in a mediated and transformed way, in other words, separately from the reality that was its basis. The article, written from the German point of view, is in the style of an expanded *fait divers*. It is distinguished, however, by the rising tension and modulation of mood that turns the trivial occurrence into a mini-story with an electrifying effect on the reader. Castorp, who is a stable, cultured, and well-brought-up young man, after all, reacts surprisingly strongly to the text, with the intensity of his sensations comparable perhaps only to those aroused by the erotic plot developed in the course of the novel. The difference between the stimuli is clear, however: Castorp's perverse fascination is provoked by a crime story rather than by a woman. The aestheticization is reversed by statements made by Castorp's travel companion, who plays a double role in the subplot; he is the observer and interpreter of Castorp's emotions and the author of the *fait divers*'s existential interpretation. It seems that the scene, secondary to the story line, serves one end: it reveals the discursive mechanism of transforming the real world and neutralizing its terror through integration into the order of a quasi-literary story with a simplified, schematic structure ("the natives kill the master"). It is concluded, in turn, with a gnomic commentary of the co-passenger on the subject of "savages" that upholds and simultaneously rationalizes the dichotomous division of colonial reality: "Give them a hand and they will grab you by the throat!" (110). This caveat leads to the final reversal of the effect of aestheticization: what was once the subject of an ordinary story in a newspaper is violently inserted into reality, creating the impression of an immediate threat.

The strategies that shape the characters' identity are integrated into the novel's narrative but certainly do not play a central role in it. They appear here and there, dispersed seemingly to be subverted by a style of presenting "otherness" that radically breaks away from traditional forms of colonial representation. They function as an overture to what constitutes the main goal of events—cognizance—as well as the means for achieving it.

In *Castorp*'s narrative a German perspective is made dominant. It is against this horizon that the reader perceives what is foreign, different, and other. The author ensures that the reader views reality through the eyes of the main character and understands it through the prism of his experience. Hence, the acquisition of knowledge can be considered to be the main theme of the novel. For this reason, the evolution of the hero's consciousness, whose point of view becomes constitutive of the reader's perspective, is crucial to the postcolonial interpretation of the work. Castorp's deeper understanding of Poles draws them out of nonexistence; it leads from their initial idealization and aestheticization, dictated by the protagonist's perspective, and toward their emancipation, which transpires on the level of the novel's representation. As a result of this process, which takes place under the surface layer of story events, Poles acquire a subjectivity in Huelle's novel that is inaccessible to them in narrations such as, on the one hand, Gustav Freytag's *Soll und Haben* (Debit and credit, 1859), which depreciates and debases Polishness, and—on the other hand—Nataly von Knobelsdorff-Brenkenhoff's *Polnisch Blut* (Polish blood, 1887), an idealizing romance written under the pen name Nataly von Eschstruth.[36]

As already mentioned, the meeting of Hans and Wanda is the turning point of the novel. It takes place in two dimensions: real and imaginary. The protagonist gives in to erotic fantasies on the subject of oriental beauty, which highlights the orientalizing aspect of the theme of an encounter between "the woman of color and the white man."[37] Here, Huelle again appears to call on colonial narrative models, in which this type of fantasy confirms on the symbolic level the "male" domination over the explored "female" territory—vulnerable, virgin, unknown, and open to penetration. The writer accomplishes this in a perverse way, however, so that the traditional polarization of power is reversed, as a result of which the woman's subjectivity is reinforced while the position of her would-be lover is problematized and jeopardized.

As previously stated, Wanda is presented in the novel as an embodiment of an oriental seductress. Taking into account the European tradition, within which Huelle's narration is located, her character plays a role analogous to the Tahitian heroines from Diderot's *Addendum to the Journey of Bougainville* (*Supplément au voyage de Bougainville*, 1772), who tempt the newcomers from the Old Continent with their mysterious, exotic beauty.[38] Wanda does not go as far as they do, however: although she ignites an uncontrollable flame of passion within the protagonist, which she is aware of, her behavior is not inappropriate in a way that could provoke the transgression of the moral code norms with which Castorp was raised. What is telling is that this violation happens in the novel within the scope of metropolitan authority, so to speak, in an institutionalized form, in the building of the "Omphalos" Society for Lovers of Ancient Culture, which lends a peculiar character to the transgression. The location conjoins in itself the traits of a Western European, elegant, middle-class brothel and of an Oriental harem. In trying to understand the specific experience with which he met there, Castorp observes that sexual arousal at the peripheries of Gdańsk is stimulated with impulses unachievable either in the metropolis or in the homes of Prussian settlers typified by another of the novel's characters, Nicholas von Kotwitz. These impulses stem from voyeurism, which is linked with breaking the cultural code that is requisite in "civilized" brothels, where a separation between what is intimate and what is public exists. The location of the orgy in the "wasteland" (150), which is a frequent attribute of a colonized space in travel journals and literature, seems to play a symbolic function: it is there that young Germans and Prussian Junkers from Gdańsk give vent to their desires and wildest erotic fantasy without any inhibitions. Noticeable here is an analogy to schematic colonial representation, in which descriptions of Asian peripheries abound in scenes of unbridled sex.[39] These scenes center on an object of a specific kind of perception that is rooted in the view of the imperial subject unable to establish a true connection with the autochthonic population. Such images were meant to suggest the "natural" sexuality of these places and their inhabitants' immorality, which stem from colonial geography and impact even the most virtuous of the metropolitan arrivals. In this manner, the code of colonial narration utilized by Huelle includes in its scope a set of meanings related to the psychosexual behavior of voyeurism.[40]

This code, however, has a referential function in Huelle's narration. It is a narrative strategy used by the author to evoke the grand European literary tradition in order to transgress it and to undermine its epistemological usurpations from a postcolonial position. The irrational actions triggered by sexual excess are played out in the space of the periphery, but they are not initiated by the "natives," in contrast to the narrations of G. Flaubert, H. M. Stanley, or T. E. Lawrence, where the locals infect the colonizers with their promiscuity.[41] To the contrary, these actions are an *import* from the metropolis: an import provided with attractive scenery (admittedly not as colorful as that of the Middle East) by the periphery. In introducing this motif into his novel, therefore, Huelle simultaneously reevaluates its semantics and backs away from developing it in the direction of cultural antagonism.

The episode played out in the house of ill repute does not serve to saturate the novel's mood with a widespread, oriental lust in the spirit of libertinism (as is the case with the oriental novels of Flaubert analyzed by Said, which abound in explicit sexual references). It should not be seen as a tribute to the colonial narrative tradition but rather as the linchpin of two independent, up until this point, storylines—Castorp's and Wanda's—that is significant from the perspective of plot construction. It is within the edifice of the "Omphalos" society that Castorp first glimpses the "mysterious Russian woman" whose Polish identity he will discover only later. It is not entirely clear, furthermore, whether her presence there is actual or Castorp's hallucination. What is certain is that Wanda appears before Castorp in her casual attire only to vanish into thin air and that her appearance and behavior are not characteristic of a harlot, in contrast to those of the remaining women, who are dressed for the duration of the intoxicating night as ancient goddesses, Bacchantes, and nymphs. Is it the Orient, embodied in Huelle's novel in the space between Gdańsk and Zoppot, that gives free rein to the instincts of the gathered guests, which are otherwise carefully hidden in the corset of civilization? Does it provoke transgression—the removal of masks imposed by a culture that is a source of such pride for the Germans in the novel? Huelle's narration does not unequivocally settle this issue. The reversal of the typical colonizer-colonized relation, wherein female promiscuity is the exclusive trait of autochthonous women of color who tempt innocent white men, is nonetheless telling. In Huelle's novel, Castorp is tempted through other channels. The eroticization of the beautiful female stranger follows from the protagonist's idealized and aestheticized view of Wanda. This perception dictates that he situate her outside of the sphere of trivial and base motives that govern the rest of the guests. Going forward, the erotic dreams that Castorp, fixated on otherness, indulges in, lead to an ever greater loss of his contact with reality. His life in the Polish province becomes ever more reminiscent of a drug-induced frenzy, in which the vision of an inaccessible woman who pulses with eroticism haunts her admirer and brings him to the brink of a psychic breakdown:

> That was when the dreadful days had set in. He had sunk deep inside himself, like falling into a bottomless well, unable to find any support. The long periods of sleeplessness had exhausted him so badly that he had no strength to go to his classes. As a result he was not eating any lunches, just breakfast and supper. Sometimes, when he did manage to get to sleep, he was haunted by images of the strange girl, lascivious and shameless as she tormented him on the beach at Zoppot or in a room at the Hotel Werminghoff. (155)

The distance toward models of colonial narration notwithstanding, the Polish-Kashubian "Orient" in *Castorp* is nonetheless marked with eroticism. It is characterized as a place of sexual adventure, with the ephemeral and sensual Wanda Pilecka becoming the central object of desire for the protagonist. Her figure is not of the world known to the protagonist, and it not only awakens strong feelings within him but also breaks out of the epistemological matrix that Castorp arrived with in Gdańsk.

Pilecka is a representative of a nation whose colonization seemed justified, even useful, to Castorp in the light of the education he received in the metropolis. Despite her ethnic background, however, she becomes elevated to the status of the protagonist's partner. Admittedly, this role is more suggested than actually performed, as the erotic thread in the story ends without fulfillment. Nevertheless, Wanda's position in relation to Castorp is sufficiently strong to speak of their complete symmetry, if not her superiority. Pilecka offers a glimpse of her life story to Castorp, and she does not lose her dignity or become dependent on him in thanking him for the offered alibi. To the contrary, she dominates him, unsettling his stable, middle-class life first as the hidden and mysterious "obscure object of desire," at times almost Buñuelian, and subsequently as a mature woman who ends their acquaintance with an elegant but decisive gesture. The novel's erotic subplot that brings Wanda and Castorp together concludes ambiguously: on the one hand, it strains the stereotype of how their respective nations perceive each other, while on the other hand it reinforces one of Poland's foundational, pre-Christian myths—that of the legendary Princess Wanda who refused to marry a German prince.[42]

For Hans Castorp, the Polish woman is an encoded text that he cannot decipher but that demands repeated hermeneutic operations by its very presence. Like the Queen of Sheba in Flaubert's *The Temptation of Saint Anthony*, she could say "I am not a woman, I am the world."[43] The book that Castorp spontaneously steals from her and expects to be "like a mysterious, inaccessible tome from the magical East" (127) turns into her metonymy; it not only stirs up fascination but also requires decoding to be understood. In the protagonist's eyes, the mythical, esoteric book and the mysterious woman, as imagined as she is real, overlap to create a coherent world of fantasy. The scenario he dreams up appears to be coming true: Wanda initially seems to be willing to agree to the young man's acquaintance. She does so only to ostentatiously "close the book" before him, however, leaving him to carry images of her sexually alluring body.

This type of representational technique implies a specific role of the protagonist in a colonial narration. Indeed, Castorp does not remain indifferent to the Polish woman's charms. His stubborn efforts to establish close contact with her can be seen as a sign of the male desire for conquest. This desire, however, meets with a resistance and transforms into a mystery, which opens for the protagonist regions of knowledge inaccessible to him and outside of colonial discourse's control—knowledge that could be granted to him only through identification with Polishness. Yet Hans Castorp will never possess Wanda Pilecka, and not because she is an embodiment of virtue but because he himself undergoes a symbolic castration in the course of the narrative. He is emasculated, stripped of his male potency, and weakened in his position as a representative of a dominant discourse. The confrontation of the two characters within the plot can be treated as a symbolic collision of a female discourse as a form of subordinate discourse with the dominant male discourse, the discourse of the empire, a collision that secures subjectivity for the "weaker" female voice and in so doing gains the upper hand over the voice of the metropolis.

## Literary Genre

Castorp's unfulfilled desire to become the Polish woman's lover, and his implied emasculation, add one more melodic line to the postcolonial resonance of the work. By transferring dominance from a German male figure to a Polish female figure, Huelle engages in a play with the *Ostmarkenroman* model of German imperial narration—a hybrid novel form about the German presence in the "eastern marchlands," which combines elements of a colonial novel with a regressive utopia typical of literature of "little homelands" (*Heimatliteratur*). Thanks to the colonial questions and the racial and spatial tropes of colonial ideology, this genre supplied propagandistic argumentation for the German civilizing project in the Polish province.[44] Novels of this type usually featured a young, inexperienced German man who, under the spell of erotic obsession with a seductive Polish woman, falls into a state of inertia, throws away his career, and is defeated, submitting himself to a woman of the "near Orient."[45] His misfortunes are a warning to readers of the contamination that relations with representatives of the "lower" Slavic race lead to: "In the imagination of the *Ostmarkenroman* authors, it is the marriage between a German man and a Polish woman that represents the greatest danger, for within the domestic parameters established by this relationship, the Polish woman is able to gain a powerfully assimilating agency."[46]

In the colonial discourse conducted by means of this genre, subalterns, presented as inherently inferior, uncivilized, and subordinate, are not only below the colonizers in social hierarchy but also incapable of overcoming their ontological defect without external intervention, as a result of which they are stigmatized and permanently subjugated. In the represented world of an *Ostmarkenroman*, determined by this axiology,

> marriage would not serve as a viable option solving political/colonial tensions in the Eastern borderlands [of the German empire]. According to Kristin Kopp's work, most of these novels tended in fact to use the topic of marriage, normally to a Polish woman, to underline the threat against

> German cultural values. German men were portrayed as victims of the Polish national cause, which used the Polish women to emasculate them. These novels coincided with an emergent discourse in the sciences of racial degeneration—addressed particularly by the then recently established *Rassenhygiene*—that was common at the turn of the century and that would target especially women in the experts' quest to culturally and biologically uplift Germany. In this context, the "horrors" of mixed marriages, so universal in the overseas colonies, were being echoed in the descriptions of German-Polish national struggles.[47]

This context also provides a complex reference point for the represented world of Huelle's novel. What implications does it have for interpreting the relationship between Hans Castorp and Wanda Pilecka along with its conclusion? Taking into consideration the ideology of the *Ostmarkenroman* current in German prose and its historical emergence at the turn of the nineteenth and twentieth centuries (which is when Huelle's protagonist undertakes his studies at the Danzig Polytechnic), Castorp *should not have been* thinking about the possibility of close relations with the Polish woman. The author, who meticulously reconstructs Gdańsk's historical climate as well as the customs, mentality, and intellectual atmosphere of the epoch, must have been aware of this literary tradition.

Tracing the evolution of Castorp's consciousness is significant for the postcolonial interpretation of the novel. Huelle provides him with a biography that underlines his identification with the metropolis. Theodor Fontane's novel *Effi Briest,* which Castorp takes from Wanda in secret, evokes memories that echo the imperial myth: "His own life, growing up in the shadow of harbor cranes and ocean-going ships, the stock exchange, world business and colonial goods, suddenly seemed to him a blaze of light in comparison with the ruts in a sandy road in Pomerania" (127). Castorp travels from a region where civilization, power, capital, and prosperity create a harmonious alliance to a periphery where these goods are confronted with other values, thus far unknown to him, discovering them in part through his encounter with the mysterious female stranger.

Until Pilecka's appearance in the story, Poles are almost unseen in Huelle's novel. They are treated incidentally: Castorp and his closest circles are German, and the exotic people of the East are basically contained in a colonial, dichotomous vision of the world; they do not present an above-average threat to German presence. When they are introduced into the plot, it is in accordance with the rules of colonial discourse that has as its aim the construction of the image of "the colonized as degenerate types on the basis of racial origin, in order to justify conquest and establish systems of administration and instruction."[48] The murder mentioned above of the German goldsmith by his Polish apprentice and his fiancé inscribes itself seamlessly into this paradigm.[49]

The colonial discourse replicated in *Castorp* can thus be evaluated in categories of the naturalization both of the Other and of the process of domination, meaning the finding of "natural" rationalizations for the conquest of lands and their inhabitants—"nature's children."[50] In this process, which is first reconstructed and then exposed on the novel's postcolonial level, the conquered people were, on the one hand, identified with the order of the natural world, which was subjected to the civilizing mission (culture taming nature). On the other hand, the realities of the subordinated population, rendered by means of colonial narration, were presented as the actual state of affairs—obvious, self-explanatory, and transparent, constituting an element of the environment that is invisible to the main protagonist. Along with the protagonist, the reader initially accepts this order, together with the structures of thought and the value system concealed in it. This initially accepted order is subsequently questioned in the light of the narrated events, which leads to the exposure of the actual character of the colonial organization of the world, starting with its epistemological usurpation and suppression and silencing of otherness.

The mysterious Polish woman and her equally enigmatic Russian lover introduce a "Polish-Russian tangle" (212) into the story, which broadens the protagonist's political horizons and shifts the narration onto a postcolonial level. Subconsciously, Castorp starts deconstructing the imperial codes with which he was equipped. In effect, he discovers the identity of the colonized and examines his own opinions on the subject and reflects—as a result of this experience—on his own identity. Huelle positions his hero in relation to people and situations that cast doubt on the canonical image of the continent's historical and political map, as formed under the influence of colonial discourse. The Orient in Huelle's novel, represented by these characters and places, is an evolving symbolic construction within which the protagonist moves from the initial warning about the Other toward fascination with and desire for the Other. This desire also evolves from its initially purely sexual basis to eventually reach the sphere of identity. In pursuit of its fulfillment, Castorp reaches a new level of consciousness that revises the worldview he held up until then. He becomes aware of the illusory supremacy of German discourse—in its colonial aspect—over its subject, and the discovery that he belongs to the nation of colonizers provokes his distaste, rather than pride or satisfaction. The process of acquiring this awareness is a significant element of narrative construction. It culminates on the final pages of the novel with the symbolic gesture of Castorp's rejection of both German and Russian imperialism: confronted with both discourses, respectively represented by a lecture on Goethe and a textbook for the study of Pushkin's language, he demystifies them and pointedly refuses to participate in the project to which they subscribe.

It is now clear that Huelle's novel also transgresses another Western European genre—the coming-of-age story, or the novel of formation.[51] In a classic bildungsroman, which belongs to "one of the most beautiful traditions in the history of narrative literature," the question of the relationship between the metropolis and the periphery is interwoven with the process of maturation and initiation into adult society.[52] The key elements of this type of a novel, beside "the maturing of the hero [and] the broadening of his intellectual, emotional, and moral horizons," also include his departure from home, often via a journey from the provinces to the metropolis, as a result of which he gains the necessary experience that subsequently makes up his nonmaterial, symbolic capital.[53]

If Castorp's later biography known from *The Magic Mountain* is set aside, the Polish prequel to Thomas Mann's novel only partially fulfills this genre model, and it does so only to ultimately undermine it. The dilemmas faced by the eponymous protagonist, his way of thinking and acting, his choices and hierarchy of values and goals, do not fit the parameters of a classic bildungsroman. Admittedly, Castorp leaves his home in Hamburg after a conflict with his uncle and as a result of the undertaken journey learns, develops, and matures intellectually, emotionally, and in terms of life experience. He travels in the opposite direction, however, from the center to the periphery, and his education culminates in an awareness that radically transforms the formative aspects of his journey. His experience up until then, necessary from the point of view of the generic requirements of the bildungsroman and based on a progressive model of social and individual development, undergoes a fundamental reevaluation. As a result of this modification, the hero changes from an unknowing representative of the colonial project into its fervent opponent. Castorp's initiation into adulthood leads him to distance himself from his compatriots and to side with the subordinated people, which constitutes a remarkable departure from a classic colonial narrative. Instead of reconciling with his society and earning its respect for his achievements, as imposed by bildungsroman poetics, Castorp feels a sense of alienation from his own community. This provokes his anger and rejection of both German and Russian imperial actions, which—as the narrator's closing comment reminds us—lead to totalitarianism. This anger and refusal to participate result from the encounter with the periphery, which is key to the hero's development. Contact with otherness that is presented from multiple angles becomes a lesson that inspires Castorp to independent, critical reflection on a double theme: the morally suspect nature of the colonial project and the subjugation of the conquered population. The maturity that he attains in the process allows him to expose the flaws in the model of a modern colonial society promoted by the ideology of the Western European novel of formation. On the basis of the novel's epilogue, it can be surmised that Hans Castorp's world will never be as stable and cohesive as bildungsroman poetics require. Huelle's modification of the genre is telling. In *Castorp*, the topos of progress and development that suggests the possibility of limitless individual activity, realized since the times of Enlightenment in part by means of the novel of formation and inscribed onto the grand narrative of colonialism, is demystified.

❧❧❧

The direction of interpretation pursued here leads to the conclusion that Paweł Huelle's *Castorp*, despite its formal referencing of a relatively distant literary tradition and, on an objective level, its recreation of the early nineteenth-century atmosphere in Gdańsk and Europe, along with the intellectual trends and social and moral climate, is ultimately the product of a twenty-first-century literary and political consciousness. Huelle deftly exploits the narrative strategies of colonial discourse; since *Castorp* imitates this discourse only to a degree in order to enter into a polemic with it, the result is a series of raptures and transgressions. Consequently, the reader is presented with a postcolonial novel: a novel that deconstructs colonial narration, that could only be written in an era of decolonization, and that perhaps is even inspired—for this cannot be entirely excluded—by postcolonial thought. The narrative strategies deployed by Huelle counter the thesis that Castorp, "in relation to Mann's prototype, rather follows in his footsteps: solidifies and supplements his portrait from the sanatorium than foretells anything of the future to the twentieth century."[54] The novel's concluding post-history (*Nachgeschichte*), presented in a form of snapshot scenes recalling Gdańsk's twentieth-century history, with its occupations and traumas, confirms that the Gdańsk episode from Hans Castorp's life is told from a specific reference point, accessible only to a writer of an epoch that began after the dismantling of first the German, then the Soviet colony in that part of the globe. In light of this conclusion and against the background of other postcolonial literatures that utilize the language of former empires, the fact that the novel was written by a Polish author is thought provoking.[55] One can therefore hope that, along with critics' enthusiasm about the language of the novel and Huelle's rendering of the climate of Gdańsk and Sopot at the turn of the twentieth century, this aspect of *Castorp* will also be noted by readers of its German and English translations.[56]

Chapter Eight

# The (East-)Central European Complex

## (Andrzej Stasiuk, *On the Road to Babadag* and *Fado*)

Andrzej Stasiuk has been called "an incorrigible partisan of Eastern European provincialism, which he traces passionately in the most peripheral regions of the Carpathians in two best-selling travelogues: *On the Road to Babadag* (*Jadąc do Babadag*, 2004) and *Fado* (2006)."[1] Stasiuk, whose style has been compared by critics to that of Jack Kerouac, is known for his fascination with the European Orient—Eastern Europe—and aversion to the Occident—Western Europe. Given the dominance of pro-European sympathies in post-1989 Polish society, his position is surprising and provocative, and it can be seen as a kind of regression and contestation of European civilizational ideals. What are the reasons behind these idiosyncrasies of Stasiuk's worldview?

Stasiuk's readers discover multiple signs of contemporary postcolonial societies within both these travelogues: the trauma of foreign hegemony, the burden of economic underdevelopment, pessimism, and passivity. These are only some of the components that constitute the complex, or rather an entire network of complexes, that these societies are trying to overcome. These complexes relate to East-Central Europe's sense of inferiority toward the West, which existed as a mythical place for East-Central Europeans during the entire Communist period: an oasis of carefree life and economic prosperity, the object of envy and aspirations both open and concealed. A reversal of this main, Western vector of cultural orientation in Polish mentality and literature is consistent with a contemporary and global postcolonial trend.

From this perspective, Stasiuk is a writer who contests the West in a manner similar to those of writers from other parts of the postcolonial world. Does it mean that Stasiuk offers this rather than another vision of the world simply because he is following a trend?

Stating that Stasiuk's narrations have long revolved around Central and Eastern European issues strikes a formulaic chord. The Slovenian Vilenica International Literary Prize that Stasiuk received in 2008 was a sign of recognition both of the place post-Soviet, post-totalitarian, and postcolonial East-Central Europe occupy in his work and of the promotion of this location in other parts of the continent and beyond it. The Austrian State Prize for European Literature, awarded to him in 2016, was the first such prize to be given to a Polish writer after the demise of Communism.[2] In a brief statement delivered on that occasion, the Austrian minister of culture Josef Ostermayer emphasized that Stasiuk is a writer who "always takes a stand on current political challenges in Poland and in Europe, and who in a resounding and eloquent voice commits himself to democratic values, such as media diversity and opinions in his homeland."[3] His statement is a clear indication that, as a writer, Andrzej Stasiuk has become internationally recognizable as a spokesman for matters related to Poland as well as the broader region of Eastern Europe, and he enjoys the attention of readers both inside and outside literary circles. He certainly does not shy away from expressing his opinions about his homeland, including political ones, to foreign (usually German) media and skillfully uses his ethnicity as a means of amplifying his voice.[4] In an interview given to Gerhard Gnauck, for instance, Stasiuk identified some of the impulses that run beneath the surface of his prose and—in so doing—one of the more significant motifs in his writing. "I fear Germans and Russians"—he admits with uncompromising honesty—"I look down at them and I admire them. Perhaps that is the fate of Poles: obsession about their own position in Europe and the world. Being a Pole means life in total isolation."[5]

Stasiuk's confession can be seen as emblematic of his work. It defines the position from which he views the "new" and the "old" Europe and indirectly also himself, his compatriots, and societies, nations, and ethnicities with whom he identifies or stands in solidarity. His disdain mixed with admiration for the former (actual or surrogate) hegemons is not a symptom of a split personality or indecisiveness.[6] Ambivalence of this kind is characteristic of attitudes held by people subjected to foreign domination regardless of their geographic location. In East-Central Europe, like in other, non-European postcolonial populations, "attitudes towards western countries are, indeed, a mix of desire and resentment, a negotiation, an ambivalent hybrid."[7] In his work, Stasiuk traverses the spectrum of these attitudes, clearly delineating its polarities of desire and resentment. Let us look at them more closely.

One effect of colonization is that the colonizer, who is equipped with a power not only physical but also, or rather primarily so, discursive (for, as a Japanese proverb states, the tongue is more painful than the sword), becomes indispensable to the self-definition of the colonized, functioning as their "Other." The process of this self-definition does not end with political decolonization, however. It is here that postcolonial theory can prove useful by supplying categories that help to recognize and describe the complex mechanisms that govern a population under foreign domination (in the sphere of the individual and the collective psyche, as well as in social life and culture). The discourse of the empire, which encompasses all of the hegemon's cultural practices aimed at the colonized, impacts the formation of ideas and social relations in a way that necessarily has long-term consequences that are difficult to eliminate quickly. The "decolonization of the mind," which is requisite for a truly sovereign and agentive functioning of people liberated from the yoke of colonial dependence, relies not only on accounting for their own individual and collective experience but also on reevaluating the structures of attitudes and relations that have become deeply ingrained in individual and collective memory. Chief among them is the sense of "inferiority" that is the natural mental and cultural consequence of long-term foreign domination. It is precisely this complex that Stasiuk gives voice to when speaking about the supposed "fate" of Poles, meaning their collective self-obsession and the isolation that stems therefrom.

Yet it is not only Poles who are condemned to isolation and loneliness in Stasiuk's work. Almost all of non-Germanic Central and Eastern Europe suffers from these illnesses and is presented by the author as uncertain of its existence and constantly seeking self-affirmation from others—the political organisms and ethnicities deemed more stable than itself. Stasiuk's East-Central Europe is a region without a future, doomed to remember the past and to transform it into myth—"a circular narrative"; it is only in the mythologized past, he seems to say, that this part of the world can find justification for its own existence.[8] The imperative of memory finds a crude expression in the author's declaration, "Screw where we're headed, I'm interested only in where we came from."[9] He makes the same point more subtly in *Fado*: "The past and memory are my homeland and my home" (122). The difference is only one of rhetoric, however. Figuratively speaking, "future tense narration" has no place in Stasiuk's Europe, for "what kind of story can be patched together in a language whose grammar has no future tense?" (24). Moreover, it is a region that fears not only the future but also the present. For victims of historical discourse, distrustful of history and pushed to the sidelines by it, the only way to compensate for the suffering they experienced is to retreat into memory—their "private history." Stasiuk's prose articulates this type of resentment of the victimized. As will become clear, however, this is a unique kind of a return and a uniquely understood history—a history that, in fact, does not exist.

This is one possible reason why in Stasiuk's vision of the European East "the present imperfect tense" rules and reality continues in a state of suspension, inconclusiveness, and decay. These characteristics apply not only to represented reality but also to the narrative order of *On the Road to Babadag*. The author seems to reject the organizing category of time, the fundamental idea of (Western) European ontology underpinning its interpretation of reality. The resulting narration, both in terms of its subject matter and the means of structuring its discourse, does not wish to owe anything to Western culture.

The issue of representation is key in Stasiuk's transnational travelogues.[10] Traveling through "his" Europe, the author observes only one kind of a person in its villages and towns—the men who stand on street corners, passive if not vegetative, suspended in inertia and torpor—and he extrapolates this psychosociological model to entire societies. It is not just that the figures he encounters neither have influence over their fate nor possess any such ambitions; their very ontology is defined by their lack of creativity and faith in even a scant possibility of forging one's own destiny. The situation is no different in Poland. After returning to his homeland, the narrator admits, "I had no sense that I was returning from somewhere" (*B*, 251). Individual, political, social, and economic subjectivity, manifested in the free, sovereign, and creative activity of societies not burdened with the experience of colonization, is subject to deformation in *On the Road to Babadag*. In Stasiuk's work, East-Central Europe's inhabitants are almost without exception losers. Admittedly, they are depicted with a large dose of empathy, as characters heroic for their time, but their heroism is the heroism of acquiescence to victimhood. The author's presentation of Central Europe's past and present is overwhelmingly pessimistic. "The story of change in this part of the continent is, after all, the story of failure" (*F*, 64)—declares a sentence from what is nearly the middle of *Fado*, in parallel with the centrally placed observation from *On the Road to Babadag* "that everyone is playing at being something other, each according to a private notion of a world not here" (120). Who is the source of this pessimism—the author or the people of Central Europe whom he encounters? This is, in fact, a false dilemma, since the two cannot be separated. Regardless of whether Stasiuk speaks in his own name or acts as spokesman for ethnic communities with which he solidarizes and that fascinate him (with one of them being his own), those familiar with postcolonial thought will recognize the clear notes of Eastern European resentment in his voice.[11] The greatest paradox of his prose is the direction that this resentment takes, for Stasiuk aims it not at the former Soviet hegemon but at the whole of the European West. In so doing, he emulates the gesture of postcolonial writers and critics from former British colonies engaged in the discourse of "provincializing Europe."[12]

Stasiuk questions whether an authentic European community can exist in contemporary times. "Is it possible to merge two streams of history that have flowed separately alongside one other for so long?" he asks rhetorically (*F*, 78). His verdict sounds harsh: the Western world does not need the "younger" Europe. Given this mentality, the unity of a continent secured by bonds stronger than feeble economic links and a motley thread of pop culture is unthinkable. Stasiuk is clearly a representative of the East, which is so vividly polarized with the West in his autobiographical and essayistic stories. His narrations, in turn, constitute an East-Central European testimony as well as a literary response to the deep asymmetry in the history of the continent along with its related discourses. Paradoxically, after 1989, this asymmetry has led to further alienation of the region and the impossibility of it finding understanding in the "West," which breeds frustration and a lack of self-acceptance among Eastern European populations. Stasiuk's above-cited phrases, such as "history of failure" and "a world not here," convey well both the East-Central European mental climate in which those who were recently colonized now live and the writer's opinions on issues of the subcontinent, with its past, present, and future. The following declaration from *Fado* is illuminating: "We hate 'now' and 'here,' and we love 'elsewhere' and 'at another time,' up to the moment at which one and the other actually arrive and become a hated present. We've never been able to accept ourselves as we are" (65). These kinds of opinions are repeated like a refrain in postcolonial societies. For members of these societies, literature provides an important forum for dealing with the residues of their colonial past.

Geography is a decisive factor for the image of the East European subcontinent in Stasiuk's narrations, as critics have often noted. The space, which was first shaped under the influence of Habsburg domination, which was indeed gentler, though not entirely innocent, and later by destructive Soviet domination, organizes the East-Central Europe of today and defines the register of dilemmas that plague the inhabitants of the territories traversed by Stasiuk. The most striking characteristic of the places encountered during Stasiuk's quasi-ethnographic and mental expeditions is the fluidity of their borders, the blurring of contours and the lack of distinction between this space's particular zones. It is a space that forms a very strange unity stripped of significant distinctions. To be sure, the countries and ethnicities it includes bring some individual features to the subcontinent's portrait, but they are not individuated to a degree that conveys even an approximation of their cultural and historical diversity, distinctiveness, and specificity. Instead of a profusion of differences, we encounter the same attributes everywhere: backwardness, dirt, slovenliness, chaos. Yet it is precisely diversity, to recall Milan Kundera's argument from his memorable essay, that forms the region's Europeanness, even Westernness: "the greatest variety within the smallest space."[13] Stasiuk radically reformulates this conceptualization. He neutralizes the differences and substitutes the Latin idea with the idea of a fundamentally anti-Latin East, which admittedly differs from Russia but also lacks ties to the West. Whereas Kundera considers "Westernness" a fundament of East-Central European identity, Stasiuk discredits the identity thus defined. He sees the occidental sentiments of the region as symptoms of an unsuccessful and harmful mimicry rather than of integrative aims and perceives the indifference toward twentieth-century upheavals of the continent's eastern regions as an argument in favor of rejecting the kind of Europe that the "West" creates.

This does not mean that Stasiuk engages in whitewashing the Eastern ex-hegemon. There is no sympathy toward Soviet Russia in his work or traces of Russophilia. Stasiuk judges Russia to be (and to have been) barbaric and uncivilized—a representation with a long tradition in Polish discourse, though this tradition does not seem to interest the author. In *On the Road to Babadag*, Russia exists only sporadically on the edges of the represented universe and is excluded from European space. The "East" that actually draws Stasiuk's attention is made up of countries located vertically to the west of the Russian metropolis and to the east of the German center.

Stasiuk's stance, however, does not bring him closer to Kundera's view. The Czech writer confronts the East, embodied in the figure of a Russian/Soviet hegemon, with the West, where he locates East-Central European nations. The Europe in Kundera's essay, that "vast seat of modern Western culture," is still capable of the heroic effort of asserting its kinship with the West: "Boxed in by the Germans on one side and the Russians on the other, the nations of Central Europe have used up their strength in the struggle to survive and to preserve their languages. Since they have never been entirely integrated into the consciousness of Europe, they have remained the least known and the most fragile part of the West."[14]

The case is different for Stasiuk, although not because of his distance toward Kundera's idea of Central Europe. The sense of uncertainty that typifies East-Central Europe forces the Polish writer to exclude this terra incognita from the Western realm. It is essentially a repetition of Europe's rejection of the East at the time of the Soviet takeover. In distinction to Kundera, Central or Eastern Europeans in Stasiuk's work do not feel European. To the contrary, they are painfully aware of their own foreignness, detachment, and alienation. They might as well have spoken the words that were uttered in an entirely different part of the world and within the context of a literally understood Western European colonial violence: "Leave this Europe where . . . for centuries they have stifled almost the whole of humanity in the name of a so-called spiritual experience. . . . We today can do everything, so long as we do not imitate Europe, so long as we are not obsessed by the desire to catch up with Europe."[15] Is Stasiuk some kind of a Slavic Frantz Fanon?

While the revolutionary stance of the Algerian intellectual is rather foreign to the Polish author and Fanon does not show even a modicum of Stasiuk's irony, the forcefulness of many of Stasiuk's formulations is not just a matter of rhetoric. Instead of reflection on the possibilities for maintaining the ties between Eastern and Western Europe, we find postulates of an intellectual secession in Stasiuk's work that do not lose their ideological edge even when marked by mockery or an ironic distance. The problem of an unbalanced, uncertain identity among postcolonial societies of Stasiuk's Europe is put forth in a declaration that leaves no question as to its author's stance: "It's hard for us to regard Europe as a whole as something that belongs to us, as our homeland, our inheritance. We are strangers in it; we come from outside, from lands about which Europe itself has only the vaguest notion and which it treats more like a threat than as a part of itself" (*F*, 73). As Stasiuk's use of plural personal pronouns in this quote shows, the author casts himself, à la Fanon, in the role of his compatriots' spokesman. A sense of rejection and marginalization reappears constantly in his work. Entering the European space comes at the risk of losing one's own distinct identity, which was formed under the influence of historical experiences, of disappearing under a layer of "cosmetics" applied by Western, postmodernist pop culture:

> We emerged from nonexistence before we were able to find ourselves a form, a character, an identity precisely; but it turned out that we didn't need to do even this. It's enough to take on the grotesque gestures of contemporary mass culture for us to be instantly absorbed into the universal community of individuals living, playing, suffering, and experiencing emotions all in exactly the same way. (*F*, 86)

The image of a looming threat from the West (which recalls the anti-European arguments of Russian Slavophiles) serves as compensation for feelings of alienation and as justification of the hesitation and the grimace with which East-Central Europeans enter Europe's salons and in their mirrors see their deformed reflection.

Given his clear lack of sentiment for the West, where does Stasiuk look for the link between "his" Europe and the rest of the continent? He seems to follow Fanon's quoted appeal and say, "Let's turn our back on Europe." The problem with this attitude is not only that "his" Europe *is* a part of the Europe that he wishes to turn away from. Its other problematic aspect is that Europeanness understood as a set of values is inscribed onto the East and Central parts of Europe in a way that is perhaps not irreversible but certainly long-lasting enough to allow for the reconstruction—based on these values—of the displaced (or else lost) East-Central European identity.

Andrzej Stasiuk would likely object to having his writing included in a discourse that formulates and assigns these types of questions and tasks to literature. He ostentatiously denies others the right to query the category of East-Central Europe in the context of his work and emphasizes this category's foreign, political, or even imperial character:

> For me, there is no Central Europe, only the place that I drive around. . . . I do not need a Central Europe. It is a German term, a cultural and political one. For me, it means the place where I drive a car and all is cool. . . . Since the unfortunate book *Two Essays on East-Central Europe*, I have never consciously used this term.[16] I do not wish to take part in this adventure. I keep getting invitations from around the world to speak about Central Europe. You can twist yourself into a pretzel, not even five thousand euros can get me to go! This is simply my space. It is my border space, my space abroad, my imaginary space, but it has nothing to do with the Central Europe of Kundera, Miłosz, or whoever else.[17]

It is not difficult for Stasiuk, an anti-Kundera by choice, to thus contest the cognitive frameworks that are imposed on Central Europe to systematize knowledge about it in a way consistent with established categories.[18] Separation from the main traditions of reflection on Central European identity is a gesture of refusing to participate in the discourse that displays, as Stasiuk believes, hegemonic aspirations—or at the very least consents to them. This gesture seemingly reinforces the sovereignty of not only the author but also the subject whom he addresses in his own tongue. Stasiuk does not wish to have a hand in the discursive appropriation of the region by the West, which happens both directly and via the work of Central European intellectuals and writers. He also manifests an aversion to becoming embroiled in a discussion about the "Europeanness" of the territories he traverses (and where he lives), although in expressing his attitude to this issue he inevitably takes a specific position on it. The coordinates of this position can be reconstructed by recalling his earlier opinions. Despite a recognizable rhetoric, it is not entirely original and does not deconstruct the dominant tradition of thinking about East-Central Europe; to the contrary, it confirms the prevailing set of stereotypes about it.

Stasiuk counters the Germanic, imperial idea of Mitteleuropa and the alternative concept of "Central Europe" as a community of cultures with Latin roots, with an image based on a specific reincarnation of the Slavic myth.[19] This myth corresponds to the orientalizing tendencies that dominated Western Europe during the Enlightenment with respect to other nations, primarily Near Eastern ones but also those of the multiethnic Polish-Lithuanian Commonwealth that had been colonized by Prussia. Stasiuk represents these populations using a series of stereotypes that emerged via Western European discourse. According to these popular assumptions, Poles are "drunken and prayerful" ("pijani i rozmodleni"), Romanians unpredictable, Ukrainians "half-wild" misogynists, and inhabitants of the Balkan region destructive (*F*, 75). In weaving self- and heterostereotypes into his work, even in the form of patronizing citations borrowed from the Western European discourse, Stasiuk becomes an inadvertent hostage of the optics that Larry Wolff describes in his work on the textual appropriation of Eastern Europe by Enlightenment's philosophers, travelers, and writers.[20] Discourse about this part of the world overlooked important differences between its inhabitants, turning a diverse populace into a monolithic, passive, and primitive mass at the mercy of the modernizing Europe.

The perspective offered in *On the Road to Babadag*, *Fado*, and some of Stasiuk's other books, including *Dziennik okrętowy* (Logbook; 2000) and *Wschód* (The East; 2014), is similar in some aspects. The author demonstratively rejects interest in high culture and in historic cities, and in their place rehashes the myth of Eastern Europe's primordial, rustic, and inherently folk culture, which is untouched by "the refinements of Western civilization" and supposedly distinct in its features from the "elitist," Latin culture of West European nations.[21] This myth takes the form of the rather unsophisticated pseudo-anthropological category of a "Slavic pigsty" (*B*, 170; orig. "słowiańskiej rozpierduchy").[22] Its cult allows Stasiuk to feel at home wherever chaos, disintegration, and fetor supposedly rule, and people are seen as resigned and inert (and at stake here is the expansive area from Poland down to Albania, which is not limited to the Slavs). Interestingly, however, this feeling of identification disappears in Slovenia, which overcame the postcolonial suspension between the past and the present and in so doing betrayed the "Slavic ideal." In Slovenia, Stasiuk feels "a barbarian from the unwashed, unfinished east" (83). Characteristically, with the exception of Ljubljana, he does not attempt to "praise the cities of Central Europe" while "on the road to Babadag."[23] This is not only because tourist narratives as a type are of no interest to him.[24] Stasiuk bypasses the metropoles with their historical monuments with premeditation (his fleeing the "hopeless Budapest" [48]) will likely enter the annals of Polish-Hungarian literary relations), for he sees them as synonymous with the despised West, as its poor imitation, and as an unnatural creation in East-Central Europe.[25]

The stereotypes that Stasiuk multiplies are not limited to ones at play in the discursive representation of the places he visits, which were established initially by French Enlightenment writers and subsequently picked up by other countries, such as England and Germany. In speaking openly against Western Europe and Westernness and supposedly sympathizing with Eastern Europe and Easternness, Stasiuk's stance is in reality consistent with the Enlightenment's division of Europe into two antagonistic parts: the "better" West and the "untamed" East.[26] Stasiuk does not critically reflect on this construction, which provides the foundation of the discursive practice that still, even today, places the "other," "younger" Europe in opposition to the "proper" Europe—the one that functions simultaneously as a prototype of Europeanness, the bearer of the myth of "progress," the center of scientific and cultural discourses, and the reference point for the various "others" relegated to positions of "pupils" vis-à-vis their mentor. The Western Europe that Stasiuk turns away from is the basis of all secondary Eurocentric constructions.

Is Stasiuk's gesture of defiance equal to freeing oneself from the jurisdiction of such constructions, however? The effects of the author's choice leave room for doubt. His rebellion seems a sign of immaturity, a demonstration of the hurt felt by an "offended" person who feeds on resentment and, entrenched in an opposing position, further entrenches the West/East binary. Reading Stasiuk's travel narratives and reflections on East-Central Europe in this context reveals the hidden ambivalence of his strategy: in protesting the prevailing dichotomy, his approach nevertheless confirms the axiology behind the emergence and the career of the construct known as "Eastern Europe."

This is not to deny the appeal of Stasiuk's prose. It is capable of stirring up sympathy for places that are forgotten, provincial, and marginalized, as readers' reviews confirm.[27] Stasiuk reconstructs a world that shows itself to be deserving of its own narration. One could almost say that the stance Stasiuk adopts approximates Christian compassion for the weak. Yet these narrations, by mythologizing space and time, have an effect that goes beyond innocent validation of the poor and disadvantaged, which is in fact ideological. Even the most autobiographical—"true" and "reliable"—of Stasiuk's descriptions of and reflections about "Others" bespeak a certain mindset. The reader has the right to query the reasons and principles behind it, since "in the colonial discourse every individual weakness has its political counterpart—uncivilized society, according to this logic, being little more than the uncivilized mind and body writ large."[28] As David Spurr notes, when considering the theme of debasement in colonial writing, a characteristic parallelism appears: "The qualities assigned to the individual savage—dishonesty, suspicion, superstition, lack of discipline—are reflected more generally in societies characterized by corruption, xenophobia, tribalism, and the inability to govern themselves. In the same way, social problems in health and sanitation, unemployment, or popular growth come to be associated with individual filth, indolence, and sexual promiscuity."[29] In effect, Andrzej Stasiuk looks at the East-Central European Other (who is the West's Other, but not his, after all) through a set of lenses supplied by colonial discourse. By doing this on the level of autobiographic representation (in *On the Road to Babadag*) and systematized reflection (in *Fado* and likewise in *Logbook*), he simultaneously carries out an ideological manipulation: sympathizing seemingly with those he represents and for whom he speaks, he actually aligns himself with the orientalizing stance of a Western intellectual. This is a peculiar paradox, since Stasiuk gives the impression of putting a lot of effort into restoring the agency of the Central European subject. The effect he accomplishes seems to run counter to the intended one, which provokes a basic question: Is freedom from the ordering and categorizing "system of truths" constructed by Westerners even possible?

It is difficult to resist the impression that Stasiuk's perspective on the Western Europeans' Other is a point of view mounted in neo-colonial discourse. Through a displacement, or else a projection, this discourse imposed on the inhabitants of East-Central Europe the image of cultural (indeed, almost racial) "misfits" and "savages." It ascribed to them characteristics that have always been a part of the human experience but that had been rejected by the discourse of modernity as undesirable and unfit for the model of a "civilized European" (who is likewise an ideological construct).[30] Stasiuk's empathetic attitude toward these figures actually strengthens such orientalizing stereotypes, for it relies on the classification strategies of the dominant discourse and the meanings that follow therefrom. As a result, his narrative subject, who also functions as the authoritative center of judgments about the narrated world, is disoriented and lost; he desperately searches for ways to buttress his identity and invests energy in diagnoses that only deepen his subservient status and make it impossible to change. This subject is implicated in a series of equivocations that overlap with each other and profoundly impact his perception of reality and the categories he relies on without being fully aware of their existence.

In light of the above, even the conclusion of *Logbook*, the essay published in the widely discussed collaboration with Yurii Andrukhovych titled *My Europe*, appears ambivalent:

> This is what it means to be a Central European: to live between the East, which has never existed, and the West, which has existed in excess. This is what it means to live "in the middle" when this middle is actually the only real ground. Only this ground is unsteady. It is reminiscent rather of an island, perhaps even a floating island. More than that, it is perhaps a ship at the mercy of currents and either Easterly or Westerly winds. . . . To live on this island, or else this ship, means constantly looking out for changes in the weather while traversing the island from shore to shore, or the ship from port to starboard. And, as happens on a sea voyage, to think only about the present and the future, since the past supplies only rational warnings of the "should have stayed home" variety.[31]

Within this frequently cited opinion of the author, the fluidity of borders that signals the difficulties, or even the impossibility, of a precise demarcation of Central Europe is not the real issue.[32] The territory described by Stasiuk "resists historical discourse and diachronic overview," becoming "a synonym of disorder, hybridity, decay, and destruction."[33] Forgoing history, Stasiuk falls into the trap of copying the clichés of colonial discourse, in which "natives" are precisely a people deprived of a past, living thoughtlessly, hic et nunc. Thus, the intentional omission of the cultural achievements of the region's inhabitants is paired with yet another factor that inscribes Stasiuk's narratives within colonial discourse: dehistoricization. Stasiuk programmatically denies the peoples of East-Central Europe the need for history, as it were, devaluing historical thinking in the name of an illusory escape from past traumas and the incomprehensibility of this history to the Western part of the world. Stasiuk seems to suggest that the victimization of East-Central Europe should be ended by doing away with the history that victimized its resident nations and ethnicities. He makes his views on this issue explicit in an interview: "You are so accustomed to the workings of history that you don't give two shits about it. You are not surprised. You treat history as a fate and a fatalism."[34] In *On the Road to Babadag*, in turn, he asks, "What is the use to anyone of chronology, sister of death?" (137). Stasiuk seems to dismiss the fact that history is understood, at least since Hegel's time, in terms of the permanent signs that nations leave behind in testimony to their existence—monuments, buildings, cities. These material inscriptions transform the landscape as well as confirm the existence of a collective. For Stasiuk, the existence of Slavs and other ethnolinguistic groups in East-Central Europe is a matter of nature and not of culture. By focusing on the primitive, primordial, anachronistic, and "natural" aspects of these societies in *On the Road to Babadag*, the author depicts them as mute, deprived of agency, and passive. They are a people without a history and with only the bare ground to stand on, on which they live without a known purpose. Nevertheless, as Stasiuk is at pains to prove, this existence has a higher value than the most refined achievements of Western culture, which is consistently and grotesquely presented as homogenous, artificial, constructed from glass and plastic, and typified by order, hyper-consumerism, and ultramodernity.[35] In an extreme antithesis, Stasiuk counters this world with one supposedly represented by East-Central Europe, which is equally homogenous, albeit mythologized by the author, rustic, made from sackcloth and straw, and characterized by poverty and filth.

What is the source of Stasiuk's open anti-occidentalism and anti-culturalism? Why does he *prefer* (by preference I mean a sui generis citation, a repeated gesture, the ironic calque of Herderian historiosophy) "sandy villages, the sticks, air stifling with pig shit" (*B*, 174) to cities, historical sites, and monuments of the past—the emblems of Western civilization's influence? What pushes him toward a frankly insistent "naturalism" and the devaluation of "civilizational markers," with industrialism and urbanization at the forefront? What inclines him to opt for the supposed primitivism and tribalism of East-Central European peoples?

Presumably, resentment toward the West and Westernness is the effect of a mélange of two kinds of Western European orientalizing discourses. On the one hand, Stasiuk ascribes to "his" Europe characteristics of the Slavic East stemming from the Enlightenment: it is an area untouched by civilization, a reservoir of simplicity and primordiality; it constitutes an antinomy of the West as a territory relegated to the function of its negative complement. (This orientalizing model has its contemporary versions, such as the ambivalent myth of Eastern Europe as the oasis of agritourism and the negative myth of it being Europe's land of extreme anachronism). On the other hand, when it comes to the actual image of the subcontinent as seen through "Western eyes," the incompatibility of the historical experiences of Europe's western and eastern regions and their resulting inability to arrive at an understanding prompts the West to reject the East as "a foreign body." This rejection meets with Stasiuk's analogous reaction to the West.

Stasiuk's absorption of theses from Western European discourse goes further. Its analysis can benefit from the theoretical category of the surrogate hegemon, which designates a characteristic component of postcolonial mentality not only of Poles but also of other East-Central European populations.[36] Perceiving themselves as culturally superior to the Eastern (now former) hegemon, these societies—in their thinking, writing, as well as social practice—"substituted" the scorned Russian/Soviet metropolis with an imagined figure of another hegemon: the mythologized West, which could model as a political organism and enjoyed prestige analogous to that granted to European empires in Asia and Africa. Andrzej Stasiuk appears to question this cultural pattern and in its place suggests that the Central European identity be constructed on the basis of rejecting the West. Does he deconstruct colonized discourse and become more postcolonial by virtue of turning away from the West in its role of surrogate hegemon?

Aleksander Fiut's opinion on Stasiuk's specific attitude toward the West and on its role in the process by which East-Central European nations and ethnicities are defining their own identities can help to answer this question:

> It is incredible just how far Stasiuk will go to not see the influence of Western culture on the territories of former communist countries! He presents a vision that seems borrowed from [Edward] Gibbon, discarding entirely twentieth-century contexts. Stubbornly and quite desperately he defends the image of a reservoir untouched by decay, and in the meantime Central Europe is not, and perhaps never was, such a reservoir; neither is Western Europe a homogenous entity—if only due to the various ethnic groups residing there or the increasing influence of Islam. As can be seen, this idealization of Central Europe feeds off a lack of both knowledge and deeper interest in the West, which appears to Stasiuk in a very superficial and long-gone form. It is as if in this author's imagination one anachronism inevitably has to follow the preceding one.[37]

One may add: it is a very peculiar idealization, which almost perversely revalorizes the central object of Stasiuk's attention. Where did it come from?

As was mentioned earlier, Stasiuk's narrations are part of a global fad of postcolonial writing, meaning literature that programmatically defies Western European cultural models as agents of Western (neo)imperial domination. In the case of Andrzej Stasiuk, however, the gesture of rejecting the "West" springs from different premises. It is a reaction to the "surrogate hegemon" rather than the actual colonizer's oppression. It must be remembered that, unlike intellectuals from former British or French colonies, Stasiuk opposes the West as a writer from a subcontinent whose current condition is determined by experiences of other-than-Western domination. As a result, instead of properly diagnosing and subsequently overcoming postcolonial mentality and culture, the author replaces it with a copied surrogate. To consider his prose as tout court postcolonial, therefore, would be possible only after a rather superficial reading, since Stasiuk has not dealt with a key issue for postcolonial literature, namely, the redefinition of the decolonized subject's identity and attitude toward itself.

It also needs to be added that postcoloniality takes on various guises in literature and should not be treated a priori as a pass not only to success but also—at the risk of striking too lofty a note—to the truth about the world and ourselves. Negating the surrogate hegemon does not lead to freedom from postcolonial resentment, and in this sense, while potent, it is actually a regress. Stasiuk bypasses the real problem by showing its substitute form in a way that is characteristic of postcolonial societies—as an aberration with an external origin, brought about by "others" and independent of us. In transferring the burden of contemporary difficulties that East-Central Europeans have with their own identities onto the universal field of the West's neocolonial hegemony, Stasiuk foregoes indicating its other historically and politically justified basis. In his work, the problem exhausts itself on the superficial attitude of the West toward East-Central Europeans; it is not recognized as something for the inhabitants of territories along the Vistula and Danube rivers to address within themselves, as part of the ballast that weighs them down because of their experience of Soviet hegemony and its far-reaching and still only partially acknowledged consequences.

Zbigniew Brzezinski once said, "In the final analysis, only Europeans can restore Europe; it cannot be done for them by others."[38] The diagnoses offered in Stasiuk's travel writing suggest that the road to fulfilling this postulate in East-Central Europe is still long and convoluted. Contrary to his suggestions, the self-image of East-Central Europeans is not a simple derivative of their dismissal by the West but a consequence of a long-term marginalization of colonial origin. True, East-Central Europeans can feel aggrieved by the West naïvely accepting the monolithic image of their countries as mere satellites of Russia, the "Eastern Bloc," and so forth, as if their societies willingly fell into Moscow's arms. Such resentment does not get to the heart of the problem, though. Stasiuk chooses not to account for the fact that the Soviet Union deprived the nations it conquered of the right to shape their own discourses and replaced it with the discourse of power and its ancillary cultural discourses, opening the field to the Western orientalizing discourse that confirmed the convictions of East-Central Europeans about their subordinate status. The lack of self-worth, the lack of faith in themselves, and finally the resentment are all consequences of precisely this phenomenon. East-Central Europeans see themselves today according to the wishes of the imperial discourse that subsumed them, and this perception, as Andrzej Stasiuk's books inadvertently confirm, is probably that residue of colonization that is the most difficult to remove.

Chapter Nine

# Colonized Poland, Orientalized Poland

## Postcolonial Theory and the "Other Europe"

The history of East-Central Europe can be conceptualized in a number of ways. It can be understood as sequence of political moves, macroeconomic decisions, and state-sanctioned military actions, taking into account also the culture forming activities of its inhabitants. It can also be interpreted as the history of contacts—diplomatic, economic, cultural, and religious—between European as well as non-European states, nations, and ethnic groups. It can be presented as a continuum that has been disrupted by great turns of events that played the role of milestones in the development of societies. It can also be understood in line with Janusz Tazbir's proposal as the history of the "monuments of human thought"—of exceptional and of "nefarious" works that decisively impacted the fate of individuals and of collectives in the eastern part of the continent.[1] Lastly, it can be viewed in categories of meta-history: as a history made up of historiographic narrations—of the constantly renewed interpretations (meaning constructions) of history of the other, younger, or, as some opine, inferior, backward, and anachronistic Europe.[2]

### "Inventing" Eastern Europe

The last, meta-historical type of historiographical reflection includes Larry Wolff's *Inventing Eastern Europe: The Map of Civilization on the Mind of the*

*Enlightenment.*[3] The book analyzes the sources and the process of constructing—"inventing"—the myth of an un(der)developed, chaotic, and barbarian "East" of Europe, an Orient in a truly Saidian sense. As Wolff argues, this myth, a product of Western European Enlightenment, contributed in an unprecedented degree to entrenching the civilizational and cultural supremacy of the West. His main thesis can be summarized as follows: to consolidate its optimistic self-image as the embodiment of the Enlightenment's ideals of progress, the West *needed* a less developed, uncivilized, backward, and immature Other, which it had to represent and name accordingly, bestowing it with the identity it generated. The "invention" of this Other was a consequence of finding excellent materials for its creation among the peripheral regions that stretched between Germany and Russia and encompassed territories from the Baltic sea to the Balkans (with small exceptions, such as Austria). The West arrived at this "invention" via the pens of its Enlightenment humanists: Fichte, Herder, Voltaire, and Rousseau, with others—diplomats, thinkers, scientists, travelers and writers—following in their footsteps. The consequences of this strategy of projection as it was applied toward the European "Orient" were predictable. The stereotypes and prejudices that have entangled East-Central Europe ever since have for decades circumscribed within prisons of thought the perception of many foreign writers, politicians, journalists, and tourists visiting that part of the world. They also calcified a significant part of academic reflection, either by tying interpretations of East-Central European social and cultural phenomena to these clichés or by not considering these phenomena at all.[4] This made recognizing and understanding the resulting cultural profile of East-Central European nations impossible or at the very least considerably more challenging. The effects of this state of affairs are still painfully felt by both average residents of East-Central Europe and the region's humanities scholars, with the latter finding their access to global "hierarchies of knowledge" more difficult than that of their Western colleagues.[5] Seen through Western eyes, the culture of the Slavic part of Europe remains the antithesis of Europeanness rather than its complement.[6]

Wolff does not coin a new theory to realize his project. He stops at repeating the main argument of Said's *Orientalism*, where the belief that "the Orient has helped to define Europe (or the 'West') as its contrasting image, idea, personality, experience" was first articulated with rhetorical prowess and the supporting analysis of dozens of source texts. Wolff's original contribution comes via a transfer of Said's conceptualization onto a territory omitted in *Orientalism.*[7] I will return to the juxtaposition of Said's and Wolff's respective frameworks, since it has more far-reaching consequences than are visible at first glance.

East-Central Europe has indeed provided an ideal training ground for the ideas of successive generations of Western European "orientalists" up until today. This is due primarily to its constitutive countries being either relatively new sovereign nation-states (Slovakia, Ukraine) or structures long absent from Europe's maps (Poland and the Baltic countries—the former Soviet republics). Since they were previously written into the history of other lands and peoples, the West has become habituated to their "soft" presence; such a presence can be effectively erased from memory, a fact that neither a well-documented martyrology nor the glory of bygone centuries can remedy.

Throughout the nineteenth and twentieth centuries, the orientalizing discourse adopted by French and German thinkers during the Enlightenment to describe Eastern Europeans constituted the dominant model of Western European narration: both literary and journalistic, which is perhaps not surprising, as well as scientific and educational, which should not only surprise but also concern, with this concern growing as we get nearer to the present day.[8] With time, a significant shift of emphasis takes place: calls for modernization in eighteenth-century journalism, documented in Wolff's book through reference to Voltaire's tirades, give way to neutralized, pseudo-objective scholarly (as well as literary) descriptions that have for decades shaped, and which to this day impact, the mental map of Western Europeans and the geographic and cultural imagination of successive generations of readers. This is how systematized knowledge about the inhabitants of the European continent's eastern regions, defined through *difference*, emerged and accumulated. The cognitive algorithm based on the East-West antithesis placed the people of East-Central Europe in a subordinate relation to paradigmatic Western Europe, both in terms of genetics and race, and in a cultural, economic, political, and intellectual sense. Taking all of this into consideration, it cannot now surprise that in *Medieval Europe: A Short History*, a popular and often reprinted four-hundred-page textbook in America, Poland is mentioned briefly in just a few places, without warranting even one full paragraph.[9] This glaring disproportion is not an isolated instance of Poland's marginalization within Western humanistic discourse; it is also true for other East-Central European nations. The example is all the more telling since it concerns a time when the Polish-Lithuanian Commonwealth existed on the European map as an independent and sovereign, if relatively late, political organism that partook in the "dawn of European nations."[10] This blatant disproportion has been defended at times as the side effect of "pedagogic convenience," a euphemism that refers to Europe's division into eastern and western parts, which has been propagated in North American historiography even after 1989.[11]

In the work of Polish as well as other Central and Eastern European scholars, the orientalization of East-Central Europe by Western humanities has for a long time mainly been overlooked, understated, or presented from a perspective that shares little with Said's methodological proposals.[12] Throughout the past two centuries, Polish thought has tended toward either epistemological exclusivism ("only we Poles know ourselves"), which in turn undermines the epistemic value of an external, "foreign" perspective ("they write about us without understanding either us or our history!"), or—to the contrary—an excessive reverence for the opinions of others ("they write about us so we must be grateful for the interest!"). Clearly, these typical attitudes could not support—and are even less able to do so now—a thorough critique of the orientalist underpinnings of Polish and other East-Central European cultural discourses; they rest on premises that are too weak and fail to address the crux of the matter. Its crux is the point of view that privileges the Western subject's attitude toward the alleged other, the exotic and underdeveloped object of its cognition, seen as incapable of reliably articulating its own opinions. It is thus that the issue of Eastern European nationalism is presented in Western historiography, for instance, which leads to a presentist and allochronic framing of the phenomenon and its invariably negative assessment in the works of American or Western European historians, political scientists, and cultural anthropologists.[13]

The work of Tony Judt is a characteristic example, in its extreme subtlety, of contemporary orientalizing discourse.[14] He approaches questions related to Central and Eastern Europe by filtering the region through a densely woven net of stereotypes used by the Soviet Union to present itself as a "good" empire to the Western world for half a century. The motif of a single center, which smothers local narrations of individual ethnicities living in East-Central Europe and is popular in Western historiography, plays a key role in these stereotypes. Filtered through such a sieve, the complicated history of East-Central Europe is framed by a discourse that, under the guise of universalism, actually accepts and replicates the hegemonic point of view. For Judt interprets the modern history of Europe primarily in categories of great-power conflicts, meaning antagonisms between powerful politico-economic systems and their interests. A careful reader will notice a belated imprint of orientalism in Judt's work, namely, the saturation of scholarly discourse, one of the most powerful Western cultural discourses, with presuppositions about the status, role, and significance of East-Central Europe for the West. The image of the European continent that emerges from his book fashions its smaller nations and ethnic groups into mere spectators of events that play out on the world's great stage without their significant participation. The decolonized societies of the post-Soviet space are relegated to a secondary role and their claims to Europeanness are mocked: "Whatever the passing brilliance of the civilizations of Prague or Vilna, they were never capitals of something definably *European* in the way that was at different moments true of Florence, Madrid, Amsterdam, London, or Vienna."[15]

Judt's rhetoric lays bare his philosophy. While writing about Communist Poland during the "Solidarity" decade, he interjects a commentary that deprives this movement of its historical agency: "The developments in Poland were a stirring prologue to the narrative of Communism's collapse, but they remained a sideshow. The real story was elsewhere."[16] Judt's subtly reconfigured perspective produces a refined, coherent, and unidirectional version of a top-down history. Such history respects, first and foremost, the vision created, or at the very least authorized, by the metropolis, and its monophonic construction would be ruptured by the uncontrolled polyphony of voices from the subordinated populations. Judt intimates that the true history of East-Central European societies (assuming that such history exists at all) rests in someone else's hands and is beyond the influence of subjects that it pertains to. This is not to say that he does not deplore the fate of Eastern Europeans. To the contrary, he himself underscores that their twentieth-century experiences were so tragic that they are difficult to describe. Nevertheless, the position from which he speaks is problematic. Even compassion can aggrieve when accompanied by a sense of superiority rather than empathy. It is perhaps here that the origin of Judt's specific, even curious, interpretation of the history of Central European nations should be sought. He sees the splendor of old capital cities (such as Prague, Warsaw, and Budapest) in the "cosmopolitanism" of their culture that was established in large part in "an international language—German—many of whose most accomplished representatives were Jews. The destruction of this genuinely central European culture has left Polish Warsaw, Lithuanian Vilnius, Czech Prague, and Hungarian Budapest as provincial as Austrian Vienna. They may be located in the middle of Europe, but their claim to a distinctive 'central Europeanness' is at best nostalgic, at worst bogus."[17] By way of contrast, Judt's opinion can be juxtaposed to a voice from within this provincialized "Central Europe" that is supposedly full of baseless grievances toward the West:

> Pointing out Central Europe's provincialism would constitute a serious misunderstanding. There is no shortage of nimble hands, wise heads, sense of values, and openness toward art here. What is left to its own fate, beyond the pale of history, languishes, however. Even a genius is marked by compromise with reality. The problem, therefore, lies not in a lack of

> culture, barbarism, or low civilization—something altogether different is at stake.
>
> Central Europe does not have the right to its own history.[18]

The above diagnosis by Josef Kroutvor is accurate. At stake is the right to narration, to one's own story, of which the "outclassed" Central and East European nations were deprived as a result of foreign hegemony that lasted decades, in some instances even centuries.[19] The examples provided above only scratch the surface of a phenomenon that is much broader in scope.[20] Analysis of this problem leads to the conclusion that attention paid to the history and cultural artifacts of marginalized societies in Western scholarship is often proportional to these societies' present-day prestige, which is in turn an offshoot of their political and economic position. The lower the status of a population in the world's hierarchy, the less audible its voice and the greater the trust placed in the metropolitan center's discourse. The lack of prestige provokes—and to some extent explains—the stubborn presence in public (including academic) discourse of statements that Hugh Seton-Watson had already summed up poignantly in 1945. He ironically encapsulated the stereotypical ideas about Eastern Europeans held by the British in his classic textbook dedicated to the interwar history of the eastern part of the continent: "They have unpronounceable names, and live in plains and forests, on mountains and rivers which might be in another world."[21] Since this kind of ignorance is still acceptable among scholars today, almost three generations later, how can those working in popular culture be held to account? In the screen adaptation of Frederick Forsyth's *The Fourth Protocol*, a British counterintelligence agent looking for a spy on the list of passengers arriving from Eastern Europe skips over the phonetically difficult Polish surnames with a telling silence. He thus repeats the rhetoric pointed out by Seton-Watson, supplementing it with a gesture of dismissal so well known to East-Central Europeans. Many of this region's intellectuals see this gesture as typical of the West; they view it as a sign of respect reserved for the USSR/Russia and things Soviet/Russian and a silencing of the populations and cultures that are located between Germany and the eastern hegemon.

On the surface, Wolff's imagological study fills in this gap. It is tempting to say that he does so while leaning mercifully over the marginalized. By showing the initial phase of the orientalization of East-Central Europe by its older and more distinguished "sister," however, Wolff's book simultaneously provokes—not with its subject matter but rather with its point of view and starting assumptions. In light of Wolff's constructivist premises, the image of East-Central Europe says more about its authors than it does about its subject. *Inventing Eastern Europe* presents the opinions and perceptions of the West about its nearest "Orient" without leaving or making any room for what that part of the continent is actually like. More so: in a methodological sense, it prevents this type of reflection. As a matter of fact, Wolff is not interested in East-Central Europe as such. He admits as much, explaining—significantly, only in his conclusions—the methodological conditions and limitations of his narration: "Eastern Europe is not the subject of this book. The grammar of the title emphasizes that Eastern Europe is considered here above all as an object, that is, the object of an array of intellectual operations practiced upon it by the Enlightenment in Western Europe."[22]

Wolff's stance does not depart significantly from the position that was the object of critical study in *Orientalism*. Said proved that the Western view of the Orient did not consider the possibility that knowledge about it could be produced and organized by its inhabitants. Within its Western vision, therefore, the actual Orient was substituted with a set of reproduced and perpetuated borrowings (clichés, interpreted images, conceptual constructions), which occlude and consequently deprive the human reality of its subjective aspect. As Said observed, in constructing a knowledge system about the object of study, these practices simultaneously perpetuate "the *strength* of Western cultural discourse."[23] *Orientalism* postulates, therefore, developing a method to "study other cultures and peoples from a libertarian, or a nonrepressive and nonmanipulative, perspective."[24]

Wolff starts from premises similar to Said's, but he moves in the opposite direction of the one suggested by *Orientalism*. His work provides a methodological justification for once again eliminating the subjectivity of East-Central Europe. The region is thus relegated anew to the role of an insignificant object that does not really exist, having been deprived of its own subjectivity and narration. It is others that give it its identity, which is based on some of the perceived ethnic, linguistic, or racial traits of East-Central Europeans rather than inherent to them or the outcome of their self-perception.[25] Without engaging in a philosophical debate over essentialism, it must be stressed that Wolff's fundamental error lies in setting aside the reality of the space that he calls "Eastern Europe." He is satisfied to move in a world of simulacra and rhetorical constructs based on a unidirectional perception of some nations by others and divorced from historical, political, and social facts. The "invention" of Eastern Europe by the West did not take place in the sterile vacuum of discourse, however. It was a secondary process in relation to a whole succession of "hard" events and processes, such as Poland's partitions and its subsequent treatment by Russia as a springboard for its own politics in relation to Europe, rather than an innocent fulfillment of "fantasies of influence and domination."[26] These phenomena—with their political, economic, and cultural consequences and a clear ethical dimension—should enter into Wolff's discussion, if only to provide a minimum of context.[27] Their omission is not justified by the stated methodological arguments, and its result is that *Inventing Eastern Europe* loses the sense of proportion between purely discursive constructions and reality, becoming an homage to one of the crowning principles of Western hegemonic discourse (Prussian/German), according to which "Slavica non leguntur" (Slavic writing is not to be read).

Wolff's and Judt's perspectives require significant correction, more precisely, a contrapuntal supplementation that considers the agency of societies objectified by orientalizing discourse. The studies of both authors are not only cut off from the realities of East-Central Europe but have downright turned their backs on it, as if the people and cultures that provide Wolff with the object of the discursive practices he analyses and Judt with the object of his synthetizing conceptualizations, did not actually exist as independent, complete, and far from primitive entities. Such an approach clearly demonstrates that Western humanities has yet to come to grips with the problem of its attitude toward the history and culture of Eastern European societies.

The opinions of both scholars converge in a curious way. Their intersection allows us to better recognize the fact that Wolff's constructivist perspective is not reducible to the innocent speculation it appears to be. A look at how Judt references the questions addressed by Wolff is in order here: "But whatever distinguishes eastern from western Europe certainly did not begin in 1945, or even in 1918; those eighteenth-century travelers and observers who 'imagined' Europe's Oriental half into existence may have been imposing upon it a prejudiced interpretation deriving from their own concerns, but they did not invent the place from whole cloth."[28] Judt loyally notes in a footnote that Wolff "presents an entirely opposite opinion," referring to the above-mentioned lack of relation between the orientalizing discourse and reality in *Inventing Eastern Europe*. The dialectic between their points of views is specious, however, when it comes to the consequences for the image of Eastern Europe that result from each of the two perspectives. As the final part of this statement shows, Judt takes Wolff's constructivist theses and essentializes them, thereby accepting the limited validity of orientalist arguments, in other words, reenacting the reference that Wolff suspended. Judt's reasoning can be summarized as follows: the Enlightenment's orientalists created an *imagined* picture of Eastern Europe, but this image was not exclusively the product of their imagination; to the contrary, it *must* have had a basis in the factual world. In this manner, eighteenth-century orientalism comes full circle, returning to the stage and forcing its way into contemporary historiographic discourse. Along with it comes a store of stereotypes and ideas, including the belief that the nations of Europe's eastern regions require the guardianship and care of the West in reaching maturity, since only this will secure their economic and social success and guarantee a peaceful existence, free from unexpected and undesirable excesses, for the rest of the continent.

This amounts to a contemporary continuation of the civilizing mission's logic, a project that inherently implies unidirectional action and excludes the option of negotiating a non-subordinate place in discourse for societies that fall within the mission's scope. Just as it was during the Enlightenment, dialogue in Wolff's and Judt's work is thwarted by the fact that only one party (the West) holds the privileged place of a subject, while the other remains an Other—immature, deprived of its own voice, and reduced to the object of description.[29] This Other is enclosed in essentializing categories imposed by the dominant discourse of Western humanities, which thus inadvertently engage in the process of cultural, and in further consequence also political, hegemony of present-day Western metropoles over East-Central Europe. By accepting without protest its objectification by this type of study, the East in turn cedes a part of its identity and autonomy, also in the field of scholarly discourse.[30]

Wolff consistently avoids accounting for the point of view of East-Central European people constricted by the corset of orientalism. Is he justified in doing so? Violating accepted methodological conventions does not seem too high a price to pay for the cognitive benefits that a confrontation of Western and Eastern perspectives could bring. Wolff seems conscious of this defect of his narration given that he magnanimously decides to let Eastern Europe speak in the last paragraphs of his discussion. He does so only in the form of a reply from the "other side" to statements that were the object of his insightful analysis, which places the inhabitants of the region in an uncomfortable position: explication is after all another way of amplifying the judgments formulated earlier by the speaker. What is most interesting and telling, however, is that Wolff chooses Leo Tolstoy's *War and Peace* for this purpose, seeing this novel as a "commanding" and "overwhelming" counterpoint to the "the brilliance, the erudition, the confidence, of the philosophers."[31] In light of Ewa M. Thompson's postcolonial interpretation of the imperial undertones of Tolstoy's masterpiece, Wolff's decision to use it in support of his argument seems bitterly ironic. A passage from Thompson's *The Imperial Knowledge* comes in handy here:

> The editing-out of the Polish narrative from remembered history was given a new impetus by *War and Peace*. At the time *War and Peace* was written, that narrative was already considered irrelevant, because Polish powerlessness was evident after a series of failed uprisings. The empire had arrived, and it could speak with a powerful voice, silencing the voices of the defeated and consigning them to cultural nonexistence—even at the time when the subjugated nation did in fact play a significant role. The distortions of history inevitably caused by empires consist of a number of such small adjustments, until a picture is created where no cultures except those supported by large armies and navies are able to conduct a public conversation. The fact that Tolstoi felt no compunction in adjusting the scales as regards these matters is another sign of his imperial self-confidence. Tolstoi trivialized the Polish thorn in Russia's side and presented the empire as if it had achieved stability on its western border.[32]

By pointing to *War and Peace* as a perfect (in his opinion) antithesis to the Western orientalizing discourse on Eastern Europe, Wolff demonstrates a similar insufficiency of sensitivity and empathy for the small and midsized non-Russian nations of East-Central Europe as Tolstoy does in *War and Peace*, from which these nations are either erased or in which they are presented as the Russian Empire's grateful servants.

Here, another issue with Wolff's work rears its head: the homogenization of East-Central Europe's image and the attendant uniformist perspective, which bulldozes over the polarization of the region, which is significant, even fundamental, to the identity of Central and Eastern European societies. Wolff seems not to distinguish between smaller states, nations, and ethnic groups, on the one hand, and Catherine the Great's imperial Russia on the other, throwing them all into the same bag with the comfortable but misleading label of "Eastern Europe." He thus ignores vital historical realities, namely, that Russia was the hegemon of many of these nations and ethnicities both during and after the Enlightenment; to view Russia as having been likewise orientalized by the West is a gross oversimplification that ignores historical facts.[33]

## The Peripheries "Write Back"?

It is possible to come up with an alternative narration to Wolff's and show how non-Germanic Central Europe invented Western Europe.[34] In such a narration, it would be necessary to account for the fact that the monolithic and monochromatic image of the European "Orient," as reconstructed by Wolff and accepted as "factual" by Judt, is accompanied and simultaneously opposed by a varied gallery of images of the West, which the cultural discourses of East-Central European societies abound in. This is particularly true for those populations whose horizons were shaped in large part by Latin civilization and Occidental sympathies. This diversity undercuts the conclusions arrived at in Wolff's book and has more than one source: it arises from identity ties with the West that Poles and other East-Central European populations believe they have; from the variety of their styles of expression and vocabularies; and from the different empirical positions that shaped public discourse in the eastern and western parts of the continent. Western historians (Richard Watt, Norman Davies, Timothy Snyder, and Roger Moorhouse being the rare exceptions) usually do not appreciate the fact that European societies on the peripheries of the Soviet Empire have put great effort into rejecting the cultural influence of the metropolis and retaining their identities; they have often refused to participate in the hegemon's civilizational project and stubbornly insisted on their affinity to the traditions and values of the Western world over those of their eastern Slavic neighbor. The extent to which they succeeded in rejecting and rebuffing the empire's influence is one of the many questions that postcolonial studies should address. The Polish experience is naturally only one part of this constellation, but an important one. What makes the Polish experience of particular interest here is that it brings together two elements that in other societies usually appear separately: a strong consciousness of cultural belonging to the West (but not its hegemony) and its colonization by Western imperial powers (of Prussia/Germany and Austria). Despite some scholars' suggestions, these two phenomena should not be equated.[35] Equating cultural influence and compulsory political domination excessively stretches the notion of colonization, turning postcolonial theory from a well-honed instrument of contemporary humanities into a blunted and vague category. Most importantly, in the course of this procedure a fundamental ethical difference is lost. What disappears from view is the fact that the act of colonization is under all circumstances directed *against* the colonized population, regardless of the scale of military engagement and the role of the "civilizing mission" in the colonial project.

The problem presented here does not boil down to the postulate of a pragmatic solution, a formula that would allow East-Central European societies to take off the Gombrowiczean "mug"—that is, grimace—that the discourse of Enlightenment and its later incarnations imposed on them. The challenge lies elsewhere. In the first place, the paradoxical attempts to expose and dismantle this discourse undertaken by scholars such as Wolff and Judt lead nowhere and indeed turn into subtle extensions of the discursive practices they critique. Second, the orientalization of East-Central Europe has deeply penetrated the mentality and culture of its inhabitants. On the one hand, this brought about the emergence of sociopsychological phenomena and cultural values that took the form of (1) popular myths, opinions, concepts, and judgments (for instance, concerning the "Polish national character," Sarmatism, or the reasons behind the fall of the Polish-Lithuanian Commonwealth); and (2) standard individual and collective behaviors, reactions, and habits. On the other hand, it fueled the concepts and theories utilized to explain these phenomena. In both instances—of the sociocultural phenomena tied to the social mind-set and of the research efforts aimed at their understanding and description—there are correlations at play that neither societies nor scholars are fully aware of, the core of which should be sought in the Foucauldian power/knowledge nexus. It is there, among a set of representations, clichés, and stereotypes created and subsequently imposed by the orientalizing discourse, that one finds the origins of the Polish and Central European inferiority complex—a diminished sense of self-worth mixed with the search for acceptance from others. This pertains to the region's average "statistical" inhabitants as much as to its intellectuals, since both groups (which include liberal Euro-enthusiasts as well as conservative Euro-skeptics) are susceptible to conceptualizations with an orientalist lineage.

Pertinent conclusions would be drawn from investigating the extent to which orientalizing gnoseological models inscribed in various texts by Western European authors (scientist, diplomats, writers, travelers, etc.) penetrated Polish identity discourse at different points in time, shaping it and leaving behind their subtle imprints, which are difficult to recognize and even harder to remove. After all, foreign narrations, such as Claude-Carloman de Rulhière's *Histoire de l'anarchie de Pologne*, which objectified Poles along with Polish history and culture, were not disconnected from interpretations of history and culture produced by Polish Romantics and their nineteenth-century successors in the search for their identity.[36] It is possible to hazard a thesis that neither preempts nor narrows the conclusions such research might lead to, that the internalization of orientalist clichés popularized two prevailing self-stereotypes in Polish society—a hyper-negative and a hyper-positive one—which represent the two extreme and opposite emanations of a colonized population's defensive position.[37] These stereotypes appear not only in political discourse, sociopolitical journalism, and literature. They function also in the humanities and its metalanguage as means of interpreting reality that emerged under the pressure of the orientalizing discourse. Postcolonial criticism that resorts to these stereotypes is prone to misinterpreting and overinterpreting sociocultural phenomena of colonial origins. Maria Janion's book *Niesamowita Słowiańszczyzna* (Uncanny Slavdom) is one example of a discussion that falls into this trap. It is based on a false alternative of exclusion: a choice between either a radical ultra-Catholic nationalism or the relinquishment of the Christian (Latin) roots of identity in the name of the "Slavic Idea," a specific humanistic incarnation of Pan-Slavism.[38]

The analyses performed above on modest but representative materials are indicative of the "political circumstances obtaining when knowledge is produced," which are also at play in the contemporary, intellectually disciplined, yet clearly insufficiently self-critical academic discourse on East-Central Europe.[39] The other side of this discourse's "entelechy," meaning its social consequences today, completes the picture of the issue under discussion here. One of its most characteristic results, which may even deserve the status of a regulatory principle, should be underlined. I refer to it, succinctly, as disinterestedness toward the subject. There are gradients to its expression, from weariness, through impatience, antipathy, and overexposure, to the questioning of the value and sense of addressing the issues of Central and Eastern Europe and their ultimate elimination from discourse. One current in the American reception of Anne Applebaum's book *Iron Curtain* illustrates this issue well.[40] A review of the book published in the *New York Times* presents a telling opinion that is simultaneously representative of Western discourse about East-Central Europe. The discussion is characteristically ambiguous. It praises the book's level of detail and strikes the already familiar, if only on the basis of Judt's work, note of empathy, only to then reverse the perspective along with its initial, seemingly favorable verdict: "It is good to be reminded of these sordid events, now that more archives are accessible and some witnesses remain alive to recall the horror. Still, why should we be consuming such a mass of detail more than half a century later?"[41]

The rhetoric of this question clearly shows that the Western discourse of the humanities has trouble lifting the burden of Eastern European questions. Indeed, by questioning the very sense of the research undertaken by Applebaum, an author who is after all a Pulitzer Prize winner, this discourse is shown to repeat the failure with which Said charged orientalism: it refuses to express solidarity with a segment of human experience that Central and Eastern Europeans were forced to participate in, that the Western world prefers to push away and reject, and that it refuses to hear.[42]

## Including Experience of the Excluded

Despite the problematic production and reception mechanisms of the contemporary discourse on East-Central Europe, its disinterested and honest, meaning non-orientalizing and non-orientalized, scholarly description as the

West's Other seems possible, as the postulate voiced at the end of *Orientalism* suggests. Without such research, East-Central Europe as an autonomous subject of history will remain a troublesome, unreal, and unnecessary entity for the Western world. This kind of reformulation of research practice, however, is not only an issue of narrowly understood methodology but rather of the ethics of humanist work today. Approaching the matter in this way fundamentally alters the expectations and requirements facing the researcher. It invites further reflection that moves beyond discourse analysis.

By way of conclusion, I would like to consider a work that successfully tackles these issues. The backstory of Steven Spielberg's feature film *Terminal* (2004) is tied to a nonexistent Krakozhia, a fictional ministate of Eastern Europe (with a name that phonetically alludes to Kraków). Both the fictional Krakozhia and its representative in the film, Victor Navorski, expertly played by Tom Hanks, embody stereotypical notions about Europe's eastern part. These clichés are the constitutive elements of the actual discourse of the encyclopedic knowledge about the world that educated inhabitants of the American continent have at their disposal in a more or less superficial form. What does the viewer of *Terminal* discover about the "other Europe," or rather what adds up to its episteme for the average American, as reconstructed and "narrated" with a tinge of irony by Spielberg?[43] The region is filled with enigmatic political entities that are small and fragile, have names that are difficult to pronounce, hazy identities, and unstable systems of governance. The pitiable economic conditions of these nations, shown suggestively in the eccentric travel accessories and clothing of the film's amiable protagonist, make their citizens into the pariahs of the civilized world. Travelers who arrive from "there" are unable to communicate with "this" world, as they do not know either its lingua franca or its rules, and their personal charm (if they possess it at all) is the result of a marriage of cultural difference, inherent ineptitude, and naivety, which must be corrected by their mentor: the more mature, authoritative, and self-regulating West.[44] This example clearly demonstrates that historiographic discourse is far from an innocent reservoir of knowledge produced according to a specific "structure of attitude and reference" that precedes works of art and popular culture and provides them with the epistemological basis and scholarly authorization.[45] This discourse impacts contemporary societies powerfully not only through academic discussions but also through works directed at a general audience and popular culture across a range of media, such as film, comic books, and even advertising. It supplies Western societies today with an extensive set of (pre)judgments, or prejudices (Gadamer's *Vorurteile*, cognitive presuppositions), thus shaping their knowledge about the world, including East-Central Europe.

Until the end of the eighteenth century, conceptualizations of Poland free of orientalism were a rather rare phenomenon, as indicated by an overview of works by European historians about Poland's partitions.[46] So far, a work of nuanced scholarship that shows the scale and forms of this orientalism and traces its impact on Polish critical discourses does not exist. For the sake of counterbalance, research into the orientalization of East-Central Europe should look at works that overturn this perspective, which has been dominant for more than two hundred years now. Norman Davies's book *Europe East and West*, for instance, challenges the centuries-old thesis about the inherent "contrast" between the two parts of the continent and gives equal weight to East-Central European countries in its main narration of Europe.[47] In the process, Davies deconstructs the continent's division that typifies historiographic discourse, which is so painfully experienced by Europe's eastern populations.

Davies's take on European history has some excellent antecedents in Anglo-Saxon writing in terms of its awareness that the values constitutive of the Western tradition are a sum of a broad legacy that includes Europe's East-Central regions. For example, Gilbert Keith Chesterton acknowledges *Vorurteile*, which are deeply rooted in and propagated by the West's dominant discourse about Poland, when introducing a London lecture by Professor Roman Dyboski in 1923. As he told the British audience:

> When it comes to other European nations, the English soul is in a state of peaceful and blissful ignorance; the case is worse for Poland, since there is a lot of information about it in the English consciousness, but this information is the venom of anti-Polish propaganda that has been systematically injected into the English spirit. This venom must first be expelled from your minds before authentic information about Poland can be received.[48]

Chesterton calls the prejudicial clichés "the venom" injected into English minds, recognizing them as "anti-Polish propaganda." He does not end his address with this sweeping statement, however. He also locates the source of this discourse in the archive of knowledge created by the empires that not only swallowed up the Polish-Lithuanian Commonwealth's territory, inhabitants, and resources but also took possession of the discourse about it, in line with the mechanisms identified and theorized by postcolonial scholars. He describes it as "the calumnious inventions of German historians who were able to take control of the enlightened opinion of Europe during the nineteenth century," adding that "eighteenth-century Poland was not at all worse than other countries that remained on Europe's map, and it fell only because of the aggressive greed of its neighbors: Prussia and Russia."[49]

Particularly telling in this context is the note that Chesterton included in his preface to the English translation of Zygmunt Krasiński's play *Undivine Comedy*: "Poland was, and still remains, surrounded by barbarians."[50] In this preface, Chesterton preemptively realizes Said's postulate from *Orientalism* to account for the experience of those parts of the world that were previously excluded from discourse. Poland's historical trials and tribulations, along with its geopolitical, cultural, and moral situation following the restoration of independence in 1918, served the English writer as a system of reference in a more general reflection about the state of humanity, in particular of Christians, in the aftermath of World War II and the Bolshevik Revolution. Chesterton managed to present Krasiński's masterpiece of the Romantic era as neither "too exotic" nor "too distant" from the dilemmas of the so-called civilized world, contrary to suggestions made by the majority of nineteenth-century academic and travel writings, lexicons, and encyclopedias published from Petersburg to Heidelberg and London, which stressed the positive role of European metropoles in relation to the former Polish-Lithuanian Commonwealth and its inhabitants.

In Chesterton's opinion, the voice that reached the Thames from East-Central Europe via an English translation of the Polish Romantic classic carried equal weight to the opinions and diagnoses circulated by institutions of Western metropoles. Chesterton did not reproduce the "West-East" opposition that organized the distinctions and typologies about political, historical, economic, anthropological, ethnographic, and other issues within European discourse since the Enlightenment. In the case of this writer and thinker, the knowledge produced over centuries in Western European metropoles and distributed in the form of authoritative scientific conclusions met with a critical reception. For Chesterton, the hegemon's written word was not "a textual standard that enforces the marginality and inferiority of colonised cultures and their books," which allowed him to avoid the paternalism of the Western discourse about "so-called new nations of Eastern Europe."[51]

It should give readers pause, therefore, when Jerzy Jedlicki, a renowned Polish historian, begins an essay entitled "Stereotype of the West in Pre-partition Poland" with the words "for Polish intellectual elites, literature, and political thought, the European West has always been the main frame of reference."[52] Something more than an objective conclusion based on an analysis of Polish identity discourse as it developed under specific historical conditions is at play in this statement. Jedlicki's assertion reflects the views of part of Polish society and is grounded in the concept according to which Poland's development is conditioned by implementing the Enlightenment ideas and taking the Western European path of modernization. By so doing, scholars such as Jedlicki reinforce the doxa (that which goes without saying in a social group and which organizes worldviews and beliefs of that group, playing the role of an undebatable truth for that group) according to which the West—in this case, Western Europe—possesses not only political and economic capital but also intellectual and scientific authority that predisposes it to be a model of civilizational development for other countries, such as Poland.[53] As this discussion shows, however, the authority of Western discourse is far from obvious or self-explanatory. By treating it as such, Jedlicki sets aside the entire complex of problems related to the contemporary cultural hegemony of the West, particularly of the United States, in East-Central Europe. Clearly, the absorption and reproduction of epistemological categories and simplified interpretive schemata produced by (and for) the Western metropoles within the scholarship of "peripheral" countries such as Poland continues to be a problem that calls for further and sustained scholarly attention.

Chapter Ten

# Slavic Issues with Identity

## Marginal Notes to Maria Janion's *Uncanny Slavdom*

The cultural discourse of Central and Eastern Europe (if we accept that such a homogeneous discourse exists at all) has been described by Roumiana Deltcheva as continually "permeated by one dominant metaphor of intent, namely the road to Europe. In spite of the differentiation of manifestations the symbol has undergone in the past ten years, the semantic scope encompasses a common perception of peripherality, marginality, isolation, outsidedness."[1]

In response to this sense of exclusion, Maria Janion, a renowned Polish scholar of Romanticism, proposes her own "road to Europe," which she describes as postcolonial, in the book *Niesamowita Słowiańszczyzna* (Uncanny Slavdom).[2] Before taking a closer look at some aspects of her proposal, a look at the continuation of Deltcheva's reflections is in order: "Geographically within Europe, yet culturally excluded from it, the countries of Central and East Europe are still in a process of defining their identity based on a double binary opposition: by consciously differentiating themselves from the former center of Soviet political power, and equally strongly attempting to integrate themselves with the Western center of cultural legitimization."[3] In identifying the West as a key vector orienting East-Central European cultural space, Deltcheva picks up on a frequent and characteristic, not so say paradigmatic, tendency in post-Communist societies. Janion's intellectual proposal seems to pursue a different objective. What are the results of her engagement with postcolonial criticism?

Applying postcolonial theory to the East-Central European context is a tempting idea, but it does come with some risks. On the one hand, postcolonialism frames the history of civilizations in categories of conquest, hegemony, subordination, resistance, and emancipation, which allows, at least theoretically, for a global traverse of different histories and geographical areas that links and amalgamates them into one subject field.[4] The benefit of such a universalizing approach lies in identifying and explicating the characteristic, recurrent structures of political, cultural, and existential experience that are bound up with foreign domination. On the other hand, the planting of postcolonial theoretical concepts in an East-Central European ground can become a purely mechanical procedure that boils down to substituting phenomena specific to a given society, culture, territory, and historical period with uniformizing categories. It is not difficult to predict that applying postcolonial theory in this way can lead to the blurring, and even erasure, of significant differences.[5] Subtle differentiations are necessary if the diverse, complicated, and multitonal reality of colonization is not to be replaced by magma lacking clear contours. Theoreticians have long noted that "the concept of the 'post-colonial' must be interrogated and contextualized historically, geopolitically, and culturally."[6]

Maria Janion's *Uncanny Slavdom* certainly manages to avoid the trap of homogenizing postcolonial discourse. Her discussion does not simply transplant the conceptual network of postcolonialism into Polish historical, literary, and cultural contexts. The successful transfer of theoretical concepts to new areas of study depends on something else: their ability to illuminate phenomena in a way that frames and interprets them more fully, deeply, and subtly than other theories do it. This is also at times accompanied by a conceptual flair arising from the encounter between the themes already familiar to the audience and a new language of description; different vocabulary and syntagmatic relations are able to lend impetus to studies on even well-researched questions. There is a remarkable energy in some ideas, such as those that thoroughly reformulated humanistic discourse, as is certainly the case with Said's concept of orientalism. Regardless of its source, however, a conceptual flair cannot make up for the shortcomings revealed when theoretical intuitions do not converge with harsh reality. This confrontation constitutes the final test of every theory. When theory and reality fail to converge, the interpretive process ends with speculation rather than explication and is of questionable cognitive value even when the originality of hypotheses posed is refreshingly exciting, breaks up stabilized views, and stimulates the rethinking of methods and conclusions arrived at with their help.

Maria Janion's study represents this last case. It deploys Said's conceptualization in a way that is fundamentally flawed despite the rhetorical and intellectual effectiveness of the argument, as this chapter will show. At stake here are not the controversial minor judgments and appraisals that are particularly prominent in Janion's diagnoses of the state of contemporary Polish literature and society but issues considerably more serious.[7] My focus is on two interlinked issues: the understanding of the nature of colonization in the context of the Polish historical experience and the interpretation of Poland's postcolonial condition in light of literary texts and other discourses.

The question of the Polish postcolonial condition takes a unique form in Janion's discussion. She proposes that the experience of colonization, which constitutes the base of Polish contemporary identity, had its beginnings as early as the Middle Ages. It is then that the West Slavic tribes inhabiting territories that soon became Polish entered the realm of Western Europe's Latin influence, which Janion views in terms of trauma caused by severance from pagan tradition. In her opinion, the orientalization of Poland and its inhabitants in Western European discourses that began in the time of Enlightenment was in fact an extension of the disdain with which Latin Europe supposedly viewed political organisms in the continent's eastern region from the beginning, as entities formed later, and thus younger, less civilized, and by that token secondary, backward, and inferior. Reconstructing Janion's argument, Poles today are contending with the long-term effects of "colonization by Christianity" that dates back to the Middle Ages. This proposed Middle Ages–contemporaneity continuum is used to justify Janion's thesis that the problems with the Polish identity over the past two centuries up till now started precisely then, in the hegemony of the idea of *latinitas* that was supposedly imposed onto Slavic Poland from the outside. In one of the book's final sentences, Janion reveals the strategic aim of her discourse in the form of a creed with a clear rhetoric and transparent axiology: "Poland is a poor and flat monolith, mostly nationalistic and Catholic. This is why it wears on those of its citizens who wish to part with it for the sake of Europe understood as a space of free culture" (330). Her book tries to challenge the dominant Catholic tradition by countering it with selected works by Polish Romantics that present the picture of the Christianization of Slavs as a great historical catastrophe or, in Janion's postcolonial idiom, the source of their centuries-long colonial trauma. She claims that this "trauma has been with the Slavs since the moment of their baptism, a baptism which was badly accomplished, and which became the source of a 'fracture, a humiliation, an infirmity felt for ages.'"[8]

Like any cultural critic, Janion has the right to assess the historical role of Christianity, and Catholicism in particular, in Poland. It is clear, however, that her interpretation is grounded in a Romantic appreciation for the pre-Christian, pagan elements that she believes missing from Polish culture.

Janion's keen interest, however, can be placed in a broader social context. As a cultural gesture, it coincides with the present emergence of neo-pagan movements, which have gained in popularity in East and Central Europe after the collapse of Communism. While reading Maria Janion's study against this background would be critically stimulating, it goes beyond the scope of this inquiry.[9]

Janion declares herself a proponent of the thesis that Poland's birth in the tenth century was "late" compared to the genesis of other European nations. From this perspective, the Polish complex stems from the fact that Poles are already a "late entity on an old continent" (15) in the Middle Ages. This assertion does not hold up in confrontation with other European ethnic groups.[10] The inferiority complex that oppresses Poles and is so keenly felt by Janion does not stem from an objective status quo but rather from the author placing her trust in the dominant discourse initiated by Encyclopédistes during the reign of Catherine the Great, subsequently developed and skillfully deployed by European imperial powers to justify their influence and entrench the system enacted by the Vienna Congress in 1815. Janion seems to forget that it is precisely this discourse that eroded the self-confidence of Poles, put into question Poland's pre-partition achievements, placed the blame for the defeat and loss of the Polish state exclusively on Poles, and led to their becoming resigned to their own marginality stemming from the lack of sovereignty. One reason to question the conclusions of *Uncanny Slavdom* is the continuing impact of this discourse on the self-perception of Poles and on how they are seen by many other Western societies. Janion's book provides indirect evidence of the hold that this discourse still has on its author. The retroactive projection of the eighteenth-century image of Latinized Slavic Europe as an "inferior" part of the continent onto the Middle Ages—and looking there for the sources of its inferiority and inequality in relation to the West—makes a caricature of Polish history and culture. This image, at odds with historical facts, is actually a continuation of the discourse of orientalism rather than a polemic against it.

One of the strongest symptoms of the power of this discourse, or at least the one that is most difficult to eliminate, is its ability to arouse self-contempt in those who have been objectified by it and thereby made to feel inferior. It can be said that the aim of orientalizing discourse is reached when this happens. Janion does not specify the point at which Western writing begins to express "contempt" toward their Others (the Slavs, the Poles), from which the "Slavic," and more precisely Polish, sense of inferiority and alienation from Europe follows. She suggests, however, that the phenomenon occurs early—sufficiently early to become a painful stigma imprinted onto the Polish "Slavic" identity. By way of confirmation, Janion references twelfth-century German sources on the Christianization of the continent's eastern regions, interpreting their declarations as expressive of the idea of imperial conquest of the Slavic lands (18). She does not give enough weight to their historical, cultural, and religious context, however, nor to the fact that the poetics of these texts reference *descriptio gentium*. In other words, their role in the creation and solidification of national, ethnic, and racial stereotypes does not necessarily have a strictly imperial basis and implications. These types of written documents and oral testimonies are, rather, the inevitable result of any confrontation with a different people, other than "our own," and they are an element in a larger constellation that consists, among other things, of the stereotype-ridden linguistic "descriptions" of ethnic and cultural groups.[11] Janion's book ultimately paints a suggestive portrait of "Slavdom" that has been subjected to German colonizing influences from at least the times of Poland's creator Prince Mieszko I (second half of the tenth century) and up until the Second World War, culminating in the Nazi rhetoric that defined Slavs as "born slaves."[12]

The portrait is telling, painted with conviction and rhetorical passion. Is it entirely true, however? Is there a sufficient basis for speaking about colonialism in the Saidian sense when referring to societies and political organisms of the Middle Ages? An unequivocal answer to this question would require taking a stance on the medieval origins of nations, which has been debated for years by not only medievalists but also anthropologists and sociologists involved in nationalism studies.[13] The practice of postcolonial critics with respect to this issue reflects this. There is an observable tendency among them to shift the temporal boundary of colonialism ever further into the historical past in a risky expansion of postcolonialism's conceptual field, which begins to include all recorded acts of territorial conquest in human history. This elides the specificity of modern colonialism and in a broader perspective leads to a methodological weakening of postcolonial studies. While postcolonial theorists link colonial expansion with "the emergence of the nation-state and the imperial-capitalist economies of post-Renaissance Europe," they also acknowledge that the rise of colonialism was aided by the discovery of the New World and the "rapid development of long-distance trading ventures in the Renaissance period."[14] As Walter Mignolo points out, already in the pre-Enlightenment, "before Orientalism developed as a massive discursive formation during the eighteenth and nineteenth centuries, a similar imaginary construction flourished with the inclusion of Indias Occidentales in the map and the subsequent invention of America."[15] Edward Said, whose authority Janion frequently calls upon, was not in favor of moving colonialism's inauguration prior to early modernity, although he did look for the early sources of the orientalizing attitude in the literary imagology of ancient Greece.[16] He viewed the nineteenth century as the beginning of the colonial era that is at stake in postcolonial studies: a period of post-Enlightenment expansion of Western European empires, supported by not only political, military, and economic means but also scientific rationalizations, philosophical and ideological arguments, and cultural practices. This is important insofar as the colonial project thus understood could develop only under conditions of an already formed and entrenched modern national identity, which appeared in Western Europe as a result of the Enlightenment. (To compare, in Timothy Snyder's book *The Reconstruction of Nations: Poland, Ukraine, Lithuania, Belarus, 1569–1999*, the Union of Lublin in 1569 is given as the birth date of the modern Polish nation.)[17] In this context, the journey back to the Middle Ages in search of the sources of the "painful forgetting or lack of recognition"—the alleged Polish or "Slavic trauma" (28)—as undertaken in *Uncanny Slavdom*, seems somewhat problematic.

This journey can be mapped as follows. Maria Janion sets out to address the problem of cultural identity in a society that has experienced colonization. She forgoes, and rightly so, the discourse of victimhood, conscious that it would doom postcolonial studies in Polish literature and culture to the repetition of commonplace models that emphasize suffering. So far, so good. Janion's journey does not take a direct route to the Middle Ages, however, but arrives there via Romanticism. In the course of her expedition to the textual realm of the Polish Romantics, she discovers places of concern that, in her opinion, speak to the violence inflicted during the Middle Ages on the primeval Polish, meaning "Slavic," identity. These places are the demonic images of some alleged ancient cataclysm, rupture, suffering, and hidden revolt found in the works of Polish Romantics. The deeply anti-Latin sphere of "uncanny Slavdom," which clearly refers to the Freudian *das Unheimliche*, constitutes in her interpretation the residue of a native Slavic resentment toward the Latin West, whose religious and political expansion resulted in the destruction of Old Slavic myths and beliefs, leading thereby to a deformation of the original Polish identity and the displacement of its authentic and most ancient content. From here stems the sense of mission that consumes Janion's study and pushes her to formulate a proposal of "an alternative thinking about our place in Europe" (179).

Janion is not mistaken in pointing out that the "inferiority" of East-Central Europe is an effect of the West's long-term discursive domination. She sidesteps, however, the factual sources of this domination. Their examination would be interesting, although it would necessitate leaving the sphere of Polish literature and writing to include other discourses, which for more than two hundred years shaped and still shape the perception of Europe's east-central areas, of their past and their present, both among the people living in the region and those beyond it. The orientalization of this region occurred not directly through the writing of Western intellectuals, as was the case with the Middle Eastern peoples but rather with the active participation of the empires involved, primarily Russia and Germany (Prussia). As is well known, colonialism, like other dominant discourses, constructed convenient representations of the Other, which fetishized it, having presented it as a dangerous entity to be feared and subjugated. In this way, the Western European Enlightenment came to the aid of the empires that took over Poland's territory from the second half of the eighteenth century until 1918. It provided them with discursive tools of stereotypes and descriptions that classified the subordinated ethnic groups as civilizationally lower, insubordinate, and flawed—in other words, as the elemental, unpredictable Other who "needs" the care and supervision of the enlightened European subject. The empires reciprocated in turn with the production and propagation of knowledge about the conquered territories, which for a long time fed masses of students, scholars, politicians, and average readers with stereotypes of the "backward peripheries" and the "trustworthy hegemon" on a "civilizing mission." One of the merits of postcolonial studies is the attention it brings to the difficulties faced by the colonized people in overcoming or evading the cognitive models that helped to structure their world.[18]

It is not altogether surprising, therefore, that Janion's study is simultaneously intended as a collective therapy project for Poles. She does not hide her ambition of restoring Polish self-perception to free the Poles both from their inferiority complex concerning the West and from stereotypical ideas about the allegedly barbarian and wild East. According to Janion, Poles as a nation found themselves "in a vicious circle of domination, imposition, oppression, exaltation and debasement, a constant fight for recognition of some mythical greatness and superiority, and an unceasing display of pride and a desire to tower over others" (329). The author suggests that Poles can escape this vicious circle by overcoming the system of binary oppositions that they rely on when perceiving and describing their surrounding reality and their identity, which they define in relation to this reality. At the base of this system of differences stands the central opposition of "West-East." *Uncanny Slavdom* aims to abolish this opposition.

As a scholar of Romanticism, Maria Janion traverses this epoch with confidence and freedom in her book, putting forth hypotheses in a way that is exceptionally convincing, impressive, and attractive for the reader. By letting Romantic writers speak on the subject of the "etiology" and "therapies" of Polish issues with identity, however, she privileges a specific interpretation of history derived from an extremely rich Romantic manufacture of historiosophical ideas (among others, by Zorian Dołęga Chodakowski and some works of Ryszard Berwiński, Zygmunt Krasiński, and Józef Ignacy Kraszewski). In so doing, Janion is guilty of a methodological abuse. She extrapolates concepts born under specific conditions of foreign domination and loss of sovereignty, with participation of Romanticism's main philosophical and aesthetic doctrines, onto earlier centuries. For instance, her thesis that "the subordination of colonized Slavs in European culture had been taking place for centuries" (18) is grounded in the Romantic philosophy of history rather than in the contemporary research of Polish and German historians, who frame the mutual relations of the two nations differently.[19]

Examples of such projections, or else excessive privileging of ideas with a Romantic lineage, can be multiplied. Janion's approach serves to underline a hypothesis proposed in the book, namely that Polish identity is built on the deep scar tissue of the feeling of lack—the elimination of a primordial and inherent "Slavic" element under the pressure of Latin Christianity. The nature of this element remains unclear even for the author, however. At times, it seems to consist of "original" myths, beliefs, and pagan customs with Old Slavic roots, preserved in the reservoir of Romantic folk culture, and analogous to those that the Irish people—in contrast to Western Slavs—were able to preserve.[20] At other times, it refers to the alleged non-Latin Christian identity and is tied to the influence of Eastern Orthodox Christianity on Polish lands. With regard to the latter, Janion calls extensively upon speculations and suppositions regarding the possible existence of another competitive tradition of Byzantine Christianity in medieval times, with Western Slavs finding themselves within its sphere of influence. Janion seeks a continuation of this tradition—the "anti-Latin episode in Polish culture" (58), as she calls it—and finds it in the works of the above Romantic writers, as well as some post-Romantic writers, among them Stanisław Ignacy Witkiewicz (Witkacy) and Stanisław Wyspiański. By emphasizing the anti-Latin thread in Polish literature, she argues in favor of an antagonistic vision of the development of Christianity on Polish lands.[21]

I am not going to discuss here the character, scale, and reach of Byzantine influences on the territories ruled by the Piast dynasty. Debating this issue and other issues related to the religious beliefs during the Middle Ages remains a matter for medievalists.[22] The arguable nature of Janion's chosen direction in her postcolonial peregrinations depends on a methodological problem that is fundamental from the point of view of postcolonial theory. Although the book foregoes narration from the point of view of a victim, with martyrdom overtones, typical of this discursive strategy—it does not renounce the concept itself. It is a recurring concept in reflections on the causes of Poland's fall since the time of the so-called Kraków school of history (Józef Szujski, Michał Bobrzyński, and others) in the late nineteenth century.[23] At stake is a view that assigns responsibility for the loss of the Polish state to Poles themselves, which could be called today the "victim syndrome."[24] By accepting a priori the legitimacy of the Romantic idea about Poles' primordial, proto-Slavic identity and extending this idea to the rank of a foundational principle of Polishness, Janion supplants an actual problem with an ostensible one. The real issue from a postcolonial viewpoint is that of foreign domination (with its sociocultural, psychological, economic, and other consequences), not the supposed loss of "Slavic" roots of Polish identity that Janion focuses on and approaches in a largely speculative way. Indeed, *Uncanny Slavdom* aspires to be a comprehensive study of the postcolonial dimension of Polish identity in literature and social life. However, in a telling shift of emphasis, the book moves to the sidelines the issue that is critical from a postcolonial perspective. In the process, the cultural manifestations and implications of foreign imperial hegemony within the Polish-Lithuanian Commonwealth's multinational society almost totally disappear from the horizon of inquiry. They are replaced with the argument that the Polish national misfortune lies in a defective construction of identity, in which Poland's Eastern roots are denied instead of being assented to and accepted in their undervalued and rejected "Easternness."

Janion appears not to notice that the burden of responsibility for the postcolonial condition of Poles is thus transferred from Poland's former hegemon—Russia—and the comprador intelligentsia co-opted by it, onto a subordination population. She defines this postcolonial condition as follows:

> Our situation is concretized in the fact that we are Slavs, meaning that as "Orientals" we belong to "organically imperfect" nations from the perspective of Western European civilization. The Latin complex results in a sense of dispossession from Slavic culture. At the same time, the notion of a cultural Slavic community arouses fear of "imperial Russia" and its once official Slavophilia. . . .
>
> We are a postcolonial country that simultaneously, as sometimes happens, feels superior to its colonizer—Russia. In this regard, we have felt, and still feel, like Europe struggling against Asian barbarism. As true Latin, Catholic, Mediterranean Europeans we cannot identify with Slavdom too much, for this would bring us close to the "inferiority" of Russia. But, as a postcolonial country, we are not after all true Europeans, since—as

> Slavs—we are secondary to them, being marked by the Russo-Slavic bastardization. We were at once a colonial state and a colonizer of our kindred Slavdom. We have always felt superiority towards it but at the same time some kinship with its "inferiority." (325, 328)

It is difficult not to agree with the vast majority of these observations. Indeed, they are not the only such articulations in Polish critical discourse. Similar observations are framed as a series of questions in a book older by several years and written by Jan Prokop, another Polish literary critic:

> The fragility of the national "I"—the crisis of national identity—would stem from an imbalance fueled by an inferiority complex in relation to the more developed West, and a superiority complex in relation to Russia, half Asiatic, less civilized, yet stronger? Or perhaps from the victimhood of the persecuted, in many regards reminiscent of the Old Testament, as well as the later, diasporic, Jewish victimhood? Or finally from the tensions between the periphery and the center, expressive of the specific *spasticity* and prickliness of the *weak* and small toward the *strong* and mighty?[25]

Prokop's direction of inquiry differs from Janion's in broadening its spectrum of possible answers. Recalling his thoughts here seems appropriate since the axis around which Janion builds her argument can arouse objections. The category on which the diagnosis proposed in *Uncanny Slavdom* rests is intellectually empty and ineffective, and its value as a contemporary research tool is questionable in the context of current postcolonial, Slavic, and comparative studies.[26] This category, of course, is the titular "Slavdom." Pushing this "anti-essentialistic" (22) concept of obscure content and scope, Janion extrapolates an ideologically laden idea with a Romantic lineage onto the present and suggests that Slavdom can serve as both an adequate tool of description for the current state of affairs and a panacea for the Polish "identity disease." She views Slavdom as a community supposedly rooted in the Romantic anti-Latinism and Slavic folklore, the extraction and recognition of a "collective amnesia" about Polish prehistory, and finally the Slavs' reservation toward the rest of Europe. Notably, these elements were introduced into the consciousness of Europeans through the Western orientalizing discourse, which successfully came to dominate the "reception style" of East-Central Europe, its societies and cultures, and imposed on them its own categorizations with a Hegelian lineage. The criteria with which Janion delineates the category of "Slavdom," however, remain unclear. Are they racial? Ethnic? Anthropological? Or perhaps linguistic? Surely, they are not geographic.

This is not a polemic against the obvious fact that Slavic tribes with their own origin myths about common ancestry once existed in Europe. Such a debate would be clearly unproductive. Janion is a refined humanist and certainly aware of twentieth-century discussions around the idea of Mitteleuropa, which the extensive footnotes in her book confirm. She purposefully chooses not to place her argument in this context, however, proposing "Slavdom" as a new, alternative conceptualization of the specificity of Polish identity in the postcolonial era. In so doing she references a different set of ideas and values than those behind concepts such as "Central Europe," or "East-Central Europe." Yet the bonds between Slavic nations, with the exception of Russian Slavophilia, were characterized by the lack of attempts to form any kind of a Pan-Slavic community, as Janion well knows.[27] Despite renouncing Pan-Slavism on the level of a declaration, her concept of "Slavdom" clearly evokes this idea, which takes her discussion down a risky track. It seems impossible to use the category of "Slavdom" today and disconnect it from that of "Slavophilia," the crowning argument of the Russian imperial discourse on the nations of Europe's Slavic region. Despite Janion's claims, the existence of aims within the "Slavic idea" other than Pan-Slavic ones does not justify deploying the category of "Slavdom" when analyzing these phenomena. To the contrary, it taints academic discourse with undesirable ideology and situates it within a specific worldview and political context, something that Aleksandr Lipatov warns against:

> The "Slavic idea" in its finished form represents the opposite of the "German" and "Western-centric" paradigms and rests on the same intellectual foundation. By dismantling and discarding inimical concepts that exclude Slavs from Europe, this idea sustains this intellectual foundation—though this seems paradoxical, it is actually perfectly logical—since it also excludes Slavic nations from the circle of European civilization (identified with the Roman-German "West"), viewing Slavs in terms of a mythologizing "self-containedness."[28]

The paradox of Maria Janion's study is that the concept of "Slavdom" that she employs is not ideologically neutral. Both the Slavophilic discourse of imperial Russia and the German historiographic discourse supportive of German imperialism made use of this category to further realize these powers' political goals. It was only in 1923 that Oskar Halecki, a Polish historian who introduced the term "East-Central Europe" to world historiography, questioned the use of the "Slavic" category in research into East-Central Europe, undermining its legitimacy along with the opinion voiced by German historians that there existed one "Slavic nation." He emphasized that a "Slavic point of view" does not exist as a historiographic principle of regional structuring in the framework of Europe's history, and that the opposition between a "Slavic world" and its supposed antithesis of Western Europe is an extreme consequence of Russian Pan-Slavism.[29] Janion's proposal, which substitutes the category of Central or East-Central Europe with the concept of Slavdom, comes dangerously close to the tactic of the Russian/Soviet hegemon, which pacified the independence movements of societies in this part of Europe with the doctrine of the "unity of Slavs."[30] Given this context, relying on a notion this ideologically laden in postcolonial studies of Polish literature and culture raises questions.

*Uncanny Slavdom* is inarguably a bold attempt to address a question of significance not only for Polish literature but also for the contemporary self-consciousness of Poles. Its charged reception, as reflected in its polarized reviews, is partially due to its ambivalent assessment of the role played by Christianity in the formation of national identity. It also stems from the specific way in which the postcolonial repository functions in the book. For this reason, *Uncanny Slavdom* can be seen as a peculiar and refined display of postcolonial "necessary fictions"; the book speaks to the need for a myth that confirms the subjectivity of a postcolonial population and strengthens its sense of autochthonism.[31] While in a "standard," intellectually unrefined version, these "fictions" revitalize myths about the former magnificence of the Polish-Lithuanian Commonwealth, of Poland "from sea to sea," in Janion's rendering they have a reversed form. In *Uncanny Slavdom*, references to Romantic interpretations of Slavic prehistory, along with speculations on the subject of Poles' present-day postcolonial identity that they give rise to, are an argument against Occidental views in reflections on Polish history and culture. Still, they do not explain these issues in a satisfying way.

Janusz Sławiński, a renowned Polish literary theorist, used the lighthouse as a metaphor of research activity.[32] Lighthouses vary in their strength: some cast a beam that brightens distant horizons, others glimmer dimly or flicker intermittently, and others only pretend to be lighthouses, not shedding any light at all. This list can be extended by yet another type: lighthouses that shine with a false light. Ships that follow them are at risk of getting lost or even of crashing, for they move in a light that gives rise to phantasmagoria instead of making actual objects visible in the darkness; the direction can be attractive and tempting, but it is illusory on closer inspection.

Maria Janion advocates an interpretation of Polish history that views Poland's acceptance of Christianity in terms of violence inflicted on a primeval, pagan social organism, rather than a sovereign political and religious choice that resulted in its admittance to a community of independent and equal states.[33] Perhaps the author was inspired by the faith of the Romantics; after all, the "idealization of primordial Slavdom is one of the most apparent characteristics of historical thought during the time of Romanticism."[34] Or perhaps she fell under the spell of a postmodern belief in the existence of an "original identity," the supposed antithesis of the "outdated" identity founded on religion. Neither possibility nullifies the other. It is here that the ambivalence of the intellectual proposition offered in *Uncanny Slavdom* is most clearly visible. On the one hand, the book's stated ambition is to overcome the temptation of a "defiant and puerile rejection of imperial cultures," while on the other hand it feeds off a "nativist" longing—the nostalgic exhumation of tradition as a formula for the strengthening of Polish identity.[35] Paradoxically, it does so by referencing pagan as well as Byzantine traditions interpreted in an anti-Latinist vein.

Setting aside Janion's motivation in using Saidian concepts, it must be said that her book performs a radical reevaluation of Polish history and culture with the help of postcolonial theory and offers its readers a kind of a scholarly, retrospective, Slavic utopia. The study is radical since Janion's interpretive direction neutralizes two ideas that were key to Polish writing from the end of eighteenth century onward: the republican will to self-determination without the interference of foreign powers and the awareness of belonging to Western culture.[36] The claim that Poles' identity as a decolonized society has components that are integral to Russian culture as the former hegemon's culture is not only a negation of Polish literature's raison d'être for at least two centuries but also a perverse application of postcolonial theory. The use of this theory is problematic to such a degree that the interpretation of events, texts, and alleged "blind spots" of old history undertaken in *Uncanny Slavdom* comes dangerously close in its conclusions to those derived from Soviet imperial discourse during the Stalinist period. In one of the Soviet history textbooks translated into Polish at that time, we find these passages about the Christianization of Western Slavs:

> The adoption of Christianity from the unenlightened and half-barbaric Germans rather than cultured Byzantium stalled the development of national culture in Western Slavdom. The clergy suppressed books written in Slavic languages and writing was developed entirely in the Latin language, which was incomprehensible to the people. . . .
>
> A mass of German clergy, who held Slavs in deep contempt and thought only of accumulating riches, flowed into Poland and Bohemia. Tithes were levied on the people and German monasteries took possession of vast lands in the Slavic countries.[37]

The Soviet imperial project, woven into the history textbooks for Polish youth during the Communist period, used two codes to articulate its civilizing mission: Great Russian and Marxist, both imperial, though the former explicitly and the latter implicitly so. Despite rhetorical differences, they likewise aimed to present the empire in ways that obstructed counterhegemonic discourse. Perhaps unwittingly, the narration of *Uncanny Slavdom* references a similar model; it offers an interpretation that is attractive because of the aura of mystery emanating from distant Polish premodernity and close to the deforming manipulatory conceptualizations within the hegemonic discourse. Janion's proposal loses sight of the Russian nationalism that served as the driving force behind the imperial activities of Poland's Eastern hegemon. Instead, the author attaches attention to an artificially isolated Polish nationalism, with its impact on the "real," meaning primordial, pagan Polish identity framed as purportedly destructive or at least problematic.

If postcolonial research of identity problems among societies such as the Polish one is to step outside of the conceptual frameworks and horizons drawn by the discourse of Russia / Soviet Union as the former hegemon, it must consider the dynamic of the complicated relations between Central and Eastern European peripheries and the metropoles, on which East-Central Europe was and continues to be dependent in many ways. Central to this dynamic is the fact that the Soviet colonization of this region enabled the process of "triangular identity formation" to take place across these territories by adding a new flagpole to the traditional network of postcolonial oppositions (West-Orient / Third World; we-them; center-periphery).[38] As a result, the East-Central European subject found itself situated between three mutually antagonistic reference points. These reference points, or centers of discourse, are characterized by a significant ambivalence, since they:

> were at once repulsive and hypnotically powerful. The West was both coveted for its freedom and opulence and vilified for its betrayal and naiveté. The Soviet Union was on the one hand a national adversary and criminal oppressor and, on the other, an impressively massive and sly victor, as well as the champion of the poor and the unexceptional many. The Orientals / Third World colonial subjects were at once the spectre of the Eastern Europeans' own failure and barbaric backwardness, but they were also natives of a romantic paradise of exotic opulence, as well as former subalterns who had gained their freedom just as the Eastern Europeans were losing theirs. All of the three reference points had something that the Eastern European lacked: a definite identity. The Sovietised Eastern European was neither a clear winner, nor a clear victim, neither Western, nor Eastern, neither entirely civilized, nor an utter barbarian or natural man.[39]

This perspective is missing from Maria Janion's intellectual proposal in *Uncanny Slavdom*. Further works on the subject of Polish identity, its sources, and its present condition are certain to come out, and some will hopefully engage with the perspective of Janion's book while also relying on postcolonial theory. Such works could cast a different light on those areas of Polish literature and culture that reveal their postcolonial entanglement. In this context, attention is due to the conservative current in Polish literature, which includes the work of Cyprian Norwid, one of the greatest Polish and European poets and artists, is expressive of the Christian attitude, and locates the core of Polish national self-identification within Christianity.[40]

Chapter Eleven

# The Melancholia of Borderlands Discourse

La mélancolie est le regret d'un autre monde mais
je n'ai jamais su quel était ce monde.

(Melancholia is a regret felt for another world,
but I am yet to discover which one.)

—Emile M. Cioran, *Cahiers 1957–1972* (June 27, 1958)

## Nostalgia, Melancholy, and Psychoanalysis

The atmosphere that prevails in Polish critical discourse on the literature and culture of the Borderlands is tangibly nostalgic. In the Polish context, the Borderlands refer to the former commonwealth's eastern and southeastern territories, which are located outside Poland since the end of World War II and presently fall within the boundaries of Lithuania, Belarus, and Ukraine. There is even a Polish neologism coined to describe the unique emotional aura that characterizes Borderlands discourse: "kresonostalgia," which translates rather awkwardly into English as "borderland nostalgia." This supposedly unique type of nostalgia is defined as "an important differentiator of literature after the November Uprising as well as the First and the Second World War. Purely elemental, it does not lend itself to commonsensical persuasion and control of reason. Borderland nostalgia was an everyday torture and torment that brought on states of depression while also, paradoxically, becoming sometimes an energizing and patriotic feeling."[1] The ambivalent character of nostalgia for the lost Borderlands conveyed by this quote—its torment and depressiveness on the one hand and its elemental nature, irrationality, and energy on the other—suggests that this affect is a specific variant of a well-known, intersubjective psychological experience that has been the subject of numerous philosophical and psychological studies. The affect in question is melancholia.

Among various types of melancholia there exists one called "postcolonial melancholia."[2] Paul Gilroy describes it as "cultural disorientation that accompanies the collapse of imperial certainties into postcolonial nihilism," and looks for the reasons behind this "collapse" in the end of the British Empire's colonial enterprise and its consequent loss of dominance on the world stage.[3] The Polish case is more complicated both from a historical and a geopolitical perspective. Poland, formerly the Polish-Lithuanian Commonwealth that included large parts of present-day Ukraine and Belarus, lost its imperial position at the end of the eighteenth century as a result of the partitions. Its territory was divided and subordinated to the rule of Russia, Austria, and Prussia. This was the case until 1918, when the Polish state appeared on Europe's map once again. Twenty years later, it was invaded by Nazi Germany and the Soviet Union in September 1939 and emerged from its ruins as a state under Soviet control, much transformed in nature, with its borders significantly shifted westward. This historical fluctuation of Poland's statehood, from a premodern empire to a country colonized by other empires, had unavoidable consequences for the Polish view of the past and experience of the present day. The category of "postcolonial melancholia" of interest in this chapter refers to precisely this (Polish) point of view and experience, although my understanding of the term differs in some ways from that proposed by Gilroy with reference to the British.

I suggest viewing postcolonial melancholia as a historically and geopolitically grounded case of a collective "disease of the soul," to reference Julia Kristeva's phrasing.[4] It affects not only those who experience "cultural disorientation" on losing their imperial status but also those who view themselves as backward, powerless, and weak as a result of having been colonized.[5] In confrontation with others, the latter display a lowered sense of self-esteem and a lack of self-respect. In the main, postcolonial melancholia affects those societies where colonial trauma manifests itself in a "loss of vitality," lack of faith in its own abilities, and a consequent low sense of self-worth. Of course, this set of negative parameters does not encompass the entire identity of postcolonial societies such as the Poles. Nevertheless, these elements are deeply ingrained in the fundaments of their collective identity.

Self-perception plays a key role in the process of reclaiming or reconstructing the postcolonial identity of a given population and is communicated via this population's cultural discourse: literature, film, journalism, and science. In the Polish case, this self-perception is characterized by an ambivalence typical of the postcolonial condition. On the one hand, it is expressed by reminiscing on greatness lost and on the other by blaming oneself for present-day shortcomings, failings, and flaws. The melancholia that arises from such historical experience can manifest itself as an unsolvable conflict between the actual condition of a collective, perceived by it as deplorable, and a memory of its former great accomplishments. This phenomenon affects societies of East-Central Europe to a particular degree, since they experienced foreign domination as a cultural and civilizational step backwards. David Chioni Moore terms this colonial model as "reverse-cultural colonization."[6]

In this chapter, I am treating melancholia as an analytical concept useful in exploring contemporary Polish discourse concerning the Borderlands, with a view to how this discourse participates in the formation of the Polish postcolonial subject. As we have learned from Freud, melancholia, like mourning, is "the reaction to the loss of a loved person, or to the loss of some abstraction which has taken the place of one, such as one's country, liberty, an ideal, and so on."[7] Melancholia is not identical with mourning, with the latter understood as a "normal affect."[8] Freud thus makes a key distinction between (healthy) mourning and (unhealthy) melancholia. Normally, the work of mourning leads to giving up the lost object or subject one yearns for—returning it to itself, in a sense. Melancholia, in turn, leads the grieving subject to construct an identity based on constant remembering and hyperbolization of the experienced loss. This has different consequences from those proper to mourning. As Freud explained, melancholia stems from a "pathological disposition" and is primarily distinguished by a "profoundly painful dejection, cessation of interest in the outside world . . . inhibition of all activity, and a lowering of the self-regarding feelings to a degree that finds utterance in self-reproaches and self-revilings."[9] Notably, some of the notes sounded in this description resonate with those struck by the opening diagnosis of "borderland nostalgia."

Borderlands discourse refers to writing on the literature, culture, and life in the territories of the former Polish-Lithuanian Commonwealth that were traditionally called "Kresy"—the Borderlands.[10] The nostalgia and vitality inherent in this writing arise from the interplay of three factors: (1) memory of the former glory of the Great Commonwealth, stretching "from [the Baltic] sea to [the Black] sea"; (2) the loss of the majority of its eastern and southeastern territories (now part of Lithuania, Belarus, and Ukraine) to the Soviet Union, first as a result of the Treaty of Riga (1921) and later due to the Yalta Accords (1945); and (3) the relegation of "the memory of Kresy and of the Polish presence in the region . . . to a strictly private sphere, while institutionally it was sustained by the Polish diaspora in the West . . . in a clearly pathetic and non-reflexive mode."[11] As a result, "the notion [of] kresy that dominated Polish émigré sociopolitical journalism and memories after the Second World War was saturated with nostalgia for the lost 'homeland' [*mała ojczyzna*]. At the same time it was almost absent in the historiography of the Polish People's Republic."[12] The model reader of Borderlands discourse is a member of the national collective who shares and subscribes to the axiology implied by this discourse. This axiology sees "the Borderlands" as having an absolute and unquestionable value as the defining element and part of the essence of Polishness, with the term itself being heavily loaded. The Borderlands symbolize an area diversified in terms of nationalities, ethnicities, culture, and religion, and because of its location on the frontier, additionally exposed and thus vulnerable to systematic contact with Others. Their symbolic position breathes new life into the myth of Poland as the *Antemurale Christianitatis*—the once-Christian Europe's last bulwark of defense against Turkish Islam and, between 1918 and 1939, Soviet atheism. During a time of Russian domination and the Soviet threat (the Polish-Bolshevik war of 1919–21), the Borderlands in particular became a place that cultivated the idea of "Polishness." Borderlands literature composed in Polish by writers with links to the region was the depository of the memory of Polish hegemony; it preserved the cultural and political "civilizing mission" that the gentry's emblematic residence—the manor house—was seen to fulfill in relation to other nations and ethnicities living in the Eastern peripheries of the Commonwealth. In fact, as Christoph Mick argues:

> For the Polish elites, Polish culture was . . . the solution for Eastern European "backwardness." They viewed Ukrainians, Belarusians and Lithuanians similar to the way Poles were perceived in Germany: as culturally inferior, incapable of state building and in need of someone who would lead them towards European civilisation, progress and modernity. While the German elites believed they brought culture and civilisation to Poland, the Polish elites in turn believed that *they* had brought culture and progress to Ukraine, Lithuania and Belarus, the former eastern borderlands of the Polish-Lithuanian Commonwealth. The borderlands (in Polish: *kresy*) discourse was a strange combination, in which fascination and longing for the "wild" and "natural" in these borderlands was commingled with a belief in the backwardness and inferiority of the East and its peoples.[13]

One of the foremost myths that aided Polish hegemony in the Borderlands was the myth of an idyllic, peaceful coexistence of national and ethnic groups whose members supposedly perceived the cultural supremacy of Poles as valuable and desirable. This myth, moreover, was supposed to neutralize darker memories of the Polish presence in the Borderlands, such as the Polish exploitation and maltreatment of Ukrainians and suppression of their drive for independence, which enraged the Ukrainian population and led to the massacres of Poles (Uman in 1768 and Volhynia in 1943).

Borderlands discourse became an affirmative discourse in relation to the values and ideas conveyed in Borderlands literature and culture. During the period of Soviet domination, the very term "Borderlands" was prohibited as politically forbidden and was even missing from the dictionaries.[14] The Communists considered it a threat to the region's alliance with the "brotherly Soviet nation" and an expression of a revanchist attitude toward the new, post–World War II political order. The politics of the Communist leadership in the Polish People's Republic precluded the possibility of a public debate about either historical events or the sociocultural processes linked to the Polish presence in the Borderlands. As a result, before 1989, neither Polish historiography nor public discourse had much space for critical reflection and debate about the colonial character of Poles' presence in the Borderlands and the implications of the Polish "civilizing mission" for other nationalities and ethnicities. The politics in place during the period of Soviet domination manipulated, and even "confiscated," Polish memory of the Borderlands by erasing relevant facts, figures, and places from public discourse.

In fact, even after 1989, the issue of Polish hegemony in the Borderlands has not been sufficiently addressed by Polish society. The removal of political censorship set off a wave of interest in the previously officially forbidden topic, which only entrenched the Borderlands legacy and prevented its critical reassessment. The Borderlands became a popular and fashionable theme that was explored as a new continent would be, aided by the publication of works by Józef Mackiewicz, Andrzej Chciuk, Florian Czarnyszewicz, Zygmunt Haupt, and Michał Kryspin Pawlikowski—authors banned by Communist authorities. This fascination arose from two interrelated factors: a collective nostalgia for the glorious pre-Communist and pre-partitions past and recourse to the Sarmatian idea to support contemporary Polish postcolonial identity.[15] The Sarmatian idea has been inextricably intertwined with the Borderlands myth of Henryk Sienkiewicz's *Trilogy* (published in the 1880s), a canonical Polish national narrative set in the Borderlands during the seventeenth century—a turbulent period of the Polish-Lithuanian Commonwealth's existence. It was through the *Trilogy*, which glorifies the heroism and bravery of the Polish gentry's defense of their homeland, that generations of Poles obtained their patriotic upbringing. Consequently, literature still plays a key role in the Polish political debate, focused, for example, on the legitimacy of including Sienkiewicz's work on compulsory reading lists in schools.

Polish nostalgia for the past, which refuses to be extinguished, is not just a symptom of a general, universal need for rootedness or, as Zygmunt Bauman says, for "rerooting the uprooted."[16] At stake is not just the pursuit of "dwelling"—the overcoming of a basic sense of ontological "homelessness"—which according to Heidegger typifies the existence of every human being.[17] After 1989, this nostalgia, in a restorative rather than a reflective version, is one of the factors shaping the postcolonial identity of societies that were cut off from their own traditions, to a greater or lesser extent, during the period of the Communist experiment.[18] It is also akin to the nostalgia that affects postcolonial societies.[19] As Pierre Nora writes, for certain "peoples, ethnic groups and even certain classes of individual in the world today" (such as Poles), "rehabilitating their past is part and parcel of reaffirming their identity," which is being rebuilt after the decolonization that "followed the collapse of twentieth-century totalitarian regimes, whether communist, Nazi, or just plain dictatorial." Nora calls this form of decolonization "an *ideological* decolonization which has helped reunite these liberated peoples with traditional, long-term memories confiscated, destroyed or manipulated by those regimes: this is the case with Russia and many countries in Eastern Europe, the Balkans, Latin America and Africa."[20]

As Nora further notes, this decolonization "has enhanced the very notion of 'collective memory,' hitherto little used." His perspective significantly modifies the current understanding of collective memory among postcolonial nations. It allows us to note the ambivalence that typifies postcolonial nostalgia:

> Like all forms of nostalgia, postcolonial nostalgias have both positive and negative aspects: usually the latter is foregrounded, as the source of an insecure idealism or sentimentality, casting a beneficent glow over past suffering and anxiety; but there is also a positive side, which admits the past into the present in a fragmentary, nuanced, and elusive way, allowing a potential for self-reflexivity or irony appropriate for former colonial . . . subjects trying to understand the networks of power relations within which they are caught in the modern world, and beyond which it often seems impossible to move.[21]

Regardless of whether we are dealing with its sentimental or ironic aspect, however, postcolonial nostalgia allows the subject to attain a more or less illusory fulfillment. In the case of literature, this fulfillment is achieved by calling forth the object of longing in the form of a story, allegory, or stylized language. In contrast to nostalgia, postcolonial melancholia as understood here does not allow this kind of fulfillment. Its implications are also different, as a later part of this chapter will show.

## Attitudes toward the Borderlands Legacy

Two antithetical images of the Borderlands coexist in Polish literature. Both are founded on Romantic representations and both call on the poetic idiom and rhetoric of Romanticism. The first crystallizes in an image of the Borderlands as a Polish paradise, foregrounding its idyllic aspects. This version of the Borderlands is represented chiefly by the Lithuania of Mickiewicz's poetry and by the work of Władysław Syrokomla and Ignacy Chodźko, among others. The second approach presents the Borderlands as an inferno and is symbolically embodied in the Ukraine of Juliusz Słowacki's play *The Silver Dream of Salome* and in the poetic tale *The Castle of Kaniv*, by Seweryn Goszczyński.[22] These versions of the Borderlands are opposed in terms of their meaning and emotional charge, yet they do have a common characteristic. Both construe the Borderlands as an imagined space that is prone to mythologization and aestheticization. It is this kind of a space that provides the setting of Sienkiewicz's *Trilogy*—"a 'meta-space of adventure' in which the chivalrous characters, wild scenery and dynamic plot made up a kind of a European western."[23] And it is from this space that Poles have been removed as a result of twentieth-century disasters such as the Second World War, genocide, and forced displacements.

The loss of the Borderlands had two effects. First, the cultivation of their memory became a collective imperative for Poles. Initially, during the Communist period, this imperative was communicated covertly, primarily in the form of family transmissions and through the circulation of literature through unofficial channels; after 1989, it entered public space openly. Second, the remembered image of the Borderlands did not undergo critical revision or reevaluation after 1989. Even writers known for their uncompromising attitude did not dare to take a mocking, ironic stance toward it, despite a strong tradition of "scoffers" in Polish literature (Witold Gombrowicz, Sławomi Mrożek, Stefan Kisielewski). "No one wished to 'scoff' at 'Borderlands' history and no one could. It would simply be too painful."[24] This is precisely the reason why Borderlands discourse is saturated with melancholia. It allows for basically one stance: the acceptance of the Borderlands legacy as a central and indispensable ingredient of "Polishness."

This is precisely where the Borderlands legacy becomes a problem in Polish cultural and critical discourse. On the one hand, it seems that Poles are doomed to accept this legacy, leave it intact, and continuously remember and rehearse its content. In this case, the recipient is seen to lack influence over the received legacy, which comes via an act that does not involve his or her choice. One might say that it is rather the legacy that *chooses* us for itself.

On the other hand, however, inheritance from the "spirits of the past," to use Jacques Derrida's apt wording, always consists in borrowing. This entails responsibility on the part of an heir, since "there is no inheritance without a call to responsibility."[25] Legacy, for this reason, is "never a *given*, it is always a task."[26] Following Derrida's understanding, we are not forced to preserve a legacy in an untouched state unless we choose to remain bound in its fetters and deprive ourselves of the opportunity to critically assess, revise, and perhaps even transgress our heritage. To repeat after Derrida:

> Heritage is not something you are given as a whole. It is something that calls for interpretations, selections, reactions, response and responsibility. When you take your responsibility as an heir, you are not simply subjected to the heritage, you are not called to simply conserve or keep this heritage as it is, intact. You have to make it live and survive, and that is a process—a selective and interpretive process.[27]

The problematic legacy of Borderlands discourse in Poland evidently calls for such "interpretations, selections, reactions, response and responsibility." The debate on how to best address it continues, particularly in literary criticism.[28] Following the threads of this debate suggests that attempts at critical reflection on this legacy can be perceived as attacks on the very core of Polishness, by the same token considered a violation of the national "code of honor." Indeed, bringing Borderlands discourse into the orbit of postcolonial studies is sometimes actually treated as a manifestation of apostasy.[29]

Historical arguments have a leading place in the conflict between Borderlands discourse and postcolonial criticism.[30] For the most part, they repeat the hoary theses of Polish historians, a canonical version of which can be found in this claim: "Polishness took root in Lithuania and Kievan Rus' primarily on a native, Lithuanian or Rusyn ground. It thus represented not an extension of Polishness brought along with the families of the arrivals, but a variant of spiritual life created on the spot, on one's own accord and on the initiative of the locals."[31] On the opposite end of the spectrum lies the perspective of those critical of Borderlands discourse in its dominant form. They view the Polishness of the Borderlands not as a stimulus to culture and civilizational development but as the beginning of the exploitation of these territories and their inhabitants:

> The "Borderland" nations that . . . within this knowledge paradigm were denied the right to an independent existence and deprived of their freedom were the "ignorant" native masses. In a cultural sense, the partial sovereignty of Lithuania in the Commonwealth of Both Nations

> was a fiction. . . . These "masses" were offered one path to civilization—Polonization through the loss of their own identity that, as a sign of cultural inferiority, could not be accepted.[32]

This interpretation of Borderlands history finds its epistemological as well as ethical justification in Said's category of orientalism:

> It is worthwhile to look at interwar politics toward the Borderlands using the Saidian conceptual apparatus, as the struggle of an all-encompassing system of knowledge/power (Polish orientalism) with the awakening consciousness of the Other—Ukrainian, Lithuanian, and Belorussian nationalisms. This greatly shifts the balance of force to the detriment of Poles, since the Polish state's physical force was bolstered with extensive layers of structural force expressed in a homogenous knowledge, culture, and language and in denying "foreigners" the right to them.[33]

Despite the objections of Polish postcolonial critics, the Borderlands are still a symbol of an irrevocable loss in the common mentality of Poles and one of the greatest and most painful traumas that Polish society experienced during nineteenth and twentieth centuries. Inscribed in this framework, Borderland-themed narrations repeatedly refer to the lost eastern territories and consequently the lost part of Polish national genealogy and Polish subjectivity. The Borderlands in these narrations are a mythical space in which various national and ethnic groups lived together in harmony once upon a time, as a community that presently exists only in individual and collective memory as well as in artistic invention. As Stanisław Uliasz puts it, "The Borderlands have broken away in a sense from territories and ethnic groups, living and developing only in the minds of people," as a result of which they "appear in the present in a symbolic and sublimated form."[34] This peculiar "derealization" of the Borderlands space, which is especially striking in texts written after 1945, in moving the material world of tangible places to a mental world of reminiscence and imagination—a world of "collective memory"—paradoxically only amplifies the "absent presence" of the Borderlands and the interpretive, axiological character of references to it.[35] Tellingly, such references are not decreasing in number:

> In our [Polish] literature, the Borderlands are still a fecund and reliably fruitful area. Although they now exist only as a historical concept, having been deprived of their political vitality and geographical position, the Romanticism that had sprung there still attracts with its spontaneity, the diversity of cultures that constituted it, the exoticism of contrasts and broadness of customs. More, the Borderlands have grown larger,

> proliferating psychologically and mentally, and entering the realms of philosophy and metaphysics. After all, they have become a land of memory, both promised and lost. They are an Arcadia, the country of cultural childhood, but also a realm of accursed problems on both national and human scales.[36]

It is thus neither physical nor political geography but the coordinates of psychology and philosophy that determine and justify the presence of Borderlands themes in contemporary Polish discourse. The Borderlands provide a formula for the universalization of cultural questions: they become "a tool for describing and thinking about the world and a means of ordering issues of importance for East-Central Europe."[37] While this thinking extends beyond issues of history and geopolitics to the cultural sphere, it is nevertheless strongly rooted in Polishness, and it is precisely Polishness that it chooses as the vantage point and aim of its observations. In addition, it privileges one trajectory of interpretation of the Borderlands heritage and experience over all others: that which accentuates the incurred loss. This loss is by no means limited to the loss of territory: it is as much cultural, spiritual, and metaphysical as it is geographic. Jan Błoński called this phenomenon of returning to the Borderlands, observed in the works of Polish writers in the 1980s, "the emigration of imagination."[38] An opinion voiced in 1986 by another literary critic, Jerzy Jarzębski, still seems timely: "In Polish literature, 'the eastern theme' is, so to speak, an attempt to describe an amputated limb that still aches."[39]

The nature of this loss is not unequivocal, and the loss itself requires further differentiation. For those who have kept the traumatic reminiscence of forced displacement in their (personal or familial) memory, the loss has become a key formative experience or simply an inerasable component of their psychological archive.[40] Evidence of this can be found in works of Włodzimierz Odojewski, Aleksander Jurewicz, or Włodzimierz Paźniewski, among others, which try to deal with the trauma of expulsion from the Borderlands. Narrated in various forms—autobiographical, fictional, historiographic, and documentary, as memoirs, stories, reportages, and interviews—this experience is expressed in nostalgia for lost space and time. This nostalgia is admittedly still tied to a concrete geographical area, but it has at its core a longing "not so much for the place that was lost, but for one's past self in that place."[41] The writer Józef Wittlin, who was born in Podolia and did not return to his birthplace following World War II but died as an emigrant in New York, wrote in 1946: "Weakness for those places in the world where the years of our youth had passed is often only self-love in disguise. It is not for Lviv that we long after years of separation, but for our own selves in Lviv."[42]

Viewed in this light, the Borderlands become something more than just a "poetologic space of freedom" or "unreal reality" subject to aestheticization.[43] For those who did not personally experience the particular kind of displacement that was expatriation from the Borderlands homeland, the loss became an experience stored in and accessed through collective (post)memory. Separated from individual biography, it evolved into an intersubjective lack sensed by the entire population and became a key part of collective Polish biography and identity. The fissure, or rather breach, created in the process led to a specific paralysis of identity—a paresis manifested by falling into a fundamental impotence that is difficult to describe yet felt by the community—a sign of melancholia. It is not the mourning after lost territories, or the nostalgia tied to their former (political, cultural, or economic) role, that requires the critical reflection enabled by postcolonial studies; it is rather this melancholia, which is transmitted by Borderlands discourse irresistibly and consistently, if often with subtlety that neutralizes possible critique. This melancholia is not innocent. To the contrary, it conceals traces of resentment that make it difficult in turn for the Polish subject to recognize and tackle its current postcolonial condition. It is this melancholia that forces its subject to wander constantly within a world of simulacra, the substitutes of reality, cultivating its suffering as a result of experienced deprivation. This deprivation is understood not as, or not only as, the loss of physical territory but more in categories of the individual and collective trauma of cultural disinheritance, as the lack mentioned above—an ontological incompleteness.

Under such circumstances, it becomes clear that Borderlands-based melancholia reveals its Freudian characteristics. Instead of stimulating healthy mourning that, according to Freud, is oriented toward grieving a loss in order to accept it and transition to normal functioning, a significant portion of Borderlands discourse finds itself in the grip of melancholia—the pathological substitute of mourning: "Differently . . . than in the case of a person in mourning, the melancholic is unable to work through the loss of the loved object and to accept it. The object in a sense continues to live within him and carries out its destructive work from the inside, so to speak."[44] Looking at this issue on a social level, one can say that a population experiences melancholia when its discourse does not provide a narrative framework that would allow it to come to terms with a loss. As a result, this loss appears difficult to define, elusive, and intangible. It shocks with its totality, encompasses all aspects of collective existence, and annihilates. The issue here is not just that Poles lost an extensive part of their former dominion. The loss celebrated by means of Borderlands literature and criticism leads to a "phantom pain" that is analogous to that experienced by amputees: detached from its original base, the pain becomes autonomous. As Freud describes it, instead of remaining outside of the subject, it transforms into an object that is internal and psychic. The place of the lost object is taken up by its painful memory. Cultivating this memory opens up an entire field of self- and hetero-stereotypes, through which Poles view themselves and their imagined "Others." As happens with stereotypes, the knowledge they provide turns out to correspond in part with reality and in part to depart from it. The subject that attains knowledge via Borderlands discourse is frustrated on discovering that it cannot undertake any actions to restore the lost object. In effect, it oscillates between two opposite feelings: pride and shame. These emotions are particularly strong whenever the subject attempts to face challenges arising from the outside. In this way, the melancholic subject in the postcolonial era grows painfully aware of its lack of agency. Passive and silent, the subject consequently finds comfort in dwelling on the unchanging images from the past and questioning its melancholic condition. This is true even when these questions are dressed in a universalist rhetoric, as happens in Adam Zagajewski's poem "To Go to Lviv":

> I won't see you anymore, so much death
> awaits you, why must every city
> become Jerusalem and every man a Jew.[45]

How to overcome this phantom pain?

The melancholic subject remains in a state of narcissistic identification with the lost object after its prior internalization and inclusion into the realm of its identity. The melancholic subject experiences an internal "rupture" as a result of which "it can never come fully to terms with itself, with others, and with the past."[46] In a state of deprivation, it *needs* an object to complete it. It needs it to such an extent that this object becomes the main factor that defines the subject's identity. In this regard, the term "Borderlands" turns out to be doubly misleading. It suggests peripherality even though it refers to the cultural and mental space seen as the core of Polish identity that marks "a line of defense of Polishness."[47] Jan Kieniewicz rightly emphasizes that "Borderlands are a way of thinking among Poles, an essential element of their identification. In this sense, they are incredibly important for the definition of Polishness and its manifestations, which naturally includes Polish literary works."[48]

The subject experiencing postcolonial melancholia suffers from a stubborn lack that cannot be compensated for and that cannot be dealt with otherwise than through constant reminiscence of past collective trauma spurred on by hope for the return of the lost fragment of the collective "I." Is such a return even possible? Would it be better if, following Lacan's logic, the dream remained an unrealized fantasy, since its fulfillment would become a nightmare?[49] Trying to rationalize this situation on a metaphysical basis, or accepting it on historiosophic grounds, entrenches this lack rather than helps to overcome it. Its tragic nature is too inconceivable to submit to the logic of some order. The forced displacement and dispossession lead the subject of Borderlands discourse to settle within an experience of untreatable pain inflicted on its community. This experience is retained in discourse, immobilized and preserved with the means of various literary genres: lyrical poetry and narrative fiction, autobiographical relations and reportages, essays and epistolography.

The essayist Jerzy Stempowski already grasped this ambivalent awareness of lack, along with the hope for its compensation with the aid of discourse used as an instrument of conceptual appropriation, in 1967: "The most beautiful and least troublesome form of possessing land in historical terms seems to me to be our present possession of the former eastern borderlands. We hold them still in memory, in literature, and in museums."[50] An explicit literary proof of the colonial character of Polish presence in the Borderlands comes, in turn, from Jarosław Iwaszkiewicz, who delivered the following criticism through one of the heroes in his *Sława i chwała* (Fame and glory) trilogy: "Our lords sure wanted Ukraine. Native Poland did not and could not bring profits like those of the Podolian and Ukrainian estates. It was difficult to give up our colonies. . . . Others searched beyond the seas. Here it was right on hand: a land flowing with milk and honey."[51] Setting aside the possible historical reasons evoked in these arguments, which arise from the geopolitical and ideological context of Iwaszkiewicz's novel, it still needs to be noted that his reasoning augurs a present-day current in discussions of Polish postcolonial critics. It concerns the specificity of Polish imperial ambitions both toward neighboring territories of the present-day Ukraine, Belarus, and Lithuania ("here it was, right on hand") and in the context of the overseas conquests in the planning stages before World War II, when the Polish Maritime and Colonial League sought overseas colonies, notably Madagascar.[52] The protagonist's cited opinion also highlights the surprising ability of art to offer insights that anticipate, sometimes by a long shot, the scholarly frameworks developed over time. Stempowski, who was an emigrant essayist and a cosmopolitan unburdened by Polish-centered obsessions, can be read in the passage above as the ultimate conclusion drawn from the matter pointed out by Iwaszkiewicz. This opinion confirms at the same time one of postcolonialism's main theses, that colonial discourse does not have to arise directly from actual territorial ambitions but can also be rooted in a certain mental map. In the cited letter from 1952, shortly before Iwaszkiewicz wrote *Fame and Glory*, Stempowski admits honestly that "possessing the land" is still the issue. He thus not only allows for the possibility of what I have called here "conceptual appropriation" but applies a telling double superlative to this form of textual possession, presented as "the most beautiful" and "the least troublesome" form of ownership. From here, it is not far to the idea that "melancholy is not simply the attachment to the lost object but the attachment to the very original gesture of its loss."[53] One can dare to propose that postcolonial melancholia is a significant source of this strong presence of texts oriented by the vector of loss in Polish writing. This loss is debated and restaged in its ever-new aspects, sometimes becoming the subject of admiration. This is true also for writers and critics with only secondhand experience of the expulsion from the Borderlands, one passed down the generations in line with the laws of postmemory and often purely aesthetic, an experience mediated by reading.[54] We are not dealing here with a closed set of personal testimonies. Borderlands discourse proliferates in texts that demonstrate "the patriotism of loss," as one might call it, with its canonical expression coming via Mickiewicz's invocation to *Pan Tadeusz*: "Lithuania, my fatherland!"[55]

## Wherein the Allure?

Given all that has been said thus far, Borderlands discourse had to become an object of interest for Polish postcolonial studies. This reflection is accompanied by an air of "imperial guilt," which makes Borderlands research seem a form of partial compensation granted to the Polonized (meaning colonized) nations of the former multinational commonwealth: the Belarusians, Lithuanians, Ukrainians, and Jews.[56] Postcolonial studies aims to reveal aspects of these groups' subalternity in relation to the Polish center and in so doing to restore their subjectivity in discourse. They are also meant to rebuild the conceptual framework in which Borderlands discourse has functioned thus far.

This process has begun. In this regard, Daniel Beauvois's categorical comments that the time has come to break away from "Borderland-mania," which he sees running amok in Polish historiography and beyond it, have had their impact.[57] In his introduction to a new edition of *The Ukrainian Triangle*, Beauvois complains:

> Six years [after the first edition] . . . and the wide world of science and politics is not yet familiar with its contents and is sometimes still guided by prejudice and stereotypes. Despite my energetic exhortations from the previous introduction, the myth of the eastern Borderlands of the former Commonwealth, the visions of false Arcadia, are still common. . . . [I]t must be said that images of a Ukraine centered on the Polish landowners still prevail. The stream of Borderland-mania flows only in this direction.[58]

Understandably, the aesthetization of the Borderlands typical of Borderlands discourse meets with resistance of non-Polish readers. Polish readers have long become accustomed to comments such as this one, that "Lithuanian, Belarusian, and Ukrainian rivers flow most beautifully in Polish literature."[59] Both writers and critics, from whom one expects distance and reflexivity, participate in this mythologization or mystification. Even among the younger generation of critics, some passively give into the nostalgic, memorial atmosphere of Borderlands narrations, as if they were rendered helpless and incapacitated by the rhetoric of its literature. This is reflected in their use of an emotionally charged idiom: "The Borderlands are like a tome in which nature, humans and time have inscribed their marks, which speak as much to fashion as to their value for Polish culture and for their Polish life as far as this value can be rationally and emotionally defined."[60] Clearly, Polishness in the texts of Borderlands discourse is dominant not just as a theme but as an ethnocentric perspective: it justifies, absolves, removes doubts, and disallows any point of view that is based in an identity other than Polish.

Given the clash between historical facts and their artistic representations in literature, the following question seems reasonable: "Are literary returns to the realm of nostalgic images of pastoral life inevitable in the face of a reality filled with poverty, conflicts, and hate?"[61] This question can also be applied to nonliterary forms of expression, as well as extended to foreground aspects of the antinomy signaled above: Can the substitution of a self-reflexive, "not fabricated," and unmystified version of Borderlands discourse for its "retouched," mythologizing version help to prevent the instrumentalization of the past while also avoiding the trap of ethnocentrism?

The problem in question here cannot be reduced to the incommensurability of two orders: of (artistic and critical) narrations on the one hand and of historical facts on the other. It cannot be resolved with a reevaluation of Borderlands discourse in terms of tolerance or sensitivity to otherness. The need for such an open attitude is difficult to argue with. It seems absolutely necessary to meaningful research activity on any ethnic periphery.[62] While in itself noble and right, limiting ethnocentrism in the contemporary discourse of the humanities in favor of a pluralistic approach respectful of multiethnicity and multiculturalism does not solve the basic difficulty of the troublesome position of the Borderlands in Polish writing—not only of the artistic or autobiographic kind but also journalistic and scientific, including Borderlands discourse. This troublesomeness is already signaled by the emotional tone of the term "Borderlands" and the attachment as much to it as to its hazy referent, which is nevertheless full of complex content and affective energy. Is the cause of this state of affairs rooted only in the national pride of postcolonial Poles? In the longing after the imperial past of the commonwealth?[63] Commenting on Polish society's attitude toward the Borderlands, Beauvois notes with surprise, "To be honest, it is not clear why Ukraine continued to fill the soul of the average Pole with nostalgia and allure even during Communist times."[64] The reason why the French historian cannot understand Polish "Borderlands melancholia" will come up again since it is significant for reasons basic to this discussion. Here it is enough to point out that Beauvois's opinion is symptomatic of a more general attitude, held by those who wish to see Borderlands discourse as a glaring example of an ethnocentric hegemonic discourse, one that orientalized—and still orientalizes, according to numerous popular science publications—ethnic groups other than Poles and any non-Polish culture.[65] From this perspective, Borderlands discourse duplicates the model of territorial and cultural domination typical of empires by activating a mechanism of appropriation and control within a textual space. This kind of interpretation does not state directly that Borderlands discourse can feed the imperial aspirations of Poles; it positions this imperial, or quasi-imperial, episode of Polish history, however, as a menacing memento that reveals a discursive violence hidden in innocent-sounding, descriptive terms. This is the reason why one hears, from time to time, calls to strip the language of academic and popular Borderlands scholarship of its hegemonic coating, for instance, by putting the term in quotation marks. These linguistic traces of hegemony belong to a realm of "soft" concepts rather than of "hard" historical facts, but they have an impact as great as the actions of governments and militaries: they limit, bind, deny both sovereignty and subjectivity, eliminate.

Indeed, once one reads *Orientalism*, it is difficult to accept the continued use of categories that distort Others and show a lack of understanding and respect for their otherness. This also pertains to Polish Borderlands discourse, which needs to reach for a higher standard of self-awareness now than it did in the late 1980s. While the standard social practice of premodern times lacked such acceptance, continuing this state of affairs today raises reasonable doubts. It is impossible to retain the delusion that a scholarly description of a fragment of reality can be offered from a neutral, universalistic position. We are well aware of the limited horizon of our knowledge and the existence of factors that condition it. Critical arguments against Borderlands discourse are justified on these grounds. Does it follow, however, that inscribing this discourse into the context of Polish hegemony is its only correct interpretation? Is this discourse deserving only of critique as an archive, or else nursery, of ethnocentric and imperial attitudes?

The presence of "nostalgia" and "allure" in Borderlands discourse, which is unfathomable to Beauvois, can be explained with reference to the understanding of cultural melancholia. To develop Beauvois's thought in a direction he probably did not foresee, one can say that, filled with such elements, the "soul of the average Pole" falls ill with melancholia that takes two forms without ever ceasing to be a disease requiring a cure: of "sublime beauty" in Borderlands literature and of intellectual pursuits in Borderlands discourse.[66] Like all melancholia, this one also makes the subject unable to "not want" what is necessary for its self-knowledge and self-definition. The melancholia of which we speak is the longing of a portion of the population for part of its lost self-image. The search for a collective self-portrait is hindered, and sometimes even made impossible, by recognizing the Other as the object of former domination, even if this domination were to be "only" discursive. Based on this understanding of melancholia, the view of the Borderlands that is presently characteristic of Polish Borderlands discourse opens the way to mythologization and stereotyping, both of the Other and of the Polish subject's attitude toward it. Idealizing narrations are its fruit, which interweave "Polishness" with "otherness" in a natural and mutually beneficial symbiosis and make the Borderlands appear as the model space of encounter, dialogue, and openness; as if Aleksander Fiut's thesis about the "'velvet' colonization" of the Grand Duchy of Lithuania could be applied with impunity to all of the Borderland territories.[67] In an essay tellingly titled "Poland Is Still the Borderlands," Zbigniew Żakiewicz put it thusly: "Over the years, the Borderlands became my soul's homeland, a mythic and metaphysical land. Until finally, when already mature, I understood that 'Borderlandness' [*kresowość*] is something dear to Polish nature if this nature is to be alive, open to otherness, loving toward 'little homelands,' and oriented toward the Universe."[68] The role of the Borderlands in Polish culture has been described similarly by many writers and critics. Zbigniew Bieńkowski emphasized the memory and myth-making function of this peculiar locale, using—with admittedly great finesse—arguments characteristic of an ethnocentric attitude:

> The Borderlands, having lost their political and geographical position, take possession of and absorb ever larger realms of accumulating memory as

> they descend into history, legend, and myth. As a purely temporal category now, as a term and a concept, they encompass everything that has passed, all that the element of eternity has blown over and covered. Lithuania, Belarus, Ukraine [have been] classically historical realms of Polish culture. . . . The concept of the Borderlands contains everything that constitutes diversity, richness of ideas, receptivity and readiness to accept the world, the fertile psychological complexity and attractiveness of Polish culture. Perhaps now more than at any other time, doomed to a diet of homogenous culture, we are aware of the values brought by Lithuanians, Belarusians, Ukrainians, and Jews in cocreating the [Polish] language, custom, and imagination. It is to them that our culture owes its unique position in European culture.[69]

This type of mythologization obscures the fact that Borderlands discourse centers on the Polish subject and is conducted from its position. As a result, the ideas, values, and meanings assigned to Others by this discourse are a projection of this subject's point of view. This means that they are regulated by claims with a particular nationalistic and ethnocultural basis despite their camouflage of universalism. This line of argumentation posits Others as a function of dominant culture, and the thought that they should seek to construct their own, sovereign culture, one not necessarily built on the Polish cultural model's values, is not within the subject's discursive horizons.

## Revisionism? Imperial Nostalgia?

The subject of Borderlands discourse is historically and geographically, and even geopolitically, determined. These preconditions likely escaped Daniel Beauvois's attention when he pointed to the imperial tinge of Polish-Ukrainian relations. The former multinational commonwealth lost the Borderlands to Russia in the first partition (1772). After the recovery of its lesser part at the Treaty of Riga in 1921, the Second Republic lost it again to the Soviet Union in the Soviet invasion of Poland in September 1939. The resulting loss destabilized the Polish subject, deprived it of its potency, and made it susceptible to the melancholia at issue here. The term "Borderlands" has become the beacon and the emblem of this melancholia. If the historical Polish-Ukrainian or Polish-Lithuanian relations are to be viewed today as relations between a former empire and a decolonized periphery, the above-noted Russian factor has to be part of the context. Russian hegemony touched all nationalities and ethnic groups on the territories of the former Borderlands.[70] In the case of Poles, its primary implication was that the commonwealth as an empire was subject to "forgetting," in the sense of the forced exclusion from memory of the more unpleasant aspects of Polish dominance in the Borderlands, such as the disenfranchisement of the Ukrainian population, social and economic oppression, and instances of brutality.[71] At the source of this peculiar amnesia lies the aforementioned melancholia. Poles' memory about the realities of being an empire has been erased by the experience of fourfold loss: of territory, political status, self-confidence, and international prestige. Both the very term "Borderlands" and the discourses it inspired point to a significant lack, deficit, or rupture in Polish identity. This rupture confirms that the subject of melancholia had been split or broken apart. As a result, it no longer views itself or its community as representative of the empire and does not feel responsible for the imperial past of its country. To the contrary, it sees itself and its nation as more of a victim. Borderlands discourse becomes the place where this self-understanding is articulated.

Both Borderlands literature and Borderlands discourse thus meet at a shared juncture: they perform the gesture of mourning for a loss. The subject and the ideal reader of both discourses, by participating in and through writing or reading, attempt to rescue the identity and integrity that have been put in harm's way as a result of Russian and Soviet hegemony. They demonstrate at the same time that they have regained the right that was lost owing to this hegemony—the right to such a narration about the past in which the substance of the Borderlands is the pinnacle of the hierarchy of values. The form these efforts inevitably take is narcissism, which can be seen as a side effect of subordination. The narcissistic, (post)colonial self is a self that, in celebrating the *lieux de memoire* of the Borderlands, celebrates also itself *in relation to* these places. The melancholia that flows from this narcissism appears here as a cultural self-defense instrument used by a population to guard against loss. It is not the loss of a place, which has been lost already, but the loss of its memory. This memory constitutes the postcolonial identity of a dislocated subject. Melancholia is an attempt to overcome—by means of aestheticizing and mythologizing the Borderlands—a defect in the collective identity caused by colonial subordination. From this perspective, Borderlands discourse appears not so much "denotatively empty," as Edward Kasperski, a renowned scholar of this topic, postulates, as akin to a deforming mirror in which the postcolonial subject looks at itself without being fully aware of its postcolonial condition.[72] When looking at this phenomenon on an individual level, contemporary psychology calls attention to the specific character of this narcissism. It results from disturbed self-expression caused by multiple acts of humiliation.[73] The same principles that reflect individual mental development can be observed on the level of social attitudes and behaviors. "All narcissistic individuals live with the unresolved polarity of grandiosity and worthlessness."[74] These two polarities strike at the core of Polish literature and public discourse of the nineteenth and twentieth centuries. At the very basis of the melancholia discussed in this chapter lies the humiliation performed on Polish society, first by the Russian, and subsequently Soviet, oppressors. The weakening, or loss of self-confidence, which is especially visible in the subject's contacts with Others, is noticeable in the work of Maria Rodziewiczówna, Zygmunt Haupt, Andrzej Chciuk, Włodzimierz Odojewski, and Julian Wołoszynowicz, among many others. The Polish "I" often appears in their writing to be defensive and withdrawn, affected by a complex of believing itself to be "a backwater of Europe."[75] It has traits that can be described as symptomatic of a "false self": characteristics of a subject that is resigned to its fate even during acts of heroic rebellion and that constantly looks for the approval of others, anticipating their expectations and demands and reacting sensitively to even "slight disapproval or failure."[76] Thus understood, narcissism can be perceived both in the psychological structure of literary characters and in the "narcissistic style" in which their histories are narrated.[77] The "false self" that develops under conditions of foreign domination is prone to indulge in narcissistic self-illusions. Heinz Kohut has formulated a theoretical framework of this defense mechanism.[78] He indicates two of its main and complementary forms: idealizing and depreciation. To maintain a cohesive self that is authentic rather than false, the individual depreciates the value of others, which boosts his or her self-esteem. The self that Donald Winnicott named the "false self" undergoes depreciation and denigration. Stretched between the poles of idealization and devaluation, the postcolonial subject's illusions, which can be granted the status of "necessary fictions," become the main source of national self-esteem and sense of self-worth.[79] Simultaneously, these illusions are a type of compensation that is actualized in Borderlands discourse, whose specific, affirmative reception style they also project.

Opponents of a postcolonial revision of Borderlands discourse seem to be led by the same melancholia that has fueled Polish identity discourse in its anti-colonial aspect (opposition to partitioning empires) as well as the imperial one (physical and textual appropriation of the Borderlands and low sensitivity to the national aspirations of their non-Polish inhabitants) since the times of Romanticism—which indeed still fuels it. This melancholia makes itself known in stubborn language structures and clichés, as well as the methodological paths and procedures routine in times before the emergence of postcolonial theory. These elements have entered literary practices in the form of reproduced descriptive and interpretive models, and they play the role of transparent and seemingly ideologically neutral means of understanding. In actual fact, however, they store the charge of discursive domination, even when it is not intended or has been openly rejected. This argument offers sufficient support for the thesis that identity discourse based on the uncritical foregrounding of the Polishness of the Borderlands has an exclusive character and bears the marks of colonial discourse. To some extent, even when it does not lead directly to the reawakening of imperial sentiments, it replicates former relations of dependency.

The issue is still more complex, however. In reality, it is a variant of melancholia that leads Polish opponents of postcolonialism to question the postcolonial theorizing of the Borderlands. The melancholia characteristic of their anti-colonial stance can be viewed as a means of resisting the possibility of losing control over the discourse of loss. It seems that the melancholia of contemporary Borderlands discourse, in opposition to the narcissistic melancholia of the Romantic and post-Romantic Borderlands literature, cannot be reduced to the repetition of the gesture of loss when faced with a threat to collective identity. This melancholia is accompanied by a different attitude, which arises from the awareness that the subject's desires are incompatible with the possibilities provided by the discourse. The subject wants to grasp and describe the cultural space of the former Borderlands, but it has only two means at its disposal: it can either draw on the available archive of Borderlands discourse with its traditional, ethnocentric categories, which opens it to charges of supporting Polish domination, or it can escape from this archive and instead risk the charge of abandoning its native scholarly discourse and subservience toward a new methodological fashion, which postcolonialism is still seen to be. The second option, interpreted as a kind of treason, sometimes meets with sharp rebukes:

> I call "apostates" those critics who attempt to "rechristen" and rename Borderlands literature as postcolonial literature. They write that it is an expression of Polish colonialism, a symptom of colonial (postcolonial) consciousness. It supposedly always shows "ours" as better and civilized and "theirs" (meaning all of the Borderlands nations) as worse and barbaric. Borderlands literature supposedly still accentuates Polish sense of superiority and the unalienable right to govern over the Borderlands nations, negating their ability to live independently and foregrounding its own imperial "Polonocentrism" and xenophobia. The apostates want to prove that Borderlands literature has a "colonial core" and is not capable of leading to true dialogue with Ukrainians, Belarusians, and Lithuanians (who are fully ready for such a dialogue). It is necessary, they say, to decolonize

> our mentality, thought, imagination, and language, and to allow Others to speak. . . . In the end, these are divagations that obscure the truth. The Commonwealth of the Borderlands did not colonize by means of bloody, offensive wars and the conquests of cruel conquistadors; it did not trade slaves, plundering and destroying, as Spain, Portugal, or England did in America, Africa, and India. Each Borderlands country was annexed by means of voluntary unions and settlements on wild and ownerless lands, good organization of political and economic life, and its own culture and education. And Borderlands literature? The countless pages dedicated to the unique values of different nations living in the Borderlands more than return what was owed.[80]

The skepticism toward applying the category of postcolonialism to the studies of Borderlands literature is at times expressed with more muted rhetoric: "It seems . . . that these tools, brought over from studies of relations in colonizing countries during the nineteenth century, which formed colonial empires, do not entirely fit research into less violent processes that at different times included the 'exchange' of submission-domination rule."[81]

The methodological dilemma just outlined highlights a fundamental problem that scholars of Borderlands writing and culture must confront: the reflexive attitude toward one's own identity and toward the object of exploration. This problem cannot be sidestepped. It has to be faced and addressed to prevent further studies of the Borderlands from becoming mired in melancholia. Doing so requires confronting the Polish point of view with that "of other participants in social communication, represented by artists of other cultures and nations who co-inhabited the areas of the former Commonwealth's eastern borderlands."[82] The proposal to read the Borderlands as a multiethnic and multicultural palimpsest is a far cry from textual appropriation and discursive domination. The diversity of the human experience, including the historical experience of collectives, makes it imperative for the ethos of a contemporary humanist to practice sensitivity toward this delicate subject and take a critical stance that is respectful of the fate of others, aware of cultural difference, and accepting of the diverse narratives that other lives inspire. The postcolonial position has the advantage of uncovering the traps of monocentrism and monoperspectivism in discourse (here, Borderlands discourse) and finding ways of avoiding them. Said's warning from the final pages of *Orientalism* fits perfectly the issue at hand:

> Modern thought and experience have taught us to be sensitive to what is involved in representation, in studying the Other, in racial thinking, in unthinking and uncritical acceptance of authority and authoritative ideas, in the socio-political role of intellectuals, in the great value of a skeptical

> critical consciousness. Perhaps if we remember that the study of human experience usually has an ethical, to say nothing of a political, consequence in either the best or worst sense, we will not be indifferent to what we do as scholars. And what better norm for the scholar than human freedom and knowledge? Perhaps too we should remember that the study of man in society is based on concrete human history and experience, not on donnish abstractions, or on obscure laws or arbitrary systems.[83]

In this way, having realized its key critical idea, *Orientalism* outlines a general framework for studies in the humanities. Applied to Borderlands discourse, this framework translates into overcoming its ethnocentric limitations.

As already noted, some critics maintain a reserved stance toward including the Borderlands in postcolonial studies. For them, applying a postcolonial perspective to the Borderlands is not only a misapplication of theory but also a manifestation of a subversive, even anti-Polish, revision of Poland's cultural heritage. Their antipathy for "postcolonizing" the Borderlands, which breeds hostility and irony, is rooted in three interconnected factors. The first is the belief in the incontrovertible value of Borderlands literature to the discourse of Polish identity. The second is the fear that the postcolonial method is harmful to Polish national culture in its supposed disavowal of Borderlands writing, since this undermines contemporary Polish identity, which has been weakened by Soviet colonialism and buttressed by the myth of the Borderlands' Polishness. For example, Bolesław Hadaczek argues:

> What is to be done about this far-fetched interpretation of Borderlands literature from the doubtful perspective of "postcolonial studies"? Well, to do one's job, objectively, based in Polish studies and from the obvious Borderlands studies perspective. One must tirelessly plant and nurture the robust Borderlands oaks and elms. . . . It is likely that various mistletoes will parasitically feed off them and cawing rooks will roost in their branches.[84]

The third factor is sentiment. Some critics explicitly reach for the linguistic register of melancholia, claiming that "it is hard to agree with Daniel Beauvois' conclusion that it is time to dispel the myths of the Borderlands, to end for once with nostalgia after an irretrievably lost paradise where the good God turned a blind eye to the sins of its inhabitants."[85]

Can the critics who object on such grounds be accused of having colonial ambitions or nurturing imperial nostalgia? Not really. Among them are those who see arriving at a more grounded and complete multifaceted understanding of the past enriched with multiple points of view as the aim of criticism. They realize that this understanding requires consideration of the "osmosis, interpenetration of cultures, . . . a departure from Polonocentric formulas, and [adopting] a perspective on the Borderlands myths that includes both "foreign" and "own elements."[86]

Nonetheless, in practice, the line between radical and explicit ethnocentrism and its implied and moderate versions turns out to be difficult to demarcate in these types of approaches. Hence, the need to rethink the theoretical assumptions of the discourse on Borderlands literature and culture. The current direction of global reflection on the intercultural contact of people burdened with a colonial past makes possible the thesis that participating in Borderlands discourse without accounting for issues raised by postcolonial critics, for the sake of protecting or defending the unique value of Borderlands culture to Poland, is possible only if the perspectives of Others are ignored. Such dismissal leads to paternalism and cultural imperialism that also ails Polish academic discourse. This paternalistic attitude is rooted in the defensive Polonocentrism inherent to this discourse, and it takes on more or less subtle forms. The following comment of art historian Tadeusz Chrzanowski on the prospects of reconciliation between the nationalities engaged in the intercultural encounter in the Borderlands is an example of a more subtle kind of paternalism:

> Brethren Ukrainians, Belarusians, Lithuanians, Latvians, brethren Romanians, Hungarians, Czechs, brethren Germans and whoever else also belongs to this bizarre community [*koine*]: the history that rolled and unceasingly rolls through here is our shared history. The monuments that lasted on these lands, so cruelly destroyed and violated, are ours. Ours in common. I lay no claim on lands that once were part of our state just as I do not wish for anyone to lay a claim on lands that are now part of the Third Republic [of Poland]. Yet I will never give up the memory of facts that constitute the elements of my native history, just as I do not deny you the right to what has survived between the Bug, San, and Vistula rivers being part of your history.[87]

This fragment is taken from a work expressively titled *Kresy, czyli obszar tęsknot* (The Borderlands, a realm of longings), which can be seen as an example of the colonial legacy in Polish humanistic thought.[88] Seemingly compatible with Said's quoted warning against uncritical acceptance of authoritative ideas, Chrzanowski's proposal in fact contradicts it. Instead of admitting that the perspective of Others is as epistemologically valuable as, and therefore parallel to, ours, Chrzanowski performs what can be called strategic inclusion of Others in the dominant Polish discourse. This inclusion takes place through emphasizing the commonality of the past, both in its nonmaterial and material aspects ("our shared history," "the monuments . . . are ours"). Otherness, therefore, is used to reinforce the institutional legitimacy of Polish colonial patronage, which is fostered by the diminishing of differences and the appeal to the alleged community of origin and fate ("brethren"). Speaking in Bhabha's terms, Otherness is perceived by Chrzanowski as "an articulation of difference contained within the fantasy of origin and identity."[89] As a result, no space is left for the self-articulation and self-representation of Others. Instead, national differences are silenced under the guise of pluralist inclusion and consequently further marginalized. Polish Borderlands discourse contains many examples of such strategic inclusion of Poland's Others.[90]

## "Phantom Pain": What Now?

The problematic position of the subject of Borderlands discourse toward the object of its exploration should not be seen as a result of ill will or some hazy "national character." It is also not a scourge of some undefined historical fate. The source of the problem lies elsewhere, in the still inadequately identified, analyzed, and theorized postcolonial condition of the Polish subject. The results of psychological research are not necessary to assert that "we often edit or entirely rewrite our previous experiences—unknowingly and unconsciously—in light of what we now know or believe."[91] Likewise, what the subject is unaware of, what does not (yet) fit the horizon of its perception of itself and others, also shapes and even determines the profile of its memory discourse. Poles have a specific way of remembering, and of understanding and organizing their knowledge about, the Borderlands; they weave certain kinds of literary and critical narratives as a result of their current postcolonial status, even when they are not fully cognizant of this being the case. Borderlands discourse is thus trapped between two extremes: of postcolonial studies in a version that does not recognize the postcolonial melancholia burrowing through this discourse, and of a traditional, ethnocentric criticism propelled by this melancholia's covert and unrecognized force. Is there no way out of this deadlock?

One solution is to incorporate the notion of melancholia into postcolonial research of the Borderlands and its discourse. This solution neither justifies this Freudian means of cultural self-defense nor condemns it. The point is rather to develop an understanding of the mechanism behind this melancholia. Its functioning involves both the critics who explore Borderlands literature and culture and their audiences. They all participate in the same cultural code by virtue of belonging to the same interpretive community. They can only benefit from the recognition that the entire social organism, including to some extent the humanities, suffers from a disease that counts melancholia among its symptoms. This symptom is both spectacular and troublesome in its manifestations, as attested to by the reactions of neighboring nations to Polish Borderlands discourse. Still, it is only one of many, including identity crisis, inferiority complex, and compensatory behaviors. This disease, with its clearly colonial etiological roots, has been named the postcolonial syndrome. It is viewed as a phenomenon "more or less typical of all the countries that have regained their independence . . . characterized by a variety of emotions, ranging from euphoria brought about by the belief that freedom would automatically solve all problems created by the previous regime, down to a complete loss of illusions, bitter disappointment and depression."[92] The melancholia of Borderlands discourse falls within the postcolonial syndrome's broad range. Like other affects, it also feeds off the memory of foreign domination and bears its mark. Edward Kasperski pointed to the paradoxical situation of Borderlands literature as an apt subject of Borderlands discourse:

> The paradox of nineteenth-century Borderlands literature becomes a paradox of the Hegelian unhappy consciousness, since the mythologization of the Borderlands revives and flourishes generally *ex post*, in a situation where the historical reality of the Borderlands is becoming problematic or indeed has disintegrated and ceased to exist. It appears the moment that Poland loses its hegemony in the Borderlands and when the agony of the Borderlands reality begins for good, impacted by the territory's partition between the occupying powers and the rapid awakening of national consciousness among Ukrainians, Lithuanians, and Belarusians.[93]

If the Hegelian *das unglückliche Bewußtsein*, the unhappy consciousness, is chosen as a departure point for describing Borderlands discourse, then the proposed Freudian category of melancholia is certainly an appropriate instrument for analyzing this discourse. Looking at Borderlands discourse through the prism of Freudian melancholia allows one to grasp the dynamics of the process by which a population reconciles itself to loss in this discourse. Moreover, it indirectly answers the urgent questions posed by opponents of traditional research frameworks. This leads to the following conclusion: a non-ethnocentric exploration of the culture and writing of the Borderlands is conditional on accounting for the postcolonial situation of Polish scholarly discourse, that is, on recognizing the position from which scholars speak and the idiom they use.

I want to end this discussion with one more conclusion that organizes the chaos created (not only in the consciousness of literary critics) by projects that submit the Borderlands and its discourse to a postcolonial dissection. The discussion thus far has shown that the particular disease of the "Polish soul," postcolonial melancholia, cannot be reduced to a fixation on an object once lost by the empire of the Polish gentry. The opinion that the Borderlands, which once belonged to the Polish-Lithuanian Republic, constitute an equivalent of the Saidian Orient, meaning a space subjected to the mechanisms of textual violence, does not hit the nail on the head. Instead, the analogy needs to be problematized and extended by one more component. In keeping with the language of psychoanalysis, the ensuing conceptual construction of the Borderlands can be redefined as the essence of the narcissistic part of the Polish subject and the idealized object of Polish melancholia, nourished in cultural memory under conditions of long-term colonization. Some see this melancholia as pathological, and others as part of a collective "memory politics," which is realized within the framework of the nation-building processes described by Anthony Smith.[94] In either case, one thing seems certain: any attempt to prove the imperial character of Polish Borderlands discourse that does not pay sufficient attention to its context—of Russian and Soviet colonialism—will not only misuse postcolonial theory but also deform historical processes and render them incomprehensible. This can be counterbalanced with the awareness that

> both sides of the represented conflict, meaning Russians and Poles, did not take into consideration the national interests of the Belarusian population, which they treated as part of their nations and wanted to either Polonize or Russify. . . . Given the existing legal and constitutional situation that favored the Russians, they were certainly more able to promote education among the people. The Poles were left only with the goal of eliminating the harmful influence, from their point of view, of Russification.[95]

It is impossible to omit the influence that the encounter with Russia and the USSR had on the Polish identity when looking at the colonial dimension of the Polish presence in the Borderlands. Juliusz Mieroszewski, an émigré political writer associated with Jerzy Giedroyc's journal *Kultura*, pointed this out, seeing the Borderlands as a realm of competition between Polish and Russian politics. He underlined the impossibility of discussing "Polish-Russian relations in isolation from the ULB [Ukraine, Lithuania, and Belarus] territories, for Polish-Russian relations were always a function of the situation on these lands during a given historical period."[96] The proposal presented in this chapter can be seen as a mirror reflection of Mieroszewski's conceptualization: if present-day Borderlands discourse is to productively and adequately utilize postcolonial theories, it must consider the Russian background of Polish colonial relations as well the historical and contemporary dynamics of Polish-Russian interactions; these dynamics are, admittedly, unfavorable to either nation. In light of the Russian-Ukrainian conflict that commenced in 2014, this is a burning issue given that debates between Polish and Ukrainian historians about the Volhynia Massacre and its instrumentalization by politicians have been inconclusive thus far. The stance on the massacre is still a basis on which many Polish groups, including those that make up the Borderlands movement, assess the possibility of supporting independent Ukraine in its pro-European aspirations and as a defense against the Russian threat. The international weight of this problem is revealed by the discussion that followed the premiere of Wojciech Smarzowski's 2016 feature film *Hatred* (Polish title: *Wołyń* [Volhynia]) in Poland, Ukraine, Germany, and Russia, as well as in the cosmopolitan space of the internet.[97] This discussion, along with the ongoing debate in Poland on the legacy of Stepan Bandera in present-day Ukraine and the responsibility of the Ukrainian nation and state for the Volhynia Massacre, has demonstrated that, with rare exceptions, there is little recognition in Polish political and intellectual circles of the colonial nature of historical Polish-Ukrainian relations and the continued use of stereotypes and clichés dating back to Communist times.[98]

Given the complexity of problems raised by Borderlands discourse, it is worthwhile to look at a sociological interpretation of the Borderlands' role in the postcolonial reconstruction of Polish identity:

> Borderlands discourse, especially its renaissance after the fall of Communism, can be defended also from a postcolonial perspective. For the memory of the Borderlands is one of the key elements of Polish national culture and Polish identity. Its amputation completed the symbolic violence of the Second World War, when Poles were exiled from these regions, deprived of all property and practically denied the possibility of any access to it, and when the memory and traces of Poles on these lands were erased to a large extent. The return to a somewhat idealized image of the Borderlands can be seen largely as a postcolonial restoration of memory that was taken away by the imperial censor. If it is not tied to any territorial claims or used for other current political aims, it can be in great measure justified and absolved of its Polonocentrism, since other, non-Polish aspects of these lands' description are mostly taken care of by their current owners.[99]

Considering the destructive force of Borderlands discourse, the stipulation that it keep its distance from territorial claims and current political ambitions seems too weak.[100] A fundamental change on the level of discourse is needed, which would prevent Borderlands discourse from being a monophonic, one-sided discourse glorifying Polishness. Postcolonial studies create this possibility.

With this change, the identity aspect of Borderlands discourse should become the object of Polish postcolonial studies. The problem of melancholia in Borderlands discourse is certainly one of the key issues here. From this perspective, the "zero point"—the initial moment in a process whose cultural scale, reach, and resonance exceeds narrow, historical conditions and their immediate effects—would be marked by "the physical and spiritual move from a multicultural community to a homogenous state with a narrowed realm of a living tradition."[101] These factors affect the national community as an entity that stores by means of cultural discourses the memory of its own experiences in its repository, fashioning at the same time an image of Others using various models. It is the task of future, reflective Borderlands critics to describe and typologize these models with the help of postcolonial theoretical categories.

How can the phantom pain of an "amputated arm" be overcome to liberate Borderlands discourse from the constantly restaged source of its melancholia? This question should be posed differently. It is necessary to consider the irrevocability of the experienced loss, which despite various diagnoses and prognoses of its nearing end or exhaustion continues to energize Borderlands writing and, indirectly, all of Borderlands discourse: Can "the 'pathological' case of feeling a hand one does not have"—and will never have again—become a "key to the 'normal'"?[102] Or, reversing the perspective, does melancholia have to remain the main modus operandi of Borderlands discourse? It seems that awareness of the melancholic underpinning of Borderlands discourse can help to answer these questions and cut the troublesome (not only for Poles) "Borderlands knot." The point, after all, is not to replace the "work of melancholia" entirely with the "work of mourning" but to ensure that the past "continues to live in the most solid form of memory, which is the identity of the subject itself."[103] Recognizing the melancholia that has been interiorized in the depths of Polish identity constitutes one of the most important moments of reflection on this identity, which—whether Poles like it or not—is based in a significant part on this melancholia today.

# Afterword

## Three Warnings

I began this book with a personal reminiscence and want to do likewise in these concluding remarks. The day of September 11, 2001, remembered well by the entire world perhaps, was also a unique experience for me. As a freshly minted Kosciuszko Foundation Fellow at Rice University in Houston, Texas, I heard the first, still uncertain news about the attack on New York's Twin Towers on National Public Radio (my favorite American radio station) while en route to my lecture. Everything became clear soon thereafter. When I entered the lecture hall in which I taught a course on East-Central European film on Tuesday and Thursday mornings, the students were behaving differently than they normally did. They were very serious and sad—I could see barely held back tears in their eyes. This was to be expected since the group consisted almost entirely of American students. Almost, since there was also one Australian among them. He always stood out a little from the rest: he reacted differently to the films we studied, gave different answers to questions, and spoke with an accent that was difficult to understand even for Americans, as a result of which he sometimes became the butt of the joke for the group. In a word, he was a version of the classic Other—an alienated newcomer from a foreign culture. On this day, however, he too became part of the community that came together in the small hall of the Fondren Library. Like the others, he refrained from an outburst of emotion. The psychological, mental, and cultural differences among students disappeared in the face of a human tragedy, the size and significance of which we were not yet able to comprehend.

This is a recurrent memory. It returned to me, for example, when I reflected on the significance of difference in the context of postcolonial theory and studies. It is difficult, of course, to question the role of this category in the construction of the conceptual framework of postcolonialism, where it has the rank of an epistemic principle that permits the description of social and cultural phenomena tied to discrimination, colonial oppression, and cultural supremacy. Yet the absolutization of difference makes the tangible reality of its opposite difficult to observe. It diverts attention away from sameness, identicality, the unity attained via fostering an empathetic attitude toward the Other, and the community, which is not restricted to extreme situations even if it is experienced most powerfully when "collectively struck." Excessive emphasis on difference obscures our view of human solidarity, which is the opposite of alienation. My experience belies this one-sided stance.

Postcolonial studies, as I propose to view it, has an enduring value, which is more than interventional when accompanied by sensitivity toward the human dimension of reality. A significant, if not the most important, characteristic of this dimension is the human subject's ability to transcend itself, its own limitations, and its own conditioning. Postcolonial criticism should not reduce culture to the realm of political and economic antagonisms between nations, countries, and institutions of power. Its value lies in seeing this aspect of culture as one in a series of contexts and meaning-making factors, and in not becoming exhausted on analyses of its fissures, stratifications, and perforations, however subtle, but leaving space for arriving by their means—as if in the Heideggerian "clearing" (*die Lichtung*)—at the mystery of humanity, which they undoubtedly in part reveal. The value of postcolonial studies is greatest when, in unmasking the harm of the colonial system, its horizon remains open to reflection on what enables human beings to counter this harm: to forgive the oppressor and encourage the conquered, to overcome colonial temptations and one's own weakness, and to give up improperly acquired advantages. As mentioned in earlier chapters, Polish literature has been partially infused with a Christian attitude in the course of its historical development. This is part of the reason why it also offers these types of "heroic" diagnoses in works that can be classified in terms of both "anti-colonial resistance" and "Polish imperial pursuits." A contrasting background is necessary to diagnose these issues, of course, which involves recognition of human cruelty, faint-heartedness, and dalliance, and an awareness of human susceptibility to evil in forms both apparent (colonial violence) and subtle (delusion of colonial prosperity).

I am inclined to view postcolonial studies in terms of the already invoked Heideggerian "clearing." Such studies submit the complex system of colonial dependencies to multifaceted inquiry; delving into processes of cultural production on both sides of the colonial divide, they deconstruct the dialectic of the colonial encounter and articulate the ambivalence of a subject's position and consciousness. Often the critical energy of such postcolonial studies is hereby exhausted, however. From the perspective at stake here, the constitutive parts of this "clearing"—the structure of colonial and anti-colonial discourses untangled by means of the postcolonial apparatus, the mechanism of differentiation, and so forth—are subservient to truths perceived in the clearing's illuminating light. These truths pertain to human beings in a broader perspective than those of postcolonial and other emancipatory theories—a perspective that exceeds categories imposed by the optics of oppressiveness founded on the notion of difference.[1] Without this wider perspective, postcolonial criticism turns one sided. Focused on what is different and on the divisions resulting from otherness, it overlooks the shared core of human experience built around identity, integrity, and the dignity of personhood.[2] A personalistic understanding of the obligations of the humanities views this form of postcolonial studies as deficient for focusing on the "deviances" sanctified by imperialist cultural practices. In the meantime, the (post)colonial aberrations of social and individual behaviors that postcolonialism reveals should make it apparent that all of these irregularities, disorders, and anomalies are only one component of a much more varied human reality, and at most its reverse.

In formulating this first warning, I am not questioning the intellectual project that rests at the foundation of postcolonial studies or the results of accepted analytical processes that this book presents. Instead, I am pointing to the possibility of a different contextualization of this current of inquiry from the one that is usually adopted; content with only a general suggestion, I propose that this context be located in personalistic thought. Such a move also seems justified in a historical perspective: between the initial phase of postcolonialism, which is marked on the theoretical map by Said's enduring concept of orientalism, and its present form, a *sea change* has taken place. Its spectacular signs include the forking of this current into numerous branches and their subordinate idiolects, as well as the departure—despite continued formal references—of a significant portion of postcolonial critics from Said's position. I think the perspective presented in these closing remarks is congruent in part with the humanistic intuitions of *Culture and Imperialism*. I am speaking of its postulate that cultural reality be treated in categories of "humanly made structures of both authority and participation" with a concurrent understanding that it consists in "estimable and admirable works of art and learning, in which I and many other readers take pleasure and from which we derive profit," and that in trying to understand these works, which are an ingredient of a certain human reality, we seek to comprehend this reality.[3]

I see postcolonial theory as being in the service of this kind of inquiry. "The human experience" as a subject of studies inspired by postcolonialism is a broader and more complex whole that cannot be described exclusively in the categories of domination and subordination: "totalizing theories, not marked and limited by doctrinal or national lines, not confined once and for all to analytical constructs."[4] I share this outlook and think that its consequences need to be taken seriously. Human experience, which admittedly possesses an "irreducible subjective core" yet "is accessible to analysis and interpretation" by virtue of its historicity, cannot be enclosed in postcolonial conceptualizations.[5] The explicatory constructions based on postcolonial theory should not be vested with the function of analytical "skeleton keys"—seemingly universal tools of explaining social and cultural reality. This runs the danger of diminishing reality's scope and even, in the most caricatured form, of reducing its interpretation to Lenin's "Who, whom?" slogan. A reference to Said is once again appropriate, since his comments prompt reflection on the role of literary critics in the transformations on the world stage of political domination: "Exactly as in its triumphant period imperialism tended to license only a cultural discourse that was formulated from within it, today post-imperialism has permitted mainly a cultural discourse of suspicion on the part of formerly colonized peoples, and of theoretical avoidance at most on the part of metropolitan intellectuals."[6] The "discourse of suspicion" mentioned by Said, from which he distanced himself, has acquired a specific form and significance today, claiming an ever-broader expanse of postcolonial studies. Its base is less national than social and political, however: it gravitates toward a radical, neo- or else post-Marxist critique of contemporary, supranational capitalism in the age of globalization. This type of criticism has loosened the historical and political determinants of the subject of postcolonial studies, redeveloping and redefining it in line with the position propagated by Terry Eagleton: "Do we really need to argue that what is happening when the ethnically marginalized of the globe assert themselves against the [W]est's clientelist states *is* a matter of class struggle?"[7] As a result, postcolonialism has transformed itself from an analysis of Western domination as realized by means of imperial conquest into research undertaken at multiple universities into the possibilities of a contemporary, global, and transnational mutation of the past "class struggle." Presently, it engages in a critique of capitalism as a system that "centrally involves the imposition of a particular mode or modes of production and specific regimes of accumulation, expropriation and exploitation in the form of the extraction of surplus value, commodification and the generalization of commodity production."[8] Given their Marxist vocabulary, these types of cultural analyses still tend to arouse objections in post-Communist East-Central Europe; they certainly cannot be considered representative of the region's academic discourses.

Nevertheless, the present-day changes within Western humanities make it necessary to consider the possibility that Eastern European postcolonial discourse will also head in that direction.[9]

Admittedly, anxieties around the increasing hegemony of the West, including its main powerhouses of Germany and the United States, as well as of the East, meaning Russia and China, are usually expressed in a language that does not shy away from either antagonistic rhetoric or a fighting spirit. Yet this anxiety often has the marks of authenticity and sincerity. In Poland, it is frequently voiced by a generation of young scholars and critics who do not view Marxism in the humanities in personal terms. They do not associate it with the oppressive power system in East-Central Europe of the second half of the twentieth century. Instead, they see it as an intellectually refined and attractive ideological option that helps to interpret the contemporary world in uniform, apparent, and clear-cut materialistic categories.[10] This attitude also manifests in indignation at the discriminatory practices of the contemporary world, which swapped conflicts of races and civilizations for the zone of political and economic rivalry that can implicate, and sometimes even directly involve, culture. These views have the stars of contemporary Marxist thought as their patrons, among them Fredric Jameson, Terry Eagleton, and Étienne Balibar.

The second warning is connected to this point. Neo-Marxism has at its disposal a vocabulary seen as a precise descriptive tool for approaching some of the questions that affect the contemporary world and is seen today as central to culture. I am referring here to the struggle for hegemony of political, economic, and military powerhouses, also within East-Central Europe, which is taking place on multiple levels. Marxist scholars believe that these issues have a decisive impact on the direction of cultural development both in Western countries and other parts of the globe. Whether the contemporary frameworks that reference the ideas of Marx and his twentieth-century successors can serve as an effective means of positive social change is not an issue that can be addressed here. I will suggest that the lesson derived from Communism has not been properly processed by the humanities yet. (Doubt whether this will ever happen is justified since the most intellectually mature critique of communism came from East-Central European thinkers, whose voices are largely discounted in the contemporary discourse of the humanities if they do not identify, or openly sympathize, with neo-Marxist thought.) There is yet another argument that supports the warning about neo-Marxism's explicatory capabilities issued here, at least in regard to East-Central Europe. The supranational conflict of a global nature noted above exists alongside tensions, antagonisms, and conflicts of interest that impact contemporary national communities, whose self-definition still appears to be one of the key issues in the identity discourses of East-Central European societies. Despite the post-national prognoses of philosophers such as Habermas, nation-states on the European continent have no intention of dissipating. To the contrary, one contingent of philosophers sees them as the optimal form of a community's political existence.[11] Even if one considers the nation-state to be an "abstract entity," one cannot deny that "we live in a nation-centric time and space."[12] Humanities in the academia have to consider this state of affairs, whatever their judgment of these phenomena, revising perhaps some of their assumptions.

The strong polarizations that have taken place in recent years, both in relations between European and global political organisms and in the discourses of specific national and ethnic groups, warrant supposing that the postcolonial questions presented in this book with reference to the cultural aspects of collective identity, especially in its national aspect, will gain rather than lose in currency. I am not thinking of the *politics of identity* here but rather of identity itself, along with the processes on which it depends and the reflection it provokes among members of the community it defines. The work that postcolonial criticism in its "pedagogical" dimension needs to undertake in this respect has not been completed yet: the "really free man" has not yet emerged from the colonial ruins of Europe's eastern regions.[13] Albert Memmi's formula, popular in postcolonial studies, is also an ideal postulate and the strategic aim of all anti-imperial movements, as well as the final horizon of postcolonialism's emancipatory reflection, which transcends temporal and local (including national) limitations.

It is time for the third and last warning. I understand this "really free man" not in the spirit of Marxist quasi-religious "eschatology" but rather as the realization of an ideal borrowed by Said, with the intercession of Auerbach, from the *Didascalicon*, the Medieval philosophical treatise by Hugo of St. Victor. The fragment cited at the conclusion of *Culture and Imperialism* defines in almost poetic language the stance that formed Said's credo as a contemporary intellectual: the imperative of overcoming the limitations arising from a bond to the nation. This overcoming must be properly understood if it is to avoid turning into its neoliberal caricature, however. It is not undertaken in the name of superficially understood cosmopolitanism, which calls for a disposal of its source identity as if it were a ballast, nor as the result of shifting polemical energy toward a Marxist struggle with neo-imperialism during the age of globalization. It is realized instead as a result of possessing a sufficient reservoir of other values: values that are transcendent in relation to the visible and the transient and that allow—in relation to temporal conditions dictated, for example, by membership, loyalty, or affiliation—to achieve "independence and detachment by *working through* attachments, not by rejecting them."[14] I hope that placing this fragment of Said's text at the closing of this book and its considerations will be received by its readers as more than a gesture of respect for another's authority or a purely rhetorical act.

> It is therefore, a source of great virtue for the practiced mind to learn, bit by bit, first to change about in visible and transitory things, so that afterwards it may be able to leave them behind altogether. The person who finds his homeland sweet is still a tender beginner; he to whom every soil is as his native one is already strong; but he is perfect to whom the entire world is as a foreign place. The tender soul has fixed his love on one spot in the world; the strong person has extended his love to all places; the perfect man has extinguished his.[15]

# Notes

## Prologue

1. Fiut, *"Polonizacja? Kolonizacja?"*; Cavanagh, "Postcolonial Poland." Cavanagh's paper appeared in Polish prior to that of Fiut.
2. Skórczewski, "Postkolonialna Polska."
3. Cornis-Poppe, "Local and Global Frames," 146.
4. As Joep Leerssen noted in a lecture given at the Sorbonne in 2016, "In the current climate of intense 'identity politics' and resurging nationalism, imagology is quickly regaining the urgency it had in the post-1945 years" ("Imagology: On Using Ethnicity," 14). For imagology as method, see Leerssen, "Imagology: History and Method."

## Chapter One

1. "Emancipation" here, and throughout the book, is identical with "liberation" and refers to the elimination of systematic domination or oppression. Its goal is freedom.
2. Duma, "Personalism," 378.
3. Ibid., 368.
4. My point of view on this issue is close to that of the Polish philosopher Barbara Skarga, as she expresses it, for example, in her book *Tożsamość i różnica: Eseje metafizyczne* (Identity and difference: Metaphysical essays):

    > I do not agree with the thesis of the death of man, or with reluctance toward humanism in its various dimensions. . . . I reject determinations that see the human being as neither the source of experiences or thoughts, nor the author of these or other events. I do not think that all philosophies who say something about human beings should be considered as mistaken, or prone to illusion, or that all terms, such as self-identity, the subject of given operations, present in what she articulates, should be seen as empty. For this philosophical current there is no subject and no author. There is thus also no individual human being, the concrete person that lives, thinks, and suffers. He or she becomes an abstraction, perhaps even nothing. (5–6)

5. In their introduction to *Postcolonial Theory in the Global Age*, Dwivedi and Kich make it clear that postcolonial theory "has now become increasingly

defined by interdisciplinary studies. Scholars and critics seem ever ready to align this theory with fresh political, socio-economic, cultural, and aesthetic perspectives—and, more provocatively, with new syntheses of such perspectives—emerging across an increasingly globalized world" (9).

6. Cf. Rüsen and Laass, *Humanism.*
7. This issue was raised in the work of Edward Said, whose questions about the possibility of constructing "noncoercive knowledge" still remain current. See Abraham, "Introduction." For a recent take on the "new" humanism in a global world, see Rüsen and Laass, *Humanism.*
8. Cf. Huggan, *Interdisciplinary Measures*, 12f.
9. I am using the term "speculum" without its psychoanalytical superstructure.
10. In this respect, I endorse Marko Pavlyshyn's view on postcolonialism ("Postcoloniality as Method").
11. Said, *Culture and Imperialism*, xiii.
12. Ibid.
13. Ibid., xii.
14. Ibid., xxiii.
15. Ibid., 278.
16. Said, *Orientalism*, xiii.
17. This question has been the subject of many works, including Gandhi, *Postcolonial Theory*, 70–74; Loomba, *Colonialism/Postcolonialism*, 20–35; Bartolovich, "Global Capital," 126–61. Cf. Wolfe, "History and Imperialism."
18. See Zagorin, "History," 5–7.
19. Aquinas, *Summa Theologiae*, Ia–IIae, q. 91, a. 2.
20. Said stressed the significance of the secularity of scholarship, treating the postulate as a warranty against the subordination of a scientific discourse to explicatory systems with a high degree of ideology. Emily Apter, however, points to the Christian indicators of Said's humanism in his capacity as reader and commentator of Auerbach's work in her article "Saidian Humanism," 44. I focus on Said because the achievement and unwavering influence of his work transgress the framework of one narrowly conceived theory. I do so also because the inherent logocentrism of his position, which is moderate, implicitly anti-postmodernist, and combined with a moral sensibility that is rare in contemporary scholarship, is often overlooked in criticism.
21. Young, *Postcolonialism*, 6.
22. On the legacy of Christian thought in Marxism, see MacIntyre, *Marxism and Christianity*.
23. As Zdzisław Pawłowski explains in his explication of the sermon's stance on violence:

> All forms of aggression directed against another human being, from murder through anger and up to verbal violence, are at the core an attack on the dignity of the other. They not only humiliate him, but, in denying him a fundamental respect, annihilate him in the sphere of social relations, amounting to

murder as a result. Jesus thus changes the qualification of violence by placing the figure of a brother at the center of his law. The violence ceases to be anonymous and impersonal, inflicted somewhere, at some point, against someone. It is always preceded by a brotherly relation between the oppressor and the oppressed. The meaning of murder, anger, and insulting language comes precisely from a previous existence of a relationship that, independently of the degree of kinship, established bonds, or personal sympathies, is rooted in the fact of creation and sourced in the ontology of the human being. . . . This structure of Jesus' commandment reflects the conviction that a social relation is not only one of many relations that can occur in the course of existence, but a remarkable and ultimate event. It brings with it an ethical surplus that calls for the radicalism of greater justice. For this reason nothing can excuse the use of violence in human relations.

24. Exceptions to this rule are postcolonial studies oriented toward the theology of liberation, studies inspired by postcolonial theory in the areas of human rights and social theology, as well as Bible studies. See, for example, Sugirtharajah, *The Postcolonial Biblical Reader*; and the special issue "Religion and Postcolonialism" of the *Australian Religious Studies Review* 25, no. 2 (2012). See also Pilario, "Mapping Postcolonial Theory."
25. See, for example, Crouch and Stökl, *In the Name of God.*
26. Habermas, "Secularism's Crisis of Faith"; During, "Toward the Postsecular." See also Huggan, "Is the 'Post' in 'Postsecular.'"
27. "Metaphysics" in my understanding is the multidimensional realm of spirituality, which is related but not confined to institutional religiousness and the object of a "metaphysical longing" (cf. Tarnowski, "Metaphysical Longing").
28. Skarga, *Ślad i obecność*, 222.
29. "Metaphysics sensitizes us to a different dimension of the world, irreducible to the materiality of things, a world of values, but also a world of conceptual and intellectual constructs that, regardless of our inclination toward either conceptualism or Platonism, arouses admiration with its abstract beauty, as if the thought of a supreme mind, or everything that is lasting and necessary, became most manifest within it. If this is a delusion or quackery, then this delusion has lasted for over two thousand years already and European culture was built precisely by it. Metaphysics is a fundamental fact of this culture and a requirement of every thinking person" (Skarga, *O filozofię bać się nie musimy*, 19). See also Skarga, *Przeszłość i interpretacje*, 99. In *Kwintet metafizyczny* (Metaphysical quintet, 180–83), Skarga links the anti-metaphysical position of contemporary humanities to tendencies that Foucault's ideas have made way for, in which the linguistic character of cognition is excessively emphasized.
30. I am referring here to the community around the Catholic weekly *Dziś i Jutro* (Today and tomorrow; published between 1945 and 1956), which

later established the pro-Communist secular Catholic PAX Association. Czesław Miłosz wrote about the ambiguity of their position in *The Captive Mind*, 69.

31. This issue invites discussion about the possibility of engaging in self-critical and open reflection on culture from standpoints that account for a scholar's religious beliefs without compromising its status as an academic discourse. Darren E. Dahl wrote on the subject in the context of Said's postulate of "secular criticism," with his remarks serving as inspiration for some of the conclusions presented here ("Criticizing 'Secular Criticism'"). Undoubtedly, my proposal as presented here exceeds the framework of Said's "secular" conceptualization of humanistic discourse. This transgression, however, is the result of Said's specific understanding of religious discourse rather than of bias against issues of transcendence. For the author of *Orientalism* understood religious discourse as a discourse that camouflages its resistance toward the possibility of criticism directed at itself and thus systematically excludes it through the mystification of its ultimate, incontrovertible authoritativeness, which it secures via access to a "higher knowledge" sanctioned by revelation. The logocentrism of Said's opinions mentioned above, which constitutes their unarticulated, but nevertheless significant and tangible foundation, remains a separate issue; in this context, the author of *The World, the Text, and the Critic* would be "guilty" of practicing within his own writing what he theoretically excluded. This issue, however, greatly exceeds the issue under discussion here.
32. See Dahl, "Criticizing 'Secular Criticism,'" 367.

## Chapter Two

1. One example is Kledzik, "Inventing Postcolonial Poland."
2. Studies that apply postcolonial frameworks to Polish literature have also been authored by Slavic and Polish literary scholars at universities outside of Poland, such as Ewa Thompson, Bożena Karwowska, Janusz Korek, German Ritz, Alfred Gall, Dirk Uffelmann, as well as Polish modern languages and comparative scholars, such as Dorota Kołodziejczyk, Bogusław Bakuła, and Paweł Zajas, the author of a book on the postcolonial South African imaginarium of Polish and Dutch literature (*Postkolonialne imaginarium*). A separate mention is due to foreign scholars in comparative and other fields of study, such as the French historian Daniel Beauvois and the professor of American German and Russian studies Kristin Kopp, for the role their work plays in introducing the Polish brand of postcolonialism to the global network of the humanities.
3. For example, Borkowska, "A Post-colonial Perspective on Polish Soil."
4. The influence of Marxist thought (primarily of Antonio Gramsci, Theodor Adorno, György Lukács, and the Frankfurt school) on postcolonial theory is widely acknowledged. Timothy Brennan considers the impact of political

orientation on the shaping of intellectual positions among American academic elites in *Wars of Position*, a book dedicated to the memory of Said and itself not entirely free of a Marxist bent.

5. When it comes to Polish contributions to literary studies, Roman Ingarden's conceptualization of the literary work remains the only entirely independent theoretical formulation. It was first explicated in German in the work *Das literarische Kunstwerk* (1931; Polish translation published in 1960).
6. Said's *Orientalism* was originally published in 1978, while Fanon's work first came out in 1961 (1963 in English translation). The reasons why the Third World responses to colonialism were ignored by the majority of Polish society during the Communist period were purely political. The notions raised in these works were rejected for being grown "on the basis of ideas imported mostly from Moscow," which, according to Adam Kola, contributed to an "amnesia" and disavowal of the indigenous Polish roots of postcolonial thought in Communist Poland, among them theoretical proposals of the historian Marian Małowist, who was recognized by Immanuel Wallerstein as the initiator of world-systems theory (Kola, *Socjalistyczny postkolonializm*, 470).
7. Łubieński, *Porachunki sumienia*, 5.
8. Tellingly, the earliest attempts to transplant Western postcolonial categories onto a Polish ground were tied to the interpretation of sociocultural reality and the field of critical pedagogy rather than literary studies, where they went unnoticed:

> Decolonisation encompassed also areas of the "other Europe," up until now delivered into the hands of Russia's mysterious elements and kept safely hidden behind the Berlin Wall. The decolonised "buffer" of Central Europe become entangled in the tragic conflict of democratic openness, which constitutes a platform for emulative identification with the West and in the feverish construction of fundamentalisms that can provide a basis for such painfully absent, unequivocal self-identification. We are torn between liberalism and democracy constructed from transplanted icons of the West, and nostalgia for our own "authenticity," uniqueness, and cultural purity, between McDonald's hamburgers and the longing for milk bars [cheap cafeteria-style eateries characteristic of Communist Poland], between fascination with, and scorn for, America and the West. (Szkudlarek, "Dialektyka Innego," 34)

9. Considering the case of Romania as a postcolonial country, Bogdan Ştefănescu writes about a "narrow and exclusive" sense of coloniality, namely one related to "the practice of capitalist or modern Western imperial powers (most of the times British and American) of acquiring, exploiting, and controlling overseas lands that were inhabited by racially non-white populations." He juxtaposes it to, on the one hand, a broader, "all-encompassing generic meaning" of coloniality and, on the other, "a *relatively particular*

instance of invasion and domination: the illegitimate acquisition, exploitation, and control of a foreign territory." He emphasizes the following as a common denominator of all colonialisms: "Whether formal or informal, overseas or accretive, territorial or political, economic or ideological, ethnic or transnational, colonialism is always an aggressive, persistent act of collective submission and domination that inflicts physical and psychological traumas and constrains the victims' process of identity (re)construction" (*Postcommunism*, 57, 73). Ştefănescu's view on the topic seems applicable to the whole of East-Central Europe, including Poland.

10. Among social, political, and economic factors that speak to the colonial status of regions subjected to Soviet hegemony are lack of sovereignty in domestic and foreign politics, the threat of military intervention, economic exploitation, forcible adaptation of a foreign education model and compulsory instruction in the oppressor's language, as well as the creolization of the elites, that is, the hegemon's handing over of some responsibilities for the functioning of conquered territories into the hands of selected "natives" through the repression of anti-colonial activity and by rewarding subservience. See Chioni Moore, "Is the Post- in Postcolonial," 121.
11. For reasons for that dissociation, see Kola, *Socjalistyczny postkolonializm*.
12. Kelertas, *Baltic Postcolonialism*, 4.
13. Ashcroft, Griffiths, and Tiffin, *The Empire Writes Back*, 1.
14. "Modern European colonialism was distinctive and by far the most extensive of the different kinds of colonial contact that have been a recurrent feature of human history. By the 1930s, colonies and ex-colonies covered 84.6 per cent of the land surface of the globe. Only parts of Arabia, Persia, Afghanistan, Mongolia, Tibet, China, Siam and Japan had never been under formal European government" (Loomba, *Colonialism/Postcolonialism*, xiii).
15. Kołodziejczyk and Şandru, "Introduction," 114.
16. A list of the most characteristic and frequently posed objections can be recreated from the opinions expressed by Borkowska in "A Post-colonial Perspective on Polish Soil" and Koczanowicz in "Postcommunism and Cultural Wars." Central among these objections are territorial distance in "classic" colonial conquests; the issue of settlements; and the problem of a lack of cultural authority on the part of Russia / the USSR among the subordinated nations of Central and Eastern Europe, which supposedly undermined the colonial character of Russian domination. Compare with Ewa M. Thompson's polemic "It's Colonialism after All."
17. Najder, "Kultura i imperializm." Najder's arguments were taken up by Koczanowicz.
18. Chioni Moore, "Is the Post- in Postcolonial," 121.
19. Doyle, *Empires*, 45.
20. Pavlyshyn, "Andrukhovych's *Secret*," 190.
21. Said, "Afterword," 177.
22. See Kelertas, *Baltic Postcolonialism*.

23. Şandru points to one more context for this skepticism:

> The Orientalising rhetoric so pervasive amongst the educated elite of East-Central Europe . . . regards this particular [Soviet] form of colonisation as one effected by a barbaric, "Asian" power. This "discourse of superiority" is compounded by a variety of "nesting Orientalisms" which seek to disavow all things Eastern in a process of identity-construction predicated on the desire to be recognised by and admitted into a highly selective European club. This attitude, quite widespread among the peoples of East-Central Europe, explains the rejection of the postcolonial paradigm outside relatively small pockets of (generally literary) scholarship. (*Worlds Apart?*, 24)

24. See, for example, Butkiewicz, *Dylematy rozwoju.*
25. See, for example, Kołodziejczyk, "Post-colonial Transfer."
26. See, for example, Cleary, "'Misplaced Ideas?,'" 22.
27. The erroneousness of these criteria has been noted before, for example, in Chioni Moore's "Is the Post- in Postcolonial" and Ewa M. Thompson's "It's Colonialism after All."
28. See, among others, Kelertas, *Baltic Postcolonialism*; Korek, *From Sovietology to Post-coloniality*; Ştefănescu, *Postcommunism*; Şandru, *Worlds Apart?*
29. Authors who claim that post-Communist realities should be addressed by an array of locally specific methodologies rather than modified versions of Western postcolonial theories conduct their research under the auspices of the Post-Dependence Studies Centre (www.cbdp.polon.uw.edu.pl/index_eng.html). For a "manifesto" of the "post-dependence" stance, see, for example, Kołodziejczyk, "Post-colonial Transfer." For a critique of replacing postcolonialism with post-dependence, see Ewa M. Thompson, "It's Colonialism after All."
30. I am referencing here the category of the "surrogate hegemon." See Ewa M. Thompson, "W kolejce po aprobatę."
31. See Jan Kieniewicz, *Ekspansja.*
32. Descriptions of the specific, non-classic colonial encounter that was Russian/Soviet domination abound in Polish literature and are articulated in different ways. They can be situated between two poles, representative of two antinomian aesthetic tones: of extreme gravity, such as what marks Gustaw Herling-Grudziński's poignant testimony of his Gulag experience titled *A World Apart: The Journal of a Gulag Survivor* (published first in English in 1951 with a preface by Bertrand Russell and in Polish in London in 1953); and of the grotesque, which permeates Sergiusz Piasecki's *Zapiski oficera Armii Czerwonej* (The memoirs of a Red Army officer), published in London in 1957. Cf. Zarycki, "Uses of Russia."
33. Kundera, "The Tragedy of Central Europe" (orig. "Un Occident kidnappé"). Although Kundera's concept has been broadly discussed and is one of the best-known attempts at defining Central Europe from a literary-cultural

perspective, it does not exhaust the issues raised in the lengthy and diverse Central European debate. See Trencsényi, "Central Europe."

34. Zarycki, "Poland and the East," 83.
35. While Kundera's once-successful "victimizing narrative" can be seen as passé from today's perspective, it was essential in shaping the discourse on the region's identity. It left an imprint of Central Europe's distinctiveness on this discourse and contributed to the fact that "the very concept of Central Europe has prevailed and transformed itself, emancipated from the political power of the Soviet Union, especially after the 2004 EU enlargement" (Moskalewicz and Przybylski, "Making Sense," 2). Indeed, the debate on Central Europe has taken another direction since the demise of the Soviet Bloc, first with the withdrawal of the Red Army from these countries, and then with their acceptance into the European Union. For a recent overview of the rebirth and collapse of the concept of Central Europe, see Melegh, "Positioning," 26–31.
36. For more on the Lisbon Conference, see the thematic cluster in *Zeitschrift für Slavische Philologie* 72, no. 1 (2016), with papers by Dirk Uffelmann, Heinrich Kirschbaum, Mark Lipovetsky, Daniel W. Pratt, Vitaly Chernetsky, and Dariusz Skórczewski.
37. *Correspondence: Letters between Frederick II and M. D'Alambert*, London: G. G. J. and J. Robinson, 1789, 454; quoted after Healy, "From Commonwealth to Colony?," 113.
38. Mickiewicz, *Dzieła*, 322–23.
39. Said, *Culture and Imperialism*, 10.
40. Chioni Moore explains the concept of reverse-cultural colonization in the following way:

    > The standard Western story about colonization is that it is always accompanied by orientalization, in which the colonized are seen as passive, ahistorical, feminine, or barbaric. However, in Russian-Central European colonization this relation is reversed, because for several centuries at least Russia has, again, been saddled with the fear or at times belief that it was culturally inferior to the West. Mittel-European capitals such as Budapest, Berlin, and Prague were therefore seen in Russia, at least by some, as prizes rather than as burdens needing civilizing from their occupiers. In return, the Central Europeans often saw the colonizing Russo-Soviets as Asiatics. ("Is the Post- in Post-colonial," 121)

41. Ewa M. Thompson, *Imperial Knowledge*, 36.
42. Feuer, *Imperialism*, 104.
43. Forrester, Zaborowska, and Gapova, *Over the Wall*, x.
44. Said, *Culture and Imperialism*, xix.
45. Forrester, Zaborowska, and Gapova, *Over the Wall*, x.
46. See Jan Kieniewicz's studies: *Ekspansja*; "Con nes y fronteras"; "Situation, Colonialism, Backwardness."

47. Nowak, "From Empire Builder to Empire Breaker"; *Od Imperium do Imperium*; "Between Imperial Temptation"; *History and Geopolitics*; *Ofiary, imperia i historycy*.
48. Gandhi, *Postcolonial Theory*, 143.
49. See, for example, the English edition of *Teksty Drugie* entitled "Postcolonial or Postdependence [*sic*] Studies?," no. 1 (2014). The Poznań-based periodical *Porównania* (Comparisons) features regular articles on postcolonial topics, and volumes in postcolonial studies are part of a series by Biblioteka Porównań, among them the English volume edited by Bakuła, Dabert, and Kledzik, *Comparisons and Contexts*.
50. The presence of colonial aspirations in Poland's political and journalistic discourse during the period 1918–39 is discussed, among others, by Borkowska, "Polskie doświadczenie kolonialne"; Kowalski, *Dyskurs kolonialny*. See also Hunczak, "Polish Colonial Ambitions."
51. Tucan, "The Adaptability of Theory," 104.
52. In the context of Polish literature, the first formulation of the postcolonial issues comes in Clare Cavanagh's article "Postcolonial Poland." (Its Polish version appeared under the title "Postkolonialna Polska: Biała plama na mapie współczesnej teorii" in 2003). It is impossible to overlook here the role played by Ewa Thompson's *Imperial Knowledge*. Even though Thompson's book does not deal with Polish literature, it contributed significantly to clearing the way for postcolonial reflection on Poland and East-Central Europe by virtue of posing the problem of Russian colonialism. It is also worthwhile to point to an article by Elwira M. Grossman, "Navigating the New Landscape for Slavonic/Polish Studies," part of which is dedicated to the perspective of postcolonial studies of Polish literature.
53. Cf. Surynt, "Post-colonial Research." Mention should also be made of the postcolonial interest in Central and Eastern Europe expressed by American German studies. See, for instance, Kristin Kopp's works: "Ich stehe jetzt hier" and *Germany's Wild East*.
54. See Tiffin, "Post-Colonial Literatures," 23.
55. Which is precisely how some German scholars view it—see, for example, Hentschel, "Überlegungen zur Polonistik," 22. For more on the topic, see Zduniak-Wiktorowicz, *Filologia w kontakcie*.
56. Fiut, *Być (albo nie być)*, 24.

## Chapter Three

*Epigraph*: Skarga, *Tożsamość i różnica*, 12.

1. See, for example, Ratti, *The Postsecular Imagination*; Jackson, *Postcolonial Critique*.
2. The collaborative research projects of scholars from the region's nations are one manifestation of this momentum. See Bakuła, *Dyskurs postkolonialny*; Bakuła, Dabert, and Kledzik, *Comparisons and Contexts*; Pucherová and Gáfrik, *Postcolonial Europe?*; Uffelmann and Smola, *Postcolonial Slavic Literatures*.

3. In contrast to scholars such as Benedykt Zientara, who place the beginning of Poland's national history in the medieval period, Timothy Snyder points to 1569 as its "starting point" (*The Reconstruction of Nations*, 3).
4. "Central Europe longed to be a condensed version of Europe itself in all its cultural variety, a small arch-European Europe, a reduced model of Europe made up of nations conceived according to one rule: the greatest variety within the smallest space" (Kundera, "The Tragedy of Central Europe," 33). On the anti-colonial appeal of Kundera's essay, see Uffelmann, "The Imprint."
5. Kołodziejczyk and Şandru, "Introduction," 115.
6. Mochnacki's key phrase "uznanie się w jestestwie" is difficult to translate, conveying self-recognition and the understanding of oneself as one is. See Mochnacki, *O literaturze polskiej*, 46.
7. See, for example, Charles Taylor, *Sources of the Self*; Leary and Tangney, *Handbook of Self*; Bamberg, De Fina, and Schiffrin, *Selves and Identities*; Calhoun, *Social Theory*; Benwell and Stokoe, *Discourse and Identity*; Straub, "Personal and Collective Identity"; Stryker and Burke, "The Past, Present, and Future."
8. See Hall and du Gay, *Questions of Cultural Identity*.
9. For more on identity discourse, see Shi-xu, *A Cultural Approach to Discourse*.
10. Loomba, *Colonialism/Postcolonialism*, chapter titled "Colonial and Postcolonial Identities."
11. See, for example, Guha and Spivak, *Selected Subaltern Studies*; Ahmad, *In Theory*; Parry, *Postcolonial Studies*; Chibber, *Postcolonial Theory*.
12. Ştefănescu, *Postcommunism*, 34.
13. Cf. Popescu, "Translations."
14. See, for example, Krasnodębski, *Postmodernistyczne rozterki*, 151. Cf. Krasnodębski, "Waiting for Supermarkets."
15. Charles Taylor, *Sources of the Self*, 27.
16. Ibid., 27–28.
17. Skarga, *Tożsamość i różnica*, 12.
18. Brubaker and Cooper, "Beyond 'Identity.'"
19. Łuczewski, "What Remains for Nationalism Studies," 5. Łuczewski refers to Znaniecki's essay "Elementy rzeczywistości praktycznej."
20. Fanon, *The Wretched of the Earth*, 293–94.
21. In 1998, Habermas predicted that "we ourselves now approach the threshold of a postnational form of collective political life" (*The Postnational Constellation*, 17).
22. Holdsworth, *Theatre and National Identity*, 1.
23. Gandhi, *Postcolonial Theory*, 113.
24. Ibid., 122. It must be stressed that Said's evaluation of nationalism is ambivalent. Said warned against nationalism not in and of itself but against its possible degeneration after the restoration of a subjugated population's sovereignty. He saw this process, which he described as "a kind of fetishization of the native essence and identity," as the main threat to the nation's existence in the postcolonial phase (*Power, Politics, and Culture*, 175).

25. Gandhi, *Postcolonial Theory*, 129.
26. Malešević, *Identity as Ideology*, 90.
27. Jaskułowski, *Nacjonalizm bez narodów*, 138. As Jaskułowski notes, such explanations are "highly naïve from a theoretical perspective" since they rest "on premises that themselves require explanation. Instead of showing why the need to belong to the same nation arises for both the governed and the governing, this need is taken for granted and used to explain the explosion of anti-colonial wars" (ibid.).
28. Kapralski, "Oświęcim," 162.
29. "One of the most well-known and fervent proponents of cosmopolitan Europe is Jürgen Habermas and his supporters, who believe that the European Union can be based on a 'thin' collective identity stemming from a set of abstract universalistic principles such as human rights, but evolves and thickens from this Kantian cosmopolitan conception into the European constitutional patriotism, which is expected to replace the ethnic bonds of European nations" (Karolewski, *Citizenship and Collective Identity*, 56). Cf. Habermas, *The Postnational Constellation*. The notion of post-national identity is often placed in the context of European citizenship. See Delanty, *Inventing Europe*.
30. Kapralski, "Oświęcim," 162.
31. Jan Kieniewicz, "What Kind of Identity," 145.
32. For more on the refugee crisis in the Polish context, see Jaskułowski, *The Everyday Politics*.
33. See, for example, Hobsbawm, *Nations and Nationalism*, 192. Anthony Giddens ties the present growth of nationalisms directly to globalization: "The revival of local nationalisms, and an accentuating of local identities, are directly bound up with globalizing influences, to which they stand in opposition" (Giddens, *Beyond Left and Right*, 5).
34. See Hacking, *Social Construction*.
35. Walicki, *Polskie zmagania*, 387.
36. See Kohn, *The Idea of Nationalism*, 234–37.
37. Baár, *Historians and Nationalism*, 9.
38. Ibid., 7.
39. Said, *Culture and Imperialism*, 216.
40. Straub, *Personal and Collective Identity*, 72.
41. Three groundbreaking works for nationalism studies were published in 1983: Gellner's *Nations and Nationalism*, Anderson's *Imagined Communities*, and Hobsbawm and Ranger's *The Invention of Tradition*. Deutsch's *Nationalism and Social Communication*, which at times aligns with Gellner's ideas, was written in 1953.
42. Gellner, *Nations and Nationalism*, 6.
43. Hobsbawm and Ranger, *The Invention of Tradition*, 13.
44. Łuczewski, *Odwieczny naród*.
45. As Nikodem Bończa Tomaszewski observes, according to Gellner's theory, "modernization produces nationalism, which in turn creates nations. The

problem consists in the fact that nationalism comes into being suddenly, *deus ex machina*, leaping like Athena from Zeus' head. Gellner waves aside a fundamental problem: how to tie the material process with transformations of consciousness, how the material is joined with the spiritual in human society" (Tomaszewski, *Źródła narodowości*, 15).

46. Staniszkis, *Antropologia władzy*, 118–19.
47. Łuczewski, *Odwieczny naród*, 630.
48. Spivak, *The Postcolonial Critic*, 51.
49. Smith, *The Ethnic Origins*.
50. Hall, "The Question of Cultural Identity," 613.
51. Cassirer, *An Essay on Man*, 43.
52. Smith, *The Ethnic Origins*, 16ff.
53. Ibid., 178–79.
54. Ibid., 206.
55. Andrew Thompson, "Nations, National Identities," 20.
56. Notably, this sense appears convergent with Said's affirmation of the role of national movements in decolonizing processes, even given his caution toward the nationalism phenomenon. See *Power, Politics, and Culture*, 175, 220.
57. As Smith indicates, the symbolic and cultural expressions of a nation, despite appearing to depend on the consciousness of those who utilize them, are graspable in the *longue durée* perspective. This allows to overcome the problem of the subjective nature of perception, beliefs, or memories (Smith, *Myths and Memories*, 14).
58. Smith, *National Identity*, 40.
59. Smith, *National Identity*, 77. "And the nation is a type of identity whose meaning and priority is presupposed by this form of culture." Ibid., 91–92.
60. A reference to Adam Mickiewicz's *Forefathers' Eve*, part 3, and Konrad's infamous demand: "Give me the rule of souls!" (*Polish Romantic Drama*, 78).
61. Gellner speaks about "the age of universal high culture" (*Nations and Nationalism*, 35). The works of Polish sociologists (Florian Znaniecki, Stanisław Ossowski, and Antonina Kłoskowska), in turn, assume that the nation is a product of national ideology. The unidirectionality of cultural transmission within the realm of national community is a limitation of both perspectives.
62. See Ewa M. Thompson, "Sarmatism."
63. Smith, *Nationalism*, 52.
64. Ibid., 90.
65. Ibid., 126.
66. Ibid.
67. See, for example, "Subject/subjectivity," in Ashcroft, Griffiths, and Tiffin, *Post-colonial Studies*, 219–26.
68. For a discussion of the subject's freedom in Foucault, see Gordon, "Foucault's Subject."
69. Foucault, "The Order of Discourse," 67.

70. "Unlike Michel Foucault, to whose work I am greatly indebted, I do believe in the determining imprint of individual writers upon the otherwise anonymous collective body of texts constituting a discursive formation like Orientalism" (Said, *Orientalism*, 23).
71. The complex issue of Said's stance on Foucault's thought has been taken up by Timothy Brennan in *Wars of Position* (chapter 3, "Humanism, Philology, and Imperialism").
72. Said, *The World, The Text, and the Critic*, 39–40.
73. Foucault, "The Order of Discourse," 52.
74. Said, *The World, the Text, and the Critic*, 214.
75. Hall, "Cultural Identity," 222.
76. Ibid., 225.
77. Sawicki, . . . *Quo magis*, 13ff.
78. Skarga, *Granice historyczności*, 141.
79. Smith, *The Ethnic Origins*, 207.
80. See Staniszkis, *O władzy i bezsilności*, 64.
81. See Bernhard, *The Origins of Democratization*, 136.
82. Falk, *The Dilemmas of Dissidence*, 18.
83. One recent example is Hanusiewicz-Lavallee's study of the history of cultural interactions among Poland, England, and Scotland from sixteenth to eighteenth century: *W stronę Albionu: Studia z dziejów polsko-brytyjskich związków literackich w dobie wczesnonowożytnej* (Toward Albion: Studies from the history of Polish-British literary connections in the early modern period).
84. Porter-Szűcs, *Faith and Fatherland*, 4–5.
85. Staniszkis, *O władzy i bezsilności*, 65.
86. Cf. Rusecki, *Personalizm polski.*
87. Staniszkis, *O władzy i bezsilności*, 58.
88. Ibid., 61–62.
89. For more on the significance of Thomism for the culture and mentality of Central and East European nations as well as for Polish subjectivity, see ibid. 49–99 and 113–46. See Markowski, "Wpływ chrześcijaństwa," 84. See also Czerkawski, "Arystotelizm"; Swieżawski, "Początki nowożytnego arystotelizmu." The memoirs of Barbara Toruńczyk, the editor of *Zeszyty Literackie*, provide interesting evidence of the contemporary continuations of Polish intellectual culture's penetration by Aristotelianism ("Opowieści o pokoleniu 1968"). In addressing the intellectual climate at the turn of the 1960s and 1970s, Toruńczyk notes that "ideas that looked to commonsensical methods of world analysis adopted in Aristotle's practical philosophy became ever more tempting. The foremost intellectual hunger of those times was for metaphysics and its instruments, such as the classical criterium of truth, and questions about the sense and value of human life, the social order, and culture."
90. See Pietrzyk-Reeves, "Podstawy wspólnotowego ładu."
91. Kizwalter, *O nowoczesności narodu*, 46.

92. Sawicki, "Ethos polskiej literatury," 28.
93. On the foundational and long-term role of medieval thought and culture in the formation of the Polish subject's identity, see Markowski, *Wpływ chrześcijaństwa*, 84–91.
94. Jędrychowska, *Widzieć Polskę*, 173.
95. See chapter 10, "Slavic Issues with Identity," in this book. See Stanisław Kowalczyk, *Filozofia kultury*, 107–14.
96. Said wrote repeatedly about the role of geography as a fundamental factor that "organizes" all of human culture, for example, in *Power, Politics, and Culture*, 195.
97. "For Fichte, Germany was the cradle of Europe and heir of Latin civilization. The Germans, by which he meant the Prussians, were 'to serve Europe' by bringing it under their control. . . . Hegel saw Europe as a spiritual synthesis of Christianity and Germanic culture whose highest embodiment was in the state" (Delanty, *Inventing Europe*, 80).
98. Thematization of the conflict between these two vectors, which delineate the field and establish the limits of self-definition, appears in many Polish literary texts since the time of the Enlightenment. One example is the unfinished novel of Prince Adam Jerzy Czartoryski, *Judge Deluty*.
99. Nowak, *Od imperium do imperium*, 192.
100. Some critics attribute such "failed transplantations" to the whole of Polish culture, viewing it as imitative, derivative, and lacking its own cultural patterns. See Sowa, *Fantomowe ciało króla*, 18–19. Such critique rests on similar premises to those underlying Alexander Kiossev's theory of the putative "imported" values and civilizational models of East-Central European populations (cf. Kiossev, "Notes on the Self-colonising Cultures," 114–17). A crucial shortcoming of Sowa's approach is its ignorance, and disparagement, of the political tradition of republicanism mentioned earlier in this chapter.
101. Charles Taylor, *Sources of the Self*; MacIntyre, *After Virtue*.
102. Charles Taylor, *Sources of the Self*, 27.
103. Ibid., 20.
104. With reference to Taylor and MacIntyre, it is more appropriate to state that they are conscious of the role of narration in the process of identity formation rather than that they uphold a narrative concept of identity (cf. Rosner, *Narracja, tożsamość, czas*, 29, 35).
105. Cf. Skarga, *Tożsamość i różnica*, 163–276.
106. Kołakowski, "Sprawa polska," 204.
107. Ibid., 209.
108. Fanon, *The Wretched of the Earth*, 236.
109. Ibid., 244–45.
110. Ibid., 233.
111. Kołakowski, "Sprawa polska," 214.
112. Ibid.; Fanon, *The Wretched of the Earth*, 246, 247.

113. For a discussion of the recent growth of nationalistic and neo-tribal tendencies in Poland, see Radziejewski, "Od Polaków do neo-Polan?"; and Kledzik, "Inventing Postcolonial Poland."
114. For a critical discussion of the alleged transition from a national to a post-national era, see Wang, "Mind the Gap."
115. Stróżewski, *Istnienie i wartość*, 295–96.

## Chapter Four

*Epigraphs*: Fanon, *The Wretched of the Earth*, 238; Radliński, "Nasza umysłowość," 1538.

1. See, for example, Stefan Kieniewicz, *Dziedzictwo zaborów*. For more on the subject, see Nowak, *Od imperium do imperium*, 113.
2. See, for instance, Janusz Maciejewski, *Z domu niewoli*.
3. Works about treason and collaboration among Poles during the partition period include Andrzej Chwalba's *Polacy w służbie Moskali* (Poles in Muscovy's service) and Magdalena Micińska's *Zdrada córka nocy: Pojęcie zdrady narodowej w świadomości Polaków w latach 1861–1914* (Treason the daughter of night: The notion of national treason in Poles' consciousness in the years 1861–1914).
4. Legutko, *O czasach chytrych*, 29.
5. The initial stage in contacts between the Soviets and Poles involved the collaboration of Polish writers with the Soviet occupation press in Lviv and Vilnius during 1939–42. Naturally, it has been entirely omitted and silenced in public discourse in Poland up to the 1990s. Yet as Gustaw Herling-Grudziński observed in his diary, the Lviv-Vilnius episode was the "testing ground of postwar reality in the country" (*Dziennik pisany nocą 1973–1979*, note dated January 2, 1977, 192): it allowed the occupiers to work out a formula for harnessing Poland's creative elites to the Soviet effort of assuming social control. For more, see Bolecki, "Realizmu socjalistycznego początki," 265.
6. One example of a work that toes the Communist Party line is Fijałkowska's *Polityka i twórcy*.
7. These publications include, among others, Fijałkowska, *Borejsza i Różański: Przyczynek do dziejów stalinizmu w Polsce* [Borejsza and Różański: A contribution to the history of Stalinism in Poland]; Hass, *Inteligencji polskiej dole i niedole: XIX i XX wiek* [The ups and downs of Polish intelligentsia: 19th and 20th centuries]; Hirszowicz, *Pułapki zaangażowania: intelektualiści w służbie komunizmu* [Pitfalls of commitment: Intellectuals serving Communism]; Krajewski, *Między współpracą a oporem: Twórcy kultury wobec systemu politycznego PRL (1975–1980)* [Between collaboration and resistance: The cultural sector and the political system of the Polish People's Republic (1975–1980)]; Murzański, *Między kompromisem a zdradą: Intelektualiści wobec przemocy 1945–1956* [Between compromise and treason: Intellectuals in the face of violence 1945–1956]; Prokop, *Wyobraźnia pod nadzorem* [Imagination

under surveillance]; Prokop, *Klerk i diabeł: Literatura—ideologie—mity* [The clerk and the devil: literature—ideologies—myths]; Prokop, *Pisarze w służbie przemocy* [Authors in service of violence]; Siedlecka, *Obława: Losy pisarzy represjonowanych* [Manhunt: The vicissitudes of the repressed authors]; Słabek, *Intelektualistów obraz własny w świetle dokumentów autobiograficznych 1944–1989* [Intellectuals' Self-portrait in light of autobiographical documents 1944–1989]; Szymański, *Uroki dworu* [The court's charm]; Trznadel, *Kolaboranci: Tadeusz Boy-Żeleński i grupa komunistycznych pisarzy w Lwowie 1939–1941* [Collaborators: Tadeusz Boy-Żeleński and the group of Communist authors in Lviv 1939–1941]; Urbankowski, *Czerwona msza czyli uśmiech Stalina* [The red mass, or Stalin's smile].

8. Słabek, *Intelektualistów obraz własny*, 194–95.
9. Ibid., 65, 80, 176.
10. Ibid., 198.
11. Tomasz Zarycki's studies in the cultural capital of the Polish intelligentsia are one example of exploring these issues. Zarycki et al. point to the continuation of the intelligentsia's ethos, part of which is struggle for spiritual leadership, placing the role of the intelligentsia in the context of post–Worl War II political, social, and economic developments in East-Central Europe:

    > After the establishment of communism in Poland, the new political capital elite (including mainly the communist bureaucratic apparatus) and the cultural capital elite (represented by different factions of the intelligentsia) became the two major actors remaining in the game. These were rarely the same intellectuals who dominated the interwar or post-communist period but they had not undermined the key role of intelligentsia identity as the model of the ideal Polish citizen, even if communist Poland was established under the slogan of a classless society. First, a major part of the political and intellectual elite was recruited from the prewar leftist intelligentsia. Second, the communists declared that they were building a specific social system composed of two non-antagonistic social classes: the working class and the peasantry as well as one further stratum: namely the intelligentsia or "*the working intelligentsia*." In this indirect way the privileged role of the intelligentsia was institutionalized, even though its more conservative members had been marginalized. In effect, the intelligentsia identity also became a key political stake, and most of the political tensions of the communist period could be interpreted in terms of the conflicts over rights to be regarded as the "true" intelligentsia elite. (Zarycki, Smoczyński, and Warczok, "The Roots of Polish Culture-Centered Politics," 375)

12. Janowski, *Narodziny inteligencji*, 7.
13. MacIntyre, *After Virtue*, 127.

14. Gandhi, *Postcolonial Theory*, 4.
15. Ibid., 14.
16. Ibid.
17. Following on the proposals of Jan Kieniewicz (*Ekspansja*, 261), this "situation" implies an external set of circumstances and conditions, independent of the society that is tied up in it, which define the attitudes, conduct, and choices of its members.
18. These three types of the creative elites' attitudes toward the hegemon reference Marek J. Chodakiewicz's typology, as presented in the book *Between Nazis and Soviets*.
19. Jedlicki, *Narodziny inteligencji*, 15.
20. Żeromski, "Literatura a życie polskie," 53.
21. Witkiewicz, *Aleksander Gierymski*, 159.
22. Zaleski, *Towarzystwo Warszawskie*, 437; as cited in Jedlicki, *Jakiej cywilizacji Polacy potrzebują*, 265.
23. Jędrychowska, *Rozmowy niekontrolowane*, 43.
24. Kijowski, "Czytając Tischnera," 205.
25. Gandhi, *Postcolonial Theory*, 4.
26. Nandy, *The Intimate Enemy*, xi.
27. Zagajewski, "Wysoki mur."
28. This is concordant with Tomasz Zarycki's observation that the post-Communist cleavage was caused not so much by economic and political issues but by "the attitudes towards the past, in particular, the interpretation of the communist period" (*Ideologies of Eastness*, 29).
29. See ibid., 82. Zarycki notes that "Many academics saw Homo-Sovieticus as an obstacle standing in Poland's way; as the main phenomenon keeping the country from "joining Europe" (29).
30. Tyrmand, *Dziennik 1954*, 178 (entry from February 8).
31. Zagajewski "Wysoki mur," 25.
32. Gibbons, "Towards a Postcolonial Enlightenment," 90.
33. Aleksander Fiut demanded the study of the "culturally active role of censorship in the People's Republic" in the article "Oblicza tyranii, oblicza historii" (The Faces of Tyranny, the Faces of History, 397). On strategies of bypassing censorship in nineteenth and twentieth century Polish literature and on the problem of deactualizing models of working "against" censorship, see Ryszard Nycz's overview account, "Polish Literature in the Shadow of Censorship."
34. Zbigniew Herbert's volume of poetry *Raport z oblężonego Miasta* (Report from a besieged city; 1983) is one canonical example of this phenomenon.
35. Bogusław Bakuła writes, "Even colonialized cultures can create mechanisms of homeostasis that prevent their total decay, which does not mean that they are capable of thorough self-transformation" ("Polska i kolonialna przeszłość dzisiaj," 158–59).
36. Appiah, *In My Father's House*, 149.
37. Zarycki, "Ku socjologicznej analizie," 173. Cf. Zarycki, *Ideologies of Eastness*, 75; Drahokoupil, "The Rise of the Comprador."

38. Zarycki, *Ideologies of Eastness*, 75.
39. Thompson, "The Surrogate Hegemon."
40. See Zarycki, *Ideologies of Eastness* (chapter 3, "Western Hegemony and Its Naturalization in Central and Eastern Europe," 32–63).
41. Mackiewicz, *Zwycięstwo prowokacji*, 172.
42. Łapiński, *Jak współżyć z socrealizmem*, 96.
43. Dąbrowska, *Dzienniki 1914–1965*, vol. 6, *1948–1949*, 271.
44. Błoński, *Zmiana warty*, 18. This closure of the discourse of the colonized within boundaries determined by the hegemon iterates the Manichaean opposition of the colonizer and the colonized as described by JanMohamed in "The Economy of Manichean Allegory."
45. Said, "Permission to Narrate," referred to by Spivak in "Can the Subaltern Speak?," 38.
46. Fuchs, "Postcolonial Mock-Epic," 30.
47. Cf. Kołodziejczyk, "Cosmopolitan Provincialism," 152–53.
48. These issues were often the subject of analyses aimed at the post-1944 period in Poland, most notably in Miłosz's *The Captive Mind* and Trznadel's *Hańba domowa* (A domestic disgrace).
49. Cf. Świda-Ziemba, "Stalinizm i społeczeństwo polskie," 19, 71. Mimicry understood in line with Bhabha's definition of it constitutes a special instance of accommodation (in "Of Mimicry and Man," in *Location of Culture*).
50. Wyka, *Wyznania uduszonego*, 200.
51. Ibid., 203.
52. Ibid., 203, 204.
53. Todorov, *The Conquest of America*, 123. Todorov borrowed this dictum from Antonio de Nebrija (*Gramática de la lengua castellana*, 1492).
54. "Wieczór 'Zapisu' u Walendowskich: Kronika" [The Zapis' evening at the Walendowski family: A chronicle], *Zapis*, no. 1 (1978); as quoted in Szaruga, *Literatura i życie*, 143–44.
55. Gandhi, *Postcolonial Theory*, 4–5.
56. Jarzębski is in favor of studying "oppositional" literature, meaning "literature created in opposition to the officially promoted visions of historical time" (*Apetyt na przemianę*, 15).
57. Szaruga, *Węzeł kresowy*, 76–77.
58. Certainly, not all Polish authors were susceptible to the lure of benefits in return for endorsing the Soviet-backed dictatorship in Warsaw. Among those who steadfastly refused to collaborate was Zbigniew Herbert, whose "refusal to make even conditional ideological concessions to the communist regime was as absolute as it was simple. With characteristic self-deprecation, he would say later that although he needed to write, he did not need to publish—not that much, anyway. By contrast, Miłosz, before his emigration to the West, served briefly (and without distinction) in the diplomatic service of communist Poland. Szymborska managed to produce two rather embarrassing books of socialist twaddle. Herbert was one of the very few Polish writers of that time who chose the Joycean stratagem of 'silence, exile

and cunning' rather than compromise" (Anders, *Between Fire and Sleep*, 88). The steadfastness of Herbert's uncompromising stand toward the regime has recently been challenged in Andrzej Franaszek's *Herbert: Biografia* (Herbert: A biography).

59. Besides the books listed in note 7 in this chapter, one can mention biographies and the most recent studies where the problem of collaboration of Polish writers during the Communist period has been addressed, among them Adamowska, *Różewicz i Herbert*, 9–46; Franaszek, *Miłosz: A Biography*; Franaszek's mentioned biography of Zbigniew Herbert (see note 58); Pasierski, *Miłosz i Putrament*; Romaniuk, *Inne życie: Biografia Jarosława Iwaszkiewicza* (A different life: Jarosław Iwaszkiewicz's biography); Shore, *Caviar and Ashes*; Siedlecka, *Biografie odtajnione. Z archiwów literackich bezpieki* (The declassified biographies: From the literary archives of secret police). See also Pasierski, "Czesław Miłosz i Jan Nowak-Jeziorański."
60. Macaulay, "Minute on Indian Education," 249.

## Chapter Five

*Epigraph*: Gombrowicz, *Dziennik 1953–1956*, 173.

1. Cf. Bhabha, *Nation and Narration.*
2. Bhabha, *The Location of Culture*, 140.
3. Ibid., 142.
4. Ibid., 148. The opposition between pedagogy and performativity would correspond, in a generalized way, to the contrast between two concepts of the ontology of the nation: primordialism (the nation as a category of describing an objectively existing community "as an a priori historical presence") and constructivism (nation as defined by Anderson, namely an *imagined community* constructed "in the performance of narrative, its enunciatory 'present' marked in the repetition and pulsation of the national sign" [ibid., 147]).
5. On this subject see, for example: Chwalba, *Polacy w służbie Moskali* [Poles in the service of Moskals]; Nowak, *Ofiary, imperia i historycy: Studium przypadków (od XVIII do XXI wieku)* [Victims, empires, and historians: Case studies (from the 18th to 20th century)].
6. Strzyżewski, *Music and Infinity*, 7.
7. Ibid., 8.
8. Halecki, *The Limits and Divisions*, 120–21.
9. This was noted by Aleksandra Niewiara in the book *Kształty polskiej tożsamości* [Forms of Polish Identity], 187–88.
10. Pieróg, "Mesjanizm," 540.
11. Walicki, *Filozofia i mesjanizm.*
12. Bednarczuk and Rudaś-Grodzka, "W poszukiwaniu utraconej wielkości."
13. Żmigrodzka, *Przez wieki idąca powieść*, 154.

14. Pigoń, *Poprzez stulecia*, 217.
15. Czesław Miłosz's letter dated November 13, 1973, in Walicki, *Zniewolony umysł po latach*, 412.
16. Walicki's phrasing (Walicki, *Mesjanizm Adama Mickiewicza*, 65).
17. Walicki, *Zniewolony umysł po latach*, 414.
18. Miłosz, *Szukanie ojczyzny*, 107.
19. Miłosz, *Ziemia Ulro*, 134.
20. Kiślak, *Walka Jakuba z aniołem*, 206.
21. Chłędowski, *Pamiętniki*, vol. 1, *Galicja (1848–1880)*, 132–33.
22. Norwid, "List do Józefa Bohdana Zaleskiego," 62.
23. Davies, *God's Playground*, vol. 1, *The Origins to 1795*, 401.
24. Ibid.
25. Przybylski, *Słowo i milczenie*, 206.
26. Iwanow, "Polski mesjanizm," 188.
27. Norwid, "List do Józefa Ignacego Kraszewskiego," 223.
28. Paźniewski, "Eseje wędrowne," 189.
29. Bogdan Zakrzewski writes, "For the independent existence of the homeland, the Napoleonism of the author of *Pan Tadeusz*, bound to the legionary idea and the Kościuszko tradition, and despite the emperor's defeat (and thus the frustration of hopes proclaimed in the *Mazurka* [now Poland's national anthem]), was and still is remarkably constructive, innovative, and fruitful for the historical future of the nation" (*Hajże na Soplicę!*, 24).
30. For a recent discussion of *Pan Tadeusz*'s values as interpreted by critics, including ideological values, see Kuziak, "*Pan Tadeusz* Adama Mickiewicza."
31. Cf. Tazbir, "*Pan Tadeusz*, a więc—jakoś to będzie."
32. Kijowski, "Listopadowy wieczór," 80.
33. Prokop, *Universum polskie*, 27.
34. Jan Nepomucen Miller, *Zaraza w Grenadzie*. As cited in Miller's *Bez kropki nad "i,"* 285.
35. Zakrzewski, *"Hajże na Soplicę!,"* 168–74.
36. Troszyński, "On the Shoulders of Giants."
37. Słowacki, *Raptularz*, 143.
38. Sawicki, "O znakach," 29.
39. For more on the relations between Poles and Lithuanians during the First Republic, see Litwin, "Nations of Polish-Lithuanian Commonwealth."
40. Sawicki, "O znakach," 29.
41. Miłosz, *The History of Polish Literature*, 227.
42. Cf. Chwin, "*Trans-Atlantyk* wobec *Pana Tadeusza*."
43. Gombrowicz, *Dziennik 1953–1956*, 356.
44. Trznadel, *Polski Hamlet*, 72.
45. Indeed, new and updated interpretations of Romantic conceptualizations do emerge from Poland. See, for instance, Bachórz, *Jak pachnie na Litwie Mickiewicza*, 61–83 (chapter titled "Mickiewiczowska idea Europy"); Cieśla-Korytowska, *O Mickiewiczu i Słowackim*, 106–19 (chapter titled "Co Mickiewicz i Słowianie mają do ofiarowania Zachodowi").

46. Artwińska, *Poetry in the Service of Politics*, 7.
47. Ibid., 10.
48. Witkowska, "Czytanie Mickiewicza," 19.
49. See Sobczak, *Kryzys polskiej tożsamości*, 247. The author notes that this phenomenon concerns the generations born after 1981.
50. Miłosz, *Szukanie ojczyzny*, 103.
51. Ibid.
52. Ibid., 110, 111.
53. See Kuziak, *O prelekcjach paryskich*; Kuziak, "Wartość kulturowego braku."
54. See Waśko, "Geopolityka."
55. See, for example, Aleksandravičius, "Tożsamość Mickiewicza."
56. Kowalczykowa, "Słowacki współczesny," 9. In the introduction to her book, Kowalczykowa characterizes Słowacki's work as having "chameleon changeability" (Kowalczykowa, *Słowacki*, 5). Amendable to a variety of readings, his oeuvre is also open to postcolonial interpretation.
57. Kowalczykowa, *Słowacki*, 58.
58. See Łaszkiewicz, "Pojęcie honoru."
59. Kiślak, *Car-trup i król-duch*, 130.
60. Kowalczykowa, "Słowacki współczesny," 10.
61. See Weintraub, *Od Reja do Boya*, 192–202 (chapter titled "Dwa *Paryże*").
62. For a definition of Sarmatism, see Ewa M. Thompson, "Sarmatism."
63. Gombrowicz, *Dziennik 1953–1956*, 173.
64. See Porter-Szűcs, *When Nationalism Began to Hate*.
65. Said, *Orientalism*, 328.
66. Kowalczykowa, *Słowacki*, 173. Emphasis mine.
67. Nicoll and Wilmurt, *World Drama*, 367–68.
68. Herling-Grudziński, *Dziennik pisany nocą 1973–1979*, 218 (dated October 11, 1977).
69. Gombrowicz, *Trans-Atlantyk*, 12.

## Chapter Six

1. Hochschild, *King Leopold's Ghost*, 294.
2. Fortunately not in its entirety; it is possible to learn about the scale of the Belgian colonial endeavor when visiting the Royal Museum for Central Africa in Brussels.
3. See Chowdhry, "Edward Said and Contrapuntal Reading."
4. Kubacki, *Z Mickiewiczem na Krymie*, 141.
5. Ibid., 12.
6. Such is Rolf Fieguth's proposal in his book *Rozpierzchłe gałązki*, 94.
7. Koropeckyj, "Orientalism in Adam Mickiewicz's *Crimean Sonnets*," 666, 667.
8. See Marian Maciejewski, "Od erudycji do poznania"; Kalinowska, *Between East and West*, 46.

9. Filipowicz, "Mickiewicz: 'East' and 'West,'" 618.
10. Opacki, *Poezja romantycznych przełomów*, 18–19.
11. The motto of *The Crimean Sonnets* is a citation from the notes and explanations to Goethe's collection *West-östlicher Divan* (Goethe, *Berliner Ausgabe*, 3:293): "Wer den Dichter will verstehen, muß in Dichters Lande gehen."
12. Borowy, *O poezji Mickiewicza*, 234.
13. Adam, "*The Crimean Sonnets* of Adam Mickiewicz," 429 (sonnet 15, vv. 12–14). All further citations from Mickiewicz's cycle refer to this translation and follow this format: sonnet number, verse number, page number. Polish orig. "Droga nad przepaścią w Czufut-Kale," vv. 12–14: "Mirzo, a ja spójrzałem! Przez świata szczeliny / Tam widziałem—com widział, opowiem—po śmierci, / Bo w żyjących języku nie ma na to głosu" (Mickiewicz, *Wybór poezyj*, 2:108).
14. Witkowska, *Mickiewicz*, 65.
15. Makowski, *Świat "Sonetów krymskich,"* 174.
16. Witkowska, *Mickiewicz*, 62.
17. "Ruiny zamku w Bałakławie": "człowiek podlejszy od gadu" (Mickiewicz, *Wybór poezyj*, 2:113). In Adam's English translation, this fragment is rendered as "Here reptiles roost, and men more odious" (17, 4, 431).
18. "Ałuszta w dzień," v. 2: "Rannym szumi namazem niwa złotokłosa." Mickiewicz, *Wybór poezyj*, 2:99.
19. "Bajdary," vv. 2–3: "Lasy, doliny, głazy, w kolei, w natłoku / U nóg mych płyną, giną jak fale potoku." Ibid., 98.
20. See Kubacki, *Z Mickiewiczem na Krymie*, 75.
21. Said, *Orientalism*, 59.
22. As Said remarks (ibid., 70), the Orientalist attitude "shares with magic and with mythology the self-containing, self-reinforcing character of a closed system, in which objects are what they are *because* they are what they are, for once, for all time, for ontological reasons that no empirical material can either dislodge or alter."
23. Kubacki, *Z Mickiewiczem na Krymie*, 157.
24. Said, *Orientalism*, 86.
25. Ibid.
26. "Ałuszta w nocy," vv. 12–14: "Nocy wschodnia! ty na kształt wschodniej odaliski / Pieszczotami usypiasz, a kiedym snu bliski, / Ty iskrą oka znowu budzisz do pieszczoty." Mickiewicz, *Wybór poezyj*, 2:101.
27. Said, *Orientalism*, 63.
28. Ibid., 40.
29. See note 19.
30. Samuel Bogumił Linde's dictionary gives the following definitions: "not worth much, low cost, low, common, simple" (*Słownik języka polskiego przez M. Samuela Bogumiła Linde*, 804). The so-called *Słownik wileński* ([The Wilno dictionary] 1861) distinguishes between a historical meaning ("not worth much, low cost, trifling," "low, common, ordinary, ignoble," and the then-current meanings that "refer only to the immoral side" ("wicked,

base, lacking character, excessively obsequious, cringing") (Zdanowicz et al., *Słownik języka polskiego*, 1065). The so-called *Słownik warszawski* ([The Warszawa dictionary] 1900–27) provides a broader and more diversified sets of meanings: (1a) "shameful, wicked, villainous, ignominious, infamous, dishonorable"; (1b) "petty, low, servile, poor, groveling"; (2) "ugly, nasty, hideous, bad, bleak, cheerless, insufferable, awful"; and the archaic forms of "banal, slight, insignificant, scant, petty, nit-picking, shabby, slapdash, mediocre, paltry, poor, flimsy, humble, inferior, second-rate" (Karłowicz, Kryński, and Niedźwiedzki, *Słownik języka polskiego*, 4:375). The meaning of Mickiewicz's phrase could be the subject of a separate essay.

31. On the difficulties that this fragment of sonnet 17 still causes for Mickiewicz's interpreters, see Piwińska, "*Sonety krymskie* czytane na Krymie," 28–29. In opposition to Koropeckyj, who sees this phrase as having a clearly pejorative tone ("less than human . . . presence in Mickiewicz's Orient," "Orientalism in Adam Mickiewicz's *Crimean Sonnets*, 670), Piwińska ties the employed means of poetic description to a memento mori topos and proposes that the entire work be seen as aiming at the universalization of the experience of servitude: "the man lower than vermin" would serve here as a warning against the belittlement that comes with foreign domination (Piwińska, "*Sonety krymskie* czytane na Krymie," 29).
32. See Ewa M. Thompson, *Imperial Knowledge*, 102–3. This analogy is imperfect because of clear genre differences: the act of exclusion in a novel, which is structurally conducive to multiple motifs and polyphony, is not the same as exclusion in a lyric form, which is subordinated to the rule of subjective representation.
33. See Seweryn, *O wyobraźni lirycznej*, 6.
34. See Koropeckyj, "Orientalism in Adam Mickiewicz's *Crimean Sonnets*," 664.
35. Ibid., 670.
36. This is how Koropeckyj interprets the tone of Prince Viazemskii's review of *The Crimean Sonnets* ("Orientalism in Adam Mickiewicz's *Crimean Sonnets*," 671). Viazemskii's review can be found in his *Polnoe sobranie sochinenii*.
37. Świdziński, "*Sonety krymskie*, czyli sposób."
38. Mickiewicz's sense of strangeness of Crimea has been noted by, among others, Zgorzelski in "Pielgrzym 'w krainie dostatków i krasy,'" 47.
39. Witkowska, *Mickiewicz*, 66–67.
40. See, for example, Piwińska, "*Sonety krymskie* czytane na Krymie," 36.
41. Świdziński, "*Sonety krymskie*, czyli sposób," 79; Zgorzelski, "Pielgrzym 'w krainie dostatków i krasy,'" 45; Kleiner, *Mickiewicz*, 1:575.
42. Świdziński, "*Sonety krymskie*, czyli sposób," 81.
43. Kubacki, *Z Mickiewiczem na Krymie*, 172.
44. Dixon, "How the Poet Sympathizes," 684.
45. Pruszyński, "Trębacz z Samarkandy." The heroes of Pruszyński's narration are the Uzbeks who live under Soviet rule. The author "permits" their own

"narration" to constitute an incredible complement to the "Polish narration," in its specific, myth-making function, no less (Pruszyński references the legend of Kraków's St. Mary's Basilica bugler). As a result, the Orient in Pruszyński's text has a sovereign existence that "answers back" to the West; in reinterpreting the Western "text," it is presented as a place with its own logic and history, which parallels and is symmetrical to that of the Occident. In comparing Mickiewicz's and Pruszyński's texts, it would clearly be necessary to account for differences stemming from genre-specific characteristics of both works.

46. Cf. Grudzińska-Gross, "How Polish Is Polishness." Grudzińska-Gross notes that Mickiewicz's *Grażyna* undermines both nineteenth-century and contemporary axioms relating to markers of nationality, such as "common past, common territory, common ancestors, language, religion" (6). This complicates the stable, consistent, and clearly defined Polish identity postulated by the discourse of nation.
47. Said, *Culture and Imperialism*, xxiii.
48. Koropeckyj, "Orientalism in Mickiewicz's *Crimean Sonnets*," 670.
49. "Bakczysaraj," v. 1: "Jeszcze wielka, już pusta Girajów dziedzina!" Mickiewicz, *Wybór poezyj*, 2:91.
50. Ibid., v. 11: "I perłowe łzy sącząc woła przez pustynie." Mickiewicz, *Wybór poezyj*, 2:92.
51. Kubacki notes that "the fountain is assigned a role of the poet's lyrical mouthpiece" (*Z Mickiewiczem na Krymie*, 307).
52. "Bakczysaraj," v. 12: "Gdzież jesteś, o miłości, potęgo i chwało!" Mickiewicz, *Wybór poezyj*, 2:92.
53. Said, *Orientalism*, 207.
54. Koropeckyj, "Orientalism in Mickiewicz's Crimean Sonnets, 671.
55. Zgorzelski, "Pielgrzym 'w krainie dostatków i krasy,'" 41.
56. I am borrowing these terms from Opacki (*Poezja romantycznych przełomów*, 18).
57. Zgorzelski speaks of Mickiewicz's Crimea as a "charming land, but very foreign to him" ("Pielgrzym 'w krainie dostatków i krasy,'" 47). Notable here are Józef Sękowski's arguments against the anti-Muslim prejudice of Poles (which stretches back to the seventeenth-century wars with Turkey), which he made in the spirit of the Enlightenment's tolerance (see Sękowski's *Collectanea*). Sękowski was a Polish Orientalist whom Mickiewicz knew personally and whose works he read (see Segel, "Mickiewicz and the Arabic Qasidah," 280).
58. By putting forth this thesis, I incline toward a more moderate stance than that of Izabela Kalinowska. Starting from the same premises, Kalinowska arrives at the overly radical conclusion that the cultural exchange presented in *The Crimean Sonnets* is hybrid in character: "The displacement that came with exile allowed Mickiewicz to recognize and respect the difference of the Other and to embrace the otherness within himself. Within a postcolonial theoretical perspective, *The Sonnets* occupy a space that 'opens up

the possibility of a cultural hybridity that entertains difference without an assumed or imposed hierarchy" (Homi K. Bhabha, *The Location of Culture*, London: Routledge, 1994, 4)' (*Between East and West*, 58). From my perspective, it is not hybridity but the ambivalence of the West-East encounter that *The Crimean Sonnets* reveal.

## Chapter Seven

1. This is how Michał Głowiński refers to *Castorp* in the essay "Nad *Castorpem*," 68, referencing the work of Theodor Ziolkowski ("Figures on Loan").
2. See, for example, Bagłajewski, "Miasto—palimpsest"; and Halikowska-Smith, "The Past as Palimpsest."
3. For instance, Marek Zaleski writes, "As an author, Huelle, it must be admitted, places himself in a very difficult position. He stirs our appetite for literature already with the title, and this appetite is, moreover, not of a general, everyday kind, but an insatiable one. Does not the word 'Castorp' sound like a mantra, a magical spell, and the promise of a wonderful adventure to every lover of literature?" ("Niedoszła miłość").
4. This is how Gayatri Spivak interprets Rhys's novel in the essay "Three Women's Texts"; see also Rushdie, "The Empire Writes Back," 8.
5. See, for example, Thieme, *Postcolonial Con-texts*; Lewis, "Postcolonial 'Writing Back.'"
6. In his definition of contrapuntal critical reading, Said claims that such reading implies the "awareness both of the metropolitan history that is narrated and of those other histories against which (and together with which) the dominating discourse acts" (*Culture and Imperialism*, 51). A "contrapuntal reading must take account of both processes, that of imperialism and that of resistance to it, which can be done by extending our reading of the texts to include what was once forcibly excluded" (66–67).
7. "Without accounting for the German colonization of the East and its continuation, we will never properly understand German colonial fantasies and practices" (Uerlings, "Kolonialer Diskurs und Deutsche Literatur," 40).
8. For example, we encounter this type of narration in nineteenth-century novels such as Jane Austen's *Mansfield Park*, William Thackeray's *Vanity Fair*, Charles Dickens's *Great Expectations* and *David Copperfield*, or in the work of Robert Louis Stevenson, all of which have been frequently analyzed by postcolonial critics. It also appears in nineteenth-century German *Ostmarkenromane* (see Kopp, "Constructing Racial Difference," 84–86).
9. Fanon, *The Wretched of the Earth*, 38, 39.
10. Marek Zaleski, "Niedoszła miłość," 11.
11. Huelle, *Castorp*, trans. Antonia Lloyd-Jones, 184. Further quotations from this work are indicated in the text.

12. Britta Schilling notes that "historians are increasingly finding parallels between racialist attitudes, paternalist ideology and policies of German colonialists overseas and 'colonial-like' attitudes towards Poles in Prussia and the Eastern borderlands since the mid-1880s" (*Postcolonial Germany*, 70); she mentions Robert Nelson's term 'adjacent colonialism' as applicable to this type of colonial expansion (Nelson, *Germans, Poland*, 2). On Africa as a source of inspiration for German art, see N'guessan, *Primitivismus und Afrikanismus*.
13. See Mosse, *The Crisis of German Ideology*, 180ff.
14. Cf. McClintock, *Imperial Leather*, 30.
15. Spurr, *The Rhetoric of Empire*, 28.
16. "Interestingly enough, the Wandervogel's love of nature sharply contrasted with that depicted in the idyllic scenes which, as children, they must have seen in their homes. For them, it was not a pastoral union with a benign force in nature. Rather, it was a conquest" (Mosse, *The Crisis of German Ideology*, 175).
17. Said, *Orientalism*, 207.
18. See Kontje, *German Orientalisms*, 179.
19. See Orłowski, "Ein feines Netz."
20. See Pennycook, *English and the Discourses.*
21. Similarly to the Arab in Camus's *The Stranger*, who "is not named and seems to be without a history, let alone a mother and father" (Said, *Culture and Imperialism*, 175).
22. The concept of the civilizing mission was introduced for the first time as early as 1840 by Richard Roepell in *Geschichte Polens* (A history of Poland), which refers to the transfer of culture by the allegedly superior *Kulturvolk* (the Germans) onto the allegedly inferior *Naturvolk* (the Poles) from the Middle Ages onward. As Kristin Kopp writes, "For the project of imagining and justifying the Polish regions as a German colonial territory, constructing a radicalized—and racialized—conception of Polish difference was of central importance" ("Constructing Racial Difference," 83). Language played a pivotal role in this construction (see, for example, Liulevicius, *The German Myth*; Kopp, "Gray Zones"). See also Thun, "Mythische Landschaften."
23. Orłowski, *Z modernizacją w tle*, 104; emphasis mine.
24. Cf. McClintock, *Imperial Leather*, 163–66.
25. Meaning the question posed in the title of Spivak's famous essay from 1988, "Can the Subaltern Speak?"
26. See Homi K. Bhabha's *The Location of Culture*, 85–92 (chapter 4, "Of Mimicry and Man: The Ambivalence of Colonial Discourse").
27. The views held by Castorp concerning Poles and the Polish lands are reflective of Bismarck's *Kulturkampf* policies, which included the escalation of the German government's already stern anti-Polish offensive during the 1880s (see Davies, *God's Playground*, 2:92–95; Berghahn, "Germans and Poles," 27; and Blanke, *Prussian Poland*, 55–91). To some extent, these views replicate parts of the program outlined by the German philosopher Edward

Hartmann in his 1885 article "Rückgang des Deutschtums" (Retreat of Germandom). Hartmann promulgated arguments for "strengthening the cohesiveness of Germany and germanizing the minorities" as well as demanded that "alien and inimical elements be eliminated (*ausrotten*)" (as quoted in Wandycz, *The Lands of Partitioned Poland*, 236).

28. For example, Siegfried Hüppe in *Verfassung der Republik Polens* (Berlin: F. Schneider, 1867), a work dedicated to Bismarck, argued that the Polish system defies "the principles of a modern state" and is "characterized, as all of inner life, in comparison to the West and Germany, by primitivism, the Slavs' civilizational immaturity and lack of political experience" (as per Serejski, *Europa a rozbiory Polski*, 332).
29. Anna Kochanowska-Nieborak writes about this in her monograph *Das Polenbild*.
30. Said, *Orientalism*, 42.
31. Ibid., 70.
32. See Kopp, *Germany's Wild East*. Cf. Rash, *The Discourse Strategies*. For a discussion of the "noble savage" myth, see Ter Ellingson's study *The Myth of the Noble Savage*.
33. Spurr presents these and other colonial discursive practices in *The Rhetoric of Empire*.
34. Ibid., 128.
35. Ibid., 47.
36. Depreciation and debasement are part of another colonial discourse practice, as analyzed by Spurr in *The Rhetoric of Empire*, 76–91. For a postcolonial analysis of Freytag's novel, see Kopp, *Germany's Wild East*, 29–56 (chapter 1, "Constructing German Colonial Space in the East: Gustav Freytag's *Soll und Haben* as Colonial Novel").
37. See Fanon, *Black Skin*, 28–44 (chapter 2, "The Woman of Color and the White Man").
38. See Pal-Lapinski, *The Exotic Woman*, 1–34 (chapter 1, "Designing/Desiring the Exoticized Woman").
39. Cf. Chari, "Colonial Fantasies," 277.
40. Cf. Metzl, "From Scopophilia to Survivor."
41. See Said, *Orientalism*, 188–90; Spurr, *The Rhetoric of Empire*, 170–83 (chapter 11, "Eroticization: The Harems of the West").
42. The legend of Wanda, the legendary daughter of King Krak, was first recorded in Mistrz Wincenty Kadłubek's *Chronicae Polonorum* (Bishop Vincentius of Cracow's *The Polish Chronicle*), which was written around 1223. It was developed further by historiographers, including the Polish Renaissance historian Jan Długosz (Ioannes Dlugossius, Joannis Longinus) in *Chronica Poloniae Maioris* and *Annales seu cronicae incliti Regni Poloniae* (Annals or chronicles of the famous kingdom of Poland) during the fifteenth century. According to Długosz's version of the legend, instead of marrying the German prince Rytigier and to prevent him from becoming Poland's ruler, Wanda chose to commit suicide by throwing herself into the

Vistula river (*Kronika wielkopolska*, 9; *Ioannis Dlugossi Annales*, 132). See also Davies, *God's Playground*, 1:52; Banaszkiewicz, "Mistrz Wincenty."

43. Cf. Said, *Orientalism*, 187.
44. Kopp, *Constructing Racial Difference*, 82.
45. Ibid., 81.
46. Ibid., 82.
47. Ureña, "Mobilizing German Women," 6. Ureña's inference is based on Kopp, *Contesting Borders*. See also Lieskounig, "'Branntweintrinkende Wilde.'"
48. Bhabha, *The Location of Culture*, 70.
49. The representation of Poles in the novel corresponds with texts of scientific character, such as the work of Fedor Ivanovich Smitt, a Baltic German in the service of Russia, entitled *Suworow und Polens Untergang*, vol. 2 (Leipzig: C. F. Winter, 1858). As Serejski summarizes it, Smitt described the Polish national character as follows: "rowdiness, recklessness, quarrelsomeness, and the lack of discipline and obedience toward authorities, greed, deceitfulness, cunning extreme individualism, an anarchic spirit" (*Europa a rozbiory Polski*, 367).
50. Spurr, *The Rhetoric of Empire*, 156.
51. It is only fair to note here yet another model that is part of the genealogical background of Huelle's novel, and which coalesced at the turn of nineteenth and twentieth centuries, namely, the travel and adventure novel. The central character in this genre is an active explorer-practitioner (in a telling coincidence, Castorp is called "Practitioner" by the narrator), and every piece of land is conquered by European travelers and eccentrics of the type represented by Phileas Fogg in *Around the World in Eighty Days* or Captain Nemo in *Twenty Thousand Leagues Under the Sea*, by Jules Verne. Novels that take place entirely in the colonies were also written at that time, as exemplified by Rudyard Kipling's *Kim* and Joseph Conrad's *Nostromo* (see Childs, *Postcolonial Theory*, 15).
52. Głowiński, "Nad *Castorpem*," 66.
53. Ibid., 66; Peiker, "Post-Communist Literatures," 6.
54. Drewnowski, "Czarodziejski brzeg," 14.
55. In the article "Between Theory and Reality," Ania Spyra offers an interpretation that goes beyond the Polish-German dialectic to consider the cosmopolitan aspect of the novel.
56. Huelle, *Castorp*, trans. into German by Renate Schmidgall. Favorable reviews of Huelle's novel in the German press passed over in silence the novel's postcolonial overtones. It seems that the immediate reasons for this stem primarily from the fact that German postcolonial studies has been focused on Germany's colonial enterprise in Africa (see, for example, Berman, *Enlightenment or Empire*). The issue of writing a postcolonial German history from the perspective in which the "German East, especially Poland [is] a site for colonial expansion from the late eighteenth century onwards" has been raised in Schilling, "German Postcolonialism," 437n29. It still

remains in the sphere of postulates rather than of academic research practice, however. Studies dedicated to questions of "white colonialism," which was as destructive for ethnic groups bordering Germany as overseas colonialism was to inhabitants of those lands, are scarce. One example of such research is the work of Kristin Kopp referenced in this chapter (cf. Ewa M. Thompson's review of Hodkinson and Walker, *Deploying Orientalism*). For a discussion of recent Polish-German postcolonial theoretical and methodological exchanges, see Zduniak-Wiktorowicz, *Filologia w kontakcie*.

## Chapter Eight

1. Kołodziejczyk, "Cosmopolitan Provincialism," 154.
2. The previous Polish recipient of the Austrian State Prize for European Literature was Andrzej Szczypiorski in 1988.
3. "Andrzej Stasiuk laureatem."
4. For example, Stasiuk, "Das Kaczynski-Theater."
5. Stasiuk, "Die Kaczynskis."
6. On the concept of the surrogate hegemon, see Ewa M. Thompson, "The Surrogate Hegemon."
7. Mayblin, Piekut, and Valentine, "'Other' Posts," 71.
8. Stasiuk, *Fado*, 24. Further citations and references marked in text (*F*).
9. Stasiuk, *On the Road to Babadag*, 29. Further citations and references marked in text (*B*).
10. For the transnational dimension of Stasiuk's writing, see Iwasiów, "(Trans) national Journeys."
11. On resentment in the Eastern European postcolonial context, see Hundorova, "Postkolonial'nyi melankholiinyi *ressentiment*." Cf. Mayblin, Piekut, and Valentine, "'Other' Posts."
12. See Chakrabarty, *Provincializing Europe*.
13. Kundera, "The Tragedy of Central Europe," 33.
14. Kundera, "Zakład czeski," 29; Kundera, "The Tragedy of Central Europe," 34.
15. Fanon, *The Wretched of the Earth*, 311, 312.
16. The proper title of the book mentioned by Stasiuk is *Moja Europa: Dwa eseje o Europie zwanej Środkową* (My Europe: Two essays on the Europe called Central).
17. Stasiuk, "Filozofia nicości," 177.
18. "Stasiuk is what we what we might call an anti-Kundera, the latter being a Slavic writer who left his home region and enjoyed the rare success of adapting to a foreign place and culture so thoroughly that he now writes in French, a true cosmopolitan who believes that literary fiction must aim high at a notional standard of 'world literature'" (O'Keeffe, "Mitteleuropa Blues," 1643).

19. On the significance of "Central Europe" from the Czech perspective, see, for example, Kroutvor, "Potíže střední Evropy."
20. Wolff, *Inventing Eastern Europe*. For more about this work, see chapter 9, "Colonized Poland, Orientalized Poland," of this book.
21. Berger, *A Winter in the City*, 118, as cited in Hammond, "Typologies," 206.
22. Stasiuk, *Jadąc do Babadag*, 215.
23. I am borrowing this phrase from Brix, "Pochwała miast."
24. For more on tourist narrative as a subgenre, see Rickly-Boyd, "The Tourist Narrative."
25. Somewhat humorously, one may note that the marriage of geopoetics and the postcolonial situation led to the birth of a new topos of the Central European city in contemporary literature. Yurii Andrukhovych writes, for example, about "putrid Warsaw" (*Dwanaście kręgów*, 50).
26. I refer here to the title of Norman Davies' essay "West Best, East Beast."
27. See Bagłajewski, "Mapa, podróż, czas"; and Frankowiak, "Środkowoeuropejska świadomość."
28. Spurr, *The Rhetoric of Empire*, 76.
29. Ibid.
30. Ibid., 77.
31. Stasiuk, "Dziennik okrętowy," 136. For a comparative analysis of Andrukhovych's and Stasiuk's essays, see Wierzejska, "Central European Palimpsest."
32. Norman Davies addressed this fluidity of external and internal borders of Europe and its regions in the lecture "Fair Comparisons, False Contrasts: East and West in Modern European History": "In exploring a subject which the Enlightenment called 'philosophical geography,' one has to put aside the physical map of Europe, or at least to treat it with considerable elasticity. For on the mental map which people carry in their heads Western Europe and Eastern Europe are not just determined by points of the compass. They are terms of orientation in a shifting intellectual landscape, where all bearings are relative and paradoxes abound" (42). For an evaluation of this territory in Stasiuk's work, see Marszałek, "'Pamięć, meteorologia,'" 546.
33. Marszałek, "'Pamięć, meteorologia,'" 543.
34. Stasiuk, "Filozofia nicości," 177.
35. For example: "Gold chains, gaudy shirts, glossy buckles on boots and belts, the shine of cheap watches, showiness . . ." (Stasiuk, "Dziennik okrętowy," 129). Stasiuk reached an apogee of the grotesque in the play *Noc czyli słowiańsko-germańska tragifarsa medyczna* (Night or a Slavo-Germanic medical tragifarce), which was commissioned by the Düsseldorfer Schauspielhaus for a theater festival celebrating the enlargement of the European Union in 2004. Stasiuk's play drew extensively on Polish and German national stereotypes and playfully juxtaposed the two nations in a symbolic clash of Europe's East and West.
36. See Ewa M. Thompson, *The Surrogate Hegemon*.

37. Fiut, "Powrót do Europy Środkowej?," 162.
38. Brzezinski, "A Divided Europe," 301.

## Chapter Nine

1. See Tazbir, "Kamienie milowe," 321, 340.
2. The concept of "the other Europe" and of the terms related to it has a long lineage that cannot be analyzed here. Its genesis was linked to the erasure of the First Commonwealth of Poland and Lithuania from the map of eighteenth- and nineteenth-century Europe as a result of its partitions. This led to a discursive utilization of the resulting "vacuum," as noted by Oskar Halecki: "The partition of the Polish Commonwealth between the Russian and German Empires made that third region disappear completely for more than a hundred years, creating the impression that there was nothing between Western European Germany and a new Russia, identified with Eastern Europe" (Halecki, *The Limits and Divisions*, 120–21). The Cold War division of the continent during the twentieth century only further perpetuated clichés and stereotypes of a "second," or else "inferior" Europe in world historiography, the social and political sciences, as well as in Russian-dominated Slavic studies.
3. Wolff, *Inventing Eastern Europe*.
4. The "sources" that Wolff lists (travelogues, philosophical writing, and literary texts) were used by German historians, among others, and seen as an argument for the "civilizing mission" that justified the German expansion into Polish lands (see Topolski, *Jak się pisze*, 182).
5. See Cervinkova, "Postcolonialism, Postsocialism." Cervinkova points to a debate between Chris Hann and Michał Buchowski as a "nuanced example of an argument between western and central European anthropologists about the former's orientalizing practices" (161n1).
6. Cf. Bobrownicka, "Antyteza słowiańsko-europejska," 13.
7. Said, *Orientalism*, 1–2.
8. Interesting inferences can be drawn from Anna Kochanowska-Nieborak's book *Das Polenbild in Meyers Konversationslexika des "langen" 19. Jahrhunderts*. Her analysis of the most influential nineteenth-century high-circulation German publications unequivocally shows that, beside an obvious negative evolution of the perceptions of Poles and Poland, which was tied directly to politics and began with the establishment of the German Reich, the theme of German superiority in relation to the Poles and their alleged need for a civilizing mission was notably and steadily present in all of the editions of Meyers's lexicons, including those from before 1871.
9. Bennett and Hollister, *Medieval Europe*.
10. Cf. Zientara, *Frühzeit der europäischen Nationen* (Polish orig. *Świt narodów europejskich: Powstawanie świadomości narodowej na obszarze Europy*

*pokarolińskiej* [The dawn of European nations: The emergence of national consciousness in post-Carolingian Europe]).

11. Wolff, "Teaching 'Eastern Europe,'" 1.
12. This issue was taken up by Janusz Korek in the essay "Central and Eastern Europe from a Postcolonial Perspective." See also Cervinkova, "Postcolonialism, Postsocialism"; Neuger, "Central Europe as a Problem."
13. See, for example, Todorova, "The Trap of Backwardness."
14. See Judt, *A Grand Illusion?*
15. Judt, *A Grand Illusion?*, 50.
16. Judt, *Postwar*, 590.
17. Judt, *The Grand Illusion?*, 54.
18. Kroutvor, "Europa Środkowa," 244.
19. This is the term used by Juliusz Mieroszewski in the article "Polityka narodów zdeklasowanych" (The politics of outclassed nations), 9.
20. On the absence of Polish history in American academic textbooks and the reasons behind it, see Kulczynski, "Dzieje Polski w amerykańskiej historiografii." Cf. Tazbir, "Polska a Europa," 39–40.
21. Seton-Watson, *Eastern Europe between the Wars*, xv.
22. Wolff, *Inventing Eastern Europe*, 358.
23. Said, *Orientalism*, 25.
24. Ibid., 24.
25. In writing about Herder's role, for instance, Wolff states that "he gave Eastern Europe its modern identity as the domain of the Slavs" (*Inventing Eastern Europe*, 11).
26. Ibid., 362. Cf. Zernack, "Ostgrenze."
27. Cf. Ricoeur, *Evil.*
28. Judt, *The Grand Illusion?*, 60.
29. See Gandhi, *Postcolonial Theory*, 32.
30. Cf. Zarycki, *Ideologies of Eastness*, 64–88 (chapter 4, "The intelligentsia doxa: the hegemony of the intelligentsia and its naturalization").
31. Wolff, *Inventing Eastern Europe*, 373.
32. Ewa M. Thompson, *Imperial Knowledge*, 103.
33. Ezequiel Adamovsky formulated a thesis similar to Wolff's about Russia's orientalization by the West in *Euro-Orientalism*. See also Boss's review of this book in *Sarmatian Review*, 1333, as well as the author's reply: "What Is Eastern Europe?," 1399–401; and the reviewer's response: "Ms. Boss Responds," 1401.
34. A proposal outlined in a discussion of Wolff's work by Dupcsik in "Postcolonial Studies and the Inventing of Eastern Europe."
35. Jerzy Jedlicki writes, "Poland was colonized by Western civilization, to be sure, but also by the partitioning powers, after all; and only in the Prussian partition did these two conquests converge" (*Jakiej cywilizacji Polacy potrzebują*, 207). See also Jedlicki, *A Suburb of Europe*. A similar view is represented by Maria Janion, who sees Poland's baptism into Latin Christianity as key to its loss of the Slavic core of its identity and, simultaneously, to its

subordination to the West (*Niesamowita Słowiańszczyzna*, 17 passim). Cf. chapter 10, "Slavic Issues with Identity," in this book.

36. According to WorldCat, Rulhière's original work (full French title: *Histoire de l'anarchie de Pologne, et du démembrement de cette république*) had fifty-nine editions between 1807 and 1843. It was published in Polish in 1808 as *Historia bezrządu w Polsce* (The history of anarchy in Poland). See http://www.worldcat.org/identities/lccn-n50-52509.
37. I am referencing terms used by Mykola Riabchuk to describe Ukraine's postcolonial condition in the article "Od 'Małorosji' do 'Indoeuropy,'" 116.
38. See chapter 10, "Slavic Issues with Identity," in this book.
39. Said, *Orientalism*, 10.
40. Applebaum, *Iron Curtain*.
41. Frankel, "Stalin's Shadow," 16.
42. "I consider Orientalism's failure to have been a human as much as an intellectual one; for in having to take up a position of irreducible opposition to a region of the world it considered alien to its own, Orientalism failed to identify with human experience, failed also to see it as human experience" (Said, *Orientalism*, 328).
43. Spielberg's film was made the same year that Poland and seven other nations from the former Soviet sphere of influence joined the European Union.
44. I cannot consider here all of the aspects of *Terminal* that are significant to its polysemic message, among them the two-way processes involved in cross-cultural encounters.
45. Said, *Culture and Imperialism*, xxiii.
46. See Serejski, *Europa a rozbiory Polski*.
47. Davies, "Fair Comparisons, False Contrasts."
48. Dyboski, *O Anglii i Anglikach*, 93.
49. Ibid.
50. Chesterton, preface, vi, as cited in Ewa M. Thompson, "On Zygmunt Krasiński's *Undivine Comedy*," 500.
51. Gandhi, *Postcolonial Theory*, 144; Dyboski, *O Anglii i Anglikach*, 93.
52. Jedlicki, "Stereotyp Zachodu," 100.
53. I borrow the concept of doxa from Pierre Bourdieu—see Bourdieu, *Outline of a Theory of Practice*. For reasons of space it is not possible to outline here the lengthy debate in Poland on the ways of modernization. For a most recent discussion of this debate, see Magdalena Nowicka-Franczak, "Was Another Modernisation Possible?"

## Chapter Ten

1. Deltcheva, "Comparative Central European Culture," 149.
2. Janion, *Niesamowita Słowiańszczyzna*. Further citations are indicated in the text.
3. Deltcheva, "Comparative Central European Culture," 149.

4. See chapter 2, "Postcolonialism in Poland," in this book.
5. Kołodziejczyk, "Post-colonial Transfer."
6. Shohat, "Notes on the Postcolonial," 111.
7. For example, do novels such as Wojciech Kuczok's *Gnój* (Manure) actually present the realities of contemporary Poland (309)? Is xenophobia really an integral element of the character of contemporary Polish society, as Dorota Masłowska's *Snow White and Russian Red* suggests (311)? Are Mariusz Wilk's books about Russia and Russians, such as *Wilczy notes* (Wolf's notebook or Wilk's notebook) and *Wołoka*, more "true," for example, than Ryszard Kapuściński's *Imperium* (235–41)?
8. Gajda, "Romanticism and the Rise of Neopaganism," 57.
9. Piotr Wiench proposes a theoretical framework for such a reading of *Uncanny Slavdom* in "A Postcolonial Key."
10. For instance, despite the shorter history of the Russian nation, Russians do not display the same sense of inferiority in relation to the rest of the continent, as evidenced by their cultural and critical discourses. Beside the long-lasting efforts of Russian historians in extending "Russianness" to the ancient Rus' territory, including Kievan Rus', a significant role here is likely played by the sense of pride stemming from the political position and status of an empire of Russia and the USSR. See Miller, Sdvizhkov, and Shirle, *"Poniatiia o Rossii"*; Obolensky, "Russia's Byzantine Heritage"; Perrie, *The Cult of Ivan the Terrible*; Platt, *Terror and Greatness*. The "syndrome of defeat" that has been inscribed onto Polish identity from the end of the eighteenth century and is so difficult to overcome is a doubtful counterweight to the Russian consciousness of belonging to a "nation of winners" (see Prokop, *Polak jaki jest*, 50).
11. Zientara sees an example of such texts in the satirical poems that circulated Europe during the Middle Ages, snidely mocking the supposedly inherent characteristics of neighboring nations (*Świt narodów europejskich*, 337). See also Leszek Kołakowski's essay "On National Stereotypes."
12. See Borejsza, *A Ridiculous Hundred Million Slavs*, 44.
13. Among theoreticians, Anthony D. Smith is a proponent of the thesis about an early, pre-Enlightenment genesis of nations (see chapter 3, "National Identity in a Postcolonial Framework" in this book). Among Polish historians, the thesis of medieval sources of nationality has been supported by Zientara, among others, who stressed that the formation of nations within the sphere of the Latin Christian community began in the eleventh century (*Świt narodów europejskich*, 341). Interestingly, Zientara states that, even though regional ties, including those between Slavic nations and ethnic groups, lasted alongside national bonds for a long time, it was the community of Latin Christianity, which declined only in the sixteenth century, that served as the strongest nonethnic link (339). This counters Janion's thesis of the Latin idea being an "alien element" for Western Slavs.
14. See Ashcroft, Griffiths, and Tiffin, *Post-colonial Studies*, 125. Cf. Mignolo, *The Darker Side*.

15. Mignolo, *The Darker Side*, 325.
16. Said, *Orientalism*, 56.
17. Snyder, *The Reconstruction of Nations*, 3.
18. Cf. Tiffin and Lawson, *De-scribing Empire*, 1994, 6. Postcoloniality is tied primarily to power that resides in discourse and textuality. Resistance to this power thus appears primarily in the sphere of textuality, since "the contestation of post-colonialism is a contest of representation" (10). For more on the orientalization of Eastern Europe in Western discourses, see chapter 9, "Colonized Poland, Orientalized Poland," in this book. See also Davies, "West Best, East Beast"; Bobkov, "To the East from the Center."
19. For example, Klaus Zernack defines the years 1000–1700 as a period of balance and normalcy in Polish-German relations on a European scale, locating the onset of German hegemony toward Poland only in the eighteenth century ("Deutsch-polnische Beziehungen").
20. Notably, a fundamental discussion of Irish literature from a postcolonial perspective omits the issue of pagan prehistory (Kiberd, *Inventing Ireland*, 1996). The Irish trope is certainly worth taking up in further postcolonial studies of Polish literature. This research direction is well justified by numerous parallels between the political and economic history of Ireland and Poland, and the role played by literature, language, and religion in preserving both nations' identity. In this context, it is also worth recalling a remark made by Lloyd George, a former British prime minister of Welsh origin, that a Pole is "the Irishman of continental Europe" (as quoted in Wandycz, "Western Images," 9). For comparison between postcolonial Poland and Ireland, see Róisín Healy's studies, among them "Colonial Ambivalence and Its Aftermath: Colonialism and Anticolonialism in Independent Poland and Ireland."
21. The Russian scholar Aleksandr W. Lipatov presents Poland's role on the medieval map of European Christianity differently: "Poland was not only a connective link between cultures of Catholic and Eastern Orthodox Slavs, not only an intermediary in, and propagator of, contacts between the Latin West and the Byzantine East, it was also itself actively co-creating the synthesis of cultural and artistic values entering this sphere within the scope of its own ideas and needs" (*Rosja i Polska*, 128).
22. The issue of the existence of Slavic rites on Polish lands, and the two-track nature of Polish Christianity that supposedly derives therefrom, was raised by Julia Tazbir and Janusz Tazbir in their review entitled "Cienie zapomnianych przodków: O *Niesamowitej Słowiańszczyźnie* Marii Janion; Czy Polacy zostali 'źle ochrzczeni'?" (The shadows of the forgotten ancestors: On Maria Janion's *Uncanny Slavdom*; Have Poles been 'badly baptized'?). On contemporary views on the Middle Ages, "in particular the recent revival of interest in strange and extreme forms of belief and behavior now perceived as characteristic of medieval civilization," see, for example, Freedman and Spiegel, "Medievalism Old and New" (quote from p. 677).

23. See Brock, Stanley, and Wróbel, *Nation and History*.
24. "The leading historians of the Cracow school in the 1860s put the blame for the partitions squarely on Polish noble democracy for failing to build a strong state and drew the conclusion that Polish national interests were best served through loyalty to an Austrian Empire that after 1869 provided a considerable measure of Polish home rule in Galicia" (ibid., 127).
25. Prokop, *Polak jaki jest*, 161.
26. Bakuła, *Historia i komparatystyka*, 13–14.
27. On the subject of these relations in medieval times, Zientara writes, "The ideology of a Slavic community did not go . . . further than the thesis of the necessity of helping 'kindred' people: Pan-Slavic plans of the political union of all Slavs were not being created at that time" (*Świt narodów europejskich*, 340–41). Basically, inter-Slavic bonds were limited to the Latinists: Poles, Czechs, Slovaks, and Catholic southern Slavs (Croats and Slovenes).
28. Lipatov, *Rosja i Polska*, 415.
29. Halecki, *The Limits and Divisions*. To support his theses about Pan-Slavism, Halecki referenced Wacław Lednicki's "Pan-Slavism."
30. Czesław Miłosz pointed to this tactic in a discussion about Central Europe as an "anti-Soviet concept," which developed during the "Central Europe and Russian Writers" conference held by the Wheatland Foundation in Lisbon in 1988. For a transcript of Miłosz's contribution to the discussion, see "The Lisbon Conference on Literature," 120–21.
31. As Homi K. Bhabha uses the term in "Representation and the Colonial Text," 97.
32. At a lecture given at the Catholic University of Lublin in 2007 on the occasion of the bestowment of the Honorary Doctorate Degree.
33. "When Poles joined Western civilization in the tenth century (966), they did so in an act of free choice and not as a historical necessity" (Koehler, "The Heritage of Polish Republicanism," 1662). A considerable number of historiographic studies explore this issue, to mention only the works of Jerzy Kłoczowski. They include *Młodsza Europa: Europa Środkowo-Wschodnia w kręgu cywilizacji chrześcijańskiej średniowiecza* (The younger Europe: East-Central Europe in the domain of medieval Christian civilization), with which Janion polemicizes (*Niesamowita Słowiańszczyzna*, 215–17), and *A History of Polish Christianity*.
34. Wierzbicki, *Spory o polską duszę*, 124.
35. Gandhi, *Postcolonial Theory*, 108.
36. This remark pertains not only to Polish identity but also to identity issues among other ethnicities of East-Central Europe. As Norman Davies points out, "The existence of the Soviet Bloc concealed the fact that in many ways the captive peoples of the east were more conscious of their European heritage than the Westerners were. . . . It would be no accident that the most convincing declarations of attachment to Europe as a civilisation were to be made by dissident intellectuals from the Soviet Bloc like Milan Kundera" (Davies, *Europe East and West*, 20).

37. Kosminski, *Historia wieków średnich*, 60 (as cited in Stobiecki, "Między marksizmem a wielkoruskim szowinizmem," 235, 241).
38. Ştefănescu, "Reluctant Siblings," 22.
39. Ibid., 23.
40. On the conservative current in Polish literature, see Ewa M. Thompson, "Why the Conservative Tradition"; Urbanowski, *Prawą stroną literatury polskiej*. On the national dimension of Norwid's work as a Christian poet, see Sawicki, "Norwid—od strony prawnuków," 119–21. Norwid's poetry, "in whose works a clear classical-humanistic inspiration is inextricably interwoven with Christian ideals" (Hanusiewicz-Lavallee, "*Humanitas* and *Christianitas*," 105) remained unknown to the English-speaking world for a long time because of its specific, idiosyncratic style and purposefully archaic language, which made it difficult to translate. *Studia Norwidiana*, the journal uniquely dedicated to studies of Cyprian Norwid's life and oeuvre, established in 1983 and published by the Cyprian Norwid Literature Research Center at the John Paul II Catholic University of Lublin, has recently introduced a parallel English edition (2016, 2017): http://czasopisma.tnkul.pl/index.php/sn.

## Chapter Eleven

*Epigraph*: Cioran, *Cahiers 1957–1972*, 26.
1. Hadaczek, *Kresówki* (Borderlands sketches), 159.
2. See, for example, Paul Gilroy's books *After Empire* and *Postcolonial Melancholia*; Eli Sorensen, "Postcolonial Melancholia."
3. Gilroy, *After Empire*, 125.
4. Kristeva, *New Maladies*. Cf. Fiała, Skórczewski, and Wierciński, *Melancholia*.
5. See chapters 8 and 9 of this book.
6. Chioni Moore, "Is the Post- in Postcolonial," 121. The term was coined to describe the nature of Russian/Soviet hegemony in the Baltic and East-Central European countries. Their specific situation was tied to the fact that Russia saw the annexation of better-developed Central European territories as a specific kind of payment for its own sense of degradation stemming from its centuries-old inferiority complex toward the West.
7. Freud, "Mourning and Melancholia," 243.
8. Ibid., 237.
9. Ibid., 243, 244. Stefan Żeromski identified some of these traits in Polish writing and commented on them critically in his famous lecture "Literatura a życie polskie" (Literature and Polish life), which he delivered in Zakopane in 1915. The place of Freud's melancholic resignation in Żeromski's lecture was taken by "abnegation . . . of rights to creative freedom, both forced and voluntary" (4:53). According to the author, this abnegation marked the modernist work of Polish writers during the period of subjugation because of their lack of access to reflections on the universal human condition.

10. "The concept of the Borderlands as a 'guardhouse,' 'an outpost of Polishness,' and a 'besieged fortress' was not just a reaction to the imperialist oppression of Polishness on these territories. It was also an answer to Lithuanian and Belorussian revivalist and separatist movements, as well as to the ideas of the 'krajowcy' group, who proposed the creation of a modern cantonal state on the territories of the former Kingdom. In this sense, the Borderlands mentality was an element of nationalistic and Poland-centered thought" (Bujnicki, "Życie pośmiertne," 171).
11. Zarycki, *Ideologies of Eastness*, 116–17.
12. Klich-Kluczewska and Seweryn, "Rediscovering Ourselves," 89. Cf. Nina Taylor, "Dziedzictwo kresowe," 130–43.
13. Mick, "Colonialism in the Polish Eastern Borderlands," 128.
14. Owsianowska, "Tourist Narratives," 172. Owsianowska quotes Robert Traba ("The Kresy as a Realm," 76), who argues that this politics of erasure "shows the mechanism of creating a phantomic reality in the system of monopolized history by the ideology of socialist state: everyone knew that the Kresy existed, but nobody would mention them publicly" (172).
15. For more on the role of the Sarmatian idea in the Polish identity discourse and the context of contemporary debate about the Borderlands, see Zarycki, *Ideologies of Eastness*, chapter titled "The Kresy (Old Borderlands) Discourse," 115–51.
16. Bauman, *Community*, 21.
17. "Dwelling is the manner in which mortals are on the earth"; "dwelling . . . is the *basic character* of Being" (Heidegger, "Building Dwelling Thinking," 245, 254.
18. This is the typology proposed by Svetlana Boym in her book *The Future of Nostalgia*.
19. See Walder, *Postcolonial Nostalgia*, 16ff.
20. Nora, "The Reasons for the Current Upsurge."
21. Walder, *Postcolonial Nostalgias*, 16. A similar ambivalence can be noted also in Polish literature.
22. Czesław Miłosz linked the name of "Polish paradise" as applied to Borderlands literature with the seminar presentation of Jan Błoński in Lille, which was organized by Daniel Beauvois in 1987 (*Szukanie ojczyzny*, 213). For more on the Borderlands' infernal image, see Sapa, *Między polską wyspą*, 44.
23. Owsianowska, *Tourist Narratives*, 174). The phrase "meta-space of adventure" as related to the Borderlands was coined by Kolbuszewski, "Legenda Kresów" (The legend of Borderlands) 69.
24. Bakuła, "Colonial and Postcolonial Aspects," 106.
25. Derrida, *Specters of Marx*, 136, 114.
26. Ibid., 67.
27. Derrida, "An Interview with Jacques Derrida."
28. See Bakuła, "Colonial and Postcolonial Aspects."
29. Cf. Hadaczek, *Kresówki*, 145–46.

30. The difficulties tied to transferring the categories of Western postcolonialism and applying them to the history of contacts between the Polish-Lithuanian Commonwealth and Europe's southeastern regions have been discussed by Jan Kieniewicz in *Ekspansja*, 170–71ff.
31. Wielhorski, "Stosunki językowe," 36.
32. Szulecki, "Inna Europa."
33. Ibid.
34. Uliasz, *O literaturze Kresów*, 14.
35. See Szacka, "Pamięć zbiorowa."
36. Bieńkowski, *Przyszłość przeszłości*, 82.
37. Uliasz, *O literaturze Kresów*, 14.
38. Błoński, "Bezładne rozważania," 16.
39. Jarzębski, *W Polsce czyli wszędzie*, 129.
40. See, for example, Ciesielski, *Przesiedlenie ludności polskiej*, 2000.
41. Zaleski, *Formy pamięci*, 17. Zaleski references the views of Jean Starobinski as presented in the essay "On Nostalgia."
42. Wittlin, "Mój Lwów" [My Lviv], 364.
43. Ritz, "Kresy polskie," 118; Dąbrowski, *Nierzeczywista rzeczywistość*.
44. Dybel, *Urwane ścieżki*, 155.
45. Zagajewski, *Without End*, 80.
46. Dybel, *Urwane ścieżki*, 150.
47. Bakuła, *Colonial and Postcolonial Aspects*, 102. On the paradox of the centrality of the Borderlands in Polish identity discourse, despite their peripheral locale, see Miłosz, *Szukanie ojczyzny*, 21; Święch, "Kresy i centrum," 35–53; and Uliasz, "Kresy," 303–5). Controversy surrounding the term "Borderlands," which "will always be a thorn in the side of Poland's eastern neighbors," has been noted by, among others, Daniel Beauvois in the article "Mit kresów wschodnich," 94.
48. Jan Kieniewicz, "Polskie pogranicza," 78.
49. See Lacan, *Écrits*, 624.
50. Andrzej Stanisław Kowalczyk, "Rozpad języka," 105.
51. Iwaszkiewicz, *Sława i chwała*, vol. 2, 421–22.
52. The issue of Poland's colonial plans during the interwar period is raised by, among others, Hunczak ("Polish Colonial Ambitions"), Borkowska ("Polskie doświadczenie kolonialne"), and Kowalski (*Dyskurs kolonialny w Drugiej Rzeczypospolitej*).
53. Žižek, "Melancholy and the Act," 660.
54. I am referring to a generation of writers who know the Borderlands only from familial reports and artifacts, such as Aleksander Jurewicz, Marek Ławrynowicz, Anna Bolecka, Adam Zagajewski, Włodzimierz Paźniewski, and Stanisław Srokowski. Cf. Dąbrowski, "Reguła kompensacji," 183.
55. See Bujnicki, "Życie pośmiertne," 170.
56. I approach this term metaphorically rather than literally. Discussions on the political form of the Polish-Lithuanian Commonwealth are ongoing

among historians. See, for example, Nowak, *Od imperium do imperium*, 337–55 (chapter titled "Czy Polska była imperium? Rozmowa z Romanem Szporlukiem" [Was Poland an empire? Conversation with Roman Szporluk]); Bömelburg, "Die polnisch-litauischen Magnaten."

57. Beauvois, "Kresomania," 15.
58. Beauvois, *Trójkat ukraiński*, 7, 8.
59. Wierciński, *Przywracanie pamięci* [Restoring the memory], 42.
60. Łozowska, *"Obca" ojczyzna*, 33.
61. Marek Zaleski, *Formy pamięci*, 214.
62. For instance, this is the position taken by Władysław Panas in the article "O pograniczu etnicznym w badaniach literackich" (On ethnic Borderlands in literary studies).
63. As Marek Zaleski suggests in *Formy pamięci*, 215.
64. Beauvois, *Trójkat ukraiński*, 17.
65. See Wasyl, "Kresy wschodnie jako kolonialna metafora," 77.
66. Cf. Kristeva, *Black Sun*, 99 ("beauty emerges as the admirable face of loss, transforming it in order to make it live").
67. Fiut, "In the Shadow of Empires," 39.
68. Żakiewicz, "Polska jest wciąż Kresami," 293.
69. Bieńkowski, *Przyszłość przeszłości*, 84.
70. Hence, the search for "new coordinates" in Lithuanian and Ukrainian historiographies and identity discourses. See, for example, Sirutavičius, "The Grand Duchy of Lithuania"; Riabchuk, "'Two Ukraines' Reconsidered."
71. Rudnytsky, "Polish-Ukrainian Relations." It should be borne in mind, however, that, as Mick emphasizes, Polish colonialism in the Borderlands "was neither exploitation colonialism nor surrogate colonialism. . . . The region was not drained of resources; instead subsidies flowed into the area, and there was no Polish expectation of being able to exploit the region in the immediate future. . . . Polish rule in the eastern borderlands was different from Russian colonial rule in Central Asia and Siberia or the overseas colonialism of the western European powers where the colonizers came from an ethnically and culturally diverse centre" ("Colonialism in the Polish Eastern Borderlands," 138, 139).
72. See Kasperski, "Dyskurs kresowy," 102.
73. Johnson, *Character Styles*, 42.
74. Ibid., 41.
75. See Paczoska, "Polskość w dobie niewoli."
76. Winnicott is referenced in this context by Johnson (*Character Styles*, 42). Winnicott believed that "other people's expectations can become of overriding importance, overlaying or contradicting the original sense of self, the one connected to the very roots of one's being" (as quoted in Klein, *Our Need for Others*, 241). Johnson, *Character Styles*, 42.
77. I use this expression in a sense analogous to "the narcissistic personality style" when referencing texts that clearly privilege the Polish point of view on the level of narrative structure (for example, in the novels of Józef Weysenhoff

and Florian Czarnyszewicz), which leads to a foregrounding of an ethnocentric perspective.

78. Kohut, *The Analysis of the Self.*
79. Bhabha, "Representation and the Colonial Text," 97.
80. Hadaczek, *Kresówki*, 145–46.
81. Bujnicki, "O problemach kultury," 185. From a comparative historical perspective, Jan Kieniewicz objects to the postcolonial revision of the Borderlands on different grounds, pointing to the unique "precolonial" expansion of the commonwealth along its border territories ("Polskie pogranicza," 71). Sowa does not voice these types of objections. While he acknowledges that Polish expansion into the Borderlands differs from the Western European model, he also categorically underlines that "this does not negate the similar nature of the colonial efforts of Poland and other European nations, which is why there is no excess in equating the Borderlands with—for instance—the British Raj" (*Fantomowe ciało króla*, 322).
82. Uliasz, *O literaturze Kresów*, 35.
83. Said, *Orientalism*, 327–28.
84. Hadaczek, *Kresówki*, 148–49.
85. Łozowska, *"Obca" ojczyzna*, 89.
86. Bujnicki, "Literackie obrazy pogranicza," 137.
87. Chrzanowski, *Kresy czyli obszar tęsknot*, s. 16, 18.
88. Sowa points to three characteristics of colonial discourse in Chrzanowski's book: the Borderlands nostalgia that erases Others, the foregrounding of the Borderlands as a realm of adventure, and the erotic and sexual connotations tied to these regions (*Fantomowe ciało króla*, 507–13).
89. Bhabha, *The Location of Culture*, 63.
90. These strategies have been discussed in Bakuła, "Colonial and Postcolonial Aspects."
91. Schacter, *The Seven Sins of Memory*, 5.
92. Ankrava, "The Postcolonial Syndrome," 26.
93. Kasperski, "Dyskurs kresowy," 97.
94. See Smith, *The Ethnic Origins.*
95. Tarasiuk, "Polsko-rosyjska rywalizacja," 155.
96. Mieroszewski, "Rosyjski kompleks," 316. On the concept of federalism in *Kultura*'s program, see Snyder, *The Reconstruction of Nations*, 222–25. Research into the analogous influence of this encounter on the Ukrainian identity is being undertaken as part of Ukrainian postcolonial studies. See, for example, Shkandrij, *Russia and Ukraine.*
97. See Puto, "A Film Which Divides."
98. "One can have doubts about the very level of public discourse on the history of Volhynia, the degree of objectivity and presentation of various aspects of the Polish-Ukrainian conflict during World War II. One can get the impression that from the end of the 1990s, the *Kresy* movement, and a considerable part of Polish politicians, historians and journalists, in their thinking

about the reasons for the bloody conflict in the Borderlands, have unquestioningly adopted the patterns of thought that were partially elaborated in the Communist period (modified and supported by scholarly work and a large number of Polish testimonies and memoirs)" (Tyma, "The Volhynian Problem," 329).

99. Zarycki, "Polska i jej regiony," 35–36.
100. Zarycki's opinion was preceded by the political ideas of Giedroyc and Mieroszewski, which they developed in *Kultura* since the beginning of the 1950s. Their vision assumed Poland's cessation of territorial claims toward former areas of Ukraine, Lithuania, and Belarus and the future creation of a regional union of East-Central European countries. The ULB program—the idea of the political and cultural independence of Ukraine, Lithuania, and Belarus, which made up an important part of Giedroyc's program—can be viewed as a postimperial component of "postimperial therapy" in the political discourse of the Polish diaspora and its present-day continuers.
101. Jarzębski, "Exodus," 129.
102. Žižek, *The Plague of Fantasies*, 183.
103. Bielik-Robson, *Inna nowoczesność*, 81.

## Afterword

1. Traditional postcolonial oppositions (of domination-subordination and center-periphery, for instance) are ever more often applied to categories and relations separate from those of traditionally understood colonial domination, such as the oppression of animals and of objects. See Braidotti, *The Posthuman*.
2. Cf. Charles Taylor, "The Concept of a Person."
3. Said, *Culture and Imperialism*, 15, xiv.
4. Ibid., 31.
5. Ibid.
6. Ibid., 194.
7. Eagleton, "Postcolonialism and 'Postcolonialism,'" 26.
8. Lazarus, "What Postcolonial Theory Doesn't Say," 10. Cf. Parry, *Postcolonial Studies*.
9. See, for example, Sowa, "Forget Postcolonialism."
10. Michael Hardt and Antonio Negri assert, for example, that the new, neo-imperial order is characterized by "the idea of a single power that overdetermines all [categories], structures them in a unitary way, and treats them under one common notion of right that is decidedly postcolonial and post-imperialist" (*Empire*, 9).
11. See Scruton, *England*.
12. Malešević, *Nation-States*, 159.

13. Memmi, *Dominated Man*, 88; quoted after Gandhi, *Postcolonial Theory*, 6. I forego here analyzing the varied, even antithetical conclusions that arise in interpretations of Memmi's category depending on the worldview onto which it is projected.
14. Said, *Culture and Imperialism*, 336.
15. Hugo of St. Victor, *Didascalicon*, 101; quoted after Said, *Culture and Imperialism*, 335.

# Bibliography

Abraham, Matthew. "Introduction: Edward Said and After; Toward a New Humanism." *Cultural Critique* 67, no. 1 (Fall 2007): 1–12.

Adam, Christopher. "The Crimean Sonnets of Adam Mickiewicz—a New Translation." *Canadian Slavonic Papers* 40, nos. 3–4 (September–December 1998): 401–32.

Adamovsky, Ezequiel. *Euro-Orientalism: Liberal Ideology and the Image of Russia in France (c. 1740–1880)*. Oxford: Peter Lang, 2007.

Adamovsky, Ezequiel. "What Is 'Eastern Europe'?" *Sarmatian Review* 28, no. 2 (April 2008): 1399–401.

Adamowska, Joanna. *Różewicz i Herbert: Aksjologiczne aspekty twórczości*. Kraków: Universitas, 2012.

Ahmad, Aijaz. *In Theory: Classes, Nations, Literatures*. New York: Verso, 1992.

Aleksandravičius, Egidijušius. "Tożsamość Mickiewicza w świetle historiografii litewskiej." *Przegląd Wschodni* 5, no. 4 (1999): 725–44.

Anders, Jarosław. *Between Fire and Sleep: Essays on Modern Polish Poetry and Prose*. New Haven, CT: Yale University Press, 2009.

Anderson, Benedict. *Imagined Communities: Reflections on the Origin and Spread of Nationalism*. London: Verso, 1983.

Andruchowycz, Jurij. *Dwanaście kręgów*. Translated into Polish by Katarzyna Kotyńska. Wołowiec: Czarne, 2005.

Andruchowycz, Jurij, and Andrzej Stasiuk. *Moja Europa: Dwa eseje o Europie zwanej Środkową*. Wołowiec: Czarne, 2007.

"Andrzej Stasiuk laureatem austriackiej nagrody literackiej." Accessed November 8, 2017. https://culture.pl/pl/artykul/andrzej-stasiuk-laureatem-austriackiej-nagrody-literackiej.

Ankrava, Sigma. "The Postcolonial Syndrome and Identity Crisis in Latvia." *Scientific Papers University of Latvia* 666 (2004): 24–35.

Appiah, Kwame Anthony. *In My Father's House: Africa in the Philosophy of Culture*. New York: Oxford University Press, 1992.

Applebaum, Anne. *Iron Curtain: The Crushing of Eastern Europe 1944–56*. London: Penguin, 2012.

Apter, Emily. "Saidian Humanism." *Boundary 2* 31, no. 2 (Summer 2004): 35–53.

Aquinas, Thomas. *Summa Theologiae*. Edited by Thomas Gilby and Thomas C. O'Brien, 60 vols. London: New Blackfriars, 1964–73.

Artwińska, Anna. *Poetry in the Service of Politics: The Case of Adam Mickiewicz in Communist Poland and Johann Wolfgang von Goethe in East Germany*. Translated by Kalina Iwanek. Frankfurt am Main: Peter Lang, 2015.

Ashcroft, Bill, Gareth Griffiths, and Helen Tiffin. *The Empire Writes Back: Theory and Practice in Post-colonial Literatures*. London: Routledge, 1989.

Ashcroft, Bill, Gareth Griffiths, and Helen Tiffin, eds. *Post-colonial Studies: The Key Concepts*. London: Routledge, 2000.

Baár, Monika. *Historians and Nationalism: East-Central Europe in the Nineteenth Century*. Oxford: Oxford University Press, 2013.

Bachórz, Józef. *Jak pachnie na Litwie Mickiewicza i inne studia o romantyzmie*. Gdańsk: Słowo/obraz terytoria, 2003.

Bachórz, Józef, and Alina Kowalczykowa, eds. *Słownik literatury polskiej XIX wieku*. Wrocław: Ossolineum, 1991.

Bagłajewski, Arkadiusz. "Mapa, podróż, czas." *Kresy*, no. 60 (2004): 95–101.

Bagłajewski, Arkadiusz. "Miasto—palimpsest." In *Miejsce rzeczywiste, miejsce wyobrażone: Studia nad kategorią miejsca w przestrzeni kultury*, edited by Małgorzata Kitowska-Łysiak and Elżbieta Wolicka, 317–38. Lublin: TN KUL, 1999.

Bakuła, Bogusław. "Colonial and Postcolonial Aspects of the Polish Borderlands Studies: An Outline." Translated by Anna Warso. "Postcolonial or Postdependence Studies?," special issue, English version, *Teksty Drugie*, no. 1 (2014): 96–123.

Bakuła, Bogusław, ed. *Dyskurs postkolonialny we współczesnej literaturze i kulturze Europy Środkowo-Wschodniej: Polska, Ukraina, Węgry, Słowacja*. Poznań: Biblioteka Porównań, 2015.

Bakuła, Bogusław. *Historia i komparatystyka: Szkice o literaturze i kulturze Europy Środkowo-Wschodniej XX wieku*. Poznań: Poznańskie Studia Polonistyczne, 2000.

Bakuła, Bogusław. "Polska i kolonialna przeszłość dzisiaj." *Nowa Krytyka*, nos. 26/27 (2011): 146–80.

Bakuła, Bogusław, Dobrochna Dabert, and Emilia Kledzik. *Comparisons and Contexts: Essays on Central-Eastern European Literature and Culture*. Poznań: Biblioteka Porównań, 2015.

Bamberg, Michael, Anna De Fina, and Deborah Schiffrin, eds. *Selves and Identities in Narrative and Discourse*. Amsterdam: John Benjamins, 2007.

Banaszkiewicz, Jacek. "Mistrz Wincenty i naśladowcy—wizje najstarszych dziejów Polski XIII–XV wieku." In *Przeszłość w kulturze średniowiecznej Polski*, vol. 1, part 1, *Przeszłość obrazowana w tradycjach zapisanych i ujęciach historiograficznych*, edited by Piotr Węcowski, 269–306. Warsaw: Instytut Historii PAN and Neriton, 2018.

Bartolovich, Crystal. "Global Capital and Transnationalism." In *A Companion to Postcolonial Studies*, edited by Henry Schwarz and Sangeeta Ray, 126–61. Malden, MA: Blackwell, 2000.

Bauman, Zygmunt. *Community: Seeking Safety in an Insecure World*. Malden, MA: Polity Press, 2001.

Beauvois, Daniel. "Kresomania." Interview by Agnieszka Sabor. *Tygodnik Powszechny*, no. 13 (2006): 15.

Beauvois, Daniel. "Mit kresów wschodnich, czyli jak mu położyć kres." In *Polska myśl polityczna XIX i XX wieku*, vol. 9, *Polskie mity polityczne XIX i XX wieku*, edited by Wojciech Wrzesiński, 93–105. Wrocław: Wydawnictwo Uniwersytetu Wrocławskiego, 1994.

Beauvois, Daniel. *Trójkąt ukraiński: Szlachta, carat i lud na Wołyniu, Podolu i Kijowszczyźnie 1793–1914*. Translated into Polish by Krzysztof Rutkowski. 2nd ed. Lublin: UMCS, 2011.

Bednarczuk, Monika, and Monika Rudaś-Grodzka. "W poszukiwaniu utraconej wielkości." *Teksty Drugie*, nos. 1–2 (2009): 318–34.

Bennett, Judith M., and C. Warren Hollister. *Medieval Europe: A Short History*. 10th ed. Toronto: Harper Collins, 2005.

Benwell, Bethan, and Elizabeth Stokoe. *Discourse and Identity*. Edinburgh: Edinburgh University Press, 2006.

Berger, Florence K. *A Winter in the City of Pleasure; Or, Life on the Lower Danube*. London: Richard Bentley and Son, 1877.

Berghahn, Volker R. "Germans and Poles, 1871–1945." In *Germany and Eastern Europe: Cultural Identities and Cultural Differences*, edited by Keith Bullivant, Geoffrey Giles, and Walter Pape, 15–36. Yearbook of European Studies 13. Amsterdam: Rodopi, 1999.

Berman, Russell A. *Enlightenment or Empire: Colonial Discourse in German Culture*. Lincoln: University of Nebraska Press, 1998.

Bernhard, Michael H. *The Origins of Democratization in Poland: Workers, Intellectuals, and Oppositional Politics, 1976–1980*. New York: Columbia University Press, 1993.

Bhabha, Homi K. *The Location of Culture*. London: Routledge, 1994.

Bhabha, Homi K., ed. *Nation and Narration: Post-structuralism and the Culture of National Identity*. London: Routledge, 1990.

Bhabha, Homi K. "Representation and the Colonial Text: A Critical Exploration of Some Forms of Mimeticism." In *The Theory of Reading*, edited by Frank Gloversmith, 93–122. Brighton, Sussex: Harvester, 1984.

Bielik-Robson, Agata. *Inna nowoczesność: Pytania o współczesną formułę duchowości*. Kraków: Universitas, 2000.

Bieńkowski, Zbigniew. *Przyszłość przeszłości: Eseje*. Wrocław: Wydawnictwo Dolnośląskie, 1996.

Blanke, Richard. *Prussian Poland in the German Empire (1871–1900)*. New York: Columbia University Press, 1981.

Błoński, Jan. "Bezładne rozważania starego krytyka, który zastanawia się, jak napisałby historię prozy polskiej w latach istnienia Polski Ludowej." *Teksty Drugie*, no. 1 (1990): 5–24.

Błoński, Jan. *Zmiana warty*. Warsaw: PIW, 1961.

Bobkov, Igor. "To the East from the Center: Configurations of Modernness in Eastern European Borderland." *Crossroads Digest* 5 (2010): 94–105.

Bobrownicka, Maria. "Antyteza słowiańsko-europejska: Z problemów stereotypu." In *Kategoria Europy w kulturach słowiańskich*, edited by Teresa Dąbek-Wirgowa and Andrzej Z. Makowiecki, 13–19. Warsaw: Uniwersytet Warszawski, 1992.

Bolecki, Włodzimierz. "Realizmu socjalistycznego początki (Lwów, Wilno)." In *Słownik realizmu socjalistycznego*, edited by Zdzisław Łapiński and Wojciech Tomasik, 265. Kraków: Universitas, 2004.

Bömelburg, Hans-Jürgen. "Die polnisch-litauischen Magnaten als imperiales Personal und übergreifende Herrschaftselite." In *Die Anatomie frühneuzeitlicher Imperien: Herrschaftsmanagement jenseits von Staat und Nation; Institutionen, Personal und Techniken*, edited by Stephan Wendehorst, 195–210. Berlin: De Gruyter Oldenbourg, 2015.

Borejsza, Jerzy W. *A Ridiculous Hundred Million Slavs: Concerning Adolf Hitler's World-view*. Translated by David French. Warsaw: IH PAN, 2017.

Borkowska, Grażyna. "Polskie doświadczenie kolonialne." *Teksty Drugie*, no. 4 (2007): 15–24.

Borkowska, Grażyna. "A Post-colonial Perspective on Polish Soil: Some Questions of a Skeptic." "Postcolonial or Postdependence Studies?," special issue, English version, *Teksty Drugie*, no. 1 (2014): 41–54.

Borowy, Wacław. *O poezji Mickiewicza*. 2nd ed. Lublin: TN KUL, 1999.

Boss, Sally R. "Ezequiel Adamovsky, *Liberal Ideology and the Image of Russia in France (c. 1740–1880)*, Oxford and Bern: Peter Lang, 2007." *Sarmatian Review* 27, no. 3 (September 2007): 1333.

Boss, Sally R. "Ms. Boss Responds." *Sarmatian Review* 28, no. 2 (April 2008): 1401.

Bourdieu, Pierre. *Outline of a Theory of Practice*. Translated by Richard Nice. Cambridge: Cambridge University Press, 1977.

Boym, Svetlana. *The Future of Nostalgia*. New York: Basic Books, 2001.

Braidotti, Rosi. *The Posthuman*. Malden, MA: Polity Press, 2013.

Brennan, Timothy. *Wars of Position: The Cultural Politics of Left and Right*. New York: Columbia University Press, 2006.

Brix, Emil. "Pochwała miast Europy Środkowej." Translated into Polish by Antoni Baniukiewicz. *Krasnogruda*, no. 9 (1998): 13–19.

Brock, Peter, John D. Stanley, and Piotr J. Wróbel, eds. *Nation and History: Polish Historians from the Enlightenment to the Second World War*. Toronto: University of Toronto Press, 2006.

Brubaker, Roger, and Frederick Cooper. "Beyond 'Identity.'" *Theory and Society* 29 (February 2000): 1–47.

Brzezinski, Zbigniew. "A Divided Europe: The Future of Yalta." *Foreign Affairs* 63, no. 2 (1984–85): 279–302.

Bujnicki, Tadeusz. "Literackie obrazy pogranicza: Litewski raj i krwawy mit Ukrainy." In *Krainy utracone i pozyskane: Problem w literaturach Europy Środkowej*, edited by Krzysztof Krasuski, 127–39. Katowice: Wydawnictwo Uniwersytetu Śląskiego, 2005.

Bujnicki, Tadeusz. "O problemach kultury i literatury pogranicza: Kilka impresji badawczych." In *Aktualni problemy inozemnoi filolohiji: Linhvistyka ta literaturoznavstvo*, 178–85. Nizhyn: Aspekt-Poligraf, 2007.

Bujnicki, Tadeusz. "Życie pośmiertne Wielkiego Księstwa Litewskiego." In *Kresy—dekonstrukcja*, edited by Krzysztof Trybuś, Jerzy Kałążny, and Radosław Okulicz-Kozaryn, 167–82. Poznań: PTPN, 2007.

Butkiewicz, Ewa, ed. *Dylematy rozwoju: Porównywalność doświadczeń krajów słabiej rozwiniętych i Polski*. Warsaw: SGH, 1992.

Calhoun, Craig, ed. *Social Theory and Identity Politics*. Cambridge, MA: Blackwell, 1994.

Cassirer, Ernst. *An Essay on Man. An Introduction to a Philosophy of Human Culture*. Garden City, NY: Doubleday Anchor, 1953.

Cavanagh, Clare. "Postcolonial Poland." *Common Knowledge* 10, no. 1 (Winter 2004): 82–92. Translated into Polish by Tomasz Kunz as "Postkolonialna Polska: Biała plama na mapie współczesnej teorii." *Teksty Drugie*, nos. 2/3 (2003): 360–71.

Cervinkova, Hana. "Postcolonialism, Postsocialism and the Anthropology of East-Central Europe." *Journal of Postcolonial Writing* 48, no. 2 (May 2012): 155–63.

Chakrabarty, Dipesh. *Provincializing Europe: Postcolonial Thought and Historical Difference*. New ed. Princeton, NJ: Princeton University Press, 2007.

Chari, Hema. "Colonial Fantasies and Postcolonial Identities: Elaboration of Postcolonial Masculinity and Homoerotic Desire." In *Postcolonial, Queer: Theoretical Intersections*, edited by John Ch. Hawley, 277–304. New York: State University of New York Press, 2001.

Chesterton, Gilbert Keith. Preface to Zygmunt Krasiński, *The Un-Divine Comedy*, translated by Harriette E. Kennedy and Zofia Umińska, 5–11. London: George Harrap, 1924.

Chibber, Vivek. *Postcolonial Theory and the Specter of Capital*. New York: Verso, 2013.

Childs, Peter. *Postcolonial Theory and English Literature: A Reader*. Edinburgh: Edinburgh University Press, 1999.

Chioni Moore, David. "Is the Post- in Postcolonial the Post- in Post-Soviet? Toward a Global Postcolonial Critique." *PMLA* 116, no. 1 (January 2001): 111–28.

Chłędowski, Kazimierz. *Pamiętniki*. Vol. 1, *Galicja (1848–1880)*, edited by Antoni Kot. Kraków: Wydawnictwo Literackie, 1957.

Chodakiewicz, Marek J. *Between Nazis and Soviets: Occupation Politics in Poland*. Lanham, MD: Lexington, 2004.

Chowdhry, Geeta. "Edward Said and Contrapuntal Reading: Implications for Critical Interventions in International Relations." *Millennium: Journal of International Studies* 36, no. 1 (December 2007): 101–16.

Chrzanowski, Tadeusz. *Kresy czyli obszar tęsknot*. Kraków: Wydawnictwo Literackie, 2001.

Chwalba, Andrzej. *Polacy w służbie Moskali*. Warsaw: PWN, 1999.

Chwin, Stefan. "*Trans-Atlantyk* wobec *Pana Tadeusza*." *Pamiętnik Literacki* 66, no. 4 (1975): 97–121.

Ciesielski, Stanisław, ed. *Przesiedlenie ludności polskiej z Kresów Wschodnich do Polski 1944–1947: Wybór dokumentów*. Warsaw: Neriton, 2000.

Cieśla-Korytowska, Maria. *O Mickiewiczu i Słowackim*. Kraków: Universitas, 1999.

Cioran, Emile M. *Cahiers 1957–1972*. Paris: Gallimard, 1997.

Cleary, Joe. "'Misplaced Ideas?' Locating and Dislocating Ireland in Colonial and Postcolonial Studies." In *Ireland and Postcolonial Theory*, edited by Clare Carroll and Patricia King, 16–45. Notre Dame, IN: University of Notre Dame Press, 2003.

Cornis-Poppe, Marcel. "Local and Global Frames in Recent Eastern European Literatures: Postcommunism, Postmodernism, and Postcoloniality." *Journal of Postcolonial Writing* 48, no. 2 (May 2012): 143–54.

Crouch, Carly L., and Jonathan Stökl, eds. *In the Name of God: The Bible in the Colonial Discourse of Empire*. Leiden: Brill Rodopi, 2014.

Czartoryski, Adam Jerzy. *Judge Deluty: Scenes from the First Years of Stanisław August's Reign (Pan Sędzia Deluty: Sceny z pierwszych lat panowania Stanisława Augusta)*. Edited by Richard Sokoloski. Lublin: TN KUL and Slavic Research Group at the University of Ottawa, 2005.

Czerkawski, Jan. "Arystotelizm na wydziale sztuk Uniwersytetu Krakowskiego w XVI i XVII wieku." In *Nauczanie filozofii w Polsce w XV–XVIII wieku*, edited by Lech Szczucki, 45–85. Wrocław: Ossolineum, 1978.

Dąbrowska, Maria. *Dzienniki 1914–1965*. Edited by Wanda Starska-Żakowska. Warsaw: PAN, 2009.

Dąbrowski, Mieczysław. *Nierzeczywista rzeczywistość: O twórczości Andrzeja Kuśniewicza*. Warsaw: Elipsa, 2004.

Dąbrowski, Mieczysław. "Reguła kompensacji: O nowej formule kresowości literackiej." In *Krainy utracone i pozyskane: Problem w literaturach Europy Środkowej*, edited by Krzysztof Krasuski, 179–94. Katowice: Wydawnictwo Uniwersytetu Śląskiego, 2005.

Dahl, Darren E. "Criticizing 'Secular Criticism': Reading Religion in Edward Said and Kathryn Tanner." *Studies in Religion / Sciences Religieuses* 31, nos. 3/4 (September 2002): 359–71.

Davies, Norman. "Fair Comparisons, False Contrasts: East and West in Modern European History." In *Europe East and West*, 22–45. London: Pimlico, 2007.

Davies, Norman. *God's Playground: A History of Poland*. Vols. 1–2. Rev. ed. New York: Columbia University Press, 2004.

Davies, Norman. "West Best, East Beast." *Oxford Today* 9, no. 2 (1997): 28–31.

Delanty, Gerard. *Inventing Europe: Idea, Identity, Reality*. Basingstoke: Palgrave Macmillan, 1995.

Deltcheva, Roumiana. "Comparative Central European Culture: Displacements and Peripheralities." In *Comparative Central European Culture*, edited by Steven Tötösy de Zepetnek, 149–68. West Lafayette, IN: Purdue University Press, 2001.

Derrida, Jacques. "An Interview with Jacques Derrida." Interview by Nikhil Padgaonkar. Universitat de Valencia (1997). Accessed November 8, 2017. http://mural.uv.es/mibosa/DerridaInterview2.htm.

Derrida, Jacques. *Specters of Marx: The State of the Debt, The Work of Mourning & the New International.* Translated by Peggy Kamuf. London: Routledge, 1994.

Deutsch, Karl. *Nationalism and Social Communication: An Inquiry into the Foundations of Nationality.* Cambridge, MA: Technology Press, 1953.

Dixon, Megan. "How the Poet Sympathizes with Exotic Lands in Adam Mickiewicz's *Crimean Sonnets* and the *Digression* from *Forefathers' Eve, Part III.*" *Slavic and East European Journal* 45, no. 4 (Winter 2001): 679–94.

Długosz, Jan. *Ioannis Dlugossi Annales seu Cronicae incliti Regni Poloniae, Liber 1–2.* Edited by Jan Dąbrowski, Wanda Semkowicz-Zarembina, Krystyna Pieradzka, and Bożena Modelska-Strzelecka. Warsaw: PWN, 1964.

Długosz, Jan. *Kronika wielkopolska (Chronica Poloniae Maioris).* Translated into Polish by Kazimierz Abgarowicz, edited by Brygida Kürbis. Warsaw: PWN, 1970.

Doyle, Michael W. *Empires.* Ithaca, NY: Cornell University Press, 1986.

Drahokoupil, Jan. "The Rise of the Comprador Service Sector: The Politics of State Transformation in Central and Eastern Europe." *Polish Sociological Review* 162, no. 2 (2008): 175–89.

Drewnowski, Tadeusz. "Czarodziejski brzeg." *Europa—Tygodnik Idei* 264, no. 32 (2004): 14.

Duma, Tomasz. "Personalism in the Lublin School of Philosophy." *Studia Gilsoniana* 5, no. 2 (2016): 365–90.

Dupcsik, Csaba. "Postcolonial Studies and the Inventing of Eastern Europe." *East Central Europe* 26, no. 1 (January 1999): 1–14.

During, Simon. "Toward the Postsecular." *PMLA* 120, no. 3 (May 2005): 876–77.

Dwivedi, Om Prakash, and Martin Kich, eds. *Postcolonial Theory in the Global Age.* Jefferson, NC: McFarland, 2013.

Dybel, Paweł. *Urwane ścieżki: Przybyszewski—Freud—Lacan.* Kraków: Universitas, 2000.

Dyboski, Roman. *O Anglii i Anglikach.* Warsaw: F. Hoesick, 1929.

Eagleton, Terry. "Postcolonialism and 'Postcolonialism.'" *Interventions* 1, no. 1 (1998): 24–26.

Ellingson, Ter. *The Myth of the Noble Savage.* Berkeley: University of California Press, 2001.

Falk, Barbara. *The Dilemmas of Dissidence in East-Central Europe: Citizen Intellectuals and Philosopher Kings.* Budapest: Central European University Press, 2003.

Fanon, Frantz. *Black Skin, White Masks.* Translated by Charles Lam Markmann. London: Pluto Press [1952 (1967)], 2008.

Fanon, Frantz. *The Wretched of the Earth.* Translated by Constance Farrington. New York: Grove Press, 1963.

Feuer, Lewis S. *Imperialism and the Anti-imperialist Mind*. Buffalo, NY: Prometheus, 1986.

Fiała, Edward, Dariusz Skórczewski, and Andrzej Wierciński, eds. *Melancholia: The Disease of the Soul*. Lublin: KUL, 2014.

Fieguth, Rolf. *Rozpierzchłe gałązki: Cykliczne i skojarzeniowe formy kompozycyjne w twórczości Adama Mickiewicza*. Translated into Polish by Marek Zieliński. Warsaw: IBL PAN, 2002.

Fijałkowska, Barbara. *Borejsza i Różański: Przyczynek do dziejów stalinizmu w Polsce*. Olsztyn: WSP, 1995.

Fijałkowska, Barbara. *Polityka i twórcy (1948–1959)*. Warsaw: PWN, 1985.

Filipowicz, Halina. "Mickiewicz: 'East' and 'West.'" *Slavic and East European Journal* 45, no. 4 (Winter 2001): 606–23.

Fiut, Aleksander. *Być (albo nie być) Środkowoeuropejczykiem*. Kraków: Wydawnictwo Literackie, 1999.

Fiut, Aleksander. "In the Shadow of Empires: Post-colonialism in Central and Eastern Europe—Why Not?" "Postcolonial or Postdependence Studies?," special issue, English version, *Teksty Drugie*, no. 1 (2014): 34–40.

Fiut, Aleksander. "Polonizacja? Kolonizacja?" *Teksty Drugie*, no. 6 (2003): 150–56.

Fiut, Aleksander. "Oblicza tyranii, oblicza historii." In *Kultura po przejściach, osoby z przeszłością: Polski dyskurs postzależnościowy—konteksty i perspektywy badawcze*, edited by Ryszard Nycz, 397–404. Kraków: Universitas, 2011.

Fiut, Aleksander. "Powrót do Europy Środkowej? Wariacje na temat pisarstwa Andrzeja Stasiuka i Jurija Andruchowycza." In *(Nie)obecność: Pominięcia i przemilczenia w narracjach XX wieku*, edited by Hanna Gosk and Bożena Karwowska, 155–71. Warsaw: Elipsa, 2008.

Forrester, Sibelan, Magdalena J. Zaborowska, and Elena Gapova, eds. *Over the Wall / After the Fall: Post-Communist Cultures through an East-West Gaze*. Bloomington: Indiana University Press, 2004.

Foucault, Michel. "The Order of Discourse." Translated by Robert Young. In *Untying the Text: A Poststructuralist Reader*, edited by Robert Young, 48–78. Boston: Routledge and Kegan Paul, 1981.

Franaszek, Andrzej. *Miłosz. A Biography*. Edited and translated by Aleksandra Parker and Michael Parker. Cambridge, MA: Harvard University Press, 2017.

Franaszek, Andrzej. *Herbert: Biografia*. Kraków: Znak, 2018.

Frankel, Max. "Stalin's Shadow: *Iron Curtain* by Anne Applebaum." Sunday Book Review. *New York Times*, November 25, 2012, 16.

Frankowiak, Anita. "Środkowoeuropejska świadomość przestrzeni w prozie Andrzeja Stasiuka." In *Polonistyka*, edited by Alâksandr Kìklevìč and Sârgej Važnìk, 289–302. Minsk: Vyd. Cèntr. BDU, 2009.

Freedman, Paul, and Gabrielle M. Spiegel. "Medievalism Old and New: The Rediscovery of Alterity in North American Medieval Studies." *American Historical Review* 103, no. 3 (June 1998): 677–704.

Freud, Sigmund. "Mourning and Melancholia." In *The Standard Edition of the Complete Psychological Works of Sigmund Freud*. Vol. 14 (1914–1916): *On the History of the Psycho-Analytic Movement, Papers on Metapsychology and Other*

*Works*, translated and edited by James Strachey, 237–58. London: Hogarth Press, 1957.

Fuchs, Jacob. "Postcolonial Mock-Epic: Abrogation and Appropriation." *Studies in the Literary Imagination* 33, no. 2 (Fall 2000): 23–43.

Gajda, Agnieszka. "Romanticism and the Rise of Neopaganism in Nineteenth-Century Central and Eastern Europe: The Polish Case." In *Modern Pagan and Native Faith Movements in Central and Eastern Europe*, edited by Kaarina Aitamurto and Scott Simpson, 44–61. London: Routledge, 2014.

Gandhi, Leela. *Postcolonial Theory: A Critical Introduction*. New York: Columbia University Press, 1998.

Gellner, Ernest. *Nations and Nationalism*. Ithaca, NY: Cornell University Press, 1983.

Gibbons, Luke. "Towards a Postcolonial Enlightenment: The United Irishmen, Cultural Diversity, and the Public Sphere." In *Ireland and Postcolonial Theory*, edited by Clare Carroll and Patricia King, 81–91. Notre Dame, IN: University of Notre Dame Press, 2003.

Giddens, Anthony. *Beyond Left and Right: The Future of Radical Politics*. Cambridge: Polity Press, 1994.

Gilroy, Paul. *After Empire: Melancholia or Convivial Culture?* New York: Routledge, 2004.

Gilroy, Paul. *Postcolonial Melancholia*. New York: Columbia University Press, 2005.

Głowiński, Michał. "Nad *Castorpem*." *Przegląd Polityczny*, no. 70 (2005): 65–68.

Goethe, Johann Wolfgang von. *Berliner Ausgabe: Poetische Werke*. Vol. 3: *Gedichte und Singspiele*, edited by Ursula and Manfred Beyer. Berlin: Aufbau Verlag, 1965.

Gombrowicz, Witold. *Dziennik, 1953–1956*. Edited by Jan Błoński. Kraków: Wydawnictwo Literackie, 1997.

Gombrowicz, Witold. *Trans-Atlantyk*. Kraków: Wydawnictwo Literackie, 1986.

Gordon, Neve. "Foucault's Subject: An Ontological Reading." *Polity* 31, no. 3 (Spring 1999): 395–414.

Grossman, Elwira M. "Navigating the New Landscape for Slavonic/Polish Studies." In *Perspectives on Slavic Literatures: Proceedings of the First International "Perspectives on Slavistics" Conference (Leuven, September 17–19, 2004)*, edited by David S. Danaher and Kris Van Heuckelom, 1–15. Amsterdam: Pegasus, 2007.

Grudzińska-Gross, Irena. "How Polish Is Polishness: About Mickiewicz's *Grażyna*." *East European Politics & Societies* 14, no. 1 (Winter 2000): 1–11.

Guha, Ranajit, and Gayatri Spivak, eds. *Selected Subaltern Studies*. New York: Oxford University Press, 1988.

Habermas, Jürgen. *The Postnational Constellation: Political Essays*. Translated, edited and with an introduction by Max Pensky. Cambridge, MA: MIT Press, 2001.

Habermas, Jürgen. "Secularism's Crisis of Faith: Notes on Post-secular Society." *New Perspectives Quarterly* 25 (Fall 2008): 17–29.

Hacking, Ian. *Social Construction of What?* Cambridge, MA: Harvard University Press, 1999.

Hadaczek, Bolesław. *Kresówki (Kresy w literaturze polskiej)*. Szczecin: Volumina, 2011.

Halecki, Oskar. *The Limits and Divisions of European History*. London: Sheed and Ward, 1950.

Halikowska-Smith, Teresa. "The Past as Palimpsest: The Gdańsk School of Writers in the 1980s and 1990s." *Sarmatian Review* 23, no. 1 (January 2003): 922–28.

Hall, Stuart. "Cultural Identity and Diaspora." In *Identity: Community, Culture, Difference*, edited by Jonathan Rutherford, 222–37. London: Lawrence and Wishart, 1990.

Hall, Stuart. "The Question of Cultural Identity." In *Modernity. An Introduction to Modern Societies*, edited by Stuart Hall, David Held, Don Hubert, and Kenneth Thompson, 595–634. Malden, MA: Blackwell, 1996.

Hall, Stuart, and Paul du Gay, eds. *Questions of Cultural Identity*. London: Sage, 1996.

Hammond, Andrew. "Typologies of the East: On Distinguishing Balkanism and Orientalism." *Nineteenth-Century Contexts* 29, nos. 2/3 (June–September 2007): 201–18.

Hanusiewicz-Lavallee, Mirosława. "*Humanitas* and *Christianitas* in Polish Culture." In *Humanism in Polish Culture*, edited by Alina Nowicka-Jeżowa, Wiesław Pawlak, and Piotr Urbański, 95–106. Frankfurt am Main: Peter Lang, 2011.

Hanusiewicz-Lavallee, Mirosława. *W stronę Albionu: Studia z dziejów polsko-brytyjskich związków literackich w dobie wczesnonowożytnej*. Lublin: Wydawnictwo KUL, 2017.

Hardt, Michael, and Antonio Negri. *Empire*. Cambridge, MA: Harvard University Press, 2000.

Hass, Ludwik. *Inteligencji polskiej dole i niedole: XIX i XX wiek*. Łowicz: Mazowiecka Wyższa Szkoła Humanistyczno-Pedagogiczna, 1999.

Healy, Róisín. "Colonial Ambivalence and Its Aftermath: Colonialism and Anticolonialism in Independent Poland and Ireland." In *Central Europe and Colonialism*, Leiden: Brill Rodopi, forthcoming.

Healy, Róisín. "From Commonwealth to Colony? Poland under Prussia." In *The Shadow of Colonialism on Europe's Modern Past*, edited by Róisín Healy and Enrico Dal Lago, 109–25. Basingstoke: Palgrave Macmillan, 2014.

Heidegger, Martin. "Building Dwelling Thinking." In *Basic Writings*, edited by David Farrell Krell, 243–55. London: Routledge, 2010.

Hentschel, Gerd. "Überlegungen zur Polonistik an deutschen Universitäten." In *Polonistik im deutschsprachigen Bereich*, edited by Danuta Rytel-Kuc, Wolfgang F. Schwarze, and Hans-Christian Trepte, 15–28. Hildesheim: Georg Olms Verlag, 2005.

Herbert, Zbigniew. *Raport z oblężonego Miasta*. Paryż: Oficyna Literacka, 1983.

Herling-Grudziński, Gustaw. *Dziennik pisany nocą, 1973–1979*. Warsaw: Res Publica, 1990.

Herling-Grudziński, Gustaw. *A World Apart: The Journal of a Gulag Survivor*. Translated by Adam Ciołkosz [Józef Marek, pseud.]. New York: Roy, 1951.

Hirszowicz, Maria. *Pułapki zaangażowania: Intelektualiści w służbie komunizmu*. Warsaw: Scholar, 2001.

Hobsbawm, Eric J. *Nations and Nationalism since 1790: Programme, Myth, Reality*. Cambridge: Cambridge University Press, 1992.

Hobsbawm, Eric J., and Terence Ranger, eds. *The Invention of Tradition*. Cambridge: Cambridge University Press, 1983.

Hochschild, Adam. *King Leopold's Ghost: A Story of Greed, Terror, and Heroism in Colonial Africa*. New York: Houghton Mifflin, 1998.

Holdsworth, Nadine, ed. *Theatre and National Identity: Re-imagining Conceptions of Nation*. New York: Routledge, 2014.

Huelle, Paweł. *Castorp*. Translated by Antonia Lloyd-Jones. London: Serpent's Tail, 2007.

Huelle, Paweł. *Castorp*. Translated into German by Renate Schmidgall. Munich: C. H. Beck, 2005.

Huggan, Graham. *Interdisciplinary Measures: Literature and the Future of Postcolonial Studies*. Liverpool: Liverpool University Press, 2008.

Huggan, Graham. "Is the 'Post' in 'Postsecular' the 'Post' in 'Postcolonial'?" *Modern Fiction Studies* 56, no. 4 (Winter 2010): 751–68.

Hugo of St. Victor. *Didascalicon*. Translated by Jerome Taylor. New York: Columbia University Press, 1961.

Hunczak, Taras. "Polish Colonial Ambitions in the Inter-war Period." *Slavic Review* 26, no. 4 (December 1967): 648–56.

Hundorova, Tamara. "Postkolonial'nyi melankholiinyi *ressentiment*." In *Ievropeis'ka melankholiia: Dyskurs ukraïns'koho oktsydentalizmu*, 103–17. Kyiv: Stylos, 2008.

Hüppe, Siegfried. *Verfassung der Republik Polens*. Berlin: F. Schneider, 1867.

Ingarden, Roman. *Das literarische Kunstwerk: Eine Untersuchung aus dem Grenzgebiet der Ontologie, Logik und Literaturwissenschaft*. Halle: M. Niemeyer, 1931. Translated into Polish as *O dziele literackim: Badania z pogranicza ontologii, teorii języka i filozofii literatury* by Maria Turowicz. Warsaw: PWN, 1960.

Iwanow, Wiaczesław. "Polski mesjanizm jako siła żywa." In *Dusza polska i rosyjska (od Adama Mickiewicza i Aleksandra Puszkina do Czesława Miłosza i Aleksandra Sołżenicyna): Materiały do "katalogu" wzajemnych uprzedzeń Polaków i Rosjan*, edited by Andrzej de Lazari, 184–94. Warsaw: Polski Instytut Spraw Międzynarodowych, 2004.

Iwasiów, Sławomir. "(Trans)national Journeys: A Case Study Using the Example of Selected Prose Work by Andrzej Stasiuk." *Forum Poetyki*, no. 2 (Fall 2015): 32–41. Accessed May 17, 2017. http://fp.amu.edu.pl/transnational-journeys-a-case-study-using-the-example-of-selected-prose-work-by-andrzej-stasiuk.

Iwaszkiewicz, Jarosław. *Sława i chwała*. Vol. 2. Warsaw: PIW, 1958.

Jackson, Mark. *Postcolonial Critique after Posthumanism: Sensing Other Life and the Problem of Ontology*. London: Rowman and Littlefield International, 2017.

Janion, Maria. *Niesamowita Słowiańszczyzna: Fantazmaty literatury*. Kraków: Wydawnictwo Literackie, 2006.

JanMohamed, Abdul. "The Economy of Manichean Allegory: The Function of Racial Difference in Colonialist Literature." *Critical Inquiry* 12, no. 1 (Autumn 1985): 59–87.

Janowski, Maciej. *Narodziny inteligencji, 1750–1831*. Vol. 1 of *Dzieje inteligencji polskiej do roku 1918*, edited by Jerzy Jedlicki. Warsaw: Neriton, 2008.

Jarzębski, Jerzy. *Apetyt na przemianę: Notatki o prozie współczesnej*. Kraków: Znak, 1997.

Jarzębski, Jerzy. "Exodus (ewolucja obrazu kresów po wojnie)." In *W Polsce czyli wszędzie*, 129–47. Warsaw: PEN, 1992.

Jaskułowski, Krzysztof. *The Everyday Politics of Migration Crisis in Poland: Between Nationalism, Fear and Empathy*. Basingstoke: Palgrave Macmillan, 2019.

Jaskułowski, Krzysztof. *Nacjonalizm bez narodów: Nacjonalizm w koncepcjach anglosaskich nauk społecznych*. Wrocław: Monografie Fundacji na rzecz Nauki Polskiej, 2009.

Jedlicki, Jerzy. "Przedmowa." In *Narodziny inteligencji 1750–1831*. Vol. 1 of *Dzieje inteligencji polskiej do roku 1918*, edited by Jerzy Jedlicki, 7–23. Warsaw: Neriton, 2008.

Jedlicki, Jerzy. *Jakiej cywilizacji Polacy potrzebują: Studia z dziejów idei i wyobraźni XIX wieku*. Warsaw: PWN, 1988.

Jedlicki, Jerzy. "Stereotyp Zachodu w Polsce porozbiorowej." In *Mity i stereotypy w dziejach Polski*, edited by Janusz Tazbir, 99–124. Warsaw: Interpress, 1991.

Jedlicki, Jerzy. *A Suburb of Europe: Nineteenth-Century Polish Approaches to Western Civilization*. Budapest: Central European University Press, 1999.

Jędrychowska, Jagoda [Kazimiera Kijowska]. *Rozmowy niekontrolowane*. Poznań: SAWW, 1990.

Jędrychowska, Jagoda [Kazimiera Kijowska]. *Widzieć Polskę z oddalenia*. Poznań: SAWW, 1990.

Johnson, Stephen M. *Character Styles*. New York: W. W. Norton, 1994.

Judt, Tony. *A Grand Illusion? An Essay on Europe*. New York: Hill and Wang, 1996.

Judt, Tony. *Postwar: A History of Europe since 1945*. London: Penguin, 2005.

Kadłubek, Mistrz Wincenty. *Kronika polska*. Translated into Polish by Brygida Kürbis, edited by Stanisław Sierpowski. Wrocław: Ossolineum, 1996.

Kalinowska, Izabela. *Between East and West: Polish and Russian Nineteenth-Century Travel to the Orient*. Rochester, NY: University of Rochester Press, 2004.

Kapralski, Sławomir. "Oświęcim: Konflikt pamięci czy kryzys tożsamości?" *Przegląd Socjologiczny / Sociological Review* 49, no. 2 (2000): 141–66.

Kapuściński, Ryszard. *Imperium*. Warsaw: Czytelnik, 1993.

Karłowicz, Jan, Adam Antoni Kryński, and Władysław Niedźwiedzki, eds. *Słownik języka polskiego*. Warsaw: Nakładem Prenumeratorów i Kasy im. Mianowskiego 4, 1900–27.

Karolewski, Ireneusz Paweł. *Citizenship and Collective Identity in Europe*. London: Routledge, 2010.

Kasperski, Edward. "Dyskurs kresowy: Kryteria, własności, funkcje." In *Kresy—dekonstrukcja*, edited by Krzysztof Trybuś, Jerzy Kałążny, and Radosław Okulicz-Kozaryn, 89–103. Poznań: PTPN, 2007.

Kelertas, Violeta, ed. *Baltic Postcolonialism*. Amsterdam: Rodopi, 2006.

Kiberd, Declan. *Inventing Ireland: The Literature of the Modern Nation*. New York: Vintage, 1996.

Kieniewicz, Jan. "Con nes y fronteras: El paralelo histórico a nales del siglo XX." In *Europa del centro y del este y el mundo hispánico*, edited by Ana I. Blanco Picado and Teresa Eminowicz, 13–19. Kraków: Abrys, 1996.

Kieniewicz, Jan. *Ekspansja. Kolonializm. Cywilizacja*. Warsaw: DiG & IBI AL, 2008.

Kieniewicz, Jan. "Polskie pogranicza: Próba interpretacji kolonialnej." In *Na pograniczach literatury*, edited by Jarosław Fazan and Krzysztof Zajas, 67–84. Kraków: Universitas, 2012.

Kieniewicz, Jan. "Situation, Colonialism, Backwardness: On the Possibilities of Comparative Studies of Eastern Europe and Latin America." *Estudios Latinoamericanos* 14, no. 1 (1992): 81–85.

Kieniewicz, Jan. "What Kind of Identity Are We Searching for?" In *Debaty Artes Liberales*. Vol. 9, *Syberia: Tradycja i modernizacja*, edited by Kamil Maria Wielecki, 144–58. Warsaw: Artes Liberales, 2015.

Kieniewicz, Stefan. *Dziedzictwo zaborów: Wybór tekstów*. Warsaw: KAW, 1983.

Kijowski, Andrzej. "Czytając Tischnera." In *Granice literatury: Wybór szkiców krytycznych i historycznych*, edited by Tomasz Burek. Vol. 2, 202–19. Warsaw: Biblioteka "Więzi," 1991.

Kijowski, Andrzej. "Listopadowy wieczór." In *Granice literatury: Wybór szkiców krytycznych i historycznych*, edited by Tomasz Burek. Vol. 2, 39–129. Warsaw: Biblioteka "Więzi," 1991.

Kiossev, Alexander. "Notes on the Self-Colonising Cultures." In *After the Wall: Art and Culture in Post-Communist Europe*, edited by Bojana Pejić and David Elliott, 114–18. Stockholm: Moderna Museet, 1999.

Kiślak, Elżbieta. *Car-trup i król-duch: Rosja w twórczości Słowackiego*. Warsaw: IBL, 1991.

Kiślak, Elżbieta. *Walka Jakuba z aniołem: Czesław Miłosz wobec romantyczności*. Warsaw: Prószyński i S-ka, 2000.

Kizwalter, Tomasz. *O nowoczesności narodu: Przypadek polski*. Warsaw: Semper, 1999.

Kledzik, Emilia. "Inventing Postcolonial Poland: Strategies of Domestication." In *Postcolonial Europe? Essays on Post-Communist Literatures and Cultures*, edited by Dobrota Pucherová and Róbert Gáfrik, 85–103. Leiden: Brill Rodopi, 2015.

Klein, Josephine. *Our Need for Others and Its Roots in Infancy*. London: Karnac, 1994.

Kleiner, Juliusz. *Mickiewicz*. Vol. 1, *Dzieje Gustawa*. 3rd ed. Lublin: TN KUL, 1995.

Klich-Kluczewska, Barbara, and Olga Seweryn. "Rediscovering Ourselves: Frontiers and Identities in Polish Historiography of the 19th and 20th Century (1989–2005)." In *Frontiers and Identities: Exploring the Research Area*, edited by Lud'a Klusáková and Steven G. Ellis, 87–99. Supplemental ed. Pisa: Pisa University Press, 2006.

Kłoczowski, Jerzy. *A History of Polish Christianity*. Cambridge: Cambridge University Press, 2000.

Kłoczowski, Jerzy. *Młodsza Europa: Europa Środkowo-Wschodnia w kręgu cywilizacji chrześcijańskiej średniowiecza*. Warsaw: PIW, 2003.

Kochanowska-Nieborak, Anna. *Das Polenbild in Meyers Konversationslexika des "langen" 19. Jahrhunderts*. Frankfurt am Main: Peter Lang, 2010.

Koczanowicz, Leszek. "Postcommunism and Cultural Wars." "Postcolonial or Postdependence Studies?," special issue, English version, *Teksty Drugie*, no. 1 (2014): 167–80.

Koehler, Krzysztof. "The Heritage of Polish Republicanism." *Sarmatian Review* 32, no. 2 (April 2012): 1658–65.

Kohn, Hans. *The Idea of Nationalism*. 1944. New York: Macmillan, 1967.

Kohut, Heinz. *The Analysis of the Self: A Systematic Approach to the Psychoanalytic Treatment of Narcissistic Personality Disorders*. Chicago: University of Chicago Press, 1971.

Kola, Adam. *Socjalistyczny postkolonializm: Rekonsolidacja pamięci*. Toruń: Wydawnictwo Naukowe UMK, 2018.

Kołakowski, Leszek. "On National Stereotypes." In *Freedom, Fame, Lying and Betrayal: Essays on Everyday Life*. Translated by Agnieszka Kołakowska, 139–43. Boulder, CO: Westview Press, 1999.

Kołakowski, Leszek. "Sprawa polska." In *Nasza wesoła apokalipsa: Wybór najważniejszych esejów*, 201–14. Kraków: Znak, 2010.

Kolbuszewski, Jacek. "Legenda Kresów w literaturze polskiej XIX i XX wieku." In *Między Polską etniczną a historyczną*, edited by Wojciech Wrzesiński, 56–59. Wrocław: Ossolineum, 1988.

Kołodziejczyk, Dorota. "Cosmopolitan Provincialism in a Comparative Perspective." In *Re-Routing the Postcolonial: New Directions for the New Millennium*, edited by Janet Wilson, Cristina Şandru, and Sarah Lawson Welsh, 151–62. New York: Routledge, 2010.

Kołodziejczyk, Dorota. "Post-colonial Transfer to Central-and-Eastern Europe." Translated by Marta Skotnicka. "Postcolonial or Postdependence Studies?," special issue, English version, *Teksty Drugie*, no. 1 (2014): 124–42.

Kołodziejczyk, Dorota, and Cristina Şandru. "Introduction: On Colonialism, Communism and East-Central Europe—Some Reflection." *Journal of Postcolonial Writing* 48, no. 2 (May 2012): 113–16.

Kontje, Todd. *German Orientalisms*. Ann Arbor: University of Michigan Press, 2004.

Kopp, Kristin. "Constructing Racial Difference in Colonial Poland." In *Germany's Colonial Pasts*, edited by Eric Ames, Marcia Klotz, and Lora Wildenthal, 76–96. Lincoln: University of Nebraska Press, 2005.

Kopp, Kristin. *Contesting Borders: German Colonial Discourse and the Polish Eastern Territories*. PhD diss. University of California, Berkeley, 2001.

Kopp, Kristin. *Germany's Wild East: Constructing Poland as Colonial Space*. Ann Arbor: University of Michigan Press, 2012.

Kopp, Kristin. "Gray Zones: On the Inclusion of 'Poland' in the Study of German Colonialism." In *German Colonialism and National Identity*, edited by Michael Perraudin and Jürgen Zimmerer with Katy Heady, 33–42. London: Routledge, 2011.

Kopp, Kristin. "'Ich stehe jetzt hier als einer von den Eroberern': Soll und Haben als Kolonialroman." In *150 Jahre "Soll und Haben": Studien zu Gustav Freytags kontroversem Roman*, edited by Florian Krobb, 225–37. Würzburg: Königshausen and Neumann, 2005.

Korek, Janusz. "Central and Eastern Europe from a Postcolonial Perspective." In *From Sovietology to Postcoloniality*, edited by Janusz Korek, 32–45. Huddinge: Södertörns högskola, 2007.

Korek, Janusz, ed. *From Sovietology to Post-coloniality: Poland and Ukraine from a Postcolonial Perspective*. Huddinge: Södertörns högskola, 2007.

Koropeckyj, Roman. "Orientalism in Adam Mickiewicz's *Crimean Sonnets*." *Slavic and East European Journal* 45, no. 4 (Winter 2001): 660–78.

Kosminski, Evgenii A. *Historia wieków średnich*. Translated into Polish by Mieczysław Henryk Serejski et al. 2nd rev. ed. Warsaw: Nasza Księgarnia, 1951.

Kowalczyk, Andrzej Stanisław. "Rozpad języka poprzedził trąbę jerychońską . . . List Jerzego Stempowskiego do Marii Czapskiej." *Regiony*, no. 2 (1995): 104–13.

Kowalczyk, Stanisław. *Filozofia kultury. Próba personalistycznego ujęcia problematyki*. Lublin: Wydawnictwo KUL, 2005.

Kowalczykowa, Alina. *Słowacki*. Warsaw: PWN, 1994.

Kowalczykowa, Alina. "Słowacki współczesny." In *Juliusz Słowacki—wielokulturowe źródła twórczości*, edited by Adam Bajcar, 9–24. Warsaw: Ogólnopolski Klub Miłośników Litwy, 1999.

Kowalski, Marek Arpad. *Dyskurs kolonialny w Drugiej Rzeczypospolitej*. Warsaw: DiG, 2010.

Krajewski, Andrzej. *Między współpracą a oporem: Twórcy kultury wobec systemu politycznego PRL (1975–1980)*. Warsaw: Trio, 2004.

Krasnodębski, Zdzisław. *Postmodernistyczne rozterki kultury*. Warsaw: Oficyna Naukowa, 1996.

Krasnodębski, Zdzisław. "Waiting for Supermarkets; or, The Downfall of Communism Seen in Postmodern Perspective." *Polish Sociological Bulletin*, no. 4 (1991): 281–87.

Kristeva, Julia. *Black Sun: Depression and Melancholia*. New York: Columbia University Press, 1992.

Kristeva, Julia. *New Maladies of the Soul*. New York: Columbia University Press, 1995.

Kroutvor, Josef. "Potíže střední Evropy: Anekdota a dějiny." In *Potíze s dějinami*, 47–104. Praha: Prostor, 1990. Translated into Polish as "Europa Środkowa: Anegdota i historia" by Jan Stachowski. In *Hrabal, Kundera, Havel . . . Antologia czeskiego eseju*, edited by Jacek Baluch, 223–91. Kraków: Universitas, 2001.

Kubacki, Wacław. *Z Mickiewiczem na Krymie*. Warsaw: PIW, 1977.

Kuczok, Wojciech. *Gnój*. Warsaw: W.A.B., 2003.

Kulczynski, John J. "Dzieje Polski w amerykańskiej historiografii Europy: Królestwo Nigdzie." In *"O nas bez nas": Historia Polski w historiografiach obcojęzycznych*, edited by Witold Molik and Henryk Żaliński, 19–48. Poznań: Wydawnictwo Poznańskie, 2007.

Kundera, Milan. "Un Occident kidnappé, ou la tragédie de l'Europe centrale." *Le débat*, no. 5 (1983): 3–23. Translated into English as "The Tragedy of Central Europe" by Edmund White. *New York Review of Books* 31, no. 7 (April 26, 1984): 33–38.

Kundera, Milan. "Zakład czeski." Translated into Polish by Agnieszka Kołakowska. *Zeszyty Literackie* 1, no. 1 (1983): 26–31.

Kuziak, Michał. *O prelekcjach paryskich Adama Mickiewicza*. Słupsk: Akademia Pomorska, 2007.

Kuziak, Michał. "Pan Tadeusz Adama Mickiewicza: Naiwny? Sentymentalny? (Glosa do komentarzy)." *Słupskie Prace Filologiczne, Seria Filologia Polska*, no. 3 (2004): 73–92.

Kuziak, Michał. "Wartość kulturowego braku: Syndrom kolonialny w twórczości Mickiewicza." *Porównania*, no. 5 (2008): 43–54.

Lacan, Jacques. *Écrits: The First Complete Edition in English*. Translated by Bruno Fink. New York: W. W. Norton, 2006.

Łapiński, Zdzisław. *Jak współżyć z socrealizmem: Szkice nie na temat*. London: Polonia, 1988.

Łaszkiewicz, Hubert. "Pojęcie honoru w Carstwie Moskiewskim i w Rzeczpospolitej w XVI–XVII wieku." In *Dusza polska i rosyjska: Spojrzenie współczesne*, edited by Andrzej de Lazari and Roman Bäcker, 89–97. Łódź: Ibidem, 2003.

Lazarus, Neil. "What Postcolonial Theory Doesn't Say." *Race & Class* 53, no. 1 (2011): 3–27.

Leary, Mark R., and June Price Tangney. *Handbook of Self and Identity*. New York: Guilford Press, 2003.

Lednicki, Wacław. "Pan-Slavism." In *European Ideologies*, edited by Feliks Gross, 808–912. New York: Philosophical Library, 1948.

Leerssen, Joep. "Imagology: History and Method." In *Imagology: The Cultural Construction and Literary Representation of National Characters*, edited by Manfred Beller and Joep Leerssen, 17–32. Amsterdam: Rodopi, 2007.

Leerssen, Joep. "Imagology: On Using Ethnicity to Make Sense of the World." *Iberic@l, Revue d'études ibériques et ibéro-américaines*, no. 10 (2016): 13–31.

Legutko, Ryszard. *O czasach chytrych i prawdach pozornych*. Kraków: Stalky i S-ka, 1999.

Lewis, A. "Postcolonial 'Writing Back.'" In *Post Colonial Identities*, edited by Chin Ce and Charles Smith, 80–97. Nigeria: African Library of Critical Writing, 2014.

Lieskounig, Jürgen. "'Branntweintrinkende Wilde': Beyond Civilization and Outside History; The Depiction of the Poles in Gustav Freytag's Soll und Haben." In *Germany and Eastern Europe: Cultural Identities and Cultural Differences*, edited by Keith Bullivant, Geoffrey Giles, and Walter Pape, 133–47. Amsterdam: Rodopi, 1999.

Lipatov, Aleksandr W. *Rosja i Polska: Konfrontacja i grawitacja. Historia. Kultura. Literatura. Polityka*. Toruń: Wydawnictwo Adam Marszałek, 2003.

"The Lisbon Conference on Literature." *Cross Currents: A Yearbook of Central European Culture*, no. 9 (1990): 75–124.

Litwin, Henryk. "Nations of Polish-Lithuanian Commonwealth. Controversial Questions." *Acta Poloniae Historica*, no. 77 (1998): 43–58.

Liulevicius, Vejas Gabriel. *The German Myth of the East: 1800 to the Present*. Oxford: Oxford University Press, 2009.

Loomba, Ania. *Colonialism/Postcolonialism*. London: Routledge, 1998.

Łozowska, Katarzyna R. *"Obca" ojczyzna: Szkice i eseje historycznoliterackie*. Szczecin: Wydawnictwo Uniwersytetu Szczecińskiego, 2004.

Łubieński, Tomasz. *Porachunki sumienia*. Warsaw: Biblioteka "Więzi," 1994.

Łuczewski, Michał. *Odwieczny naród: Polak i katolik w Żmiącej*. Toruń: Wydawnictwo Naukowe UMK, 2012.

Łuczewski, Michał. "What Remains for Nationalism Studies." In *Freedom, Justice, and Identity*, edited by Thomas Nesbit and Justin Steinberg. Vienna: IWM Junior Visiting Fellows' Conferences. Vol. 18, 2005. Accessed May 14, 2016. http://www.iwm.at/publications/5-junior-visiting-fellows-conferences/vol-xviii/michal-luczewski.

Macaulay, Thomas Babington. "Minute on Indian Education." In *Selected Writings*, edited by John Clive and Thomas Pinney, 237–51. Chicago: University of Chicago Press, 1972.

Maciejewski, Janusz, ed. *Z domu niewoli: Sytuacja polityczna a kultura literacka w drugiej połowie XIX wieku*. Wrocław: Ossolineum, 1988.

Maciejewski, Marian. "Od erudycji do poznania." *Roczniki Humanistyczne* 14, no. 1 (1966): 5–79.

MacIntyre, Alasdair. *After Virtue. A Study in Moral Theory*. London: Bloomsbury, 2011.

MacIntyre, Alasdair. *Marxism and Christianity*. Notre Dame, IN: University of Notre Dame Press, 1984.

Mackiewicz, Józef. *Zwycięstwo prowokacji*. London: Kontra, 1988.

Makowski, Stanisław. *Świat "Sonetów krymskich" Mickiewicza*. Warsaw: Czytelnik, 1969.

Malešević, Siniša. *Identity as Ideology: Understanding Ethnicity and Nationalism*. Basingstoke: Palgrave Macmillan, 2006.

Malešević, Siniša. *Nation-States and Nationalisms: Organization, Ideology and Solidarity*. Malden, MA: Polity Press, 2013.

Markowski, Mieczysław. "Wpływ chrześcijaństwa na kulturę humanistyczną w Polsce średniowiecznej." In *Personalizm polski*, edited by Marian Rusecki, 65–91. Lublin: Wydawnictwo KUL, 2008.

Marszałek, Magdalena. "'Pamięć, meteorologia oraz urojenia': Środkowoeuropejska geopoetyka Andrzeja Stasiuka." In *Literatura, kultura i język polski w kontekstach i kontaktach światowych: III Kongres polonistyki zagranicznej Poznań, 8–11 czerwca 2006 roku*, edited by Małgorzata Czermińska, Katarzyna Meller, and Piotr Fliciński, 539–47. Poznań: UAM, 2007.

Masłowska, Dorota. *Snow White and Russian Red*. 2002. Translated by Benjamin Paloff. New York: Grove Press, 2005.

Mayblin, Lucy, Aneta Piekut, and Gill Valentine. "'Other' Posts in 'Other' Places: Poland through a Postcolonial Lens?" *Sociology* 50, no. 1 (February 2016): 60–76.

McClintock, Anne. *Imperial Leather: Race, Gender and Sexuality in the Colonial Contest*. New York: Routledge, 1995.

Melegh, Attila. "Positioning in Global Hierarchies: The Case of Central Europe." In *Understanding Central Europe*, edited by Marcin Moskalewicz and Wojciech Przybylski, 26–31. London: Routledge, 2018.

Memmi, Albert. *Dominated Man: Notes toward a Portrait*. London: Orion, 1968.

Metzl, Jonathan. "From Scopophilia to Survivor: A Brief History of Voyeurism." *Textual Practice* 18, no. 3 (2004): 415–34.

Micińska, Magdalena. *Zdrada córka nocy: Pojęcie zdrady narodowej w świadomości Polaków w latach 1861–1914*. Warsaw: Sic!, 1998.

Mick, Christoph. "Colonialism in the Polish Eastern Borderlands, 1918–1939." In *The Shadow of Colonialism on Europe's Modern Past*, edited by Róisín Healy and Enrico Dal Lago, 126–41. New York: Palgrave Macmillan, 2014.

Mickiewicz, Adam. *Dzieła*. Edited by Leon Płoszewski. Vol. 14, *Listy*. Part 1. Warsaw: Czytelnik, 1955.

Mickiewicz, Adam. *Wybór poezyj*. Edited by Czesław Zgorzelski. Vol. 2. 4th ed. Wrocław: Ossolineum, 1997.

Mieroszewski, Juliusz. "Polityka narodów zdeklasowanych." *Kultura* 6, no. 92 (1955): 3–9.

Mieroszewski, Juliusz. "Rosyjski kompleks Polski i obszar ULB." *Kultura* 9, no. 324 (1974): 3–14. Reprinted in Paweł Kowal, ed. *Nie jesteśmy ukrainofilami: Polska myśl polityczna wobec Ukraińców i Ukrainy; Antologia tekstów*, 311–22. Wrocław: Kolegium Europy Wschodniej, 2002.

Mignolo, Walter. *The Darker Side of the Renaissance: Literacy, Territoriality, and Colonization*. 2nd ed. Ann Arbor: University of Michigan Press, 2003.

Miller, Aleksei, Denis Sdvizhkov, and Ingrid Shirle, eds. *"Poniatiia o Rossii": K Istoricheskoi Semantike Imperskogo Perioda*. Vols. 1–2. Moscow: Novoe Literaturnoe Obozrenie, 2012.

Miller, Jan Nepomucen. *Zaraza w Grenadzie*. Warsaw: Księgarnia F. Hoesicka, 1926. Reprinted in *Bez kropki nad "i."* Warsaw: PIW, 1964.

Miłosz, Czesław. *The Captive Mind*. Translated by Jane Zielonko. New York: Knopf, 1953.

Miłosz, Czesław. *The History of Polish Literature*. 2nd ed. Berkeley: University of California Press, 1983.

Miłosz, Czesław. *Szukanie ojczyzny*. Kraków: Znak, 1992.

Miłosz, Czesław. *Ziemia Ulro*. Kraków: Znak, 2000.

Mochnacki, Maurycy. *O literaturze polskiej w wieku dziewiętnastym*. Edited by Ziemowit Skibiński. Łódź: Wydawnictwo Łódzkie, 1985.

Moskalewicz, Marcin, and Wojciech Przybylski. "Making Sense of Central Europe: Political Concepts of the Region." In *Understanding Central Europe*, edited by Marcin Moskalewicz and Wojciech Przybylski, 1–21. London: Routledge, 2018.

Mosse, George L. *The Crisis of German Ideology: Intellectual Origins of the Third Reich*. Translated by Salvator Attanasio et al. New York: Schocken Books, 1981.

Murzański, Stanisław. *Między kompromisem a zdradą: Intelektualiści wobec przemocy, 1945–1956*. Warsaw: Volumen, 1993.

Najder, Zdzisław. "Kultura i imperializm: Czy Polacy są postkolonialni?" *Europa—Tygodnik Idei*, no. 26 (2005): 14.

Nandy, Ashis. *The Intimate Enemy: Loss and Recovery of Self under Colonialism*. Delhi: Oxford University Press, 1983.

Nebrija, Antonio de. *Gramática de la lengua castellana*. Madrid: Editora Nacional, 1980. (Orig. 1492).

Nelson, Robert L., ed. *Germans, Poland, and Colonial Expansion to the East*. New York: Palgrave Macmillan, 2009.

Neuger, Leonard. "Central Europe as a Problem." In *From Sovietology to Postcoloniality*, edited by Janusz Korek, 23–31. Huddinge: Södertörns högskola, 2007.

N'guessan, Béchié Paul. *Primitivismus und Afrikanismus: Kunst und Kultur Afrikas in der deutschen Avantgarde*. Frankfurt am Main: Peter Lang, 2002.

Nicoll, Allardyce, and Arthur Wilmurt. *World Drama: From Aeschylus to Anouilh*. 2nd rev. and enlarged ed. London: Harrap, 1976.

Niewiara, Aleksandra. *Kształty polskiej tożsamości: Potoczny dyskurs narodowy w perspektywie etnolingwistycznej (XVI–XX w.)*. Katowice: Wydawnictwo UŚ, 2009.

Nora, Pierre. "The Reasons for the Current Upsurge in Memory." *Transit—Europäische Revue*, no. 22. Accessed May 14, 2017. http://www.eurozine.com/reasons-for-the-current-upsurge-in-memory.

Norwid, Cyprian. "List do Józefa Bohdana Zaleskiego." April 24, 1848. In *Pisma wszystkie*, edited by Juliusz Wiktor Gomulicki. Vol. 8, *Listy, 1839–1861*, 61–63. Warsaw: PIW, 1971.

Norwid, Cyprian. "List do Józefa Ignacego Kraszewskiego." Ca. May 15, 1866. In *Pisma wszystkie*, edited by Juliusz Wiktor Gomulicki. Vol. 9, *Listy, 1862–1872*, 223. Warsaw: PIW, 1971.

Nowak, Andrzej. "Between Imperial Temptation and Anti-imperial Function in East European Politics: Poland from the Eighteenth to Twenty-First Century." In *Emerging Meso-areas in the Former Socialist Countries: Histories Revived or Improvised*, edited by Kimitaka Matsuzato, 247–84. Sapporo: Slavic Research Center, 2005.

Nowak, Andrzej. "From Empire Builder to Empire Breaker; or, There and Back Again: History and Memory of Poland's Role in Eastern European Politics." *Ab Imperio: Studies of New Imperial History and Nationalism in the Post-Soviet Space*, no. 1 (2004): 255–89.

Nowak, Andrzej. *History and Geopolitics: A Contest for Eastern Europe*. Warsaw: Polish Institute of International Affairs, 2008.

Nowak, Andrzej. *Od imperium do imperium: Spojrzenia na historię Europy Wschodniej*. Kraków: Arcana and Instytut Historii PAN, 2004.

Nowak, Andrzej. *Ofiary, imperia i historycy: Studium przypadków (od XVIII do XXI wieku)*. Kraków: Arcana, 2009.

Nowicka-Franczak, Magdalena. "Was Another Modernisation Possible? Liberal and Leftist Critique of the Transformation in the Public Debate in Poland." *Polish Sociological Review* 203, no. 3 (2018): 321–43.

Nycz, Ryszard. "Polish Literature in the Shadow of Censorship: A Lecture." "Postcolonial or Postdependence Studies?," special issue, English version, *Teksty Drugie*, no. 2 (2016): 84–104.

Obolensky, Dmitri. "Russia's Byzantine Heritage." In *The Structure of Russian History: Interpretive Essays*, edited by Michael Cherniavsky, 3–28. New York: Random House, 1970.

O'Keeffe, Terrence. "Mitteleuropa Blues, Perilous Remedies: Andrzej Stasiuk's Harsh World." Part 2. *Sarmatian Review* 32, no. 1 (2012): 1640–50.

Opacki, Ireneusz. *Poezja romantycznych przełomów: Szkice*. Wrocław: Ossolineum, 1972.

Orłowski, Hubert. "Ein feines Netz: 'Polnische Wirtschaft'—ein Diskurs (in) der deutsch-polnischen Beziehungsgeschichte." *Historie*, no. 6 (2012–13): 237–47.

Orłowski, Hubert. *Z modernizacją w tle: Wokół rodowodu nowoczesnych niemieckich wyobrażeń o Polsce i Polakach*. Poznań: PTPN, 2002.

Owsianowska, Sabina. "Tourist Narratives about the Dissonant Heritage of the Borderlands: The Case of South-Eastern Poland." *Journal of Tourism and Cultural Change* 15, no. 2 (2017): 167–84.

Paczoska, Ewa. "Polskość w dobie niewoli—gniazdo czy 'zaścianek'?" In *Przemiany formuły polskości w drugiej połowie XIX wieku*, edited by Janusz Maciejewski, 105–18. Warsaw: IBL, 1999.

Pal-Lapinski, Piya. *The Exotic Woman in Nineteenth-Century British Fiction and Culture: A Reconsideration*. Hanover: University of New Hampshire Press, 2005.

Panas, Władysław. "O pograniczu etnicznym w badaniach literackich." In *Wiedza o literaturze i edukacja: Księga referatów Zjazdu Polonistów Warszawa, 1995*, edited by Teresa Michałowska, Zbigniew Goliński, and Zbigniew Jarosiński, 605–13. Warsaw: IBL, 1996.

Parry, Benita. *Postcolonial Studies: A Materialist Critique*. London: Routledge, 2004.

Pasierski, Emil. *Miłosz i Putrament: Żywoty równoległe*. Warsaw: WAB, 2011.

Pasierski, Emil. "Czesław Miłosz i Jan Nowak-Jeziorański—protokół rozbieżności." *Archiwum Emigracji: Studia—Szkice—Dokumenty*, nos. 22/23 (2015): 27–39.

Pavlyshyn, Marko. "Andrukhovych's *Secret*: The Return of Colonial Resignation." *Journal of Postcolonial Writing* 48, no. 2 (May 2012): 188–99.

Pavlyshyn, Marko. "Postcoloniality as Method and Mind-Set: Ukrainian Literature and Literary Scholarship, 1991–2011." In *Ukraine Twenty Years after Independence: Assessments, Perspectives, Challenges*, edited by Giovanna Brogi, Marta Dyczok, Oxana Pachlovska, and Giovanna Siedina, 259–72. Rome: Aracne, 2015.

Pawłowski, Zdzisław. "Kazanie na Górze a przemoc: Utopia czy większa sprawiedliwość?" *Studia Bobolanum*, no. 2 (2005): 45–60.

Peiker, Piret. "Post-Communist Literatures: A Postcolonial Perspective," *Eurozine*, March 28, 2006. Accessed December 2, 2018. http://www.eurozine.com/post-communist-literatures-a-postcolonial-perspective/?pdf.

Pennycook, Alastair. *English and the Discourses of Colonialism*. London: Routledge, 1998.

Perrie, Maureen. *The Cult of Ivan the Terrible in Stalin's Russia*. New York: Palgrave Macmillan, 2001.

Piasecki, Sergiusz. *Zapiski oficera Armii Czerwonej*. London: Gryf, 1957.

Pieróg, Stanisław. "Mesjanizm." In *Słownik literatury polskiej XIX wieku*, edited by Józef Bachórz and Alina Kowalczykowa, 536–40. Wrocław: Ossolineum, 1991.

Pietrzyk-Reeves, Dorota. "Podstawy wspólnotowego ładu Rzeczypospolitej w XVI wieku a wpływy humanizmu i republikanizmu." In *Polska czyli . . . idee wspólnoty politycznej i tożsamości narodowej w polskiej tradycji intelektualnej*, edited by Arkady Rzegocki, 15–50. Kraków: Ośrodek Myśli Politycznej, 2011.

Pigoń, Stanisław. *Poprzez stulecia: Studia z dziejów literatury i kultury*. Edited by Julian Maślanka. Warsaw: PWN, 1984.

Pilario, Daniel F. "Mapping Postcolonial Theory: Appropriations into Contemporary Theology." *Asian Christian Review* 1, no. 1 (Spring 2007): 48–78.

Piwińska, Marta. "*Sonety krymskie* czytane na Krymie w roku 2004." *Pamiętnik Literacki* 96, no. 4 (2005): 19–40.

Platt, Kevin. *Terror and Greatness: Ivan and Peter as Russian Myths*. Ithaca, NY: Cornell University Press, 2011.

*Polish Romantic Drama: Three Plays in English*. Translated, selected, edited and with an introduction by Harold B. Segel. London: Routledge, 1997.

Popescu, Monica. "Translations: Lenin's Statues, Post-Communism and Post-apartheid." *Yale Journal of Criticism* 16, no. 2 (Fall 2003): 406–23.

Porter-Szűcs, Brian. *Faith and Fatherland: Catholicism, Modernity, and Poland*. Oxford: Oxford University Press, 2011.

Porter-Szűcs, Brian. *When Nationalism Began to Hate: Imagining Modern Politics in Nineteenth Century Poland*. Oxford: Oxford University Press, 2000.
Prokop, Jan. *Klerk i diabeł: Literatura—ideologie—mity*. Kraków: Viridis, 1999.
Prokop, Jan. *Pisarze w służbie przemocy*. Kraków: Viridis, 1995.
Prokop, Jan. *Polak jaki jest—nie(ch) każdy widzi: O rozchwianiu tożsamości na progu Europy*. Kraków: Księgarnia Akademicka, 2004.
Prokop, Jan. *Universum polskie: Literatura, wyobraźnia zbiorowa, mity polityczne*. Kraków: Universitas, 1993.
Prokop, Jan. *Wyobraźnia pod nadzorem*. Kraków: Viridis, 1994.
Pruszyński, Ksawery. "Trębacz z Samarkandy." In *Trzynaście opowieści*, 63–72. Warsaw: Czytelnik, 1995.
Przybylski, Ryszard. *Słowo i milczenie bohatera Polaków: Studium o "Dziadach."* Warsaw: IBL, 1993.
Pucherová, Dobrota, and Róbert Gáfrik, eds. *Postcolonial Europe? Essays on Post-Communist Literatures and Cultures*. Leiden: Brill Rodopi, 2015.
Puto, Kaja. "A Film Which Divides Poles and Ukrainians." *New Eastern Europe* 25, no. 1 (2017): 182–86.
Radliński, Ignacy. "Nasza umysłowość." *Myśl Niepodległa*, no. 81 (1908): 1538.
Radziejewski, Bartłomiej. "Od Polaków do neo-Polan? Nowy trybalizm a polityczność Polaków." In *Polska czyli . . . idee wspólnoty politycznej i tożsamości narodowej w polskiej tradycji intelektualnej*, edited by Arkady Rzegocki, 273–94. Kraków: Ośrodek Myśli Politycznej, 2011.
Rash, Felicity. *The Discourse Strategies of Imperialist Writing: The German Colonial Idea and Africa, 1848–1945*. London: Routledge, 2017.
Ratti, Manav. *The Postsecular Imagination: Postcolonialism, Religion and Literature*. New York: Routledge, 2013.
Riabchuk, Mykoła. "Od 'Małorosji' do 'Indoeuropy': Stereotyp 'narodu' w ukraińskiej społecznej świadomości i myśli społecznej." In *Narody i stereotypy*, edited by Teresa Walas, 113–24. Kraków: Międzynarodowe Centrum Kultury, 1995.
Riabchuk, Mykola. "'Two Ukraines' Reconsidered: The End of Ukrainian Ambivalence?" *Studies in Ethnicity and Nationalism* 15, no. 1 (2015): 138–56.
Rickly-Boyd, Jillian M. "The Tourist Narrative." *Tourist Studies* 9, no. 3 (2010): 259–80.
Ricoeur, Paul. *Evil: A Challenge to Philosophy and Theology*. 2nd ed. London: Bloomsbury Academic, 2007.
Ritz, German. "Kresy polskie w perspektywie postkolonialnej." In *Nieobecność: Pominięcia i przemilczenia w narracjach XX wieku*, edited by Hanna Gosk and Bożena Karwowska, 115–33. Warsaw: Elipsa, 2008.
Romaniuk, Radosław. *Inne życie: Biografia Jarosława Iwaszkiewicza*. Warsaw: Iskry, 2012.
Rosner, Katarzyna. *Narracja, tożsamość, czas*. Kraków: Universitas, 2006.
Rudnytsky, Ivan L. "Polish-Ukrainian Relations: The Burden of History." In *Essays in Modern Ukrainian History*, 49–76. Edmonton: Canadian Institute of Ukrainian Studies Press, 1987.

Rulhière, Claude-Carloman de. *Histoire de l'anarchie de Pologne, et du démembrement de cette république*. Paris: Desenne, 1807.

Rusecki, Marian, ed. *Personalizm polski*. Lublin: Wydawnictwo KUL, 2008.

Rüsen, Jörn, and Henner Laass, eds. *Humanism in Intercultural Perspective: Experiences and Expectations*. Bielefeld: Transcript, 2009.

Rushdie, Salman. "The Empire Writes Back to the Centre." *Times* (London), July 13, 1982, 8.

Said, Edward W. "Afterword: Reflections on Ireland and Postcolonialism." In *Ireland and Postcolonial Theory*, edited by Clare Carroll and Patricia King, 177–85. Notre Dame, IN: University of Notre Dame Press, 2003.

Said, Edward W. *Culture and Imperialism*. New York: Vintage Books, 1994.

Said, Edward W. *Orientalism*. New York: Vintage Books, 1979.

Said, Edward W. *Power, Politics, and Culture: Interviews with Edward Said*. Edited by Gauri Viswanathan. New York: Vintage, 2002.

Said, Edward W. *The World, The Text, and the Critic*. Cambridge, MA: Harvard University Press, 1983.

Şandru, Cristina. *Worlds Apart? A Postcolonial Reading of Post-1945 East-Central European Culture*. Newcastle upon Tyne: Cambridge Scholars, 2012.

Sapa, Dorota. *Między polską wyspą a ukraińskim morzem: Kresy południowo-wschodnie w polskiej prozie, 1918–1988*. Kraków: Universitas, 1998.

Sawicki, Stefan. "Ethos polskiej literatury." In *Wartość—sacrum—Norwid: Studia i szkice aksjologicznoliterackie*, 19–31. Lublin: KUL, 1994.

Sawicki, Stefan. "Norwid—od strony prawnuków." In *Wartość—sacrum—Norwid. 2. Studia i szkice aksjologicznoliterackie*, 111–24. Lublin: Wydawnictwo KUL, 2007.

Sawicki, Stefan. "O znakach aksjologicznie nacechowanych i nie tylko o nich." In *Wartość—sacrum—Norwid. 2. Studia i szkice aksjologicznoliterackie*, 29–40. Lublin: Wydawnictwo KUL, 2007.

Sawicki, Stefan. . . . *Quo magis veritas propagetur*. Toruń: Wydawnictwo Naukowe UMK, 2010.

Schacter, Daniel L. *The Seven Sins of Memory: How the Mind Forgets and Remembers*. Boston: Houghton Mifflin, 2001.

Schilling, Britta. "German Postcolonialism in Four Dimensions: A Historical Perspective." *Postcolonial Studies* 18, no. 4 (2015): 427–39.

Schilling, Britta. *Postcolonial Germany: Memories of Empire in a Decolonized Nation*. Oxford: Oxford University Press, 2014.

Scruton, Roger. *England: An Elegy*. London: Continuum, 2001.

Segel, Harold B. "Mickiewicz and the Arabic Qasidah in Poland." In *American Contributions to the Fifth International Congress of Slavists, Sofia, September 1963*. Vol. 2, *Literary Contributions*, 279–300. The Hague: Mouton, 1963.

Sękowski, Józef. *Collectanea z dziejopisów tureckich rzeczy do historyi polskiey służących*. Vols. 1–2. Warsaw: Zawadzki i Wącki, 1824–25.

Serejski, Marian H. *Europa a rozbiory Polski: Studium historiograficzne*. Warsaw: PWN, 2009.

Seton-Watson, Hugh. *Eastern Europe between the Wars, 1918–1941*. 1945. Hamden: Archon, 1962.

Seweryn, Dariusz. *O wyobraźni lirycznej Adama Mickiewicza*. Warsaw: IBL, 1996.

Shi-xu. *A Cultural Approach to Discourse*. New York: Palgrave Macmillan, 2005.

Shkandrij, Myroslav. *Russia and Ukraine: Literature and Discourse of Empire from Napoleonic to Postcolonial Times*. Montreal: McGill-Queen's University Press, 2001.

Shohat, Ella. "Notes on the Postcolonial." *Social Text*, nos. 31/32 (Spring 1992): 99–113.

Shore, Marci. *Caviar and Ashes: A Warsaw Generation's Life and Death in Marxism, 1918–1968*. New Haven, CT: Yale University Press, 2006.

Siedlecka, Joanna. *Biografie odtajnione: Z archiwów literackich bezpieki*. Warsaw: Zysk i S-ka, 2015.

Siedlecka, Joanna. *Obława: Losy pisarzy represjonowanych*. Warsaw: Prószyński i S-ka, 2005.

Sirutavičius, Marius. "The Grand Duchy of Lithuania and the Historical Region: The Search for New Coordinates in Post-Soviet Lithuanian Historiography." In *The Construction of National Narratives and Politics of Memory in the Central and Eastern European Region after 1989*, edited by Egidijušius Aleksandravičius, 41–54. Vilnius: Vytauto Didžiojo universitetas, 2014.

Skarga, Barbara. *Granice historyczności*. Warsaw: IFIS PAN, 2005.

Skarga, Barbara. *Kwintet metafizyczny*. Kraków: Universitas, 2005.

Skarga, Barbara. *O filozofię bać się nie musimy: Szkice z różnych lat*. Warsaw: PWN, 1999.

Skarga, Barbara. *Przeszłość i interpretacje: Z warsztatu historyka filozofii*. Warsaw: PWN, 1987.

Skarga, Barbara. *Ślad i obecność*. Warsaw: PWN, 2002.

Skarga, Barbara. *Tożsamość i różnica: Eseje metafizyczne*. Kraków: Znak, 1997.

Skórczewski, Dariusz. "Postkolonialna Polska—projekt (nie)możliwy." *Teksty Drugie*, nos. 1/2 (2006): 100–112.

Słabek, Henryk. *Intelektualistów obraz własny w świetle dokumentów autobiograficznych, 1944–1989*. Warsaw: KiW, 1997.

Słowacki, Juliusz. *Raptularz, 1843–1849*. Edited by Marek Troszyński. Warsaw: Topos, 1996.

*Słownik języka polskiego przez M. Samuela Bogumiła Linde*. Vol. 2, part 2. Warsaw: Drukarnia XX. Pijarów, 1807.

Smith, Anthony D. *The Ethnic Origins of Nations*. Oxford: Wiley-Blackwell, 1988.

Smith, Anthony D. *Myths and Memories of the Nation*. Oxford: Oxford University Press, 1999.

Smith, Anthony D. *National Identity*. Harmondsworth: Penguin, 1991.

Smith, Anthony D. *Nationalism: Theory, Ideology, History*. Malden, MA: Polity, 2010.

Smitt, Fedor Ivanovich. *Suworow und Polens Untergang*. Leipzig: C. F. Winter, 1858.

Snyder, Timothy. *The Reconstruction of Nations: Poland, Ukraine, Lithuania, Belarus, 1568–1999*. New Haven, CT: Yale University Press, 2003.

Sobczak, Jacek. "Kryzys polskiej tożsamości narodowej, narodziny tożsamości europejskiej—antynomie, dylematy, miraże." In *Tożsamość polska w odmiennych kontekstach*, edited by Leon Dyczewski and Dariusz Wadowski, 227–59. Lublin: Wydawnictwo KUL, 2009.

Sorensen, Eli. "Postcolonial Melancholia." *Paragraph* 30, no. 2 (July 2007): 65–81.

Sowa, Jan. *Fantomowe ciało króla: Peryferyjne zmagania z nowoczesną formą*. Kraków: Universitas, 2011.

Sowa, Jan. "Forget Postcolonialism, There's a Class War Ahead." *nonsite.org*, no. 12 (2014). Accessed May 17, 2017. http://nonsite.org/article/forget-postcolonialism-theres-a-class-war-ahead.

Spivak, Gayatri Chakravorty. "Can the Subaltern Speak?" In *Can the Subaltern Speak? Reflections on the History of an Idea*, edited by Rosalind Morris, 21–78. New York: Columbia University Press, 2010.

Spivak, Gayatri Chakravorty. *The Postcolonial Critic: Interviews, Strategies and Dialogues*, edited by Sarah Harasym. New York: Routledge, 1990.

Spivak, Gayatri Chakravorty. "Three Women's Texts and a Critique of Imperialism." *Critical Inquiry* 12, no. 1 (Autumn 1985): 243–61.

Spurr, David. *The Rhetoric of Empire. Colonial Discourse in Journalism, Travel Writing, and Imperial Administration*. Durham, NC: Duke University Press, 1993.

Spyra, Ania. "Between Theory and Reality: Cosmopolitanism of Nodal Cities in Paweł Huelle's *Castorp*." *Comparative Literature* 64, no. 3 (August 2012): 286–99.

Staniszkis, Jadwiga. *Antropologia władzy: Między Traktatem Lizbońskim a kryzysem*. Warsaw: Prószyński i S-ka, 2009.

Staniszkis, Jadwiga. *O władzy i bezsilności*. Kraków: Wydawnictwo Literackie, 2006.

Starobinski, Jean. "On Nostalgia." Translated by Kristen Gray Jafflin. In *The Emotional Power of Music: Multidisciplinary Perspectives on Musical Arousal, Expression, and Social Control*, edited by Tom Cochrane, Bernardino Fantini, and Klaus R. Scherer, 329–40. Oxford: Oxford University Press, 2013.

Stasiuk, Andrzej. "Das Kaczynski-Theater ist vorbei." *Die Welt*, November 27, 2007.

Stasiuk, Andrzej. "Die Kaczynskis, das ist die nackte polnische Seele: Interview mit Gerhard Gnauck." *Die Welt*, March 14, 2007.

Stasiuk, Andrzej. "Dziennik okrętowy." In *Moja Europa: Dwa eseje o Europie zwanej Środkową*, by Jurij Andruchowycz and Andrzej Stasiuk. Wołowiec: Czarne, 2007.

Stasiuk, Andrzej. *Fado, 2006*. Translated by Bill Johnston. Champaign, IL: Dalkey Archive Press, 2009.

Stasiuk, Andrzej. "Filozofia nicości do mnie nie przemawia." In *Rozmowa była możliwa: Wywiady z pisarzami*, by Michał Larek and Jerzy Borowczyk, 163–80. Poznań: Stowarzyszenie Czasu Kultury, 2008.

Stasiuk, Andrzej. *Noc czyli słowiańsko-germańska tragifarsa medyczna*. Wołowiec: Czarne, 2005.

Stasiuk, Andrzej. *On the Road to Babadag: Travels in the Other Europe*. Translated by Michael Kandel. New York: Vintage Books, 2012. Polish original: *Jadąc do Babadag*. Wołowiec: Czarne, 2004.

Ştefănescu, Bogdan. *Postcommunism—Postcolonialism: Siblings of Subalternity*. Bucureşti: Editura Universitatii din Bucureşti, 2013.

Ştefănescu, Bogdan. "Reluctant Siblings: Notes on the Analogy between Post-communist and Postcolonial Subalterns." *Word and Text: A Journal of Literary Studies and Linguistics* 2, no. 1 (2012): 13–25.

Stobiecki, Rafał. "Między marksizmem a wielkoruskim szowinizmem: Elementy obrazu dziejów Polski w radzieckich podręcznikach doby stalinizmu." In *Dusza polska i rosyjska: Spojrzenie współczesne*, edited by Andrzej de Lazari and Roman Bäcker, 229–43. Łódź: Ibidem, 2003.

Straub, Jürgen. "Personal and Collective Identity: A Conceptual Analysis." Translated by Anthony Nassar. In *Identities: Time, Difference and Boundaries*, edited by Heidrun Friese, 56–76. New York: Berghahn Books, 2002.

Stróżewski, Władysław. *Istnienie i wartość*. Kraków: Znak, 1981.

Stryker, Sheldon, and Peter J. Burke. "The Past, Present, and Future of an Identity Theory." *Social Psychology Quarterly* 63, no. 4 (December 2000): 284–97.

Strzyżewski, Mirosław. *Music and Infinity: Studies in Polish Romanticism*. Toruń: Wydawnictwo Naukowe UMK, 2016.

Sugirtharajah, Rasiah S., ed. *The Postcolonial Biblical Reader*. Malden, MA: Blackwell, 2006.

Surynt, Izabela. "Post-colonial Research and the 'Second World': German National-and-Colonial Constructs of the 19th Century." "Postcolonial or Postdependence Studies?," special issue, English version, *Teksty Drugie*, no. 1 (2014): 143–66.

Świda-Ziemba, Hanna. "Stalinizm i społeczeństwo polskie." In *Stalinizm*, edited by Jacek Kurczewski, 15–96. Warsaw: Wydawnictwo UW, 1989.

Świdziński, Jerzy. "*Sonety krymskie*, czyli sposób artystycznego 'łudzenia despoty.'" In *Spotkania literackie: Z dziejów powiązań polsko-rosyjskich w dobie romantyzmu i neoromantyzmu*, edited by Bohdan Galster and Janina Kamionkowa, 61–84. Wrocław: Ossolineum, 1973.

Święch, Jerzy. "Kresy i centrum." In *O dialogu kultur wspólnot kresowych*, edited by Stanisław Uliasz, 35–53. Rzeszów: WSP, 1998.

Swieżawski, Stefan. "Początki nowożytnego arystotelizmu chrześcijańskiego." *Roczniki Filozoficzne* 19, no. 1 (1971): 42–56.

Szacka, Barbara. "Pamięć zbiorowa." In *Wobec przeszłości—pamięć przeszłości jako element kultury współczesnej*, edited by Andrzej Szpociński, 17–30. Warsaw: Instytut im. Adama Mickiewicza, 2005.

Szaruga, Leszek. *Literatura i życie: Ważniejsze wątki dyskusji literackich, 1939–1989*. Lublin: Wydawnictwo UMCS, 2001.

Szaruga, Leszek. *Węzeł kresowy*. Częstochowa: WSP, 2001.

Szkudlarek, Tomasz. "Dialektyka Innego i postkolonialna tożsamość." In *Edukacja a tożsamość etniczna: Materiały z konferencji naukowej w Rabce*, edited by Maria Marta Urlińska, 25–36. Toruń: UMK, 1995.

Szulecki, Kacper. "Inna Europa i Kresowa Atlantyda: O Polsce orientalizowanej i orientalizującej." *Kultura Liberalna*, no. 95 (2010). Accessed May 17, 2017. http://kulturaliberalna.pl/2010/11/02/wolff-iskandar-wilczura-szulecki-busza-kmicic-je-kebab...-„orientalizm"-po-polsku.

Szymański, Wiesław Paweł. *Uroki dworu*. Kraków: Arka, 1993.

Tarasiuk, Dariusz. "Polsko-rosyjska rywalizacja o oświatę na ziemiach białoruskich na przełomie XIX–XX wieku." *Białoruskie Zeszyty Historyczne*, no. 23 (2005): 148–55.

Tarnowski, Karol. "Metaphysical Longing." In *The Creative Matrix of the Origins: Analecta Husserliana*, edited by Anna-Teresa Tymieniecka, 261–70. Dordrecht: Springer, 2002.

Taylor, Charles. "The Concept of a Person." In *Philosophical Papers*. Vol. 1, *Human Agency and Language*, 97–114. Cambridge: Cambridge University Press, 1985.

Taylor, Charles. *Sources of the Self: Making of the Modern Identity*. Cambridge, MA: Harvard University Press, 1989.

Taylor, Nina. "Dziedzictwo kresowe w literaturze emigracyjnej." In *Literatura polska na obczyźnie: Prace Kongresu Kultury Polskiej*, edited by Józef Bujnowski. Vol. 5, 130–43. London: Polskie Towarzystwo Naukowe na Obczyźnie, 1988.

Tazbir, Janusz. "Kamienie milowe polskiej świadomości historycznej." In *Prace wybrane*. Vol. 4, *Studia nad kulturą staropolską*, 321–40. Kraków: Universitas, 2001.

Tazbir, Janusz. "Pan Tadeusz, a więc—jakoś to będzie." In *Prace wybrane*. Vol. 5, *Szkice o literaturze i sztuce*, 147–60. Kraków: Universitas, 2002.

Tazbir, Janusz. "Polska a Europa." *Nauka*, no. 4 (2004): 39–40.

Tazbir, Julia, and Janusz Tazbir. "Cienie zapomnianych przodków: O *Niesamowitej Słowiańszczyźnie* Marii Janion; Czy Polacy zostali 'źle ochrzczeni'?" *Tygodnik Powszechny*, no. 3 (2007): 8–9.

Thieme, John. *Postcolonial Con-texts: Writing Back to the Canon*. London: Continuum, 2001.

Thompson, Andrew. "Nations, National Identities and Human Agency: Putting People Back into Nations." *Sociological Review* 49, no. 1 (February 2001): 18–32.

Thompson, Ewa M. *Imperial Knowledge: Russian Literature and Colonialism*. Westport, CT: Greenwood Press, 2000.

Thompson, Ewa M. "It's Colonialism after All: Some Epistemological Remarks." "Postcolonial or Postdependence Studies?," special issue, English version, *Teksty Drugie*, no. 1 (2014): 67–81.

Thompson, Ewa M. Review of *Deploying Orientalism in Culture and History: From Germany to Central and Eastern Europe*, by James Hodkinson and John Walker, eds. *Slavic and East European Journal* 58, no. 3 (Fall 2014): 551–52.

Thompson, Ewa M. "On Zygmunt Krasiński's *Undivine Comedy*." *Chesterton Review* 27, no. 4 (November 2001): 495–501.

Thompson, Ewa M. "Why the Conservative Tradition Is an Important Philosophical Option in Polish Intellectual Life." *Periphery* 3, nos. 1/2 (1997): 30–35.

Thompson, Ewa M. "Sarmatism, or the Secrets of Polish Essentialism." In *Being Poland: A New History of Polish Literature and Culture since 1918*, edited by Przemysław Czapliński, Joanna Niżyńska, and Tamara Trojanowska, 3–29. Toronto: University of Toronto Press, 2018.

Thompson, Ewa M. "The Surrogate Hegemon in Polish Postcolonial Discourse." Accessed May 14, 2017. www.owlnet.rice.edu/~ethomp/The Surrogate Hegemon.pdf.

Thompson, Ewa M. "W kolejce po aprobatę." *Europa—Tygodnik Idei*, no. 180 (2007): 8.

Thun, Gregor. "Mythische Landschaften: Das Bild vom 'deutschen Osten' und die Zäsuren des 20. Jahrhunderts." In *Traumland Osten*, edited by Gregor Thun, 181–212. Göttingen: Vandenhoeck and Ruprecht, 2006.

Tiffin, Chris, and Alan Lawson, eds. *De-scribing Empire: Post-colonialism and Textuality*. London: Routledge, 1994.

Tiffin, Helen. "Post-colonial Literatures and Counter-discourse." *Kunapipi* 9, no. 3 (1987): 17–34.

Todorov, Tzvetan. *The Conquest of America: The Question of the Other*. Norman: University of Oklahoma Press, 1984.

Todorova, Maria. "The Trap of Backwardness: Modernity, Temporality, and the Study of Eastern European Nationalism." *Slavic Review* 64, no. 1 (Spring 2005): 140–64.

Tomaszewski, Nikodem Bończa. *Źródła narodowości: Powstanie i rozwój polskiej świadomości w II połowie XIX i na początku XX wieku*. Wrocław: Wydawnictwo Uniwersytetu Wrocławskiego, 2006.

Topolski, Jerzy. *Jak się pisze i rozumie historię: Tajemnice narracji historycznej*. Warsaw: Rytm, 1998.

Toruńczyk, Barbara. "Opowieści o pokoleniu 1968: Kim byliśmy, kim jesteśmy, skąd i dokąd zmierzamy?" *Dwutygodnik.com*, no. 18 (2009). Accessed May 15, 2017. http://www.dwutygodnik.com/artykul/635-opowiesci-o-pokoleniu-1968-7.html.

Traba, Robert. "The Kresy as a Realm of Memory: The Long History of Persistence." *Herito*, no. 8 (2012): 50–56.

Trencsényi, Balázs. "Central Europe." In *European Regions and Boundaries: A Conceptual History*, edited by Diana Mishkova and Balázs Trencsényi, 166–87. New York: Berghahn, 2017.

Troszyński, Marek. "On the Shoulders of Giants." *Sarmatian Review* 30, no. 1 (January 2010): 1463–69.

Trznadel, Jacek. *Hańba domowa*. Paris: Instytut Literacki, 1986.

Trznadel, Jacek. *Kolaboranci: Tadeusz Boy-Żeleński i grupa komunistycznych pisarzy w Lwowie, 1939–1941*. Komorów: Antyk, 1998.

Trznadel, Jacek. *Polski Hamlet: Kłopoty z działaniem*. Paris: Libella, 1988.

Tucan, Dumitru. "The Adaptability of Theory: Postcolonialism vs. Postcommunism in Romanian Literary Studies." *Dacoromania Litteraria*, no. 2 (2015): 101–16.

Tyma, Piotr. "The Volhynian Problem: The Dilemmas of Ukrainians from Poland." Translated by Sławomir Nowodworski. In *Reconciliation through Difficult Remembrance. Volhynia 1943*, edited by Aleksandra Zińczuk, 328–33. Lublin: Stowarzyszenie Panorama Kultur, 2012.

Tyrmand, Leopold. *Dziennik 1954: Wersja oryginalna*. Warsaw: Prószyński i S-ka, 1999.

Uerlings, Herbert. "Kolonialer Diskurs und Deutsche Literatur: Perspektiven und Probleme." In *(Post-)Kolonialismus und Deutsche Literatur: Impulse der angloamerikanischen Literatur- und Kulturtheorie*, edited by Axel Dunker, 17–44. Bielefeld: Aisthesis, 2005.

Uffelmann, Dirk. "The Imprint of Kundera's Strategic Anticolonialism on the Central European Roundtable in Lisbon (1988) and the Russian Discussants' Tactical Nominalism." *Zeitschrift für Slavische Philologie* 72 no. 1 (2016): 39–53.

Uffelmann, Dirk, and Klavdia Smola, eds. *Postcolonial Slavic Literatures after Communism*. Frankfurt am Main: Peter Lang, 2016.

Uliasz, Stanisław. "Kresy." In *Po co Sienkiewicz? Sienkiewicz a tożsamość narodowa; z kim i przeciw komu?*, edited by Tadeusz Bujnicki and Jerzy Axer, 303–5. Warsaw: DiG and OBTA, 2007.

Uliasz, Stanisław. *O literaturze Kresów i pograniczu kultur: Rozprawy i szkice*. Rzeszów: Wydawnictwo Uniwersytetu Rzeszowskiego, 2001.

Urbankowski, Bohdan. *Czerwona msza czyli uśmiech Stalina*. Vols. 1–2. 2nd rev. and expanded ed. Warsaw: Alfa-Wero, 1998.

Urbanowski, Maciej. *Prawą stroną literatury polskiej: Szkice i portrety*. 2nd ed. Łomianki: LTW, 2015.

Ureña, Lenny A. "Mobilizing German Women against 'Cultural Drunkenness': Rassenhygiene and Colonial Discourse in the Prussian-Polish Provinces, 1890–1914." Paper delivered at the conference "Gender and Power in the New Europe." August 20–24, 2003, at Lund University, Sweden. Accessed May 14, 2017. https://www.atria.nl/epublications/2003/Gender_and_power/5thfeminist/paper_635.pdf.

Viazemskii, Petr A. *Polnoe sobranie sochinenii*. Edited by S. D. Sheremetev. Vol. 1, *1810g.–1827g.* St. Petersburg: M. M. Stasiulevich, 1878.

Walder, Dennis. *Postcolonial Nostalgias: Writing, Representation and Memory*. New York: Routledge, 2011.

Walicki, Andrzej. *Filozofia i mesjanizm*. Warsaw: PWN, 1971.

Walicki, Andrzej. *Mesjanizm Adama Mickiewicza w perspektywie porównawczej*. Warsaw: IBL, 2006.

Walicki, Andrzej. *Polskie zmagania z wolnością: Widziane z boku*. Kraków: Universitas, 2000.

Walicki, Andrzej. *Zniewolony umysł po latach*. Warsaw: Czytelnik, 1993.

Wandycz, Piotr. *The Lands of Partitioned Poland, 1795–1918*. Seattle: University of Washington Press, 1974.

Wandycz, Piotr. "Western Images and Stereotypes of Central and Eastern Europe." In *Vampires Unstaked: National Images, Stereotypes and Myths in East Central Europe*, edited by André Gerrits and Norman Adler, 5–23. Amsterdam: Royal Netherlands Academy of Arts and Sciences, 1995.

Wang, Horng-luen. "Mind the Gap: On Post-national Idea(l)s and the Nationalist Reality." *Social Analysis* 46, no. 2 (June 2002): 139–47.

Waśko, Andrzej. "Geopolityka i literatura romantyzmu." In *Przeklęte miejsce Europy: Dylematy polskiej geopolityki*, edited by Jacek Kloczkowski, 92–111. Kraków: Ośrodek Myśli Politycznej, 2009.

Wasyl, Franciszek. "Kresy wschodnie jako kolonialna metafora historiografii polskiej: Postkolonialna perspektywa badań historiografii narodowej." In *Obcy—Obecny: Literatura, sztuka i kultura wobec inności*, edited by Paweł Cieliczko and Paweł Kuciński, 73–78. Warsaw: IBL, 2008.

Weintraub, Wiktor. *Od Reja do Boya*. Warsaw: PIW, 1977.

Wielhorski, Władysław. "Stosunki językowe, wyznaniowe i etniczne w Wielkim Księstwie Litewskim pomiędzy XIII a XVIII wiekiem." *Teki Historyczne* 13 (1964–65): 17–40.

Wiench, Piotr. "A Postcolonial Key to Understanding Central and Eastern European Neopaganisms." In *Modern Pagan and Native Faith Movements in Central and Eastern Europe*, edited by Kaarina Aitamurto and Scott Simpson, 10–26. London: Routledge, 2014.

Wierciński, Adam. *Przywracanie pamięci*. Opole: Wydawnictwo Uniwersytetu Opolskiego, 1997.

Wierzbicki, Andrzej. *Spory o polską duszę: Z zagadnień charakterologii narodowej w historiografii polskiej XIX i XX w*. Warsaw: Instytut Historii PAN, 1993.

Wierzejska, Jagoda. "Central European Palimpsest." In *Postcolonial Europe? Essays on Post-Communist Literatures and Cultures*, edited by Dobrota Pucherová and Róbert Gáfrik, 375–97. Amsterdam: Brill-Rodopi, 2015.

Wilk, Mariusz. *Wilczy notes: Zapiski sołowieckie 1996–1998*. Gdańsk: Słowo/obraz terytoria, 1998.

Wilk, Mariusz. *Wołoka*. Kraków: Wydawnictwo Literackie, 2005.

Witkiewicz, Stanisław. *Aleksander Gierymski*. 1903. Warsaw: KiW, 1950.

Witkowska, Alina. "Czytanie Mickiewicza—dzisiaj." In *Księga w 170 rocznicę wydania "Ballad i romansów" Adama Mickiewicza*, edited by Jacek Kolbuszewski, 11–20. Wrocław: Wydawnictwo Uniwersytetu Wrocławskiego, 1993.

Witkowska, Alina. *Mickiewicz: Słowo i czyn*. Warsaw: PWN, 1986.

Wittlin, Józef. "Mój Lwów." In *Orfeusz w piekle XX wieku*, 364–403. Kraków: Wydawnictwo Literackie, 2000.

Wolfe, Patrick. "History and Imperialism: A Century of Theory, from Marx to Postcolonialism." *American Historical Review* 102, no. 2 (1997): 388–420.

Wolff, Larry. *Inventing Eastern Europe: The Map of Civilization on the Mind of the Enlightenment*. Stanford, CA: Stanford University Press, 1994.

Wolff, Larry. "Teaching 'Eastern Europe' without the Iron Curtain." *Perspectives* 31, no. 1 (January 1993): 10–13.

Wyka, Kazimierz. *Wyznania uduszonego*. Kraków: Universitas, 1995.

Young, Robert. *Postcolonialism: A Very Short Introduction*. Oxford: Oxford University Press, 2003.

Zagajewski, Adam. *Without End: New and Selected Poems*. Translated by Clare Cavanagh, Renata Gorczynski, Benjamin Ivry, and C. K. Williams. New York: Farrar, Straus and Giroux, 2002.

Zagajewski, Adam. "Wysoki mur." *Zeszyty Literackie*, no. 7 (1984): 16–42.

Zagorin, Perez. "History, the Referent, and Narrative: Reflections on Postmodernism Now." *History and Theory* 38, no. 1 (February 1999): 1–24.

Zajas, Paweł. *Postkolonialne imaginarium południowoafrykańskie literatury polskiej i niderlandzkiej*. Poznań: Wydawnictwo Naukowe UAM, 2008.

Żakiewicz, Zbigniew. "Polska jest wciąż Kresami." *Ethos*, nos. 2/3 (1992): 293–97.

Zakrzewski, Bogdan. *"Hajże na Soplicę!"* Wrocław: Wydawnictwo Uniwersytetu Wrocławskiego, 1990.

Zaleski, Antoni. *Towarzystwo Warszawskie: Listy do przyjaciółki przez Baronową XYZ*. Edited by Ryszard Kołodziejczyk. Warsaw: PIW, 1971.

Zaleski, Marek. *Formy pamięci: O przedstawianiu przeszłości w polskiej literaturze współczesnej*. Warsaw: IBL, 1996.

Zaleski, Marek. "Niedoszła miłość Hansa C." *Tygodnik Powszechny*, no. 24 (2004): 11.

Zarycki, Tomasz. *Ideologies of Eastness in Central and Eastern Europe*. London: Routledge, 2014.

Zarycki, Tomasz. "Ku socjologicznej analizie dyskursu elit peryferyjnych." In *Wartości, polityka, społeczeństwo*, edited by Marta Zahorska and Ewa Nasalska, 169–81. Warsaw: Scholar, 2009.

Zarycki, Tomasz. "Poland and the East." In *Understanding Central Europe*, edited by Marcin Moskalewicz and Wojciech Przybylski, 80–85. London: Routledge, 2018.

Zarycki, Tomasz. "Polska i jej regiony a debata postkolonialna." In *Oblicze polityczne regionów Polski*, edited by Małgorzata Dajnowicz, 31–48. Białystok: Wyższa Szkoła Finansów i Zarządzania, 2008.

Zarycki, Tomasz. "Uses of Russia: The Role of Russia in the Modern Polish National Identity." *East European Politics and Societies* 18, no. 4 (Fall 2004): 595–627.

Zarycki, Tomasz, Rafał Smoczyński, and Tomasz Warczok. "The Roots of Polish Culture-Centered Politics: Toward a Non-Purely Cultural Model of Cultural Domination in Central and Eastern Europe." *East European Politics and Societies and Cultures* 31, no. 2 (May 2017): 360–81.

Zdanowicz, Aleksander, Michał Bohusz Szyszka, January Filipowicz, Walerjan Tomaszewicz, Florjan Czepieliński, Wincenty Korotyński, and Bronisław

Trentowski, eds. *Słownik języka polskiego*. Part 2. Wilno: Maurycy Orgelbrand, 1861.

Zduniak-Wiktorowicz, Małgorzata. *Filologia w kontakcie: Polonistyka, germanistyka, postkolonializm*. Poznań: Wydawnictwo Naukowe UAM, 2018.

Zernack, Klaus. "Deutsch-polnische Beziehungen im historischen Überblick." In *Tausend Jahre polnisch-deutsche Beziehungen: Sprache—Literatur—Kultur—Politik*, edited by Franciszek Grucza, 88–102. Warsaw: Graf-Punkt, 2001.

Zernack, Klaus. "Ostgrenze." In *Deutschlands Grenzen in der Geschichte*, edited by Alexander Demandt, 140–65. Munich: C. H. Beck, 1991.

Żeromski, Stefan. "Literatura a życie polskie." In *Dzieła*, edited by Stanisław Pigoń. *Nowele i opowiadania*. Vol. 4, *Sen o szpadzie: Pomyłki*, 39–61. Warsaw: Czytelnik, 1957.

Zgorzelski, Czesław. "Pielgrzym 'w krainie dostatków i krasy.'" In *Obserwacje*, 41–48. Warsaw: PWN, 1993.

Zientara, Benedykt. *Frühzeit der europäischen Nationen: Die Entstehung von Nationalbewusstsein im nachkarolingischen Europa*. Translated into German by Jürgen Heyde. Osnabrück: Fibre, 1997. Polish original: *Świt narodów europejskich: Powstawanie świadomości narodowej na obszarze Europy pokarolińskiej*. Warsaw: PIW, 1985.

Ziolkowski, Theodor. "Figures on Loan: The Boundaries of Literature and Life." In *Varieties of Literary Thematics*, 123–51. Princeton, NJ: Princeton University Press, 1983.

Žižek, Slavoj. "Melancholy and the Act." *Critical Inquiry* 26, no. 4 (Summer 2000): 657–81.

Žižek, Slavoj. *The Plague of Fantasies*. New York: Verso, 2008.

Żmigrodzka, Maria. *Przez wieki idąca powieść: Wybór pism o literaturze XIX i XX wieku*. Edited by Maria Kalinowska and Elżbieta Kiślak. Warsaw: IBL, 2002.

Znaniecki, Florian. "Elementy rzeczywistości praktycznej." In *Pisma filozoficzne*. Vol. 1, *Myśl i rzeczywistość i inne pisma filozoficzne*, 77–112. Warsaw: PWN, 1987. Originally published in *Przegląd Filozoficzny*, no. 15 (1912): 161–89.

# Index